Epistemology

A Contemporary Introduction

Alvin I. Goldman

and

Matthew McGrath

New York   Oxford

OXFORD UNIVERSITY PRESS

Oxford University Press is a department of the University of Oxford. It furthers the
University's objective of excellence in research, scholarship, and education by publishing
worldwide.

Oxford   New York
Auckland   Cape Town   Dar es Salaam   Hong Kong   Karachi
Kuala Lumpur   Madrid   Melbourne   Mexico City   Nairobi
New Delhi   Shanghai   Taipei   Toronto

With offices in
Argentina   Austria   Brazil   Chile   Czech Republic   France   Greece
Guatemala   Hungary   Italy   Japan   Poland   Portugal   Singapore
South Korea   Switzerland   Thailand   Turkey   Ukraine   Vietnam

For titles covered by Section 112 of the US Higher Education
Opportunity Act, please visit www.oup.com/us/he for the
latest information about pricing and alternate formats.

Published in the United States of America by
Oxford University Press
198 Madison Avenue, New York, NY 10016
http://www.oup.com

Library of Congress Cataloging-in-Publication Data
Goldman, Alvin I., 1938-
   Epistemology : a contemporary introduction / Alvin I. Goldman, Rutgers University
and Matthew McGrath, University of Missouri.
      pages cm
   Includes index.
   ISBN 978-0-19-998112-0
 1. Knowledge, Theory of. I. McGrath, Matthew. II. Title.
   BD161.G643 2014
   121--dc23
                                                                                    2014015224

Printing number: 9 8 7 6 5 4 3 2 1

Printed in the United States of America
on acid-free paper

Table of Contents

Epistemology: A Contemporary Introduction

Epistemology is a very old field; it is also a young and vibrant field, with many new directions and fresh ideas. The traditional core themes of epistemology, including the challenge of skepticism and the nature of knowledge and justification, are examined in the first half of the book. Several new angles and methodologies that arose and matured in recent decades are explored in the second half. These include naturalized epistemology, experimental philosophy, and social epistemology. Also included is a substantial treatment of probabilistic epistemology, a favorite subfield of contemporary researchers that rarely makes an appearance in introductory texts. It is impossible, of course, to cover everything. We have gravitated toward the topics we know best but have tried to preserve a balance between the probable tastes and interests of potential users and what we ourselves are most excited about.

Several other balances have also served as desiderata. One is a balance between accessibility to undergraduates and relevance to (beginning) graduate students. This has meant keeping the debates challenging and of contemporary relevance while not overwhelming beginning students with excessive detail. Another balance at which we have aimed is one between a broad and fair coverage of competing positions while not hiding or refusing to articulate our own favored points of view. Philosophy is a more personal field than most academic fields, and one really gets the feel for it when one sees how a philosopher sets out and defends a perspective in some depth. The two authors do not share the same perspective in all matters discussed here. Each chapter has a primary author responsible for its content, but we have thoroughly critiqued one another's chapters—not to the point of full agreement, necessarily, but to the point of respectful satisfaction. (Actually, we probably disagree a lot less than a randomly selected pair of epistemologists.)

Given the amount of material covered in this text, there will inevitably be different ways to use it, and we encourage instructors to be experimental. A full-year course could easily cover all eleven chapters. For a one-semester course, instructors will probably want to select a subset of the chapters. A course that emphasizes the "core" of epistemology would focus on the first six chapters. A course that seeks to introduce students to the newest, most cutting-edge topics would invest a lot of time in the last five chapters. A course that seeks to sample from both of these areas could be constructed in multiple ways. Instructors should have no trouble designing courses to their own taste.

There are many people to thank for helpful guidance and/or inputs into the authorship process. Our editors, Robert Miller, Emily Krupin, Diane Kohnen, Cindy Sweeney, and Wendy Walker, displayed a nice balance of urgency and patience. They also obtained for us an excellent cast of reviewers of the manuscript's first draft, including James Beebe, David Bennett, Richard Fumerton, Peter Graham, Kristoffer Ahlstrom, Anna-Sara Malmgren, and Patrick Rysiew. The book is better because of their comments. We would also like to thank Marina Folescu, Ted Poston, Paul Weirich, Bob Beddor, and especially Jack Lyons (who gave us comments on the entire manuscript) and Patrick Rysiew (who provided extra comments on Chapter 7). Thanks are also due to the students of Alvin's epistemology class at Rutgers University, fall 2013, who road-tested the draft manuscript. Finally, Isaac Choi contributed editorial assistance and suggestions for end-of-chapter questions for Alvin's chapters.

AIG and MM

PART I

Justification and Knowledge: The Core Issues

The Structure of Justification

Alvin I. Goldman

1.1 THE CONCEPTS AND QUESTIONS OF EPISTEMOLOGY

Epistemology is the study of knowledge and related phenomena such as thought, reasoning, and the pursuit of understanding. It is less a study of customary thinking processes—although they are relevant—than a study of better versus worse ways to think, reason, and form opinions. Moral theory reflects on what is right and wrong in the sphere of action, while epistemology reflects on what is rational or irrational, justified or unjustified, in the sphere of the intellect.

Why are matters of the intellect important? This can be approached from many vantage points of ordinary life. Do I want to make good decisions in life, decisions that promote my own welfare, my family's welfare, my community's welfare? If so, I had better figure out which of the available choices would best promote favorable outcomes. In other words, I need to form correct, or *true,* beliefs about the consequences that would ensue from the performance of different actions. If I form true beliefs about the consequences of each choice, I am more likely to make choices that lead me in useful directions. If I form false beliefs, my choices may be unfortunate however good my intentions. Accurate beliefs tend to guide us down desired pathways, inaccurate beliefs down pathways we don't mean to travel. A student decides to get trained in a given field because employment opportunities are predicted to boom in that field within a few years. Training in this field should bode well for the student if the prediction is true, but a wasted effort if it is false. One hopes to act on true predictions rather than false ones.

The same point emerges when deciding whom to trust in this or that domain. In consulting a physician about an ailment, I want her to have extensive medical knowledge plus the skill of applying that knowledge to new cases. I want her to predict correctly which treatments would cure or alleviate my ailment (and have no serious side effects). The same point extends to a choice of a financial advisor or auto mechanic. The claim here is not that instrumental or practical value is the only value of true belief or the sole ground of the intellect's importance. People have intellectual interests not rooted in practical affairs. We are curious creatures. We want to know, for example, what caused the dinosaur extinction many millennia ago, even if knowing this has no immediate action implications. This curiosity does not rest on the pursuit of practical ends.

All right, you concede, we have reasons to try to get truths, and to enlist the help of others who are adept at getting truths. But how is truth to be acquired? Can one ascertain the truth by just reaching out and grasping some facts? It isn't clear how one does that. This problem is what epistemology is largely about. A customary way to approach the issue is to focus on another central topic in epistemology: *justification*. If I can get a justified or warranted belief, rather than a randomly or haphazardly chosen one, such a proposition is more likely to be true. How, then, do I go about getting justified beliefs? Some epistemologists link justification to having good evidence. Others link it to following good methods or procedures. These are among the prospects to be explored in what follows. In this chapter and Chapters 2 and 6 our discussion focuses on justification; in Chapters 3, 4, and 5 it focuses on knowledge.

As these introductory remarks make clear, epistemology talks a lot about belief. What is belief (or opinion)? It is a species of psychological attitude toward a proposition, where a proposition (roughly) is a content that purports to express a fact. The statement that the dinosaur extinction was caused by a massive asteroid impact on the earth purports to state a fact. To believe this proposition is to mentally "assent" to it, or think that what it states is so. Belief belongs to a family of psychological attitudes directed at propositions. Other members of this family include *disbelief*, which is the mental attitude of rejecting, or denying, a proposition, and *agnosticism*, or suspension of judgment, which is the mental attitude of neutrality, or indecision, with respect to a proposition's truth. Collectively, these different attitudes (plus more finely graded attitudes such as being 75 percent convinced of something) are called *doxastic attitudes*. The term *doxastic* comes from the Greek word *doxa*, meaning opinions.

It is widely thought that forming a belief that is reasonable, warranted, or justified is the best means available of forming a true belief. Hence, epistemology is particularly interested in the question of how one should go about acquiring a belief that is warranted, justified, or reasonable. *Justification* and *warrant* are examples of terms of epistemic evaluation or appraisal. To call a person's belief "justified" is to commend it, or appraise it positively, along some evaluative or normative dimension, whereas calling a belief "unjustified" or "unwarranted" is to criticize it, appraise it negatively, along the same dimension. Suppose I say that John thinks that Gregory is a terrible fellow, but this belief is totally unwarranted because it is wholly based on Gregory's appearance. I call it "unwarranted" because judging people by their looks is like judging a book by its cover. It is a poor basis for judgment (or belief). Such a normative assessment has parallels with moral discourse, in which actions are called right or wrong. Epistemologists agree, however, that epistemic terms of appraisal like *justified* and *unjustified*, *warranted* and *unwarranted*, are not terms of moral evaluation; they express evaluations along some intellectual dimension. If you believe in the absence of good evidence, or by reliance on unsound reasons, this is an intellectual failing rather than a moral one.

Although justification may be significantly related to truth, truth and justification are not equivalent concepts. A proposition can be true although nobody believes it, and it can be true although nobody is justified in believing it. Consider a precisely delimited expanse of seaside beach. Some proposition of the following form is true: "The number of grains of sand on this beach is N." But nobody is justified in believing this truth (with the correct value of N filled in) because nobody has determined or ascertained the correct value of N. A major question in epistemology is how justification is related to truth, but they are not equivalent concepts.

Truth, it may be said, is a purely metaphysical concept rather than an epistemological one. Given a proposition, what makes it true or false is simply the state of the world. Its truth-value is not affected by cognitive relations people have toward the relevant state of affairs. But cognitive relations to a proposition are precisely what are crucial in determining justification or warrant. A person's justifiedness with respect to a proposition P is never (or rarely) fixed by P's actual truth-value. Despite a proposition's truth, it is possible for someone to lack any evidence for its truth (as in the grains-of-sand example). Conversely, it is possible to have highly favorable (though misleading) evidence that justifies one in believing a proposition despite its falsity. Thus, truth and justification must be carefully distinguished.

Justified and *warranted* are not the only terms of epistemic evaluation; another familiar term of epistemic evaluation is *rational*. Some epistemologists equate rationality with justification, but we shall keep them distinct. Epistemologists who favor rationality-talk as compared with justification-talk often opt for a more finely delineated range of doxastic attitudes. Instead of the tripartite classification scheme of belief, disbelief, and withholding (or suspension), they prefer degrees of belief arrayed along a zero-to-one interval. One represents the highest possible strength of credence in a proposition, and zero represents the lowest. Our own treatment here will mainly use the tripartite classification scheme. But in Chapter 11, on probabilistic epistemology, finer gradations will often be invoked.

In addition to justification, warrant, rationality, and reasonability, a critical concept in epistemology is *knowledge*. Indeed, the term *epistemology* just means the study of knowledge (*episteme*, in Greek). According to many theories, there are intimate relations between knowledge and some of the other epistemic concepts we have introduced. Here are some points of widespread agreement. First, knowledge implies truth; you cannot know that P unless P is true. (This idea is often conveyed by saying that truth is *factive*.) If you are certain of a proposition P, in your own mind, you will be inclined to *claim* to know it. But if P is not true, as a matter of fact, then you don't really know it. (One cannot know what isn't so.) Second, a person must believe P, or have reasonably high credence in P, in order to know it. Knowledge is (partly) a psychological state. Third, most theories hold that knowledge requires justification. You do not know that P by simply believing P where P is true. Being justified in believing it is also necessary. Thus, there appears to be a web of relationships between knowledge and other important concepts. Closer examination of these matters occupies Chapters 3, 4, and 5. This book begins with justification, which some regard as the more fundamental epistemological concept.

1.2 THE EPISTEMIC REGRESS PROBLEM

Many justified beliefs attain this status when people infer them from other things they believe. Inferential relations between beliefs are often expressed in conversation or debate with others. Suppose Henry says to Tony, "I hear you believe that New York will win the basketball championship next year. How can you think that? New York was so miserable last season; how can you think it will turn things around and win next year?" Tony responds: "New York landed the top new draft pick in the league this year, and he is rumored to be the most talented player since Michael Jordan. It has also acquired one of the best big men in the league. With these crucial additions, I feel confident it will win."

Tony offers an argument featuring P1 and P2 as premises and C as conclusion:

P1: New York will have the most talented draft pick in years.
P2: New York also has one of the best big men in the league.
C: Therefore, New York will win the championship next year.

Tony defends C by appeal to P1 and P2, implying that C is a reasonable conclusion to draw from P1 and P2 (given various unmentioned assumptions). C does not deductively follow from P1 and P2, that's clear. But it may be a reasonable nondeductive inference from P1 and P2 (given the additional assumptions).

Our story presents Tony as a speaker who verbally defends his belief to a challenger, but a similar story might be told where there is no challenger and Tony makes no verbal defense of C. If he holds his belief in C in utter silence, but it is (properly) based on (justified) beliefs in P1, P2, and the additional assumptions, the same justificational upshot will hold with respect to proposition C. Thus, interpersonal speech is not required for there to be justified inferential belief. Personal justification has no essential tie to a "dialectical" situation, where verbal reasons-giving takes place.

What is the structure of Tony's justification for C? As described so far, it resembles the roots of a tree. In Figure 1.1, the belief in proposition C (labeled Bel(C)) appears as the top node of a tree, with beliefs in premises P1 and P2 (labeled Bel(P1) and Bel(P2)) shown as downward-branching roots. The arrows indicate that Bel(P1) and Bel(P2) lend joint support to Bel(C). Inferential justification is supposed to be transmitted upward from one or more root nodes to at least one higher-level node. However, if the lower-level nodes have no justification of their own to transmit—in other words, if Tony does not believe them *justifiedly*—then the higher-level node(s) cannot inherit justification from them.

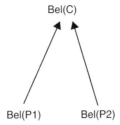

Bel(C)

Bel(P1)   Bel(P2)

FIGURE 1.1 Belief in C is Justified by Inference from Justified Premises P1 and P2.

Might the root structure of Tony's justification run deeper? If his beliefs in premises P1 and P2 are justified, how was *their* justification acquired? Perhaps Tony had other justified beliefs from which P1 and P2 were properly inferred. His belief in P1, for example, may have been based on his justified beliefs about the new draft pick's previous scoring records and the tall recruit's rebounding prowess. To depict this situation in the diagram, we would expand the root structure by adding another level of branching roots, roots that extend downward from Bel(P1) and from Bel(P2). Of course, each additional root node must also be justified if Tony's beliefs in P1 and P2 are to acquire justification from them.

What emerges here might be called a *regress* of reasons, grounds, or justification. How does this regress of justification continue? This question poses what is called the *regress problem* in epistemology. It was posed in ancient times by Sextus Empiricus, who asked about the chain of "proofs" for a person's assertion. Here we focus on beliefs rather than assertions and reasons rather than proofs, but the core idea—and worry—is much the same. Can the regress of reasons continue indefinitely, with additional beliefs being invoked at each step, with no repetition and no end points? Or must the regress eventually terminate along each root, where a terminus is a justified belief that acquires its justificational status from an epistemic source distinct from inference? What are the possible structures here, and which possibility captures the real structure of inferential justification?

Here are three views about the correct structure of a regress—that is, a structure that enables justified beliefs to be derived from other (justified) beliefs:

1. *Infinitism.* The correct structure is an unending continuation of reasons, without repetition or end. A justification tree for each inferentially justified belief contains roots that never end and never contain repetitive nodes.
2. *Foundationalism.* The correct structure is a tree with roots of *finite* length. Each root has a terminal, or final, node that represents a justified but

noninferred belief. Such beliefs are *foundational*, or *basic*, beliefs. All justified beliefs that are not themselves basic, however, ultimately derive their justification from one or more other beliefs that are basic. So, all justification ends at—or begins with—basically justified beliefs.

3. *Coherentism.* The correct structure is one in which some of the roots circle, or loop, back on themselves. In other words, some nodes reappear earlier in the chain. Thus, the regress has no end points. At the same time, it is not infinitely long. In rejecting end points, coherentism joins infinitism in rejecting the notion that justification depends on there being foundational, or basic, beliefs.

A fourth response to the regress problem belongs in a separate category because it does not purport to "solve" the problem of justification—that is, to show how inferential justification is possible (and feasible):

4. *Skepticism About the Regress.* None of the first three solutions to the regress problem is satisfactory. One cannot get justified belief via any of the structures they describe. Because those other three solutions jointly exhaust the possibilities for a positive solution, there is no way by which inferential beliefs can be justified.

In claiming that none of the three solutions works (for reasons to be examined below), the skeptical position implies that justification can never be derived by inference. This response is *skeptical* because it denies justification for a huge swath of beliefs—all beliefs based on reasoning—that we normally consider justified.

Before examining these rival responses to the regress problem, let us note a shared feature of the positive solutions. All of these theories restrict beliefs that do the justifying to ones held *at the same time* as the target belief. In the case of Tony's basketball championship belief, our question is whether his belief at the time of the conversation is justified. Obviously, Tony's justification for C depends on whether he is justified in believing that the new draft pick is as talented as he claims. This is something he might be justified in believing in, say, December, although he wasn't justified in believing it in October.

The three positive theories under discussion are all "classical" theories of justification in the sense that they center on *synchronic* reasons. A synchronic reason for a belief is a factor occurring at the same time as the target belief. Earlier or later beliefs make no justificational difference in the traditional view. Presumably everybody would agree that Tony's belief that New York will win the championship cannot be justified in the way indicated if Tony's beliefs about the new players either weren't really in place at the time he believed C or weren't yet justified at that time, say, because the draft of the super-talented player had not yet occurred or the player had not yet signed a contract. Surely the supporting premise beliefs must be held and justified at the time of the conclusion belief; so the synchronic view would have it. We can agree that justified premise beliefs that only occur *after* a target belief cannot help the latter belief (at the earlier time). However, this leaves open the possibility that earlier beliefs and their justificational statuses can influence the justificational status of a later belief (albeit indirectly). That is a prospect we shall encounter in connection with a diachronic theory of justification to be considered in Chapter 2. Diachronic theories as such do not solve the regress problem, certainly not simply by virtue of being diachronic. The point is only to indicate that theories of justification need not be purely synchronic. All classical theories of justification, however, have been synchronic, including infinitism, foundationalism, and coherentism.

1.3 INFINITISM

Infinitism is rarely given serious consideration. Two problems jump out on first encounter. First, if a justification tree goes back infinitely far (on one or more roots), there seems to be no point at which justification originates. But if there are no originating places for justification—places where justification gets "kick-started"—how can there be any justification to transmit to higher nodes? Second, if a tree contains an infinite chain of reasons, doesn't this imply infinitely many beliefs? But, surely, no human person has infinitely many beliefs.

Does infinitism have any good response to these problems? In response to the first problem, it may be argued that justification need not originate anywhere; starting points aren't needed. Just as time and the universe may each be eternal (in both directions), with no real starting points, so justification can lack starting points. In the case of synchronic justification, of course, the issue of temporal origination doesn't arise. What the critic of infinitism denies is that all beliefs on inferential trees are epistemically dependent on others. The critic insists that some beliefs must be independently justified if they are to generate any justificational "juice" to transmit to the others. This is not a proof, but it seems intuitively compelling.

What of the criticism that nobody possesses infinitely many beliefs? Here the infinitist has a bit of maneuvering room (Klein 2005). The principal maneuver appeals to a standard epistemological distinction between two kinds of justification. *Doxastic* justification is a property of existing beliefs; *propositional* justification arises from the state or condition of an epistemic agent that entitles them to believe a proposition (even if they don't opt to believe it). Proposition P may be justified "for" such an agent in the sense that they *would* be justified in believing it in virtue of their condition or situation. If you are shivering with cold on a wintry night, you are justified in believing that you feel cold, even if you fail to notice this feeling and don't assent to the proposition. Once it is conceded that propositions can be justified even without belief in them, infinitism can be interpreted as the view that there are infinitely many propositions (rather than beliefs) that form chains of inferential justification. Even if no finite being like us has infinitely many beliefs, this leaves open the possibility that there are infinitely many propositions we are justified in believing at a given time.

The propositions might be arrayed in a chain of (potential) inferential dependence. Not that we actually execute all of the corresponding inferences,
but we would be justified in executing any finite segment of them.

Does a switch from an infinite chain of beliefs to an infinite chain of propositions really work? What the infinitist presumably holds is not only that a
proposition can be justified without itself being believed but also that it can
receive (inferential) justification from other propositions without the latter
being believed. So infinitism supports the viability of a chain of propositions, each of which bears (or possesses) justification but none of which is
believed. This is extremely dubious: Unless a proposition is believed, it is
doubtful that it can convey inferential justifiedness to other propositions.
Don't *some* propositions in the chain have to be believed? Perhaps so, the infinitist might reply, but this only requires one proposition to be believed, not
infinitely many of them. Is this correct? If a single believed proposition is
inferentially justified, doesn't it have to be inferred from other beliefs earlier
in the chain? But then we are off and running on the same sort of infinite
regress of beliefs the infinitist sought to avoid.

Of course, we have already encountered an example in which a proposition is deemed (propositionally) justified without receiving that justificational status from a belief. That's the feeling-cold example of two paragraphs
back. The problem is that no infinitist can embrace this sort of case as prototypical, because it features a proposition that acquires justification from a
nondoxastic source, and hence is an example of basic, or foundational, justification. This supports not infinitism but one of the rival solutions instead
(foundationalism).

1.4 COHERENTISM

We proceed to the coherentist solution to the regress problem. Coherentism
is a minority view today but historically was an influential theory and doubt-
less retains some of that luster. In terms of the regress problem, it is commonly conceptualized as tolerating circular inference. But this may not be
the best way to introduce it; let us consider another perspective.

Coherentism depicts a body of justified beliefs as a holistic system whose
parts mutually support one another. There are no "privileged" beliefs that
play the role accorded to foundational beliefs under foundationalism
(i.e., beliefs that obtain justification from outside the doxastic system and
transmit this justificational juice to the remaining elements of the system).
Under coherentism, all justification arises from interrelations among beliefs
(or other doxastic states). Moreover, the justificational interrelations are re-
ciprocal or bidirectional rather than unidirectional.

A good metaphor for coherentism is a house of mutually supporting cards
leaning against one another. Such a structure stands upright because its components are each supported by all of the others, or at least many of the others.
Support runs in many directions. In a four-card house consisting of A, B, C,
and D, support might run from A, B, and C to D, from B, C, and D to A,

and so forth. There are no "foundational" cards that support others but are themselves wholly unsupported. The very formulation of the regress problem assumes that justificational support is linear—that is, runs in a single direction. Coherentism challenges this assumption.

Now consider how justificational coherence might be spelled out, metaphors aside. Unfortunately, there is little consensus here. One ingredient that presumably contributes to system coherence is logical consistency. Unless the beliefs in a total doxastic system are mutually consistent (i.e., their conjunction does not imply a contradiction), the system isn't coherent. But this is an extremely weak condition. Thus, consider the following set of propositions as someone's total system:

1. There are cats.
2. There are bananas.
3. Sometimes it rains.
4. There is a sun.
5. There is a moon.

These five propositions constitute a consistent system, because their conjunction entails no contradiction. But is this consistent system a highly coherent one? No; at least not in the rich sense of coherence that coherentists typically advance. The system fails to be coherent because (i) no proposition is deducible from any of the remainder (either singly or in conjunction with one another) and (ii) none of the propositions would have its probability raised by taking the truth of the others as given. In short, the five propositions are mutually independent, both logically and probabilistically. Coherence, however, is supposed to be the opposite of this; a coherent system should display a high degree of mutual interdependence.

Here is an illustration of a system with greater interdependence:

6. Edna loves cappuccinos.
7. On Tuesday afternoon Edna had a yen for a cappuccino.
8. On Tuesday afternoon Edna thought that the closest place to get a good cappuccino was Café Nero.
9. On Tuesday afternoon Edna went to Café Nero for a cappuccino.

Like system (1)–(5), this system of propositions is logically consistent. In addition, however, it also features several probabilistic support relations among various members of the system. The truth of (6) raises the probability of (7); the truth of the conjunction of (7) and (8) considerably raises the probability of (9); and arguably (9) raises the probability of (7). So there is a fair amount of mutual coherence among these propositions, and hence the system as a whole has a fair degree of systemic coherence (especially for a small system).

Now comes the jackpot question: Does a system's level of coherence guarantee or contribute materially toward a positive justificational status for the propositions that constitute the system? Does the fact that a belief system is highly coherent guarantee, or even make it likely, that each of its members (or most of them) is <u>justified?</u> No.

Notice first that the propositions constituting a consistent system need not be true, and similarly for the members of a coherent system. System (6)–(9) is more coherent than system (1)–(5), but this is no clue as to which system has more true members. Now turn to justification. Would the fact that somebody believes all and only the members of (1)–(5) and another person believes all and only the members of (6)–(9) provide any clue about which believer has a larger proportion of justified beliefs? No. It all depends on how the beliefs were formed, or arrived at, by the two believers, and nothing said thus far speaks to their respective processes or methods of belief formation. The believer in propositions (1)–(5) may have formed each of her beliefs by careful observation, whereas the believer in propositions (6)–(9) may have formed his beliefs by mere wishful thinking. Thus, the justificational quality of the member propositions does not correlate with system coherence. Contrary to coherentism, nothing follows about a belief's justifiedness—certainly not its doxastic justifiedness—from the fact that it belongs to a system that ranks high on a systemic-coherence scale. It may also fail to be propositionally justified if the relation of coherence among the propositions is too complex or obscure for the subject to appreciate it.

This point may be reinforced by considering the following possibility. Although we may believe each member of a coherent system, we might not recognize or (intellectually) appreciate the fact that they cohere. We might form each belief separately from the others, without recognizing their logical and/or probabilistic relations. In this scenario, the fact that our beliefs are mutually coherent contributes nothing to their level of justifiedness. Their justifiedness depends on whatever leads (or causes) us to believe them. Since, by hypothesis, we are not influenced by their coherence relationships, those relationships have no impact on their justifiedness.

We can highlight these points by tweaking an example often used against coherentism. Fiona loves to fantasize. She sits in her armchair weaving complex stories that rival the best detective mysteries for intricacy of plot and depth of detail. Fiona's fantasy is, in effect, itself a well-composed novel with a high degree of coherence (the plot "hangs together"). Moreover, the fantasy is so vivid and realistic that Fiona believes each of the elements in the story. Is she justified in believing them (to be true)? Surely not. Yet each such element is a member of a highly coherent system. The system would rate very high on the coherence dimension, judged, at least, by their internal relations with one another.

Here are two additional problems for coherentism, the first commonly called the *isolation* objection. According to coherentism, a given belief's justificational status is exclusively a function of the believer's other belief states. Psychological states of other kinds, such as perceptions and feelings, are irrelevant. According to coherentism, your feeling cold right now has no bearing on any of your beliefs' justificational statuses, even the status of a belief to the effect that you feel cold or feel hot. How you actually feel makes no difference, because justification is exclusively a function of *inferential* relations between beliefs, and neither feeling cold nor feeling hot is a belief. Similarly, if we hear what sounds like a motorcycle careening down the street, hearing this sound is justificationally irrelevant to any motorcycle beliefs we may have. This approach seems wrong-headed. Beliefs that are misaligned with concurrent experience (especially vivid experience) are unjustified. After all, perceptual experience is input from the world, and ignoring such experience does not conduce to sound belief. Some epistemologists (e.g., BonJour 1985) try to tinker with coherentism to avoid this counterintuitive feature, but none of them has had much success.

Finally, a seemingly small defect in coherentism shows how dramatically off-track it is. Coherentism says that a belief is justified if and only if it belongs to (is a member of) a highly coherent total system of beliefs. An obvious consequence of this is that all members of a highly coherent system are justified and all members of a weakly coherent system are unjustified. In short, all members of any total system have the same justificational status. This makes little sense: Normal people have a mix of justified and unjustified beliefs, a mix that coherentism has no obvious resources to accommodate.

1.5 FOUNDATIONALISM AND BASIC BELIEFS

Foundationalism's response to the regress problem says that every root in a tree of (successful) inferential justification terminates after finitely many steps. Each stopping point (or starting point, one might say) is a belief that possesses justification it does not get from further (premise) beliefs. Such starting points, or "basic" beliefs, have two crucial properties: (A) they are uninferred and (B) they are justified. In addition, foundationalist theories say that there are inferential relations between basic and nonbasic beliefs such that enough of the latter are justified to avert the threat of global skepticism. Roughly speaking, a wide swath of our commonsense beliefs qualify as justified under foundationalist principles.

To succeed, a developed form of foundationalism must address four questions (we shall frequently use the terms *immediate* and *mediate* justification for basic and nonbasic justifiedness, respectively):

1. What does it take for a belief to attain the status of "justified" in an unmediated or noninferential fashion?
2. Which types of belief qualify as immediately justified? (For example, what types of propositional content lend themselves to immediate justification?)
3. What strength of justification must immediately justified beliefs possess according to foundationalism? Must they exhibit the highest grade of justification (i.e., certainty or infallibility)?
4. Assuming that many immediately justified beliefs are available, does this enable epistemic agents to draw enough reasonable inferences to further beliefs to dispel the specter of skepticism often laid at foundationalism's doorstep?

The foregoing questions pose the constructive tasks confronting the foundationalist program. Can it provide satisfactory answers? Foundationalism's critics have attacked it with energy and zeal, challenging the very possibility of its delivering the goods. We shall give examples of some roadblocks erected by the critics. Do these roadblocks eviscerate all prospects for a successful foundationalism, or do the opponents' criticisms fall apart when examined closely?

1.6 BASIC BELIEFS AS SELF-JUSTIFYING BELIEFS?

Focusing on the first (and central) question, one answer is that immediately justified beliefs are self-justifying beliefs. The term *self-justifying* often crops up in attempts to explain what is distinctive to immediate justifiedness. *Self-justifying* sounds like the right contrast with inference-based justifiedness, since inference is always a relation with other beliefs. So perhaps immediate justifiedness is what accrues when a belief is self-justifying. But what does it mean for a belief to justify itself? Is this even possible? Perhaps a belief justifies itself in case its occurrence logically entails the truth of its content. A belief to the effect that one has some beliefs seems to satisfy this condition. To be sure, few beliefs exemplify this property: Believing it is going to rain tomorrow does not entail it will rain tomorrow. Still, in those few cases in which a belief has this property, maybe it is immediately justified.

Would this answer to question (1) satisfy the goals of foundationalism? It is widely assumed that paradigm cases of immediately justified beliefs concern our own current (nonfactive) mental states—for example, "I believe I am in pain," or "I believe I want an espresso." But the proposed definition will not guarantee this result, first because the desired logical entailment will rarely hold. Does the fact that I believe I am sad logically entail that I am sad? That is highly dubious. Perhaps we are always correct when we classify our own current mental states—but is this logically, or even metaphysically, guaranteed? These are problematic theses.

However, even if it is true in such cases that believing we are in mental state M guarantees that we are in M, why should this imply justifiedness of the belief? For any truth L of logic, my believing L (trivially) entails its truth (because it is necessarily true). But it hardly follows that I am justified in believing it. L might be such a complex proposition that although I manage to grasp its content, I fail to understand how or why it is true. Thus, even when the content of a belief guarantees its truth, a bit of reflection shows that this does not guarantee its justifiedness.

Here is a slightly different way to understand self-justification. If person S believes that she is currently in mental state M and S *is* in M, then S is justified in believing this proposition. Under this second conception, self-justification works a little differently: It isn't the believing that confers justifiedness, but the belief's being true that confers justifiedness. This idea was defended by Roderick Chisholm (1977). Chisholm offered the following formula: "What justifies me in thinking I know that *a* is F is simply the fact that *a* is F."

Chisholm conceded that the formula does not apply to every proposition that instantiates it:

> Thus, in answer to "What justification do you have for counting it as evident that there can be no life on the moon?" it would be inappropriate—and presumptuous—simply to reiterate "There can be no life on the moon." But we can state our justification for *certain* propositions about our beliefs, and certain propositions about our thoughts, merely by reiterating those propositions. (21, italics added)

Unfortunately, Chisholm offers no explanation of *why* it is appropriate to defend the justification for certain beliefs by reiteration but not others. Why does it work for first-person mental-state propositions but not for third-person mental-state propositions? What is the crucial difference between them?

Chisholm introduced a phrase to distinguish the one class of propositions or states of affairs from the other class. States of affairs are called *self-presenting* when it is appropriate to reiterate the fact in defense of a justification claim. This provides a label, but not the slightest explanation of the alleged epistemic difference. Perhaps such an explanation is intended when Chisholm says that a self-presenting state is one that is "apprehended through itself" (22). But this obscure notion is never explained. If the phrase of immediate justification is not explained more clearly, a defense of immediate justification remains elusive.

1.7 DEBUNKING SOME DEBUNKERS OF IMMEDIATE JUSTIFICATION

Perhaps the case for foundationalism takes on an obscure character from these unhelpful attempts to clarify the nature of immediate justification. In principle, however, this might not be a hopeless task. To get some appreciation for what foundationalism is after, consider first the following analogy.

In European history becoming a monarch was usually a matter of lineage: One became a monarch by standing in the right lineal relationship to someone else who had been a monarch. Not every monarch, however, became one by inheritance; some became monarchs by leading a conquest of new territory. So, in addition to monarchy being passed on by inheritance, it was also sometimes acquired de novo. This parallels the idea of justificational status (J-status) being generated without any justificational "juice" being transmitted from one possessor to another. This makes good sense in the abstract, and there seems no reason to preclude it, at least in principle, in the realm of epistemic justification.

Nonetheless, many epistemologists are pessimistic about the prospects for foundationalism. Several have tried to debunk immediate justifiedness by demonstrating its inherent unrealizability. William Alston (1983) has surveyed some of these attempted debunkings and undertaken to debunk those debunkings. Let us consider a few of these critical assaults and Alston's re-joinders to them.[1] We begin with the ground rules Alston lays down, more specifically the core notions of mediate justification (MJ) and immediate justification (IJ):

> (MJ) S is *mediately* justified in believing that p if and only if S is justified in be-lieving that p by virtue of some relation this belief has to some other justified belief(s) of S.
> (IJ) S is *immediately* justified in believing that p if and only if S is justified in believing that p by virtue of something other than some relation this belief has to some other justified belief(s) of S. (Alston 1989, 58)

Immediate justification is defined here purely negatively: It is justification that does not involve any inferential relation or other relation to other justified beliefs. This skeletal definition does not supply an answer to question (3) posed above; it does not provide positive conditions for immediate justified-ness. Alston goes on to argue that the relevant debunkers he addresses make sneaky attempts to substitute a different conception of immediate justification than the simple conception, (IJ). In effect he accuses debunkers of quietly seeking to impose more stringent conditions on immediate justification than foundationalism needs.

The basic maneuver may be illustrated in terms of an analogy. You are going to a concert, ticket in hand. You approach the entrance to the concert venue and hand your ticket to the ticket-taker standing at the door. The ticket-taker says, "Well, OK. You have a ticket; but that's not enough for entry. You must also produce proof that you personally purchased this ticket from an authorized ticket agency plus the date of your purchase. No such proof is on the ticket itself." You would be outraged, of course. Permission to enter public events of this kind is normally guaranteed by presentation of an applicable ticket. Further proof of how and when the ticket was acquired is not needed. Such a surprise "upping of the ante" would be frowned upon in everyday life. Analogously, Alston's plan is to rebut certain debunkers of immediate justification who (in his view) unfairly and unreasonably "up the ante" for immediate justifiedness.

Alston picks out several debunkers who offer "level ascent" arguments against the possibility of immediate justification. Level ascent is exemplified in our concert ticket example. The first-level requirement for admission—normally the only requirement—is presentation of a legitimate ticket. The ticket-taker goes up a level by requiring not only a legitimate ticket but proof that it is a legitimate ticket. A similar inflation of reasonable requirements for immediate justification is what Alston claims to detect in the work of certain critics.

The first such critic is Wilfrid Sellars (1956). Alston describes what Sellars says about a certain approach to observational knowledge, which might account for how such knowledge can be immediate. This approach would say, roughly, that an observer has perceptual knowledge of an object's being green if, in the presence of green objects, he reliably forms beliefs that they are green. Sellars, arguing to the contrary, says that Jones does not *know* that the object is green unless he is able to reflect on his own performance and take the formation of his statement or belief as a reason for supposing that a green object is present. Alston diagnoses the maneuver as follows:

> Sellars is clearly denying that observational knowledge is or can be immediate knowledge, as that term was explained above [in (IJ)]. His reason for denying it clearly falls under our Level Ascent rubric. One's belief counts as knowledge only if one knows something about the epistemic status of that belief, viz., that it counts as a reliable sign of the fact believed. And, equally clearly, this move could be used against *any* claim to immediate knowledge. (1989, 66)

As further support for his interpretation and rejection of Sellars's level ascent argument, Alston accuses Sellars (and others) of confusing two subtly different concepts that need to be kept separate. The two concepts are, first, the concept of a belief's being justified and, second, engaging in some kind of activity vis-à-vis the belief that reflects on it and establishes its legitimacy. In the concert ticket case, there is a difference between the ticket's being legitimate and the person's having an additional document to prove or establish the ticket's legitimacy. Similarly, Alston argues, it is one thing for a belief to have a certain epistemic property (e.g., being justified); it is quite another for the believer to have a higher-level justification for believing or asserting that it is legitimate. Immediate justification is a first-level property like having legitimacy. When one insists, as Sellars appears to do, that having legitimacy also involves having a higher-level justification about the belief's legitimacy, this inevitably brings in additional beliefs and keeps the original belief from being immediately justified. For the foundationalist, the proper solution is to reject the insistence on any extra, higher-level requirement.

Another epistemologist who tries to debunk basic justification by deploying a level ascent maneuver is Laurence BonJour (1985), who at the time was a coherentist. BonJour begins with the usual assumption that foundationalism can succeed only if there is a certain class of beliefs that are immediately justified. Moreover, given his discussion of justifiedness, a belief's being justified implies that it is highly likely to be true. Thus, whatever feature you might specify that promises to legitimize a belief as immediately justified, possession of that feature must imply that the belief is highly likely to be true. Call your favorite candidate for the correct feature Φ. Then for a belief to qualify as basic, says BonJour, the premises of the following argument must themselves be at least justified:

i. Belief B has feature Φ.
ii. Beliefs having feature Φ are highly likely to be true.

Therefore, B is highly likely to be true.

BonJour then continues as follows:

> And if we now assume, reasonably enough, that for B to be justified for a particular person (at a particular time) it is necessary, not merely that a justification for B exist in the abstract, but that the person in question be in cognitive possession of the justification, we get the result that B is not basic after all since its justification depends on that of at least one other empirical belief. (1985, 5–6)

In other words, BonJour is saying that it's not enough for the premises of his argument to be true—for example, that B has feature Φ (being likely to be true). It is also necessary that the believer be justified in believing that B is likely to be true. But this is an extra, higher-level belief that is said to be needed for first-order justification. If this were indeed necessary, what is initially claimed to be a basic belief depends for its justification on the justifiedness of a higher-level belief as well. If this were so, it would obviously undermine foundationalism. The argument is again a level ascent style of argument. It says that the justifiedness of any first-level belief B requires the epistemic agent also to have a justified higher-level belief B* to the effect that B is likely to be true. It is not enough for the first-level belief, B, genuinely to be likely to be true. In addition, the agent must have a different belief, B*, that justifies him or her in believing that B is likely to be true. This automatically implies that B is not immediately justified, at most only mediately justified.

Alston's response to BonJour is now predictable: He challenges BonJour's crucial step of requiring that for S's first-level belief to be justified there must be a justified higher-order belief to the effect that the first-level belief is highly likely to be true. "In other words, in order that I be justified in accepting B, I must know, or be justified in believing, the premises of the above argument. And why should we suppose that?" (1989, 73). By Alston's lights, BonJour just begs a crucial question, and doesn't really argue for it. Alston concludes, "Thus in BonJour, as in Sellars, the contention that putatively immediate knowledge really rests on higher-level reasons itself rests on a foundation of sand" (77). Alston offers no positive defense of foundationalism by specifying a particular criterion for immediate justifiedness, but he does poke a large hole in the indicated attempts to refute the very possibility of foundationalism.[2]

1.8 STRENGTH, CONTENTS, DEFEATERS, AND BOOSTERS

Our discussion has focused almost entirely on our earlier question (1): What are the necessary and sufficient conditions for obtaining immediate justification? Let us now say a few words about questions (2) and (3) in our original list of questions (Section 1.5).

Descartes was responsible for jump-starting the foundationalist picture of knowledge and justification. He also led the way with the idea that the starting point of the epistemic justification project resides in our own states of mind. His famous maxim "I think, therefore I am" and the struggles he inaugurated about how to proceed from mental states to states of the external world pervaded several centuries of epistemology. In the twentieth century, however, foundationalists started to rethink matters and decided that even physical object propositions ("There's a pear on the table") might be an immediately justified belief. A resolution of this debate is still up in the air.[3]

Roughly the same story can be told for debates over question (2). Descartes again set things in motion by identifying the epistemological project with a quest for certainty. He argued that certainty could be attained in the case of first-person current mental propositions, and certainty was just the strength of justification to demand for basic beliefs. In the last century, however, epistemologists began to have second thoughts: Perhaps immediate justifiedness need not require the highest level of justifiedness. There is no obvious connection between the type of belief content and this required justificational strength, although some such connections have long been defended.

A less explored topic is the impact of so-called defeaters on the problem of justificational types. In foundationalist lore, there are two kinds of (positive) justificational statuses, either of which can characterize a justified belief. There is immediately justified belief and mediately justified belief. This is an exhaustive and exclusive typology. All justified beliefs are justified in one manner or the other; no justified belief has its justification in both ways. But this cannot be an adequate portrait of the epistemic landscape. In fact, the justificational source for many beliefs can be both immediate and mediate, both direct and inferential.

How can this transpire? First, let's introduce some terminology. When a proposition gets an "injection" of justification from some source, let us say it is *prima facie* justified for the epistemic agent. Prima facie justification is provisional, or tentative, justification, as opposed to justification on balance, or all things considered. Whether the J-status of the proposition (for the given agent) changes to on-balance justified may depend on other sources. Some of those other sources might cut against the proposition, thereby reducing its initial positive justifiedness. If that happens (to a sufficient extent), we say that the undercutting or undermining sources *defeat* the prima facie justification arising from the original source. The beliefs (or whatnot) that perform the undermining are called *defeaters*. We might also introduce a term for factors that add justificational support to a proposition: let us call them *boosters*. Both pieces of terminology can also be used in association with the language of "reasons." Doxastic or nondoxastic reasons may be boosters for believing p. If there are both positive and negative sorts of reasons and the negative ones are strong enough, they defeat the prima facie reasons in favor of p. In that case the *ultima facie* (all things considered) J-status of the proposition is unjustified. Alternatively, though an initial injection of justifiedness may be insufficient to bring a proposition across the threshold of justifiedness, getting a booster from a new source may add enough to bring the proposition across the justificational threshold.

Suppose you are looking at the sky and spot a plane with an unfamiliar contour. Is it one of those new-fangled 829s, you wonder? That's what they look like, but the plane is partly in the clouds, it's getting dark, and your distance vision was never so good anyway. But you now recall reading that this new model was going to be flight-tested in your area today. So you conclude, firmly, that what you are seeing is an 829. Your belief is justified but its source of justification is twofold: both noninferential and inferential. The first source is visual, presumably falling in the category of immediate justifiedness. The second source is background information, falling in the category of mediate justifiedness. The two sources jointly supply enough justificational "juice" to make the belief ultima facie justified. But neither source alone would reach across that threshold. A satisfactory theory of justification, obviously, must be capable of handling cases of this kind. If foundationalism is to be such a theory, it had better be able to handle them. Fortunately for foundationalism, this seems feasible with only a slight adjustment. Foundationalism can simply take the properties of immediate and mediate justifiedness to pertain not only (or even primarily) to beliefs, but to sources, factors, or components of justifiedness. Thus, the same belief can have both a mediate source of justifiedness and also an immediate source.

Coherentists will here jump in eagerly. They will point out that for *any* belief one is tempted to form by an immediate source, its justificational status can always in principle be influenced by other beliefs one already holds. "This is just what we have been saying all along," coherentists will exclaim. A careful epistemological should resist this claim. This is not *exactly* what coherentists have said right along; at least it's not the entirety of what they say. Another, stronger thesis they endorse is that inference, or inferential relations to other beliefs, is the *only* source of justification. Coherentism denies the existence of any source of justifiedness other than inference. So what was conceded in the previous two paragraphs is not tantamount to coherentism. But it does give ground to coherentism at least to some degree. It also seems to require foundationalism to countenance the fact that many basic beliefs owe their justification, in part, to inferential sources, albeit these basic beliefs would also have *some* justifiedness arise from noninferential sources.

1.9 MOVING FROM THE FOUNDATIONS TO HIGHER FLOORS (QUESTION 4)

Cartesian foundationalism is the variant of foundationalism that confines basic beliefs to beliefs about first-person current mental states. Setting aside the question of how beliefs about mental states gain immediate justifiedness, we now ask how a subject can proceed from such beliefs to propositions about material things in the external world that also qualify as justified. Clearly, this requires there to be legitimate methods for inferring such external-world propositions from propositions about current experience. Are there such methods? Obviously, we cannot logically deduce external-world propositions from ones about our own inner experiences. According to many epistemologists and philosophers of science, however, our most important and interesting inferences are not deductive anyway. A standard kind of inference—used both in everyday life and in science—is *inference to the best explanation* (also called *abductive* inference).

After this morning's snowfall, I see some tracks in the snow. I infer that the tracks were made by a deer because they look like deer tracks and deer frequent my neighborhood. This looks like a good inference and it's clearly an explanatory inference. I regard the deer hypothesis as a good explanation of the observed tracks in the snow. But my neighbor tells me: "A company called 'Toys for Tricksters' recently marketed a machine that simulates deer tracks. Its tracks in the snow are indistinguishable from genuine deer tracks (and leave no telltale wheel tracks). These machines have become very popular among jokesters." My neighbor claims that my tracks were produced by such a machine; or, when pushed a bit, he says that it is perfectly possible that they were so caused. In either case he concludes that I am not justified in believing it was a deer.

How should we adjudicate this issue? Some inference principle is needed here, one for explanatory inference in particular. Here is a candidate principle:

> (JEI) *Justification by Explanatory Inference.* If hypothesis H purports to explain S's evidence E, and there is no incompatible hypothesis H' that provides a better or equally good explanation of E, then S is justified in believing H on the basis of E. [OR: . . . then S is justified in believing hypothesis H on the basis of E if and only if there is no incompatible hypothesis H' that provides a better or equally good explanation of E.]

If we substitute for "H" the hypothesis that the deer tracks were caused by a deer, and substitute for "E" the observed deer tracks, does JEI sanction my believing the deer hypothesis? Or does the deer-track simulator hypothesis constitute a better or equally good alternative explanation of the tracks? If my believing the deer hypothesis does not satisfy JEI, but JEI is retained as the relevant inference principle, then I should withhold judgment rather than flat-out believe it.

What is involved in one hypothesis being explanatorily superior to another? We shall briefly address this question here and return to it in greater depth in Chapter 4 (Section 4.5). Here are a few principles that have won some degree of acceptance among philosophers (Beebe 2009):

> *Explanatory Simplicity:* Other things being equal, a theory that posits fewer primitive explanatory notions should be preferred to one that posits more.
> *Coherence with Background Knowledge:* Other things being equal, a theory that fits better with other widely accepted theories and background knowledge should be preferred to a theory that fits less well.

Explanatory Depth: Other things being equal, a theory that provides a more illuminating explanation of the relevant data should be preferred to a theory that provides a less illuminating explanation.

Avoidance of Ad Hoc Elements: Other things being equal, a theory that has fewer ad hoc elements should be preferred to a theory that has more ad hoc elements.

How might these ideas be applied to the problem of inferring propositions about the external world from propositions about our own inner experiences? Most philosophers would say that the existence of genuinely material things (chairs, rocks, buildings) is the best explanation, for each of us, of our collection of mental experiences. But George Berkeley disagreed. As a better explanation he offered the hypothesis of a nonmaterial thing—namely God (an infinite mind)—that causes our sequences of experience. He defended this partly by appeal to the greater simplicity of the God hypothesis and partly by appeal to the principle of greater coherence with background knowledge. We already know that minds can cause experiences, but we don't already know that material substances can cause experiences. So it is unclear whether foundationalism can use an inference-to-the-best-explanation principle (whether JEI or another such principle) to show how beliefs about the external world can justifiedly be based on beliefs about our own mental experiences (the foundations). We shall return to this question in Chapter 4.

QUESTIONS

1. The first section of the chapter draws a parallel between moral rightness and wrongness, on the one hand, and epistemic rightness and wrongness on the other. The latter is usually described in terms of being justified or unjustified, rational or irrational in holding certain beliefs. At the same time it was said that moral and epistemic normativity are different species of normativity. Can we really hold both of these things? How can there be a strong commonality between moral and epistemic normativity if they are two different species of rightness and wrongness? How would you explain what is common to the two realms and what is different?

2. Descartes seemed to regard the foundations of his belief system as beliefs he could trust as the basis for other beliefs, on the analogy of what a houseowner does in relying on the foundations of the house to support its higher stories. Does this mean that the foundations must always be stronger than the higher floors? How would this analogy play out in the realm of belief and justification? Must a foundational, or "basic," belief be better justified than any nonbasic justified belief? Descartes said that his foundational belief was "I think." Is that better justified than any other (nonbasic) belief one might have? What property does this belief have that sets it apart from nonbasic justified beliefs and make its justification so strong? Does this property (or properties) hold for all basically justified beliefs? What should a wise foundationalist hold?

3. Suppose you are a member of a jury that is trying a murder charge against a defendant. As often happens in such cases (at least on television), much seems to depend on whether the prosecution's case "hangs together" better than the rival story of what transpired presented by the defense. The first story, of course, includes a proposition about how the defendant did the deed. The second story includes propositions about how the defendant was nowhere near the scene of the crime. Aren't you, as a juror, better justified in believing whichever story is the more coherent one, the one that "hangs together" better? If this is right, doesn't it prove the truth of coherentism? How might a foundationalist reply to this argument?

4. Sticking with the murder case example, suppose the prosecution contends that its own story of what transpired is simpler than the story told by the defense and it has fewer ad hoc elements. Suppose you agree with these claims. Is it clear that this should convince you of the prosecution's story? Why is a simpler story and one with fewer ad hoc elements more worthy of belief? Either explain why it is more belief-worthy, or indicate why it is a mistake to assign simplicity and minimization of ad hoc elements such heavy weight in determining justification.

5. At the end of Section 1.4 it was objected that according to coherentism all members of a highly coherent system will be justified and all members of a weakly coherent system will be unjustified. In other words, for any system, all of its member beliefs have the same justificational status. This is an objection because it's clear that this is not how justification usually works: Normally people have some justified and some unjustified beliefs, despite having just one current system. This appears to be a serious problem given the formulations of coherentism presented in the chapter. But maybe a new formulation of coherentism could avoid this problem. Can you suggest one?

FURTHER READING

Alston, William (1980). "Level Confusions in Epistemology." *Midwest Studies in Philosophy* 5, 135–150. Reprinted in Alston (1989). *Epistemic Justification: Essays in the Theory of Knowledge.* Ithaca, NY: Cornell University Press.

BonJour, Laurence (1985). "The Elements of Coherentism." Chapter 5 in *The Structure of Empirical Knowledge.* Cambridge, MA: Harvard University Press.

Haack, Susan (1999). "The Foundherentist Theory of Epistemic Justification." In Louis Pojman (ed.), *The Theory of Knowledge: Classical and Contemporary Readings* (2nd ed.). Belmont, CA: Wadsworth.

Huemer, Michael (2001). *Skepticism and the Veil of Perception* (pp. 98–118). Lanham, MD: Rowman and Littlefield.

Klein, Peter (2005). "Infinitism Is the Solution to the Regress Problem." In M. Steup and E. Sosa (eds.), *Contemporary Debates in Epistemology* (pp. 131–140). Oxford: Blackwell.

Lyons, Jack C. (2009). *Perception and Basic Beliefs* (Chapters 1, 2, and 4). New York: Oxford University Press.

Pollock, John, and Joseph Cruz (1999). *Contemporary Theories of Knowledge* (2nd ed., Chapter 2, "Foundations Theories"). Lanham, MD: Rowman and Littlefield.

Williams, Michael (2001). *Problems of Knowledge.* New York: Oxford University Press.

NOTES

1. Note that Alston's official target in his paper is knowledge rather than justification. But since the present chapter is devoted to justification rather than knowledge, our exposition will be an adaptation of Alston's discussion.

2. By contrast, Jack Lyons does specify a clearly stated criterion for immediate justifiedness. See Lyons (2009).

3. We return to this topic in Chapter 6.

Two Debates About Justification:
Evidentialism vs. Reliabilism
and Internalism vs. Externalism
Alvin I. Goldman

2.1 JUSTIFICATION AND EVIDENCE

As we have seen, foundationalism and coherentism are the leading theories of the structure of justification. They also constitute the dominant players in what might be called traditional epistemology. Although they disagree sharply on the question of structure, they share a number of assumptions. Much of this chapter focuses on contrasts between traditional justification theories, mainly represented by *mentalist evidentialism*, and untraditional (or less traditional) theories, mainly represented by *process reliabilism*. A lively opposition between these two theories is revealed both by a head-to-head debate between them and by an associated debate between the broader approaches they exemplify, *internalism* and *externalism*.

The term *justifier* refers to anything that helps make a belief state justified or unjustified. In other words, it's anything that contributes, positively or negatively, to the justificational status (*J-status*) of a target belief. Foundationalism and coherentism, even between them, offer only two types of justifiers. The first type is (other) *belief states* of the subject, beliefs from which the target belief can be inferred. These are the things to which we usually appeal when asked or challenged to defend a specified belief. When I reply, "I believe P because of X, Y, and Z," the reasons cited are normally propositions I *believe*. (Sometimes I also know them, but that implies belief in them.) A second type of justifier is *experiential* states, such as perceptual and memory experiences. (What is meant by a memory experience is a conscious seeming-to-remember episode.) As we saw in Chapter 1, coherentism restricts justifiers to beliefs (or other doxastic states) exclusively. It holds, in effect, that all justification takes place by inference, or inferential relations. By contrast, foundationalism allows justification to be conferred by experiences as well as by (other) beliefs.

One thesis shared by traditional foundationalism and coherentism is that all justifiers are mental states of one sort or another—more specifically, mental states of the epistemic subject. Only a subject's own mental states can make a difference to whether the subject is justified or unjustified in holding a given belief. Another point on which foundationalism and coherentism concur is the assumption that only states subject S is in at t are ones that affect the justificational status (J-status) of S's belief in P at t. Consider Jane, a 25-year-old who believes today that when she was seven years old her feelings were badly hurt by her big sister making a snide and derogatory comment. Jane has no memory experience today of those long-ago feelings, or of the sound of her sister's words being uttered. She just believes that this incident occurred. Is Jane warranted in believing that the incident occurred? In addressing this question traditional epistemology instructs us to ignore any mental state or event Jane underwent when she was seven. Such past states certainly matter to the truth of her memory belief (which isn't here in question), but they make no difference to the J-status of her current belief (precisely the matter that is in question). According to traditional theories (in particular, foundationalism and coherentism), only an agent's own current mental situation affects the justifiedness of one of her current beliefs. This may be called the *current-time-slice* assumption of traditional epistemology. ("Solipsism of the moment" is another label for this general type of view, which has dominated modern philosophy.)

The idea harks back to Descartes and other philosophers of his period, who conceptualized epistemology as the task of asking whether—and if so, how—we can start from what we think and experience at any moment and rationally reconstruct our entire corpus of belief from that position. The "problematic" of epistemology, in other words, is to confront this question: How can one legitimately infer outward (to the external world), forward (to the future), and backward (to the past) from the indicated, very limited, dataset? These are all the data we have to go on, according to the tradition, so we'd better be able to show that these inferences are legitimate. Skepticism must be answered by showing how all (or most) of one's commonsense beliefs can be justified on the basis of one's own current mental states.

Before proceeding further let us remind ourselves of an important distinction drawn in Chapter 1 between two types of justification: *doxastic* versus *propositional* justification. Doxastic justification applies to beliefs actually held by a subject, not merely a belief he or she could hold. In speaking of doxastic justifiedness, what is evaluated is a (token) belief, not the subject or the epistemic situation of the subject. By contrast, propositional justification applies to a proposition, a subject, and his or her epistemic situation; it is applicable even if the subject has no belief in the specified proposition. To say that a subject is propositionally justified with respect to P is to say (roughly) that it would be appropriate for him or her to believe P (given his or her epistemic situation). Both concepts of justifiedness are widely used, but some theorists find the doxastic sense of justification more important or congenial and others find the propositional sense more congenial. The best theories try to accommodate both senses of justifiedness but may give priority to one or the other.

Let us now return to the kind of tradition being exposited earlier and reformulate it in terms of *evidence*, a concept widely used in epistemology. There are different conceptions of evidence, but for present purposes we use the term in a sense in which it refers exclusively to mental states. Earl Conee and Richard Feldman (2004) defend a theory called *evidentialism* (or *mentalist evidentialism*), which has a lot in common with traditional theories, especially foundationalism. According to evidentialism, all (positive or negative) justifiers of a belief held by epistemic agent S at time t are evidential states S is in at t. Such states, as we have seen, are exhausted by experiences and beliefs (or doxastic states more generally).

What must the relation be between S's belief in P at t and S's evidential states at t in order for the belief in P to be justified? (*Propositional* justification is the species of justification of central focus here.) The answer offered by evidentialism is that belief is (would be) the appropriate or fitting attitude to adopt given the evidence. In other words, there must be a relation of fittingness that holds between the attitude of belief (directed at P) and S's total evidential states at t. Here we have an exceedingly simple (or simple-looking) theory of justification, which uses only two concepts: evidence and fittingness with the evidence.

Of course, the notion of fittingness is only apparently simple. On reflection, it proves to be fairly elusive, especially when pressed theoretically. Fundamentally, there are two kinds of fittingness: inferential and noninferential. Inferential fittingness holds between propositional states (like beliefs) when there is a strong enough "support" relationship between the contents of the evidential beliefs and the target hypothesis. If the evidential beliefs logically entail the hypothesis, then the support relationship is presumably strong enough to warrant belief in the hypothesis. But other kinds of support also sometimes warrant belief—for example, support of an *inductive* or *explanatory* variety. An example of inductive support is this:

E_1: In the past whenever smoke emanated from a certain location, fire was also present at that location.
E_2: Smoke is now observed at location L.
H: Fire is also present at L.

If E_1 and E_2 are the believed propositions and H is the hypothesis, H is inductively supported by the conjunction of E_1 and E_2. Inference to the best explanation, discussed in Section 1.9, provides another pattern of the support relation, at least in favorable cases. So we appear to have a reasonably clear conception of what inferential fittingness consists in (ignoring problems and complications arising in these areas).

Noninferential fittingness is a more obscure and debatable relation. This is the category to which fittingness with *experience* would belong. One question here is whether experiences (e.g., visual experiences, auditory experiences, being in pain, etc.) have propositional contents, or contents of any sort. If they lack propositional contents (i.e., contents expressible by a declarative sentence), how can they be "commensurable" with doxastic states (with propositional contents) so that the latter can fit or fail to fit the experience? And what shall we say about the epistemic impact of different perceptual modalities (e.g., vision and touch)? If vision and touch provide different "deliverances" about the shape, texture, or identity of an object of interest, which modality's deliverance should be assigned greater evidential weight? What conclusion "fits" the two perceptual deliverances taken together? Also, do perceptual experiences have such qualities as clarity and vividness, and if so how do these qualities affect the noninferential appropriateness of having a belief in their contents as opposed to suspending judgment? Finally, exactly which kinds of experience influence justifiedness? Is having a premonition that something bad will happen a type of experience that makes it fitting and proper (intellectually speaking) for one to believe that something bad *will* happen?

All such problems must be addressed by an evidentialist theory that makes fittingness a key concept. There is another important complication, however. Although evidentialists often say that beliefs are evidence, this cannot be strictly correct. Return to the smoke/fire example. Is it correct that believing E_1 and E_2 provides evidence for H? Not necessarily. Belief per se should not be considered an evidential state; only justified belief deserves to count as evidence. If my beliefs in E_1 and E_2 are unjustified, they don't give me any justification for believing H. This complicates the evidentialist story in important ways, as we shall see below.

2.2 PROBLEMS FOR EVIDENTIALISM

2.2.1 Is Evidential Co-presence Necessary and/or Sufficient?

Let us examine mentalist evidentialism by asking whether the conditions it specifies are necessary and/or sufficient for justifiedness. Evidentialism implies that if a person S believes proposition P and this belief obtains in S's mind at the same time as he or she undergoes or instantiates a set of evidential mental states for which belief is the fitting response, then this is sufficient for S to be justified in believing P. Is this correct?

Jack has worked hard for Congressional candidate Cindy, and it is now election night and he is watching the returns. They are coming in fast from many precincts. Some are rather encouraging if examined carefully. A correct tabulation of those numbers would support substantial confidence. However, Jack is very excited, and although he sees these numbers, he makes a sloppy calculation and comes up with a discouraging but faulty total. Jack's attention, meanwhile, is focused more on other precincts. Although their numbers are scanty, Jack is sure they will come in massively for Cindy. It is mere wishful thinking on his part, however, that makes him confident of this. As a result of this wishful thinking, however, Jack thinks Cindy will win the election. Is his belief justified?

According to evidentialism, it appears that Jack's belief is justified, because the numbers he saw from the first group of precincts did support belief in her ultimate victory. On the other hand, he didn't pay much attention to them. And the numbers from the second batch of precincts are scanty, and prove nothing. But that should not matter under evidentialism, because the first batch of numbers constitutes adequate evidence to support confidence in Cindy's victory. Thus, Jack's belief in victory meets evidentialism's sufficient conditions for justifiedness. Intuitively, though, this verdict is wrong. Jack's belief is *not* justified. (At least in the doxastic sense of justifiedness, his belief is not justified.) It is based on sloppy calculation and wishful thinking. Surely something has gone awry.

What has gone wrong, it appears, is that the mere *co-presence* of a belief with evidential states that it fits is not enough for its justifiedness. It is crucial that appropriate evidential states actually *cause* the belief via suitable thinking. This does not happen in the election returns example. Jack occupies an evidential position that might potentially lead to a justified belief, but he has misused this evidential position, so his confidence in Cindy's victory is the product of highly flawed thought processes. Evidentialism falters here by failing to incorporate a suitable causation condition. It tries to make do with co-presence, but this does not work.

Evidentialism has tried to accommodate this problem by introducing another concept in the vicinity of justification called *well-foundedness* and by including something like a causation condition as necessary for well-foundedness. However, the specified condition is not exactly causation. The proposed condition is that the belief be "based on" appropriate evidence, where the basing relation is left unanalyzed. Unless a causal condition is included, however (whether or not it is embedded in the basing relation), it looks like the election case cannot be handled appropriately. This is already an important shift from the tradition in which it used to be claimed that mental causation and "discovery" are purely psychological matters that have no bearing whatever on justification and no place in a theory of justifiedness (Reichenbach 1938). Causal theories of justification, of the sort we shall examine shortly, run contrary to this tradition (Goldman 1967).

Turn next to *necessity*: Is it a necessary condition of a belief's being justified that it fit some set of evidential states co-present with it? Here is a counterexample. Nora's friend Amy asks her: "What is the circumference of the Earth?" Nora replies: "It is approximately 25,000 miles." Amy continues, "Really? What makes you think that? What is your evidence for it?" Nora replies: "I don't know what my evidence is. I can't think of any evidence right now. It's just one of those facts that I know, or at least believe." Suppose, indeed, that Nora has no recollection of reading it anywhere, or hearing somebody say it. In short, Nora no longer retains any specific evidence about the Earth's circumference, although she did once learn it from an authoritative source. As far as her current mental states are concerned, the only relevant state is the belief itself. So she has neither inferential (belief-based) evidence for the proposition nor noninferential (experiential) evidence for it. Nonetheless, it is perfectly plausible that her belief in this proposition is justified. If she learned it originally from an authoritative source and retained it ever since, she is still justified in holding it. If this is right, the current possession of evidence that a belief fits is not a necessary condition for the belief's being justified. (Do you share this intuition? If not, more argument would be needed.)

A defender of evidentialism might reply as follows. Even if Nora has no current justified belief about the source of her belief in the circumference proposition, she must surely have a justified current belief *that her memory beliefs are usually reliable.* Isn't this a current evidential belief that helps support her circumference belief, since it is a belief of hers? Perhaps the italicized belief represents the needed evidence. However, it does not seem necessary for Nora's belief in the circumference proposition to be justified that she should have such a belief about her memory's reliability. Maybe she just isn't reflective in this sort of way, or isn't being reflective about it at the moment. Even if she possesses this general belief about her memory, which could be elicited if she were prompted, it plays no causal role in her current belief. Thus, it is arbitrary to insist that this is what confers justifiedness on the belief. If the assumed story is that Nora did read some authoritative source to the effect that the Earth's circumference is 25,000 miles but later forgot the identity of that source, it might be reasonable to conclude that this past piece of evidence acquisition played a crucial missing role in Nora's being justified later on. But this does nothing to show that she needs co-present evidential states to have a justified belief now.

Next we consider an argument for saying that some justified beliefs are not accompanied by any (appropriate) evidential states whatever. Almost all epistemologists agree that people have justified beliefs about their current mental states; for example, "I now have a headache" or "I think that my social security number is such-and-such." It is also generally agreed that such beliefs enjoy noninferential rather than inferential justification. So, if all noninferential evidence (about contingent propositions, at any rate) consists in experiential states, the present cases would also have to involve experiential evidence. Finally, a fairly standard view is that beliefs of the foregoing kind are justified because one introspects the mental states that the beliefs describe. Does introspection involve experiential evidence? This is dubious. Although some philosophers view introspection as a quasi-perceptual process (an "inner sense"), it surely differs from standard perceptual processes in lacking any associated sensory "feel." Introspection involves no distinctive qualitative character analogous to the qualitative character associated with vision or hearing. This suggests that no experiential evidence is present in introspection. What, then, is the experiential state that renders an introspection-based belief justified?

Evidentialists might retort: "It is the target mental state itself. In the foregoing examples this would be the headache itself, or the judgment that my social security number is such-and-such." One objection to this is that it seems improper for a target state to be evidence for itself. The very idea of a state's conferring evidence on itself is highly suspect. As we saw in Chapter 1, Chisholm proposed to deal with the problem of ending evidential regresses by quipping "what justifies me in thinking I feel sad is that I *do* feel sad." This is clever, but Chisholm offers no explanation of when or why it should work. Can we equally say "what justifies me in thinking that the fusiform gyrus of my right occipital cortex [a certain brain region] is being activated is that the fusiform gyrus of my right occipital cortex *is* being activated"? Surely not. This certainly does not work for random brain states, if any. An evidentialist needs to explain why not. How do brain states differ from feelings of sadness so that the formula "works" for the latter but not for the former? Moreover, in the social-security-number belief case the target state is not an experiential one, so how can it provide experiential evidence in the way that perceptual or memory states do?

Finally, this subsection turns to a problem of explanation rather than a counterexample. How can evidentialism explain why certain experiences confer evidence while others do not? Philosophical theories aim to explain things, especially to illuminate underlying reasons that lie behind intuitively familiar data. Here the thing to be explained is an intuitive datum mentioned earlier: Although premonitions are experiential states, they do not confer justification. If one has a premonition that P, this lends no legitimate evidential support to P. Why is this so? It is hard to find an answer in evidentialism's toolkit. By contrast, a competing theory we shall soon examine has a simple and straightforward answer.

2.2.2 What Is Meant by "Evidence"?

When we engage in philosophical theorizing, we want to be careful about our theoretical terms. A theoretical term is often open to different definitions or interpretations, and the choice of definition can be quite important. One definition might suit a given theoretical position well and another might suit it badly. So it is always appropriate to ask proponents of a philosophical theory to specify the meanings they attach to their terms.

These points apply to evidentialism. It is obviously important, in trying to assess the merits of this theory, to get straight about the intended meaning of "evidence." Although evidentialists offer clear examples of what they consider evidence, they do not provide any definition. Definitions of "evidence" have been offered by other philosophers, however, and it is instructive to see if any of these could work for evidentialism. Here is one proffered definition:

> X is evidence for Y just in case possessing X enhances a person's justification for believing Y.

Notice that this definition uses "justification" in the analysans (the clause that does the analyzing). There is nothing wrong with this in the abstract, but here we are discussing a theoretical approach that seeks to analyze justification in terms of evidence. So it would be circular to turn around and define evidence in terms of justification. It is OK to define either term by means of the other but not to do both at once. That engulfs one in circularity.

What is so bad about a circular pair of definitions? Suppose I define *wizard* as someone who produces magical events, and then define *magical* as events produced by a wizard. If I tried to figure out whether there are any wizards or magical events, this pair of definitions would be singularly unhelpful. Spotting events I suspect to be magical, the second definition tells me that I need to determine whether any of them is caused by a wizard. When I try to determine of any individual whether he or she is a wizard, the first definition instructs me to determine whether the individual produces any magic. Progress seems impossible.

Let us try a different definition of evidence. It is a matter of common observation that lightning is evidence of impending thunder. To call lightning "evidence" here seems to mean that lightning is a reliable indicator of thunder, where a reliable indicator is a sign that invariably, or regularly, gets things right. What is meant by "gets things right" is, roughly, "tells the truth." Thus, this sense of "evidence" can also be captured by the phrase "reliable mark of the truth."

Can evidentialists adopt this as their preferred sense of "evidence"? Accepting this definition would imply that a mental state (e.g., a perceptual experience) qualifies as an evidential state only if it reliably indicates the truth—presumably, the truth about the external world. But given the posited relationship between justification and truth, beliefs will get to be justified at least partly in virtue of states having truth-indicating properties, so truth-indicatorship would become relevant to the J-status of beliefs. It would follow from this that truth-indicatorship is a "justifier," something that helps determine the J-status of beliefs. But truth-indicatorship is not a mental state, so in the end, the evidentialist's core claim that only mental states are justifiers would be undercut. Thus, evidentialists cannot use this definition of "evidence." This is a fundamental theoretical problem for evidentialism: How can they define their central theoretical term so as to avoid circularity but not undercut core features of their theory?

2.3 JUSTIFICATION AND PROCESS RELIABILITY

Let us make a new start toward a theory of justification. The example of Jack the election worker illustrates that the J-status of a belief depends on how it is formed, or caused. The fact that Jack's confidence in his candidate's victory is caused by wishful thinking is clearly what leads us to assess his belief as unjustified. Evidentialism tries to accommodate this point by saying that a belief's being justified ("well-founded," in their terminology) requires not only that the belief fit the subject's evidence but also that it be based on this evidence. Does this cover the point adequately? It handles the case of Jack because although he possesses some evidence (i.e., the favorable numbers he substantially ignores) that his victory belief fits, it isn't based on that evidence. So far, so good.

Now consider another case. A simple rule of deductive logic called "disjunctive syllogism" licenses the following pattern of inference as valid:

Either P or Q.
Not-Q.
Therefore, P.

Suppose that Chad justifiably believes a proposition of the form "P or Q" and justifiably believes "not-Q." Then he has first-rate evidence for believing P; indeed, his evidence logically entails P. Hence, if he forms a belief in P based on this evidence, mustn't this belief of Chad be justified? Is that necessarily the case? No.

Suppose Chad is psychologically "wired" to deploy the following reasoning process under many circumstances. When he believes two premises of the form "P % Q" and "not-Q," where the symbol "%" is replaceable by any binary truth-functional connective (disjunction, conjunction, material conditional, etc.), then Chad infers a conclusion of the form "P." In other words, Chad employs a reasoning principle that resembles disjunctive syllogism but greatly (and ludicrously) overextends it. If deployment of this overextended principle is the process by which Chad arrives at his belief in P in the foregoing example, then his belief is definitely not justified. It follows from this that it is not a sufficient condition for a belief to be justified that it both fits one's evidence and is based on that evidence (Goldman 2012, 7).

As this and previous cases indicate, it is quite crucial to the J-status of a belief how it is causally produced. It is not just a matter of the inputs to the causal process (e.g., their being suitable evidential states). It is crucial that the belief-forming process used be of an appropriate, or suitable, kind. Which belief-forming processes are suitable and which are unsuitable?

In trying to answer this question, let's review some of the examples already covered. Forming beliefs by wishful thinking is clearly unsuitable. Forming beliefs by using invalid reasoning processes like Chad's overgeneralized inference schema is also unsuitable. Beliefs formed by these kinds of processes are always unjustified, no matter what prior mental states (or evidence) they take as inputs. What are examples of suitable belief-forming processes? Presumably, ordinary perceptual processes are suitable. We normally judge the outputs of such processes (perceptual beliefs about the external world) to be justified. Similarly, we tacitly assume that introspection is a suitable belief-forming process. Finally, using valid inference schemas to guide our reasoning is surely justification-preserving. If one starts with justified beliefs in the premises and applies a valid reasoning process to it, the output of the reasoning process will also be justified.

What do suitable ("good") belief-forming processes have in common that makes them all good (i.e., justification-conferring)? What do unsuitable ("bad") belief-forming processes have in common that makes them all bad (i.e., unjustification-conferring)? The answers seem to leap out. The good processes are highly reliable processes: A high proportion of the beliefs they generate are true. The bad processes are unreliable processes, or at least not very reliable ones: The proportion of true beliefs they generate is not very high, some of them less than 50 percent. Thus, wishful thinking is bad because the beliefs it outputs are only occasionally true. The overextended version of disjunctive syllogism is bad because it would frequently lead to erroneous conclusions even when its inputs are true. By contrast, forming beliefs by standard perceptual processes (in favorable viewing conditions) is generally reliable. And using disjunctive syllogism (in the strict sense) will always yield true conclusion-beliefs if the premise-beliefs are true. It's a good-making feature of a belief-forming process that it tends to produce a high ratio of true beliefs and a bad-making feature of a belief-forming process that it tends to produce a low ratio of true beliefs. Very plausibly, this is why belief-outputs of the former type of processes are justified and belief-outputs of the latter type of processes are unjustified. A theory of justification incorporating these core ideas is naturally dubbed *process reliabilism* (Goldman 1979).

2.4 FORMULATING PROCESS RELIABILISM

How should such a theory be formulated? For starters, consider the following principle:

> Belief B is justified if and only B is produced by a reliable belief-forming process—that is, a process that has a tendency to generate (belief) outputs with a high percentage of truths.

What is a high percentage? Eighty percent? Ninety percent? The theory can afford to be vague in this matter. After all, the concept (or property) being analyzed, justification, is itself a vague concept, so it is appropriate for its analysis to be correspondingly vague.

However, there is another problem. Some belief-forming processes are reasoning processes. These processes operate on prior beliefs of the subject (premise beliefs), which themselves can be either justified or unjustified and either true or false. Focus on their truth-values. Where the input beliefs are true, a "perfect" reasoning process (i.e., a deductively valid process) would have all of its output beliefs true as well. And we might expect inductively strong processes to have most of their output beliefs be true. But we cannot expect this for the class of cases in which the input beliefs include falsehoods. Even a first-rate inference process can't be expected to produce true outputs when applied to false inputs. As the saying goes, "garbage in, garbage out."

So let's distinguish between processes that take prior beliefs as inputs and processes that don't. Processes of the latter type should be required to be unconditionally reliable. Processes of the former type, on the other hand, should only be required to be conditionally reliable—that is, to have a high proportion of true outputs across the range of cases in which their belief

inputs are all true. Once this distinction is drawn, we can advance two principles of justification (doxastic justification is the main species of justification
at issue here):

(UR) A belief B is justified if it is produced by a belief-forming process that is
unconditionally reliable.
(CR) A belief B is justified if (i) B is produced by a belief-forming (or belief-
retaining) process that is conditionally reliable, and (ii) all of the belief inputs to
the belief-forming (or belief-retaining) process that causes B are justified.

Notice that (CR) does not specify that all the input beliefs must be true; it
only requires that they all be justified. This guarantees, however, that the
input beliefs must have been produced by prior uses of "good" processes too,
even if, as it happened, those good processes did not (all) produce truths on
those occasions. The rationale here is that one cannot expect epistemic agents
to do more than use good epistemic procedures. The idea behind reliabilism
is that good epistemic procedures are either unconditionally reliable or conditionally reliable.

It follows from (UR) and (CR) that a person can arrive at a justified belief
by a series of belief-forming or belief-retaining processes that take place over
a considerable period of time. People routinely make inferences scattered
over a period of time, each new inference drawing on old beliefs that may
have been formed quite a while earlier. Memory plays a fundamental role in
such a series—not memory in the sense of conscious episodes but memory
in the sense of a preservative or retentive process that takes belief states at
one point in time and maintains them, or "carries them over," to a later time.
(Alternatively, an imperfect memory process may result in belief modifica-
tion over time.) With this in mind, (UC) and (CR) can be fused into a single
reliabilist principle of justification:

(R) A belief B (at time t) is justified if and only if B (at t) is the output of a series
of belief-forming or belief-retaining processes each of which is either unconditionally or conditionally reliable, and where the conditionally reliable processes
in the series are applied to outputs of previous members of the series.

A simple illustration of this principle is as follows. Suppose Mary believes
that her favorite Hollywood couple is getting divorced. She acquired this
belief from reading a Hollywood magazine, *Gossip*, which reported that
Kenneth and Gwyneth had filed for divorce. She also believes that *Gossip* is
very trustworthy in such matters, which she had established previously.
Mary first used perceptual processes to form the belief that *Gossip* reports an
impending divorce (=D) and from this she inferred the truth of D. Each of
these cognitive steps involved a reliable process (unconditional in the perceptual step and conditional in the inferential step). Her belief in D was then
stored in memory and retained for at least a week. Memory storage, let us
assume, is a conditionally reliable belief-retaining process; that is, its later

outputs are usually true if the earlier inputs to it were true. Then, by princi-ple (R), Mary's preserved belief in D is justified. Suppose that Mary no longer remembers a week later that her belief in D was acquired by reading *Gossip*. At the later time of belief, she no longer possesses any such evidential source that inferentially supports D. The reliabilist principle (R), however, does not require co-present evidence. According to (R) the history, or etiology, of a person's belief in a proposition is also relevant to its J-status. Given that Mary originally formed her belief in D based on good evidence, and nothing has transpired to undercut or defeat that evidence, (R) is perfectly consistent with Mary's being justified at the later time in believing D. This seems like the intuitively right result. Unlike evidentialism, then, process reliabilism delivers a correct verdict about Mary. (At least so it strikes the present author.)

Notice that process reliabilism marks a substantial departure from earlier theories we considered (foundationalism, coherentism, and evidentialism) in introducing a novel category of justifiers, viz. belief-forming processes. Under process reliabilism, psychological processes used in acquiring and/or retaining beliefs are critically relevant to their J-status. Thus, belief-forming and belief-retaining processes are justifiers, or J-factors. They are not eviden-tial justifiers; they are not pieces of evidence, or reasons, to which a subject would appeal to defend his or her beliefs. (They just "operate" on such evi-dence or reasons to produce beliefs or other doxastic attitudes.) Nonetheless, they are relevant to the J-statuses of the beliefs they produce, which is what it takes to qualify as justifiers.

Process reliabilism is mainly a theory of what makes beliefs justified or unjustified—beliefs that are actually held. Thus, it is primarily a theory of doxastic justifiedness. However, we can also ask a question about proposi-tional justifiedness. We can ask whether a person is justified to believe P even when he or she does not in fact believe it. A visual experience someone undergoes while viewing a mountain landscape may entitle him or her to believe that there are three peaks in the distance, although he or she hasn't paid attention to the number of peaks or formed any belief on that question. We might nevertheless say that he or she is justified (or warranted) to believe that there are three. Since a proposition that is not believed has no causal his-tory, however, principle (R) cannot be used directly to assess its J-status for S. What needs to be asked, therefore, is whether the subject in question is in mental states that could be used as inputs to a reliable process and, if so used, would output a belief in the designated proposition. That's a rough sketch of how process reliabilism can be adapted to handle propositional justification (Goldman 1979).

2.5 RELIABILISM'S ATTRACTIONS AND PROBLEMS

Process reliabilism has many attractions as a theory of justification, some of which have been noted. It also faces a number of significant problems. Let us survey some of its chief advantages and most prominent problems, and ask how reliabilism might address the latter.

If the preceding discussion was right, reliabilism delivers accurate verdicts about J-statuses in a large number of cases. In addition, it has two attractive features that merit emphasis. First, it goes a long way toward reducing threats of skepticism. Epistemologists generally welcome effective rejoinders to skeptics. (At issue here is justification skepticism. Reliabilism can also be formulated, with important additions, as a theory of knowledge, as we'll see in Chapter 3.) Reliabilism is congenial to several leading responses to knowledge-skepticism as we'll see in Chapter 4. Section 1.6 posed a traditional skeptical challenge. It argued that external-world beliefs can be justified only if they offer better explanations of everyday experience than competing hypotheses such as Cartesian demons or envatted brains. Indeed, many skeptics argue that a subject must be able to exclude such competitors on explanatory grounds. These stiff requirements demanded by skeptics are hard to meet. But is it appropriate to impose them? Reliabilism proposes a milder requirement for justification, namely the reliability or truth-conduciveness of the belief processes used. This condition is much more easily satisfied than the hyperdemanding conditions often proposed by skeptics.

A second widely acknowledged desideratum for a theory of justification is that it underwrite a close link between justification and truth. Contemporary epistemologists admit that a belief's being justified rarely guarantees the truth of its content. Still, a belief's being justified should make its truth highly probable. For many theories, however, it is difficult to see how this result can be secured. BonJour, an erstwhile coherentist, explicitly accepts the truth-link desideratum, and sets out to show why his own theory has this consequence (1985). Unfortunately, it is very unclear how coherentism guarantees this. By contrast, reliabilism seems to secure it easily. If a belief is caused by reliable processes, doesn't this essentially guarantee a substantial probability of the belief's being true?

As a first line of criticism, some critics turn the tables on reliabilism by disputing the adequacy of its response to skepticism. They argue that it sets too weak conditions for justification, allowing warrant to be attained on the cheap. Serious skeptical worries are just dodged, not really met. One such line of criticism starts by saying that being caused by a reliable process is not enough for justification. The subject must also meet a "meta-justification" requirement: he or she must be justified in believing that his or her belief is reliably caused. Furthermore, such critics continue, this meta-justification condition cannot be met. In particular, it cannot be met without appealing to the self-same element of reliability that is under challenge—and this would be an unsatisfactory solution.

Reliabilists are not lacking in responses here. Reliabilism about justification is partly motivated by the idea that we need an analysis of justification in nonjustificational and nonepistemic terms. Causal reliability can meet this desideratum because it makes no appeal to justificational notions. So if we have to honor a meta-justification requirement, it might take the form of a requirement that the subject must believe reliably that his or her first-order belief is reliably caused. But why, exactly, would the satisfaction of this higher-level requirement guarantee justifiedness if satisfaction of a first-order reliable belief formation fails to do so? If "bare" reliability of first-order belief cannot do the job, why would a single higher-order element of meta-reliability succeed? Why not require an infinite series of higher-order reliably formed beliefs? Yet this would clearly be excessive. So we should reject the demand for a meta-level requirement at the very start. A related condition, however, may well be appropriate, namely the much weaker requirement that the subject not believe (or not reliably believe) that his or her first-order belief is unreliably caused. This "negative" condition, simply an anti-defeat condition, can certainly be incorporated into reliabilism without adverse consequence.

A second line of skepticism-related criticism also concerns the adequacy of the reliable-causation condition. According to one critic, this feature of reliabilism guarantees only the possibility that humans meet the justification requirement for their ordinary beliefs. Guaranteeing this mere possibility, however, should not satisfy a skeptic (Wright 2007, 31). A skeptic wants to be given something stronger than this. He or she wants to see that it is not merely possible for people to be justified in their everyday beliefs; he or she wants to be shown they *are* so justified. At any rate, the skeptic wants to be shown that they are justified in believing (if they are reflective enough) that they are so justified. And he or she wants to challenge the very possibility of this. But even Wright concedes that the skeptic is in no position to assert the impossibility of our having such second-order justifiedness when it is characterized in reliabilist terms. The skeptic cannot preclude the possibility that we should have reliably caused beliefs to the effect that our ordinary beliefs are reliably caused. What an internalism-driven skeptic wants to claim is that mere higher-order reliability does not adequately express and resolve his or her dissatisfaction. However, Wright seems to concede that it isn't obvious how the skeptic's dissatisfaction should be expressed. Wright offers no formulation of the dissatisfaction (in internalist terms) that he himself finds satisfactory.

A third line of criticism has a different focus. It casts doubt on the idea that token belief-forming processes can be assigned unambiguous degrees of reliability, an assumption that seems fundamental to process reliabilism. Without such assignments, the question of whether a given belief is caused by a sufficiently reliable process (wherever the threshold for reliability is set) cannot be resolved. The ambiguity arises from the fact that any token belief-forming process can be "typed" in many different ways. For example, the token process in which George arrives at the belief that he has won a lottery by reading this in *The New York Times* might be an instance both of the type *forming a belief by reading The New York Times* and of the type *forming a belief by reading*. The first type might have a very high reliability, enough to meet the requisite standard of justifiedness. The second type, by contrast, may not be sufficiently reliable to qualify for justifiedness. But which type should be used in fixing a token belief's justifiedness? Reliabilism hasn't supplied any (agreed-upon) formula for choosing a process type at the "right" level of generality. This is called the *generality problem*. One response by reliabilists is to point out that the generality problem, though genuine, is not peculiar to reliabilism. According to this view, in some form it is every epistemology's problem, not one peculiar to reliabilism.[1] This response can be supported by pointing out that every epistemology must acknowledge that a belief is (doxastically) justified only if it stands in the basing relation to states of evidence-possession or reasons-possession that the epistemic subject is in. But the basing relation involves some sort of causal process, and any instantiation of a causal process must be suitably typed. This introduces the generality problem in (roughly) the same way it arises for process reliabilism.

Many attempts to solve the generality problem have been tried. A novel approach emerges if one considers a general approach to justification (and other philosophical topics) that focuses heavily on the attributor, a maneuver we will consider below. For now let us postpone discussion of the generality problem until we have placed some methodological considerations on the table.

Our fourth problem for reliabilism was, historically, one of the first that was raised. It is called the *new evil-demon* problem. Descartes entertained the possibility of an evil demon that systematically deceived him, causing even his perceptual experiences to mislead him about his surroundings. Contemporary critics of reliabilism use the evil-demon hypothesis to pose a counterexample to reliabilism. Since the character in the evil-demon world is systematically deceived by his perceptual experiences, his perceptual belief-forming processes must be unreliable. Hence, according to reliabilism (it seems), he isn't justified in believing their outputs. But, these critics protest, such beliefs should intuitively be classified as justified, presumably because agents in an evil-demon world have the same experiences as people in the actual, normal world. Ostensibly, this is a major flaw in reliabilism.

At this point it may be wise to take a step back and assess the methodology we are using (not just in this immediate context, but more broadly). In assessing the merits or demerits of each theory, the evidence to which we appeal is to ask what judgments, verdicts, evaluations, or attributions people make, or are inclined to make, about the target belief's epistemic status. In so doing, however, a theorist doesn't directly detect the belief's epistemic status. It cannot be "read off" from the case description whether the belief held by a victim of the demon is justified or unjustified. The theorist's "immediate" evidence is what he or she herself intuitively judges and what other people who consider the same question judge. Do they attribute justifiedness or unjustifiedness to the victim? Or what are they inclined to attribute? In effect, the data to which we appeal are data about justification attributions. It is natural to suggest, then, that what we should be seeking is a theory that explains, or accounts for, these attributions made by people who are given the cases in question. Theories of this sort need not focus exclusively on the epistemic subject whose belief justifiedness is in question; they might equally focus on the attributor.[2] Let us see how this strategy plays out in the evil-demon case.

Here is a plausible-looking story (though admittedly a speculative one). The epistemic properties people associate with various belief-forming processes are likely to be properties that those processes display in ordinary, actual-world settings. As encountered in the actual world, perceptual processes are by and large impressively reliable over a fairly wide range of circumstances. Thus, people might naturally think of common perceptual process types (e.g., seeing, hearing, feeling) as good ways of forming beliefs—good in the sense that they usually deliver the truth (which is what people seek for the most part). Other belief-forming process types, such as forming a belief by hunch or guesswork, are presumably thought to be bad ways of forming beliefs, bad because of their error-proneness. Now if these people are presented, in conversation, with descriptions of imagined scenarios in which the protagonist's situation is highly unusual (e.g., an evil-demon type of situation), they might not evaluate the protagonist's performance in terms of what regularities prevail in his or her unusual world. Rather than abandon the classifications they have stored up based on actual-world experience, they might continue to apply them even to the bizarre hypothetical world. They might classify perceptually formed beliefs as justified and beliefs formed by guesswork as unjustified, even if these processes are described as having reversed reliabilities in the imagined scenarios. This pattern of justification attribution might be captured by a "two-stage" theory of justification attribution. In the first stage the potential attributor forms appraisals of belief-forming process types in terms of their observed (or inferred) reliability in the actual world. In the second stage the potential attributor is invited to make attributions of justifiedness or unjustifiedness about real or imagined epistemic subjects. The theory we are developing conjectures that people would make this choice by relying heavily on their mentally stored lists of approved and disapproved process types (Goldman 1992). This account would readily explain the pattern of people's attributions in the new evil-demon case. In particular, it predicts that attributors would give a "justified" verdict for the victim's belief because perceptual belief-forming types will be on attributors' approved lists.[3]

Approved-list reliabilism might also help us understand what transpires in another style of (putative) counterexample to reliabilism. Laurence BonJour advanced the example of a reliable "clairvoyant" subject, Norman, who forms beliefs—he knows not how—about the current whereabouts of the President, despite having no perceptual experiences of seeing the President at the time (or any other standard bit of evidence) (1985, 38 45). As it happens, Norman in fact possesses an extremely reliable clairvoyant power, and this power is what generates his belief about the President's whereabouts. Norman just suddenly finds himself believing that the President is in New York City. He has no evidence or reasons for thinking that he has any special cognitive power for remote detection—but he does have such a power. According to the original formulation of reliabilism, the theory seems committed to saying that Norman's clairvoyant belief is justified, but most epistemologists find this counterintuitive.

The question now arises whether the new form of reliabilism under consideration here (approved-list reliabilism) also predicts the "wrong" verdict (i.e., "justified"). The answer seems to be no: Clairvoyance would presumably not be on the approved list of normal attributors. Indeed, both clairvoyance and other mysterious and suspect powers would probably be on a normal attributor's disapproved list (along with extrasensory perception, telekinesis, etc.). This would explain the tendency of attributors to deny that Norman's belief is justified.[4]

Finally, let us return to the generality problem to see what light might be shed on it by the attributional focus. Rephrased for this approach, the principal question for approved-list reliabilism is whether attributors judge a belief to be justified when and only when they also judge it has been produced by a reliable process. As Erik Olsson (forthcoming) suggests, this is a question one might test for "experimentally," using the following method. One might first select two groups of subjects and confront them with, say, twenty episodes of ordinary life involving a person coming to believe something. The episodes could be presented as film sequences. Each subject in the first group is asked to state independently for each episode whether the character in that episode is justified in his or her belief. Similarly, each subject in the second group is asked to state independently for each episode whether the character in that episode acquired his or her belief in a reliable way. Suppose the experiment yielded the result that there was a high correlation between the reports in the first group and the reports in the second group. In other words, more or less the same episodes that were classified as justified by all or almost all members of the first group were also classified as having been acquired in a reliable way by all or almost all members of the second group. This would be clear support, at least prima facie support, for the reliabilist theory (at least in its original, one-stage version). This begins to give us an idea of how reliabilism might be tested, and it isn't obvious, argues Olsson, that it would be refuted. We shall return to this topic with further developments in Chapter 7.

A fifth problem for process reliabilism focuses on a theory of epistemic value to which it is allegedly tied. According to these critics, however, allegiance to this theory of epistemic value creates a serious problem for reliabilism's verdicts about justification.[5] The theory of value in question is epistemic teleology, or epistemic consequentialism, which says that the possession of true beliefs and the avoidance of false beliefs are valuable ends in themselves. According to the critics, reliabilism about justification is a theory of when a belief is "right" or "appropriate" very similar to the ethical theory of utilitarianism, which views an action's moral status as a function of the causal effects of that action. Applied to the epistemic case, this is said to yield intuitively incorrect verdicts of justifiedness. Consider a hypothetical case in which you are a longstanding atheist, persuaded of this view by careful intellectual reflection. Now you have an opportunity to be awarded a research grant offered by a religious organization, but winning this grant is contingent on your adopting a belief in God. By a kind of surrender of the intellect to desire, your keen desire to win the grant changes your belief around so that you now believe in God. Finally, suppose that you win the grant, and the research it supports generates an abundance of widely believed scientific truths. Does this show that your belief in God is justified? Certainly not, say the critics; but it looks like reliabilism is committed to this palpably incorrect verdict.

Clearly the critics say that the belief is not justified. But does process reliabilism imply otherwise, as the critics imply? No. As clearly indicated by the principles stated in Section 2.4, process reliabilism is a historical theory of belief justifiedness, which implies that only processes upstream of a target belief, not downstream from it, determine its justificational status. In the critics' example, however, the crucial process that leads directly to the belief in question (belief in God's existence) is quite clearly a defective process. Surrendering one's intellect to desire, whatever that amounts to, is clearly defective. The process reliabilist will explain such defectiveness in terms of unreliability. This feature is salient in the case, and process reliabilism would clearly invoke this feature to issue a verdict of "unjustified" about this belief. It does not matter at all (for reliabilism's verdict) that many true-belief states are the consequences of your forming a belief in God (at the time in question). According to process reliabilism, it is the causes of the target belief (within the agent) that are critical to its J-status, not its consequences.

2.6 INTERNALISM VS. EXTERNALISM: FRAMING THE DEBATE

Evidentialism belongs to a family of justification theories called *internalism* and process reliabilism belongs to a family of justification theories called *externalism*. Internalism and externalism are rival approaches to the nature of justifiers, or J-factors. In the original terms of debate, internalism has claimed that all justifiers are "internal" and externalism has denied this. Externalists assert that at least some justifiers are "external." Since mental states are paradigm cases of internal factors, (mentalist) evidentialism is a prime example of internalism. Since truth (or reliability) is a paradigm case of an external factor, reliabilism is a prime example of externalism. Examining the (sometimes fierce) debate between adherents of these two approaches can deepen our understanding of issues in the theory of justification.

It might help to conceptualize the topic of epistemic justification in explicitly normative terms. Ethical theory regularly talks about morality in terms of rules. For example, an action may be considered morally right just in case it conforms to right moral rules and wrong in case it violates, or fails to conform to, such rules. Analogously, in epistemology we can say that a doxastic attitude toward a proposition is justified just in case it conforms to what is permitted by correct epistemic rules and unjustified in case it doesn't conform to such rules. Presumably, correct rules permit or decline to permit doxastic choices based on an agent's epistemic conditions or circumstances. If S's circumstances include the possession of a certain body of evidence

Rules ?

relevant to P, then the correct rules may permit S to believe P. If a different body of evidence is possessed, the correct rules may not permit him or her to believe P. What kinds of conditions or circumstances are featured in correct rules and therefore play a role in permitting or prohibiting doxastic decisions? Those types of conditions or circumstances are the justification-makers or -breakers; that is, they are the "J-factors" (or some of them, anyway). We want to determine the kinds of factors these J-factors are—in particular, whether they are internal or external states of affairs.

What is meant by calling a J-factor an "internal" factor? There are two main approaches here. As we have seen, one approach holds that internal factors are mental states. An older approach is more flexible; it holds that internal factors are anything directly accessible to the agent at the time of doxastic decision making. What does it mean to be "directly accessible"? It includes being available to introspection but is usually meant to be wider than that. Sometimes it is said to be anything available "to reflection," where reflection may include a priori cognition. We shall return to this in the course of our discussion.

Why do (some) epistemologists wish to restrict J-factors to internal states, whether mental states or other directly accessible matters? Sometimes the argument proceeds by straightforward argument "from cases." In defending internalism, for example, Earl Conee and Richard Feldman (2001, 236–238) present six pairs of contrasting cases. In each pair one person is justified in believing a certain proposition and the other person is unjustified in believing it. Conee and Feldman contend that these contrasts in J-status are best explained by supposing that internal differences account for the epistemic difference. Here is one pair of such cases.

A novice and an expert bird-watcher both get a good look at a bird in a nearby tree. The expert immediately knows that it is a woodpecker, because he has fully reasonable beliefs about what woodpeckers look like. The novice has no good reason like that, so he is not justified in believing it is a woodpecker. Conee and Feldman comment: "The epistemic difference between novice and expert arises from something that differentiates the two internally. . . . The novice would gain the same justification as the expert if the novice came to share the expert's internal condition concerning the look of woodpeckers" (2001, 237).

One can see the merit in this line of argument. However, externalists (especially reliabilist externalists) have a response. They can say that what differentiates the expert and the novice is that the expert's beliefs about what woodpeckers look like give him a process that is reliable at distinguishing between woodpeckers and non-woodpeckers. If his visual representation of the observed bird is compared to his stored representation of a prototypical woodpecker, there will be a reasonably good "match." Arriving at a belief that the observed bird is a woodpecker in this fashion would be a reliable process. The novice would lack any such process. Thus, the externalist would explain the difference in terms of the ability to make accurate—that is, true—woodpecker classifications. Truth being an externalist concept, the explanation provided is externalist in contour.

Next let us consider a different slant on the internalism/externalism debate. Suppose you are writing a cookbook intended for novice cooks. You want your users to be able to follow each of your cooking instructions correctly. You want them to understand and be able to implement each direction. Otherwise, your book won't be a good guide to cooking. This places constraints on what your instructions can say. You will have to describe each operation in understandable and implementable terms. One approach to epistemology has a similar *modus vivendi*. It thinks of right rules as giving directions to which any epistemic agent can conform, which means that the rules must refer exclusively to circumstances directly accessible to the agent. This would include an agent's current mental states, and perhaps some other kinds of conditions and circumstances, but not any old circumstance or state of affairs. In particular, the reliability of a process may well be a property that is *not* directly accessible. So this kind of condition would be excluded by a conception of correct rules expressed in the "implementable recipe" model. Another possible label for this conception is the *infallible-guidance* conception. The idea is not that correct rules should infallibly lead a subject to the truth (that would be too much to expect); it's only that a careful subject would infallibly be able to follow, or conform to, the rules. This would guarantee that a careful and conscientious subject would always have justified doxastic attitudes, though not necessarily true ones.

2.7 INTERNALISM AND INFERENTIAL RULES

Without agreeing to the infallible-guidance conception of epistemic rules, let us nonetheless pursue the link between justification and conformity with right rules. Let us reflect on what right rules might look like, hoping to shed light on whether important types of justifiers are internal or external. We shall focus on rules for inference. What might be a correct rule, or rule schema, for inferential belief? Here is a first pass at a schema for inferential rules:

> (INF) If agent S has beliefs in propositions K, L, M, N (at time t), and proposition P is logically entailed by the conjunction of K, L, M, N, then S is permitted (at time t) to believe P.

Two kinds of conditions (or "circumstances") appear in this rule schema. First is a set of prior beliefs S has, and second is a relation of logical entailment between the conjunction of the contents of these beliefs and the target proposition, P. What kinds of conditions are these, internal or external?

Start with the logical entailment relation. Is it internal or external? If "internal" refers exclusively to (nonfactive) mental states, then obviously this relation or condition is not internal. The fact that a certain conjunction of propositions does or does not entail another proposition is a fact of logic, which is independent of any mental state of a random epistemic agent. In particular, such a relation doesn't consist in what an agent believes or thinks. Under this interpretation of "internal," we have already identified an external justifier. If (INF) is a correct rule schema of normative epistemology, then internalism (under the mentalist interpretation) is refuted. (Remember: Under the initial terms of debate between internalism and externalism, internalism is vindicated only if *all* justifiers are internal.)

Matters are a little less clear if we adopt the direct accessibility interpretation of "internal." But even here it is quite doubtful that logical entailment is an internal relation or condition. Logical entailment in general, at any rate, is unlikely to be a directly accessible relation, especially for all epistemic agents. Some logical entailment relations are quite complex, so whether particular complex propositions (including conjunctions) genuinely entail certain other propositions is not directly accessible in the sense that one can infallibly tell ("in a flash of intuitive insight") whether or not they are instances of entailment. So the entailment-relation component of an epistemic rule schema would apparently violate internalism. But it would be premature to conclude that internalism is mistaken. After all, we don't yet know if (INF) is a correct rule schema; if it is not correct, it is irrelevant to our deliberations. Internalists may propose a substitute schema for (INF).

Now let us consider the belief component of the antecedent of (INF)— that is, the condition that S believes a certain set of propositions. Beliefs are obviously (nonfactive) mental states, so this type of condition seems to pass the internalist test. However, this does not prove much of interest, for the same reason registered a moment ago, unless (INF) is a correct rule schema—and our discussion earlier in the chapter strongly suggests that it is incorrect. Recall the point (Section 2.1) that mere beliefs are not in themselves evidential states or justifiers; only justified beliefs qualify as evidence and hence justifiers. An inference schema is not correct that permits one to believe a proposition (e.g., P) when one merely has unjustified beliefs whose contents jointly entail it. A correct rule-schema along the lines of (INF) needs to specify that antecedent beliefs are justified. Thus, (INF) needs to be replaced by (INF*):

(INF*) If agent S has justified beliefs in propositions K, L, M, N (at time t), and proposition P is logically entailed by the conjunction of K, L, M, N, then S is permitted (at time t) to believe P.

Now the question arises whether the condition of having justified beliefs is an internalist condition. True, beliefs are mental states, but having justified beliefs may be regarded as a composite state of affairs that isn't wholly mental. In that case, (INF*) won't satisfy the requirements of mentalist internalism. Nor does it seem likely to satisfy the requirements of accessibilist internalism, because whether or not a current belief is justified is not a directly accessible matter. Why not?

Because, as we saw in the case of Nora, the J-status of a belief held at t may depend on events that occurred earlier than t. Such events may or may not be recalled by S at time t. If they are not recalled, they will not be directly accessible to S at t. Even if they are recalled at t, it is doubtful that memory qualifies as direct access. Moreover, being justified in believing something at t is not a mental state wholly obtaining at t, since the justification property of the belief does not arise from matters obtaining exclusively at t. Thus, whether internalism is interpreted in a mentalist or an accessibilist fashion, rule-schema (INF*) does not comply with internalist requirements.

Now let us return to the other condition appearing in (INF*), the logical entailment relation. We said that internalists might want to tweak the formulation so that it no longer appeals to logical entailment per se. How might this tweaking go, and would it work? The general approach would be to substitute a purely mentalist condition for the "objective" logical relation. This would "internalize" what starts out as an external fact. Here is one possibility that has been floated:

(INF**) If agent S has justified beliefs in propositions K, L, M, N (at time t), and S sees that proposition P is logically entailed by the conjunction of K, L, M, N, then S is permitted (at time t) to believe P.

However, is "seeing that" such-and-such a purely (nonfactive) mentalist condition? No; seeing that X is a factive state of affairs. It implies that X is true, which is a matter of objective fact, not mentalist opinion. So (INF**) tacitly retains a distinctly external element in its second condition of permissibility.

Here is another attempt to tweak (INF*), which unquestionably substitutes a mentalist condition for the logical entailment relation:

(INF***) If agent S has justified beliefs in propositions K, L, M, N (at time t), and S thinks that proposition P is logically entailed by the conjunction of K, L, M, N, then S is permitted (at time t) to believe P.

The problem for (INF***) is whether S's merely thinking there is an entailment relation is sufficient for a correct permission rule of this type. What if S is rather bad at determining logical relations and is totally off-base in a particular case that fits the mold of (INF***)? Should we really count S's belief in P as justified, simply because S (incompetently) thinks that an entailment relation holds? That is what (INF***) would license, which seems poorly motivated. In the end, then, it appears that this kind of condition should be an external condition, which undercuts internalism.

On further reflection, however, perhaps we should revisit internalism's own way of posing the debate as one between the claim that all justifiers are internal versus the denial of this claim. If internalism would only draw in its horns a bit, it might have a stronger position. If it took the more moderate stance—for example, that most, not all, justifiers are internal—it would have a more defensible point of view. However, it still is not clear that the position would be right. We have thus far examined two classes of candidate justifiers and it turned out that both were external rather than internal. (Well, the belief part of "justified beliefs" is internal.) Is it so clear that, under further probing, the majority of types of justifiers will be internal?

At least two other types of justifiers seem likely to fall into the external category. To explain these cases, though, more must be said about the nature of justifiers. We previously said that justifiers are factors that "make a difference" to the justificational status of a belief or other doxastic attitude. Does this mean that they make a causal difference? No. A better account of justifiers is that they are facts that explain why, or in virtue of what, a belief has a certain J-status. If this account is accepted, then right epistemic rules themselves should be among the justifiers. If someone forms a new belief in accordance with (INF*) and if (INF*) is a correct rule, then one thing that explains why the belief is justified is the fact that (INF*) is correct. In other words, the correctness or rightness of (INF*) is one of the justifiers of the new belief.

An analogy with another normative domain can be helpful here. If Jones is justly convicted of a crime, what factors explain his being guilty of the crime in question? The factors would of course include "material" facts, such as the deeds Jones committed and their circumstances and/or consequences. Another type of factor, however, is what the law says. In other words, legal facts bear on the question of Jones's guilt and (help) explain why he is guilty. Thus, the legal rule is one of the factors, or determinants, of his guilty status. Similarly, in the present case, the epistemic rule (and its rightness) that entitles the person to believe P under his existing evidential circumstances is part of what explains the fact that his belief is justified.

Now, what category does the rightness of a given epistemic rule fall into: internal or external? A rule's being right certainly isn't a mental state, nor is it likely to be a "directly accessible" state of affairs. So this type of justifier doesn't seem to be internal; it is much better understood as external. Here is yet another case where a type of justifier is best classified as external rather than internal.

Arguably, there is yet a higher type in a hierarchy of justifiers, which would be the criterion of rightness: a feature (or cluster of features) in virtue of which justification rules are right or wrong. What might be such a criterion? One attractive candidate is a pair of goals associated with belief-formation in general, viz. believing the truth and avoiding believing the false. Innumerable epistemologists of varying stripes agree that truth-attainment and error-avoidance are the twin goals of the intellect. These are closely linked to reliability, because reliability means getting the truth most of the time and erring only occasionally. All of these desiderata—obtaining the truth, avoiding error, reliability, and so forth—fall into the external family, since truth is (generally) external to the mind and not "directly accessible."

Thus, if truth-conduciveness and error-avoidance are the critical features in virtue of which the right epistemic rules are right, then the highest type of justifier is an external matter. Along with the previously identified examples of external justifiers, this solidifies the case for externalism about justification. This is not to say that all types of justifiers are external, but only that most of them are.

QUESTIONS

1. Mentalist evidentialism says that only mental states provide evidence, and hence justification for, various propositions. Presumably this is how people get basic justification for certain propositions. But which propositions do they get evidence for? This is something evidentialists have not explained very clearly. When someone has a headache, that headache has many properties or features. For each such feature, there is a true proposition describing the headache as having that feature. But is the subject (prima facie) justified in believing every such proposition? This seems dubious. At most, only the features the subject attends to seem to get justifiedness attached to them. But how exactly should this be explained? Can you fill in an appropriate story for evidentialism? At the same time, what would you say about a problem raised in Section 2.2.1, namely the problem about the brain-state? For an appropriate selected mental state, one of its features is "being an instance of the fusiform gyrus being activated." Is the proposition saying that the mental state has this feature a proposition for which one thereby has evidence? Can you state a principle that would exclude this (as evidentialists presumably would want to do)?

2. According to mentalist evidentialism, one category of mental states that constitute evidence are experiences. But do all types of experiences constitute evidence? Are they all equally weighty specimens of evidence? What about premonitions, for example? Does the premonition of an upcoming disaster constitute evidence of the truth of its content? And does this imply that, in the absence of defeaters, a person experiencing such a premonition is justified in believing there will be a disaster (soon)? Intuitively this seems wrong. How can evidentialism avoid this upshot? The natural answer seems to be this: They are not evidence because premonitions are not reliable indicators of the truth of their contents. But this account would be rejected by staunch internalists like Feldman and Conee (who don't want to appeal to externalist elements like truth). So what can they say?

3. Process reliabilism is initially presented as a theory of doxastic justifiedness. Then, at the very end of Section 2.4, it is explained how the account might be tweaked a bit to accommodate propositional justifiedness. How does this proposed account of propositional justification go? Can you identify any problems that might arise for this proposal? Discuss.

4. If process reliabilism is an "historical" theory, does this imply that if S forms a belief in P by an unreliable process at time t, S can never thereafter be justified in believing P? Would this be a correct result? Why or why not? If it would not be a correct result, can process reliabilism be formulated so as to (clearly) avoid this result? How would such a formulation go?

5. Of the several problems facing process reliabilism that might be resolved by "approved-list" reliabilism, which of these applications of approved-list reliabilism strike(s) you as most promising and which of them strike(s) you as least promising? Explain why you so classify them.

6. Concerning the generality problem for reliabilism, some people (e.g., Comesaña 2006) have suggested that it is a genuine problem but it isn't peculiar to reliabilism; rather, it is "everybody's" problem. This might be taken to mean that it's a problem for any otherwise promising approach to justification. Do you think this is correct? Show what other theories can be expected to run into the generality problem as well.

7. Addressing the novice vs. expert bird-watcher example (Section 2.6), internalists try to account for the difference in J-status between the two bird-watchers by appeal to internal differences between them where externalists try to account for the difference in terms of external differences. Explain how, specifically, their respective accounts go. Which side makes a more convincing argument for its viewpoint? Explain your appraisal of who wins that debate.

8. In Section 2.7, we examined several candidates for inferential rules of deduction-based justification. One of them was INF***, which was clearly an internalist rule insofar as it involves a condition pertaining to what the subject *thinks* about a logical relation. However, a problem was raised for INF***: It seems to allow a subject to be justified too easily. Explain how this objection goes and whether you think it is a strong or weak objection. If it is a serious one, how can internalism tweak this condition so as to improve its theory?

FURTHER READING

BonJour, Laurence (1980). "Externalist Theories of Empirical Knowledge." In P. French, T. Uehling, Jr., and H. Wettstein (eds.), *Midwest Studies in Philosophy* 5, 53–73. Minneapolis: University of Minnesota Press. Reprinted in H. Kornblith (ed.), *Epistemology: Internalism and Externalism* (2001, pp. 10–35). Malden, MA: Blackwell.

Chisholm, Roderick M. (1989). *Theory of Knowledge* (3rd ed.). Englewood Cliffs, NJ: Prentice-Hall.

Comesaña, Juan (2006). "A Well-Founded Solution to the Generality Problem." *Philosophical Studies* 129(1): 27–47.

Conee, Earl, and Richard Feldman (2001). "Internalism Defended." In H. Kornblith (ed.), *Epistemology: Internalism and Externalism* (pp. 231–260). Malden, MA: Blackwell Publishers.

Feldman, Richard, and Earl Conee (2004). "Evidentialism" (with afterword). In E. Conee and R. Feldman, *Evidentialism: Essays in Epistemology* (pp. 83–107). Oxford: Oxford University Press.

Goldman, Alvin I. (1979). "What Is Justified Belief?" In G. S. Pappas (ed.), *Justification and Knowledge* (pp. 1–23). Dordrecht: Reidel. Reprinted in A. I. Goldman (2012). *Reliabilism and Contemporary Epistemology* (pp. 29–49). New York: Oxford University Press.

Kornblith, Hilary (ed.) (2001). *Epistemology: Internalism and Externalism*. Malden, MA: Blackwell.

Plantinga, Alvin (1993). *Warrant and Proper Function*. New York: Oxford University Press.

Vogel, Jonathan (2000). "Reliabilism Leveled." *Journal of Philosophy* 97(11): 602–623.

Williamson, Timothy (2000). *Knowledge and Its Limits*. Oxford: Oxford University Press.

NOTES

1. The generality problem was noted first by Goldman (1979) and substantially elaborated by Conee and Feldman (1998). For a statement of the "everybody's problem" response, see Comesaña (2006). Other responses to the generality problem appear in Alston (1995), Heller (1995), Wunderlich (2003), Beebe (2004), Olsson (forthcoming), and Jönsson (2013). Another problem raised for reliabilism is the bootstrapping, or easy knowledge, problem (Vogel 2000; Cohen 2002; Van Cleve 2003). This problem is discussed in some detail in Chapter 6 (Section 6.6).

2. This approach is becoming increasingly popular among epistemologists, not just in connection with justification or reliabilism. Thus, DeRose (1992; 2009) couches his defense of contextualism about knowledge largely in terms of an attribution theory. A recent volume devoted to the problem of knowledge is called "Knowledge Ascriptions" (Brown and Gerken 2012), where "ascriptions" is just another label for "attributions." Chapter 5 takes up the related point that epistemology must pay close attention to the workings of epistemic language used by attributors.

3. This two-stage kind of theory is proposed in Goldman (1992), where it is called "two-stage reliabilism." Elizabeth Fricker (forthcoming) has proposed the appealing label "approved-list reliabilism."

4. One question that arises here is what the truth about justification is according to approved-list reliabilism. Is the truth of the matter still determined by the original reliabilist theory? This might imply more errors by ordinary attributors than would be welcomed by many reliabilists. Alternatively, might the truth about justification be relativized to each attributor's specific approval list? This problem is left open here.

5. See Berker (2013). For a response, see Goldman (2014).

Defining Knowledge

Matthew McGrath

Epistemologists spend a lot of time thinking about knowledge. Of course, knowledge is not the only epistemological category. Much of this book focuses on justification, for instance, but justification shares the limelight with knowledge. Why devote so much attention to knowledge?[1]

One factor is the ubiquity of the word "know" in ordinary life. According to an analysis based on the Oxford English Corpus,[2] "know" is the eighth most commonly used verb in English; it is ahead even of "see" and "think." It serves as our chief linguistic means for expressing epistemic ideas.

Another factor concerns value. As Plato's Socrates pointed out in the dialogue *Meno* (97a–98d), knowledge is more highly prized than mere true opinion. However, Socrates tells us that knowledge isn't more useful than mere true opinion in the here-and-now: True opinion about the way to get to Larissa is no less useful in getting to Larissa than knowledge about the way to get there. If there is something about knowledge that makes it more prize-worthy than mere true opinion, what is it? We also seem to prize knowledge over mere justified belief. We certainly want our beliefs to be justified, but we seem to regard knowing as better. What makes it better? We will take it as a working assumption in this chapter that knowledge is indeed more prize-worthy, in general if not in every single case, than either mere true belief or mere justified belief. This assumption motivates an inquiry into what knowledge is, how it relates to truth, belief, and justification, and why it has the value it has.[3]

Most of this chapter is concerned with attempts to define knowledge, and in particular knowledge of facts or propositions—that is, knowing that something is the case, as opposed to knowing a person, knowing a subject matter, knowing how to do something.[4] We begin with an examination of the traditional account of knowledge as justified true belief. We consider how this account fares against a number of objections, including the famous one due to Edmund Gettier. Next, we consider ways philosophers have tried to revise the traditional account to solve the "Gettier problem." The difficulty of the Gettier problem might make us wonder whether there might be ways to study knowledge without trying to define it. The last section examines this possibility.

This is a very long chapter. Not all parts of it are equally central. Two sections have been labeled optional.

3.1 THE TRADITIONAL ACCOUNT: KNOWLEDGE AS JUSTIFIED TRUE BELIEF

On the traditional account, knowing that something is the case is a matter of having a justified true belief that it is the case; in the shorthand: K = JTB. In the subsections below, we'll look at why knowledge might be thought to imply each of J, T, and B, and consider possible objections to the claim that these are individually necessary conditions on knowledge. In later sections, we'll turn to the question of whether the conjunction of these three conditions is sufficient for knowledge.

3.1.1 The Truth Condition

It is not hard to see why many philosophers consider truth a necessary condition of knowledge. We think of knowledge, unlike mere justified belief, as involving genuine possession of the truth, rather than only possessing something that seems to be the truth. If knowledge does indeed involve possession of the truth, this may well help to explain why knowledge is more prizeworthy than mere justified belief: Justified belief can be false, but what is known is true, and other things equal it is better genuinely to possess the truth than not to.

The way we talk about knowledge also supports the claim that knowledge implies truth. When someone claims to know something, which we then later find out to be false, we feel justified in complaining that he or she didn't know it after all. Suppose you and your friend are talking about an upcoming concert. Your friend declares, "The concert is this Friday." You say, "Do you know that? Maybe it's not this Friday but next Friday." Your friend assures you that he knows. Suppose the two of you go to the concert venue on Friday and find out that the concert is actually on the following Friday. You can complain to your friend, "You said you knew, but you didn't!" This makes sense if truth is a necessary condition on knowledge.

Nevertheless, sometimes when we find out that we were wrong about something, we say, "I just *knew* it, but it wasn't true." For instance, consider, "I just *knew* I wouldn't win the award, but I did!" or "I *knew* my new car would get me to Chicago without a problem, but it didn't." We make such claims about other people as well: You might notice that narrators in novels and children's stories occasionally describe characters as knowing things that turn out to be false. Should these facts about what we sometimes say lead us to conclude that subjects can know things that are false? This would be a rash inference. As Richard Holton (1997) notes, similar reasoning would lead us to draw clearly false conclusions concerning other matters. A narrator in a nonfiction book might tell the reader at one point, "The detective was satisfied. She had arrested the killer. Now she could finally get some rest," and then later the same narrator might inform us, "It turned out the man she arrested wasn't the killer; he had been framed." We shouldn't conclude from this that it's possible to arrest a killer who isn't a killer! That's a contradiction. Examples like this can be multiplied.

If knowledge requires truth—if what is known must be true—why would we talk in ways that at least suggest otherwise? Linguists refer to a phenomenon they call *free indirect speech*. We can speak from the perspective of someone with more limited or false information. There is no danger—if listeners attend to the full context in which the remarks are made—of the audience being misinformed.

Another indicator that we shouldn't take these uses of "know" to show that knowledge is compatible with falsity is that you could always get the same message across by speaking of what you *thought* you knew. Consider: "I really thought I knew I wouldn't win the award, but I guess I didn't know" or "The detective really thought she had arrested the killer, but she hadn't." Such remarks are at least as natural as claims that you did know. But both sets of remarks can't both be strictly and literally true, presumably. So, this should give us serious pause about inferring that knowledge doesn't require truth from the fact that it seems natural to say the likes of "I knew it but it turned out to be false."

3.1.2 The Belief Condition

Clearly, the mere fact that something is true isn't enough for a particular person to know it. There are many truths that you don't know. To know the truth, it seems you must somehow possess or have it. What is it to possess the truth? A natural thought is that possession at least involves belief. Clearly desire, hope, and other "conative" states are not needed. And it seems speculation or "having some suspicion" isn't enough either. We also ascribe knowledge in ways that are hard to explain unless knowledge at least usually involves belief. Why didn't John show up at the usual 1:00 time for the business meeting? Because he knew the meeting time was changed to 2:00. If knowledge didn't usually involve belief, it would be hard to see why knowing should explain action in the way it does. We also commonly conclude that a person "didn't know" something if after we tell them they express surprise. To the extent that surprise indicates previously lacking belief, this again is some reason to think belief is a condition on knowledge.

However, memory cases pose a challenge to the belief condition. Here is an example, due to Colin Radford (1966):

Quiz on English History

Jean is a French-Canadian who claims not to know any English history. He is given a verbal quiz on English history. He answers questions hesitantly, but gets many answers right. One question asks the date of Elizabeth I's death. Jean says, "I'd just be guessing, but, um, let's say 1603." That is the correct answer. Suppose in fact that Jean did learn this answer, along with many others long ago in school and that his present "guess" is based on a vague memory that in fact traces back to his learning the date of Elizabeth I's death. Does Jean know that Elizabeth I died in 1603? Does he believe she died then?

Here is one reason to think Jean knows that Elizabeth I died in 1603: He once knew this and he hasn't forgotten the information, even though he now (incorrectly) regards it as a mere guess. It isn't a mere guess: He is right, and not by luck. So, he knows. Yet he doesn't believe that 1603 is the correct date: He's more confident that 1603 is *not* the correct date than that it is. So, he knows but doesn't believe that Elizabeth died in 1603. Thus, belief isn't a necessary condition on knowledge.

Defenders of the traditional account can reply in either of two ways. They can say, first, that Jean did believe in some related but different sense of the term, and thus insist that this isn't really a case of knowledge without belief at least in that related sense. Still, Jean thinks it's more likely Elizabeth didn't die in 1603 than that she did. Can a person believe P if he thinks that P is more likely false than true? Maybe not. Still, even if Jean can't be said to "believe" P, he has something like belief. He possesses information that, if pushed, he is disposed to use to at least some extent, however hesitantly. The traditionalist could then concede that K isn't JTB but insist that it is JTB*, where B* is something belief-like. This wouldn't be a huge concession.

Another way to uphold the traditional account, due to Keith Lehrer (1974, 57), is to deny that Jean knows. Here is an argument for this claim (read this carefully—it's a subtle argument):

  i. Jean doesn't know that 1603 is the correct answer to the question of when Elizabeth I died.
  ii. If Jean knows that Elizabeth I died in 1603, then he does know that 1603 is the correct answer to this question.
  iii. So, Jean doesn't know that Elizabeth I died in 1603.

Consider the second step, (ii), first. If Jean did know that Elizabeth I died in 1603, he would know that 1603 is the correct answer to the question simply by deducing it from his knowledge that she died in 1603. Compare: If you know that class starts at 11:00, then you know through simple deduction that the correct answer to the question of when class starts is 11:00. So, (ii) seems well supported. What about step (i)? The traditionalist might simply say that (i) is plausible on its face. Perhaps in some sense Jean "knows the answer"— just as someone who guesses correctly on a quiz show could be said to "know the answer"—but Jean surely doesn't know that it is the *correct* answer to the question any more than the guesser does. This appeal to intuition, to what is "surely" so, might seem less than convincing. In his lengthy discussion of these issues, Lehrer in the end appeals to a kind of value-consideration in defense of (i). The sort of knowledge we are interested in as epistemologists is knowledge of a kind that is "characteristically human in critical reasoning and the life of reason" (1974, 41). This is knowledge that is readily available for use in reasoning, both about what to do and what is the case. Jean's "knowledge" is not readily available for such use. Note, though, that if knowledge implied belief, knowledge would be available for reasoning.

So, while Radford has by no means been decisively refuted, there are several promising replies to his argument.

There is another sort of reason for thinking knowledge doesn't require belief, quite different from the one just discussed. If you've had a course in early modern philosophy—Descartes to Kant—you might remember that philosophers of that period, such as Locke and Hume, often draw a sharp distinction between probable opinion and knowledge, taking the two not just to be distinct but incompatible. Knowledge is beyond probability. So it would follow that knowing entails not having probable opinion.

Few contemporary philosophers follow suit. It is hard to see how opinion and belief aren't compatible with knowledge. Certainty, after all, is compatible with knowledge, and surely a subject can believe with certainty. If you believe P with certainty, then you believe P. The problem here may simply be a matter of what is suggested by *saying* that you believe. If you say to a friend that you believe you'll be at the concert, you're somehow suggesting that you don't know you will be, that you "only" believe it, and perhaps that there is some doubt in your mind. Similarly, if you say to your mother, when you get off the phone, that "some man" called, you'd be implying that you don't have further relevant information about the man's identity. But suppose it was your father who called. Your statement that "some man called" would be misleading but nevertheless true. The same is plausible for claiming to believe when, in fact, you know.[5]

We see again how important it is to exercise caution in drawing conclusions about knowledge from premises about what we ordinarily say. Investigating our talk of knowledge provides evidence we should use in constructing theories of knowledge, but not simple answers.

3.1.3 The Justification Condition

The idea that knowledge is not merely true belief goes back at least to Plato's dialogues. In a memorable passage in the *Meno*, Socrates goes as far as to say:

> … that knowledge differs from true opinion is no matter of conjecture with me. There are not many things which I profess to know, but this is most certainly one of them. (*Meno* 98b)

We can see the grounds for this by thinking about examples. If you walk into a room of hundreds of people, you will feel that you don't know how many people are in the room. You will feel that if you just formed a belief that there were 368 people, then even if you were right, you wouldn't know there were

368. Why not? One good answer: It wouldn't be a reasonable thing for you to believe in the situation; you wouldn't be justified in believing it. Or consider the question whether it rained in New York City on October 23, 1838. Do you know whether it rained on that date? No. Even if you formed your best guess and it turned out to be true, still, you didn't know. Why not? A plausible answer is that you lack sufficient justification.

It's important, here, that we understand justification in terms of reasonableness of belief, and not in some stronger sense, such as being able to justify your belief through convincing verbal argumentation. Many alleged examples of knowledge without justification seem on closer scrutiny instead merely to be cases of knowledge without justification in some such strong sense. For example, consider the chicken-sexer, who can tell just by looking whether a baby chick is male or female. The chicken-sexer knows a certain chick is male, without having at her disposal anything like an argument (suppose). Still, she has a basis for her belief, a certain subtle gestalt look the chick has. This look might be enough to make the chicken-sexer justified—reasonable—in her belief, but not enough for the rest of us.[6]

Adding the justification condition helps us see what it is about knowledge that makes it better than mere true belief. We prize getting it right, but we prize getting it right through a justified belief even more. One explanation for this might be that if a true belief in P is reasonable, P can appropriately be used in reasoning about what to do and what is the case; it is among your reasons and not merely your opinions. Since whether a subject is acting or believing on the basis of genuine reasons matters, if justification is a condition on knowledge, we can see why we might care not merely about having true beliefs but about having knowledge.

3.2 THE GETTIER PROBLEM

Until 1963, the traditional account of knowledge as justified true belief seemed to be in fairly good shape. None of the examples we discussed so far seems clearly to refute it. And the view seems nicely to accommodate the greater value of knowledge over both mere true belief and mere justified true belief. When you have JTB, you have an epistemic state with value beyond merely that of TB and beyond merely that of JB. This happy state of affairs met a sad ending as philosophers absorbed the lessons of Edmund Gettier's three-page paper, "Is Justified True Belief Knowledge?"

Gettier prepares the reader for his cases by stating two assumptions he will rely on. Here is the first:

First assumption: A belief can be justified even if it is false.

This is a kind of fallibilism about justification. It is a very plausible assumption. It seems there are many situations in which people have justified false beliefs. Many in the United States had a justified false belief that Al Gore won Florida's electoral college votes in the U.S. presidential election in 2000 after all the major network news outlets (incorrectly) declared that Gore won Florida.

The second assumption Gettier makes is a principle about how justification expands through deduction:

> *Second assumption*: If you are justified in believing P, P entails Q, and you (competently) deduce Q from P believing Q as a result of this deduction, then you are justified in believing Q.[7]

In the literature this is called the principle of the "deductive closure" for justification. In general, closure principles for some epistemic status (e.g., justification, knowledge) are principles stating that if one has a given epistemic status with respect to one proposition P and then one meets a certain condition with respect to another proposition Q, one will have that same epistemic status for Q as well. Gettier's second assumption takes the "certain condition" to be deduction of Q from P. It says that if you start out justified in believing P, and deduce Q from P, you end up being justified in believing Q.

Consider some examples to motivate Gettier's deductive closure principle. If you are justified in believing that John has red hair and then you competently deduce John doesn't have blond hair, then your resulting belief that John doesn't have blond hair, too, is justified. Or again, if you are justified in believing that *your* 1983 Toyota Celica has a timing chain problem and you deduce that *some* 1983 Toyota Celicas have a timing chain problem, then the latter belief, too, is justified. It's true we wouldn't bother to carry out such simple deductions in our explicit thinking, but that's perhaps because they are so obvious, not because we wouldn't end up with a justified belief.

Gettier's second assumption is a powerful principle. Some of its implications, in particular with regard to skepticism, might seem questionable. Can I gain a justified belief that I'm not a brain in a vat [BIV] being stimulated by evil neuroscientists merely by deducing this from the proposition that I have hands? That I have hands does entail that I'm not a brain in a vat, as a mere brain lacks hands. But can I arrive at a justified belief that I'm not a BIV in this way? Let's put aside these sorts of worries for the purposes of this chapter. The assumption seems very plausible if we simply think of garden-variety deductions from things we are justified in believing, such as the humdrum examples given in the previous paragraph. These don't seem at all to involve deductive reasoning that is question-begging, in contrast to reasoning from *I have hands* to *I am not a BIV*. As we'll see, in his attempt to refute the traditional JTB account of knowledge, Gettier only considers deductive reasoning of the garden variety kind; there is no whiff of question-begging or circular reasoning in the examples he gives (as we will see). In Chapter 4 (Section 4.2.1), we consider how to formulate a closure principle that is true more generally, suitable for theorizing about skepticism.

With these two assumptions in place, Gettier gives two cases that he thinks are cases of subjects having justified true belief while lacking knowledge. If

Gettier is right, then knowledge cannot be defined as justified true belief, because justified true belief isn't sufficient for knowledge.

We'll discuss one of the cases, Case I. Here's his description of the case:

Gettier's Case I: Smith, Jones, and the Job

Suppose that Smith and Jones have applied for a certain job. And suppose that Smith has strong evidence for the following conjunctive proposition:

(d) Jones is the man who will get the job, and Jones has ten coins in his pocket.

Smith's evidence for (d) might be that the president of the company assured him that Jones would in the end be selected, and that he, Smith, had counted the coins in Jones's pocket ten minutes ago. Proposition (d) entails:

(e) The man who will get the job has ten coins in his pocket.

Let us suppose that Smith sees the entailment from (d) to (e) and accepts (e) on the grounds of (d), for which he has strong evidence. In this case Smith is clearly justified in believing that (e) is true.

But imagine, further, that unknown to Smith, he himself, not Jones, will get the job. And also, unknown to Smith, he himself has ten coins in his pocket. Proposition (e) is then true, though proposition (d), from which Smith inferred (e), is false.

Gettier concludes that in this case Smith has justified true belief in (e) but doesn't know (e) to be true. It's a matter of luck that he is correct. Other terms like "accidentally correct" or "correct as a matter of sheer coincidence" apply as well.

Let's look at an initial worry you might have about Gettier's conclusion before seeing what makes this example tick. You might object that Smith really does know (e), because when Smith thinks to himself "the man who will get the job has ten coins in his pocket," he is really thinking about Jones, and he does know Jones has ten coins in his pocket. The idea behind the objection is to take (e), at least in Smith's context of speech or thought, to mean just the same as (d).

These worries can be avoided if we make it clear how Smith is reasoning. Let us say, on behalf of Gettier, that Smith is reasoning like this: "Jones is the man who will get the job and Jones has ten coins in his pocket, so it follows that whoever it is who is the person who gets the job, he will have ten coins in his pocket." Smith's final conclusion is not merely that *this guy* has ten coins in his pocket, but that *whoever will get the job* has ten coins in his pocket.

We can use *definite descriptions*—uniquely identifying descriptions—like this even when we think we know who satisfies them. Suppose you're writing a philosophy paper. You know and of course believe that you are the author of the paper. In believing this, you do not merely believe the triviality that you are yourself; you believe that you are the unique person who satisfies a certain description. You also believe that you have other features, such as that you are, say, brown-eyed. So, you believe that the unique person who satisfies the description "the author of this paper" is also brown-eyed. This belief is not the same as the belief that *you* are brown-eyed; your teacher might know you are brown-eyed but not know that the author of the paper is brown-eyed, if, for instance, you forget to put your name on the paper.

The key thing is that even when you believe that the so-and-so is x, your belief that *the so-and-so has feature F* isn't the same as your belief that *x has feature F*. We should think of Smith in Gettier's Case I on this model: His belief that *the man with ten coins in his pocket will get the job* is not the same as his belief that *Jones has ten coins in his pocket and will get the job*. In fact, the latter belief is false, whereas the former is true.

So far, you might find Gettier's conclusion about Case I plausible, but you might doubt its significance. If this is just a one-off case with nothing more general behind it, we might conclude that one odd case can't dislodge the simple and attractive JTB definition of knowledge.

Once you understand the basic idea behind Gettier's case, though, you can see how to produce many more cases like it. Here are some presented in the literature:

Sheep on the Hill (Chisholm 1966)

You see a rock on a hill. The rock looks exactly like a sheep from your vantage point. You think, "That's a sheep, so there are sheep on the hill." As it turns out, there *are* sheep on the hill, but they are out of view behind some trees past the rock. You have a justified true belief that there are sheep on the hill, but do you know there are sheep on the hill?

Havit/Nogot (Lehrer 1965)

You see Nogot driving a Ford on a regular basis. Nogot tells you he owns the Ford. You've never seen Havit drive at all; he walks everywhere or takes public transportation. There are three people who work in the office: you, Nogot, and Havit. You don't own a Ford. You reason like this: Nogot owns a Ford, and Nogot works in the office, and so someone who works in the office owns a Ford. It turns out that Nogot *doesn't* own the Ford he's been driving at all. Moreover, Havit *does* own a Ford, but it's an old classic car he never drives. You have a justified true belief that someone in the office owns a Ford, but do you know that someone in the office owns a Ford?

In these cases, as in the original Gettier Case I, the subject reasons from a false belief to a true one. The subject has JTB but intuitively does not have K.

Let's call cases in which a person has a justified true belief but lacks knowledge *Gettier cases*.[8] Gettier's own recipe for constructing Gettier cases is to construct cases in which people make deductions from falsehoods to truths. But is this necessary to create a Gettier case? If it was, we might hope to fix the traditional account of knowledge by adding as a fourth condition that the subject's belief not be based solely on deduction from a falsehood.

Are there Gettier cases that involve no deductive reasoning at all? Consider this one:

Barn Façade Country (Goldman 1976, originally due to Carl Ginet)

Henry is driving through farmland. Unbeknownst to him, he is in barn façade country. There are numerous barn façades around that look exactly (from the road) like barns. Of course, barn façades are not barns (you can't put horses or straw in them). After believing falsely "that is a barn," "this is a barn," etc. as Henry drives along he looks at what is in fact the only remaining real barn in the area, which looks no different from the road than any of the façades. As usual, Henry thinks "and that, too, is a barn." He has a justified true belief. But does he know it is a barn?

There seems to be no deduction here, or even any explicit reasoning at all. Henry believes, based on experience, that this thing is a barn. But it can seem that Henry doesn't know. He could easily have been wrong, and was wrong many times before and after seeing the sole genuine barn.

Suppose these are indeed cases of justified true belief without knowledge.[9] How could we revise the traditional account to handle the cases? We've seen that we wouldn't avoid all counterexamples by adding a condition that the subject's belief not be based on deduction from a falsehood. What conditions might work? Here we will briefly consider some general strategies for coping with the Gettier problem and note some challenges for each of them. It is fair to say that the Gettier problem remains unsolved, although there are promising approaches. In what follows, we discuss a number of accounts. Try to get the basic idea of each account under your belt before thinking about its advantages and disadvantages.

As we proceed, we will ask not only whether the accounts we consider give acceptable results about the various Gettier cases but whether they have other virtues desirable in a theory of knowledge. It is a matter of some debate just what these other virtues ought to be. Here we will assume the list includes at least the following:

- The account should help us see why knowledge is valuable and the extent to which it is. Is it more valuable than mere justified true belief? If so, why?
- The account should enable us to see how knowledge satisfies a principle of deductive closure like that for justification.

Earlier, we discussed Gettier's second assumption, which asserts the deductive closure of justification. Similar arguments support a parallel principle for knowledge. Think about the example we gave above concerning the 1983 Toyota, but applied to knowledge rather than justification. If you know that *your* 1983 Celica has a timing chain problem, then if you competently deduce that *some* 1983 Celicas have a timing chain problem, you know that some 1983 Celicas have a timing chain problem. The same goes equally well for many other examples. Suppose you know, looking at a barn, that it is a red barn. You can deduce from this that it is a barn. So, you'll know that, too. Formulated generally, we have:

Deductive Closure of Knowledge

If you know P, P entails Q, and you competently deduce Q from P, believing P as a result of the deduction, then you know Q.[10]

As with Gettier's Assumption 2, this principle will require qualification when we consider skepticism. Can I come to know I'm not a BIV by deducing it from my knowledge that I have hands? One might well think not: I have to already know I'm not a BIV in order to know I have hands in the first place. Again, we postpone discussion of these matters to the next chapter. We are looking for an account of knowledge that retains its closure under deduction, at mundane cases that do not involve any seemingly question-begging deductions.

The traditional theory, K = JTB, upholds deductive closure for knowledge. Suppose P entails Q, assuming deductive closure for justification. If you have a JTB for P and you competently deduce Q from P, believing Q as a result of this deduction, you also have JTB for Q. However, when we add a further condition X, reaching K = JTB + X, it is by no means automatically assured that the resulting account continues to satisfy the closure principle.

3.3 JUSTIFICATIONIST SOLUTIONS TO THE GETTIER PROBLEM

One kind of solution takes off from the idea that in Gettier cases the subject's justification is faulty in some way. The subject is justified but the justification is somehow defective. We discuss two accounts of this sort.

3.3.1 The Defeasibility Account

One common feature common of Gettier cases is that the people in the examples fail to grasp the full story about their situation. There are facts about their situation that they don't know and that, if discovered, would give them good reason to revise their beliefs. In the lingo, such facts are called *defeaters*.[11] Clearly, there is a defeater for Henry's belief that he sees a barn, viz. that he is in barn façade country. There is a defeater in Gettier's Case I as well, which is that Jones will not get the job. Such defeaters make the subjects' justification defective insofar as it is vulnerable to being undermined in light of the facts of the case.

Consider then the following account of knowledge:

Defeasibility Account (simple version)

To know P is to have justified true belief in P, where there are no defeaters for your belief.

The account seems to uphold the deductive closure of knowledge. If there is a defeater of your belief in Q, and you completely deduce Q from P, it seems there will have to be a defeater of your belief in P, namely the defeater of your belief in Q together with your knowledge that if Q is false, P is, too.

As promising as the defeasibility account appears in its simple version, it is overly strong: there are cases in which subjects have knowledge despite the existence of defeaters, such as:

Tom Grabit (Lehrer and Paxson 1969)

You know Tom Grabit fairly well by sight. You see him grab a book and run from the library. The library alarms go off. Tom stole the book. It seems you know Tom stole the book. Yet suppose at the court hearing later in the week, Tom's mother testifies that Tom was out of the state that day but that he has an identical twin, Tim, who is always getting into trouble, and that Tim stole the book. It turns out that this is sheer fabrication and the university attorneys easily expose it as such in the hearing. Tom has no identical twin at all.

It is a fact that Tom's mother so testified. Now, if you knew about this fact (and only this fact), you wouldn't be justified in thinking it was Tom who stole the book. Still, you do know it was Tom, don't you? If so, the simple defeasibility account can't be quite right. Vulnerability of a justification to undermining in the light of *some* of the facts doesn't guarantee that one lacks knowledge.

If we think that there is knowledge in this case, despite the existence of defeaters, we will want to modify the simple version of the defeasibility account. In the Tom Grabit case, it seems that there is "more to the story" than merely the information that the mother testified as she did, and that the "full story" discredits the defeater provided by the mother's testimony. The defeasibility theorist might refine the account by saying that what knowledge requires is not that there is no defeater of one's justification but that there is no defeater of one's justification that is itself undefeated by "more of the story." The details can be complex. (For a sophisticated account, see Klein 1981.)

In developing a defeasibility account, we should also ask whether what distinguishes knowledge and justified true belief according to the account is something we care about. If that is what K adds to JTB, do we—should we—care about the difference between it and mere justified true belief? As Kvanvig points out (2003, chapter 5), the more complicated and comparatively artificial the distinguishing feature becomes the more we have to ask. Should we care about *that*?

3.3.2 The No-False-Assumptions Account

We saw that Gettier cases need not involve deduction and perhaps not even any reasoning. So, an account of knowledge as JTB in which the subject's reasoning isn't based on reasoning from false premises would be incorrect. However, we might think falsehood is involved in the person's thinking in a more subtle way (cf. Harman 1973). So, for instance, even in the barn façade case, which seems not to involve reasoning, Henry at least *assumes* something false, namely that he is driving through normal farmland, where things that look like barns are barns. This is a kind of defect in one's justification. Perhaps Henry doesn't know because his justification is based on a false assumption. Let us formulate this account of knowledge as follows:

No-False-Assumptions Account

To know is to have justified true belief such that your belief isn't based on a false assumption.

This account needs clarification. Just what does it take for a belief to be based on a false assumption? It doesn't require explicit reasoning from that assumption as a premise. We might think it consists in something like this counterfactual condition: Were you to learn that your assumption is false, you would no longer be justified in holding your belief. This condition is satisfied in the barn façade case. Were you to learn that the country through which you're driving isn't one in which things that look like barns are barns, you would no longer be justified in believing that you see a barn. However, notice that if we think of being based on a false assumption as a matter of satisfying this counterfactual condition, we've reverted to the simple defeasibility account, and so this version of the no-false-assumptions account will face any problems the defeasibility account faces.

What is it to be based on a false assumption if not to satisfy the counterfactual condition above? We want an account that avoids over-intellectualization. Henry needn't have any thoughts about barn façades or even know what papier-mâché is in order for him to lack knowledge in the barn façade case. What is it that Henry assumes exactly? You might say, "Things around here are the way they look." But doesn't Henry know the likes of "that's a tree, that's a fence" when he looks out at the farm containing the barn? It would seem so. Is the key false assumption, then, that what looks like a barn around here is a barn? Of course, the barn façade doesn't look like a barn from the side or behind. The assumption needs to be that what looks like a barn from this sort of vantage point and around this area is a barn. But what does it take for Henry to assume this? He needn't think it explicitly, let alone use it as a premise in his reasoning.

None of this is meant to suggest that the no-false-assumptions account is doomed to failure. Something about the account seems exactly right: After you've discovered you have been "Gettiered," you feel that your expectations— your assumptions—were false, that you were fooled. The challenge, though, is to flesh out the details of the account,[12] and to do so without delivering incorrect verdicts about cases or giving up deductive closure. And again, as we saw for the defeasibility account, as we flesh out the details, we should bear in mind the consequences for questions about value and importance: Do we, should we, care about the condition said to distinguish mere justified belief from knowledge?

3.4 RELIABILITY SOLUTIONS

Perhaps the above solutions bark up the wrong tree. Perhaps what disqualifies Gettier cases from being cases of knowledge is not faultiness in the subject's justification but rather the lack of a certain sort of objective connection between the subject's belief and the truth. We will use the term "reliability" very broadly (following Goldman [1986, 44]) to pick out any sort of objective relation between a subject's belief and the truth. This section examines reliability accounts of knowledge.[13]

Another reason we might wish to examine reliability proposals is what they promise to show us about the value or importance of knowledge as opposed to mere justified belief. In the *Meno,* Socrates speculatively suggests that the difference between knowledge and mere correct opinion is that knowledge is "tethered" to the truth, much as one must tie down the (mythological) statues of Daedalus else they run away. Objective relations to the truth give content to the metaphor of "tethering."

Finally, as we consider the various kinds of reliability accounts, we will not concern ourselves much with the justification condition on knowledge. Many advocates of reliability conditions doubt whether justification is necessary for knowledge. We will simply ignore the justification condition in this section. (A reliability theorist could add a justification condition to his or her account, of course.)

3.4.1 The Causal Account

One proposal, due to Alvin Goldman, is to take causation to be the key relation:

Causal Account

To know P is for the fact P to be causally connected in an appropriate way with your believing P. (Goldman 1967, 358)

The causal account nicely handles a number of Gettier cases. In many Gettier cases causal connections between one's belief and the truth are missing. When you see a sheep on a hill in a normal case, the sheep's being there causes you to see them and thus to believe that there are sheep on the hill. You satisfy the causal condition: Your belief that there are sheep on the hill is caused by the fact that makes it true, viz. the fact that there are sheep on the hill. In the Gettier case, though, you don't *know* there are sheep on the hill, and the causal account explains why. There don't seem to be any causal connections between the fact that there are sheep on the hill and the fact that you believe this. You believe it because of the sheep-shaped rock. But the fact that there *are* sheep on the hill has nothing to do with the sheep-shaped rock being there—the two facts are causally unrelated.

Which are the appropriate sorts of causal connections? We can ask, in particular, whether the fact P must itself be a cause of the knower's belief in P. In many cases of knowledge, including paradigm cases of perceptual knowledge, this relation holds. However, as Goldman notes (364), it would be too strong to say that only when the fact P causes your belief in P do you know P. To use an example similar to one of his, if your friend tells you on Friday that she is going sailing the next day, this testimony can give you on Saturday knowledge that she is sailing that day. But the fact that she is sailing on Saturday doesn't cause your belief on Saturday that she is sailing. Here there is a different sort of causal connection that, according to the causal theorist, gives knowledge, viz. the relation of being common effects of the same cause. The common cause of both the fact that she sails on Saturday and that you believe on Saturday that she is sailing is her intention on Friday to go sailing. Here is a diagram:

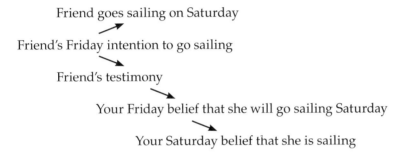

Friend goes sailing on Saturday

Friend's Friday intention to go sailing

Friend's testimony

Your Friday belief that she will go sailing Saturday

Your Saturday belief that she is sailing

To accommodate the deductive closure of knowledge, the causal theorist needs to appeal to further appropriate causal connections. Suppose the fact that there is a violin before me causes my belief there is a violin before me and I then go on to deduce that there is something that isn't a cello before me. How is my belief that there isn't a cello before me appropriately connected to the fact that there isn't a cello before me? For an account of various appropriate sorts of causal connections, the reader should consult Goldman (1967).

The causal theory has a lot going for it; however, it does face certain difficulties. There are cases in which the relevant causal relations obtain but in which the subject still seems to lack knowledge. The barn façade case is a case in point. The barn causes Henry's belief that it is a barn in a perfectly normal way, yet he doesn't know he sees a barn.

Arguably, causal relations aren't quite the relations we are looking for. A related suggestion is to appeal to modal relations. Talk of "modality" in philosophy is understood as relating to would's and could's, to what would have been, what could be the case. We will consider two modal notions that might be thought to help us solve the Gettier problem: sensitivity and safety.

3.4.2 The Sensitivity Account

The key idea behind the sensitivity account of knowledge is that knowing P requires that your belief in P be "sensitive" to the truth of P in the following sense: You wouldn't have believed P had P been false (Nozick 1981, 172–176).

A great many cases of knowledge involve sensitive belief. Look around the room. If there weren't a couch over here, weren't a chair over there, surely you wouldn't believe these things. By contrast, in many Gettier cases, it seems the subject would still believe just as he or she did even had the proposition been false. Had it been false that Henry was looking at a barn, he might well have been looking at a barn façade but would have believed he was looking at a barn. Had it been false that the man who will get the job had ten coins in his pocket—because someone in the office other than Smith or Jones was going to get the job—Smith would still have believed it was true. So, the proposal is as follows:

Sensitivity Account

To know P is to have true belief in P that is sensitive to the truth of P (i.e., were P false one wouldn't believe P).

The account seems intuitive. More subtlety is needed, however, to avoid misclassifying some cases, such as:

Grandmother (Nozick 1981, 179)

Suppose a healthy grandson visits his grandmother. He is the picture of health. Seeing him, his grandmother knows he is well. However, had he not been well his parents would have kept the grandmother in the dark about it and he wouldn't have visited her, and so she would still have believed he was well.

Here we have a case of knowledge without sensitivity. A standard solution is to appeal to methods of belief. The grandmother used a certain method of belief—say, looking at her grandson and judging health by looks. Had the grandson not been well, the grandmother would not have believed he was well using that method. She would have believed he was well using a different method, reliance on testimony. All that matters to knowledge, though, is that one's belief using method M is sensitive in this sense: Had P been false, one would not have believed P using M.

Still, aren't there cases of knowledge without sensitivity so understood? Can't you *know* that not all of the sixty amateur golfers will get a hole-in-one at the most difficult hole on a pro golf course (Vogel 2007)? Can't a professor *know* that not all students in her intro logic class of seventy-five students will get As on every exam? But if these things were false, the subject would still believe them using the very same methods. Because of worries like these, many philosophers have moved away from the sensitivity account.[14]

Moreover, as Nozick recognized, the sensitivity account predicts there are counterexamples to our deductive closure principle for knowledge. Your belief in P might be sensitive, but even if you competently infer Q from P, your resulting belief in Q might not be sensitive. This can happen, certainly, for beliefs about skeptical scenarios. You know you are awake. You can deduce from this that you are not merely dreaming that you are awake. But were you merely dreaming that you were awake, you would still believe you were awake (using the same method). As we'll see in the next chapter, Nozick regarded this feature of the account as a virtue because he saw it as providing the tools for responding to arguments for skepticism about knowledge. Again, though, we postpone consideration of skeptical arguments until the next chapter. It would be a mark against the sensitivity account if the account predicted counterexamples to deductive closure in cases in which the deductive reasoning isn't at all question-begging or circular.

Without appealing to methods, sensitivity predicts widespread counterexamples to deductive closure. I might know I don't have a lottery ticket and conclude from this that I don't have the winning ticket. This seems to be a straightforward case of expanding knowledge via deduction. However, although my belief that I don't have a lottery ticket is sensitive, my belief that I won't win the lottery isn't. Were I to have the winning ticket, I'd still believe I don't have the winning ticket. But methods help here. Were I to have the winning ticket, I'd know I have a ticket and so I'd believe I don't have the winning ticket on the basis of the fact that there's such a tiny chance of winning. However, this is different from the method I use when I know I don't have the ticket. My method when I know I don't have a ticket is deductive reasoning from *I don't have a ticket*. I reason like this: *Since I don't have a ticket, I can't win*! Appealing to methods is a *must* for the sensitivity theorist, if she is to stem the tide of examples to deductive closure.[15]

However, some problematic counterexamples might still remain. Vogel (1987) notes that on the sensitivity account, I can know that the proposition P is true but still not be in a position to know that I do not falsely believe P. Of course, I can deduce *I do not falsely believe P* from *P is true*. But the belief resulting from this deduction is not sensitive: Were you to falsely believe P, you would still believe you were right and so that you did not falsely believe P, and the method used would be the same. This counterexample is a bit tricky, and perhaps isn't an ordinary instance of expanding one's knowledge. (Is the deduction question-begging?) In Chapter 4 (Section 4.2.2), we discuss these issues again when we consider the merits of Nozick's reply to the skeptic.

3.4.3 The Safety Account (Optional)

Similar to the sensitivity account is an account that appeals to *safety*. Safety is the contrapositive of sensitivity. To take the contrapositive of a conditional ~A→~C, we swap A and C and subtract negations to arrive at C→A. So, where the sensitivity conditional is: "Were P false, S wouldn't believe P," the safety conditional is: "Were S to believe P, P would be true." Contraposition is not a valid rule of inference for conditionals involving "were, would"— that is, for what are called *subjunctive conditionals*.[16] So, the safety proposal is not logically equivalent to the sensitivity proposal.

Safety Account

To know P is to have true belief in P that is safe (i.e., were you to believe P, P would be true).

The safety account captures a natural intuition we have about many Gettier cases, which is that even though the subject has a true belief, the subject could easily have been wrong.[17] In fact, we can read the safety conditional "If you were to believe P, P would be true" as amounting to "It couldn't easily be that you believe P but are wrong." Henry in the barn façade case could easily have believed he was looking at a barn but have been wrong (because he could easily have been looking at a mere façade)—similarly for many other examples.

The examples that (arguably) refuted the sensitivity account seem not to refute the safety account. You know, for instance, that not all sixty golfers will score a hole-in-one, and this belief seems safe: The situations in which it is false are far removed from actuality, and so your belief couldn't easily be false. Moreover, the safety account appears to avoid the problem we noted concerning deductive closure. If I safely believe *P is true* and I competently deduce *I do not falsely believe P*, it appears that my concluding belief, too, is safe: Were I to believe that I do not falsely believe P, I would be right.[18]

Yet there do appear to be counterexamples to the safety account. The following example, due to Juan Comesaña (2005, 397), seems to show that knowledge is compatible with unsafe belief:

HALLOWEEN PARTY: There is a Halloween party at Andy's house, and I am invited. Andy's house is very difficult to find, so he hires Judy to stand at a crossroads and direct people towards the house (Judy's job is to tell people that the party is at the house down the left road). Unbeknownst to me, Andy doesn't want Michael to go to the party, so he also tells Judy that if she sees Michael she should tell him the same thing she tells everybody else (that the party is at the house down the left road), but she should immediately phone Andy so that the party can be moved to Adam's house, which is down the right road. I seriously consider disguising myself as Michael, but at the last moment I don't. When I get to the crossroads, I ask Judy where the party is and she tells me it is down the left road.

Comesaña claims that in this case he knows that the party is down the left road, but his belief is not safe. It could easily have happened that he was dressed as Michael, in which case Judy would have given him the same directions but called Andy, who would have moved the party. Comesaña's diagnosis is that, while knowledge does require reliable belief, the safety condition mischaracterizes reliable belief. Intuitively, Judy's word, given how Comesaña looks, is reliable despite the fact that her word in a nearby case is false.[19]

It also appears that in some cases one might fail to know while nevertheless enjoying a safe (and justified) true belief. Consider the sheep-on-the-hill case. Perhaps it is no accident that there are sheep out of sight on the hill; perhaps the property owners are playing a joke and want to "Gettierize" unsuspecting subjects. If so, it couldn't easily turn out that your belief that there are sheep on the hill is false when you see the sheep-shaped rock. Still, it seems you don't know there are sheep on the hill.

There are more complex versions of safety and sensitivity theorists that may well avoid the problems we have discussed. The book is by no means closed on these theories.

3.5 THE RELEVANT ALTERNATIVES APPROACH

Suppose we're discussing the date of Julius Caesar's birth. There is some scholarly dispute about the exact year, whether it was 100, 101, or 102 B.C. Here is a possibility scholars don't consider: It was actually 100 A.D., but later officials conspired to create evidence so that it would seem to be 100 B.C. This is what's called a conspiracy hypothesis. The conspiracy theory presents merely an irrelevant alternative to *Caesar was born in 100 B.C.* To know that Caesar was born in 100 B.C., you only have to rule out relevant alternatives. We can formulate the general idea here as follows:

The Relevant Alternatives Approach

To know P is to have a true belief in P and to have evidence that rules out all the relevant alternatives to P. (Cf. Dretske 1970, Goldman 1976)

How does this approach bear on the Gettier problem? In the Gettier cases, what is normally an irrelevant alternative is relevant, unbeknownst to the subject. For instance, normally the possibility in which you're in barn façade country is irrelevant, so you don't have to rule it out to know the thing you see is a barn. However, in barn façade country, it *is* relevant, so you *do* have to rule it out. Because you can't, you don't know.

So far, the relevant alternatives approach is quite intuitive, but it needs further fleshing out. To flesh it out, we need an account of relevance and an account of ruling out.

Let's start with ruling out. "Ruling out" an hypothesis sounds quite a bit like *knowing it is false*. If we understood it in that fashion, we would have to abandon our definitional ambitions, of course. Good definitions are not circular: They do not employ the very concept being defined. Aside from that problem, we'd also be accepting many counterexamples to deductive closure for knowledge. To say that you don't need to rule out the irrelevant alternatives to P in order to know P, on the present assumption that ruling out is knowing to be false, is to say that you can know P without knowing that certain alternatives to P are false (or being positioned to know them false through deduction). But P entails the falsity of its alternatives, so any case in which you know P but can't rule out some irrelevant alternative to P would be a counterexample to the principle of deductive closure for knowledge. Since the relevant alternatives theorist wants to say that very often, and even apart from skeptical cases, we can't rule out irrelevant alternatives, the theorist needs another way of explaining ruling out.

Another possibility, due to Goldman (1976), is to appeal to the sensitivity of the subject's evidence with respect to the alternative: Your evidence rules out an alternative just if, had that alternative obtained, you would have had (substantially) different evidence from the evidence you in fact have. For instance, to use a variant of an example of Goldman's, suppose you see a German shepherd fifty feet away in a large suburban backyard. Consider two alternatives to the proposition that what you see is a German shepherd: What you see is a dachshund, and what you see is a wolf. Your evidence rules out the dachshund alternative but not the wolf alternative. How so? It rules out the dachshund alternative insofar as had you seen a dachshund, you would have had very different visual evidence. However, had it been a wolf, it would have looked the same or very similar to you.

How should we understand relevance? One suggestion is to think of an alternative A to P as relevant just in case A might have happened had P been false. So, in a normal situation in a suburban backyard, if you weren't looking at a dog, you wouldn't be looking at a wolf and so the wolf alternative is irrelevant. However, suppose the property owner turns out to have a wolf. Then if you weren't looking at a dog, you might well have been looking at a wolf. This would make the wolf alternative relevant.

Notice how closely the relevant alternative approach resembles the sensitivity account if we understand ruling out and relevance in the ways just described. Putting it all together, replacing terms with their definitions, we would have: You know P if and only if you have a true belief in P, where your evidence is such that had P been false, you wouldn't have had that evidence. The only difference between this and a sensitivity account is that it holds the evidence is sensitive rather than the belief itself.

There are other ways we might understand ruling out and relevance. For instance, if you read the previous section, consider how the resulting account would look if you defined ruling out an alternative to P in terms of the safety of the subject's evidence with respect to the alternative and defined relevance of an alternative to P in terms of what could easily have happened were you to believe. The resulting account would look nearly identical to a safety account.

It might be best to view the relevant alternatives approach as an intuitively appealing framework within which to develop accounts of knowledge rather than as yet another rival account of knowledge in its own right. For this reason, we have labeled it an "approach" rather than an "account."[20]

3.6 THE COMPETENCE ACCOUNT

We distinguish between local and global reliability, following Goldman (1986, 44). Local reliability concerns the relationship between the subject's belief and the truth in the subject's particular or local situation. This is the sort of reliability discussed so far in this chapter. However, there is also global reliability, which is a matter of the overall truth-conduciveness of the process or method by which the belief is formed across the many situations in which the process or method is or might be used. As we saw in Chapter 2, reliabilism about justification explains justification in terms of global, rather than local, reliability.

Having distinguished these sorts of reliability, we might think knowledge requires both.[21] That is, we might think that knowledge requires both that you are related properly to the truth in your particular situation and that the process or method by which you formed your belief is generally one that produces (and would produce) true beliefs. On this sort of view, it is very natural to see justification as a condition of knowledge, for justification could be understood as the condition of global reliability. Globally reliable belief needn't be true (just as justified belief needn't) but is truth-conducive (just as many externalists think justified belief is).

We will finish our tour of accounts of knowledge by considering a recent way of conceiving of knowledge as involving both local and global reliability, the *competence account*. As we'll see, this account offers further insights about why we might care about knowledge over mere true belief or even mere justified true belief, insights beyond the desirability of being tethered to the truth.

Think about tennis. Let's assume you are a poor tennis player (perhaps contrary to fact). Now you might just happen to nail a Serena-Williams-style ace. It could happen that your motions, awkward and unlovely though they are, result in a perfect ace. In this sort of case, you succeed by sheer luck, not because of your skill, your competence in tennis. Compare Williams. Her aces derive from her competence. We care, and so do the professionals, about the difference between success through luck and success through competence. We care about this generally, not only in sports but in all our activities, including our beliefs. Now think about the Gettier cases. These are not mere oddities dreamed up by philosophers. They concern accidentality of a kind that we care about: We seem to care not just about having a successful belief—a true one—but having a successful belief due to intellectual competence. In this way, we might hope to appeal to the connection between knowledge and competence to show not only how the Gettier problem taps into something we care about but also how to solve it. Our discussion draws on work by Sosa (2007a), a leading competence theorist. Sosa sees these competences as virtues, and thus his epistemology is often described as *virtue epistemology*.

Let's formulate the account as follows:

Competence Account

To know is to have a true belief and for your belief to be true because it is an exercise of your intellectual competence.

Again, think about Williams's ace: She nails the ace because of her own competence. Similarly, when we know, we believe the truth because of our own competence. Your belief that the sun is shining today is true because of your competence for getting this right in situations like the one you're in. In the Gettier cases, though, or at least in most of them (more presently on this!), we get the truth only by luck, and not because of our competence. The subject in the sheep-on-the-hill case has a true belief, but he or she doesn't get the truth because of a competence, but because of a lucky coincidence.

The competence account also seems to do fine with respect to deductive closure. When you know P and competently deduce Q from P, the competence theorist sees this as getting a true belief in Q because of the competences involved in knowing P and in competently(!) deducing Q from P.

As appealing as the account is, it has a real sticking point: the barn façade case. Here it does seem that Henry gets the truth and that he does so because of his competence. After all, he exercises his normal perceptual skills properly in interaction with a normal barn. Suppose an expert archer, Archibald, is shooting at a target. Suppose he is one of many archers shooting at targets, each with his own target, separated by some safe distance. Suppose that gusts of wind throw off all of the other archers, but no wind affects Archibald's shot. He hits the target, using his excellent archery skills. Doesn't Archibald hit the target because of his skills, despite the fact that he could easily have been in a situation in which his skills wouldn't enable him to succeed? (Cf. Whitcomb 2007) Similarly, doesn't Henry have a true belief that he is looking at a barn because of his skills, even though he could easily have been looking at a barn façade? If so, is this a case of knowledge without belief that is true due to his competence?

3.7 SHOULD WE BE TRYING TO DEFINE KNOWLEDGE?

An increasing number of philosophers in recent years, reflecting on the many attempts to define knowledge, have come to doubt whether it is definable after all. It is not just that the attempts haven't succeeded (or at least not clearly so). How many ordinary categories can we define? Try defining "bachelor" yourself (Question: Is the Pope a bachelor? A widower?). It's not easy, even in this case.

We *can* give necessary conditions for being a bachelor, though. Perhaps we can give some for knowledge as well. Perhaps a list of some informative necessary conditions could serve as our account of knowledge. But maybe focusing exclusively on finding "conditions" for knowledge is mistaken, whether the search is for necessary or sufficient conditions or both. Consider belief. Suppose there are certain cases of knowledge without belief (e.g., the case of Jean and the quiz on English history). Then belief would not be a necessary condition for knowledge. But should we just leave belief out of our account of knowledge, as if it were entirely irrelevant?

3.7.1 The Point of the Concept of Knowledge (Optional)

Following E. J. Craig (1990), we might think that a more profitable approach to studying knowledge is to ask about the point of the concept of knowledge: Why do we have this concept? Such an investigation might free us up from the constraints of finding necessary and sufficient conditions.

Why do we have the concept of knowledge? Let's get at this by asking what good having this concept does for us. We use the concept all the time; what important functions does it serve? There are a number of functions. We consider three.

First, as we noted in our discussion of the justification condition on knowledge, knowing P seems to ensure being in a position to use P appropriately in reasoning about what to do and what is the case. One function of the concept of knowledge, plausibly, is that we use the concept to mark when a subject can appropriately use a certain proposition in reasoning. This would explain a lot of the uses of "know." Think of the detective's remark, "Let's stop a minute and think about what we know, and go from there," the child's remark, "I know that already, Daddy!" and the guarantee we attempt to provide by saying, "I know the apartment is locked; I don't need to check it again." (A similar function might explain the relevance of belief to knowledge, as we saw in our discussion of the belief condition: We might use the concept of knowledge to mark out who is prepared to use a proposition in reasoning.)

Second, as Craig himself stresses, we often use the concept of knowledge to mark good sources of information: "Ask her; she knows." Marking such sources is surely essential to our practical lives as well as our more theoretical investigations: we need to rely on one another, and it matters whom we rely on! (Chapter 9 discusses testimony in detail.)

Third, taking a page from the competence account, we might think that one of the main points of the concept of knowledge is to mark when we get the truth due to our own competence.

Understanding these functions is itself an interesting project for epistemology. Moreover, it might pay off in other ways. For instance, it might turn out that some of the valuable functions of the concept of knowledge have problematic side effects. Perhaps the arguments for skepticism about knowledge exploit otherwise valuable functions of the concept of knowledge. This is something to remember when reading Chapter 4.

What can the proponent of defining knowledge say in response to all this? He or she shouldn't deny that the concept of knowledge serves functions for us and shouldn't deny that it's a job for epistemology to explain these functions. What he or she might say, though, is that we can't do this job without thinking about what conditions people meet when they know. These two projects, the definitional project and the project of explaining the point of the concept of knowledge, go hand in hand.[22] Still, we might think, as this author does, that Craig is right about this much: Even if knowledge isn't definable, there is much work left for the study of knowledge.

3.7.2 Knowledge-First Epistemology

There is a more radical criticism of the definitional project. Perhaps we have been approaching things the wrong way around. We have tried to explain knowledge in terms of JTB + something else. Perhaps a better idea, due to Timothy Williamson (2000), is to take knowledge as a basic concept and try to explain other things in terms of it. This is *knowledge-first epistemology*.

To see knowledge-first epistemology in action, let's consider a way we might try to explain justification in terms of knowledge.[23] First, begin with a kind of evidentialism: You are justified in believing P just in case P is well supported by your evidence. Next, suppose that we explain evidence as amounting to knowledge—that is, that your evidence consists of exactly what you know, or E = K. From evidentialism and E = K it follows that you are justified in believing P just in case P is well supported by your knowledge. *Voilà*, an explanation of justification in terms of knowledge, rather than the other way around!

Why accept E = K, though? We'll sketch Williamson's (2000) argument. First, it seems that genuine evidence always consists of facts, or true propositions. Evidence must be the sort of thing that can increase the probability of what it is evidence for, can make a hypothesis more likely. And what increases probability must itself be a proposition, something true or false. The dirty dishes in the dishwasher might be said to be evidence that the dishwasher hasn't been run. However, the dishes aren't themselves evidence except in a loose sense. The real evidence is the fact that the dishes in the dishwasher are dirty. So, evidence consists of propositions.

Second, note that not just any proposition counts as a subject's evidence. If you have no idea that P is true, P is hardly part of your evidence. But merely believing P isn't enough by itself to make P part of your evidence. Suppose you and a friend are walking into a restaurant. Suppose you believe it's a vegan restaurant because you hope it is. Does this give you evidence that cheeseburgers won't be on the menu? In order to give you evidence, the belief must at least be justified.

But is having a justified belief in P enough to make P part of your evidence? Matters are subtler here. Suppose it isn't a vegan restaurant at all, but it looks like one, and you've been told it is one. You justifiably believe it's vegan, but you don't know it is. Is "it's a vegan restaurant" part of your evidence? Once you learn it isn't a vegan restaurant, if someone asks you what your evidence was for thinking the place wouldn't serve cheeseburgers, you would probably say, "Well, my evidence was that it looked like a vegan place and I was told it was." That is, you'll appeal to your previous knowledge. You won't say, "Well, my evidence was that it was a vegan place." You won't appeal, in other words, to your previous justified (false) beliefs. But if what you justifiably believe is evidence, why can't you appeal to it?[24]

Even supposing JB isn't sufficient for evidence, though, it might be that JTB is. But in Gettier Case I ("Smith, Jones, and the Job"), is it part of Smith's evidence that the man who will get the job has ten coins in his pocket? Is part of Henry's evidence in the barn façade case that what he sees is a barn? Evidence might seem to require the same nonaccidentality as knowledge.

If we add the premise that anything a person knows is part of his or her evidence, we get the conclusion that E = K. Here is the argument in full:

1. One's evidence consists of propositions.
2. Only if a proposition is known is it part of one's evidence.
3. Everything one knows is part of one's evidence.

So, 3. One's evidence consists of all and only the propositions one knows—that is, E = K.

There are various points where one might want to question this argument, but its steps appear at least initially plausible.

Notice one surprising upshot of E = K: If you were in a skeptical scenario (say, a brain in a vat [BIV]), you wouldn't have the same evidence you have. As things stand, you know you have hands, eyes, and a body. But if you were a BIV, you wouldn't know these things, because they would be false. You would only have evidence such as "it seems that I have hands." Evidence, arguably, concerning how things seem isn't as powerful as evidence concerning how things are. So, you are better justified in many—indeed all—beliefs about the world outside you than your BIV twin is. If you recall the "new evil demon" problem from Chapter 2, you can see how this is one sort of response to it. Generally, you can see how knowledge-first epistemology shakes things up!

3.8 CONCLUSION

We have covered a great deal of ground in this chapter. We've seen that despite all the hard work since Gettier's 1963 paper, it remains unclear how knowledge can be defined or even whether it is definable. No doubt this isn't a result epistemologists were hoping for, but we shouldn't underestimate the value of all this work over the past half-century and counting. Exploring the connections between knowledge, JTB, sensitivity, competence, and the rest is crucial to understanding knowledge and why it is important, even if the explorations haven't delivered a definition. We have seen that there may be something of value to knowledge beyond mere justified true belief. In particular, gaining the truth due to one's competence to do so seems to be an additional value. Moreover, all this work will put us in a good position to tackle other epistemological problems. As we will see in the next chapter, for instance, the notion of sensitivity is useful to the skeptic who argues that we lack much of any knowledge of the world around us.

QUESTIONS

1. Devise a case of your own in which a speaker uses free indirect speech to say something that is false.

2. Suppose your parents told you you've never been to Banff National Park in Canada, and you know your parents are quite reliable on your trips in general. Still, you have a very vague memory of seeing Lake Louise, a glacial lake you know to be within Banff. You think to yourself: This apparent memory is probably just based on your having seen pictures of Lake Louise in books and on the Internet. So, you dismiss the memory. However, it turns out that your parents had made a mistake (they confused Banff with Glacier). You *have* been to Banff, and yes, your vague memory does trace back to seeing Lake Louise. The

question is: Before you learned of your parents' mistake, did you know you had been to Lake Louise? If you did, was this a case of knowledge without belief? Was it a case of knowledge without justification?[25]

3. See if you can find a Gettier case in a novel, play, movie, or TV show. Hint: Shakespeare is a good source; so is *Terminator 2*.

4. On usual thinking about the pure truths of mathematics (i.e., truths such as $2 + 2 = 4$), they are necessarily true, and so true in all possible worlds. We can clearly know many pure mathematical truths. But can our belief in a pure mathematical truth be caused by the fact that makes it true? If we think mathematical facts don't stand in causal relations, how can the causal theorist explain mathematical knowledge? Mathematical knowledge is also difficult to explain under sensitivity and safety accounts. Can you explain why?

5. Some competence theorists (e.g., Sosa 2007a) have responded to the barn façade case by claiming that it is a case of knowledge. Play the part of a competency theorist. How best can you argue that Henry in the barn façade case does know he sees a barn?

6. Intuitively, if you buy a ticket in a large fair lottery that will have only one winner, you can't know in advance of the announcement of the winner that your ticket will lose. Consider this issue from the perspective of a sensitivity theorist, a competence theorist, and from the perspective of the relevant alternatives approach.

7. Is the following a Gettier case with respect to the proposition that one of the two players is guilty of a foul? Explain why or why not:

> You're watching a game of hockey. You see a scuffle between two players, a Penguin and a Red Wings player. Clearly someone committed a foul. Thinking about the two players, and knowing their foul percentages, you conclude the Penguin player is guilty of the foul. Suppose, however, that the actual fact is that the Red Wings player is guilty of the foul.

8. Where would you challenge the argument for E = K? Explain.

9. How would you reply to the following reaction to the topic of this chapter: "Look, definitions are up to us. We can define things however we like. So, we can just define knowledge as justified true belief and be done with it. Gettier just defines knowledge differently. Two definitions could both be right."

FURTHER READING

Craig, E. J. (1991). *Knowledge and the State of Nature*. Oxford: Clarendon Press.

Dretske, Fred I. (1970). "Epistemic Operators." *Journal of Philosophy* 67(24): 1007–1023.

Goldman, Alvin (1976). "Discrimination and Perceptual Knowledge." *Journal of Philosophy* 73: 771–791.

Kvanvig, Jonathan (2003). *The Value of Knowledge and the Pursuit of Understanding.* Cambridge: Cambridge University Press.

Nozick, Robert (1981). *Philosophical Explanations.* Cambridge, MA: Harvard University Press.

Pritchard, Duncan (2005). *Epistemic Luck.* Oxford: Oxford University Press.

Sosa, Ernest (2007a). *A Virtue Epistemology*. Oxford: Oxford University Press.

Stine, Gail (1976). "Skepticism, Relevant Alternatives and Deductive Closure." *Philosophical Studies* 29.

Williamson, Timothy (2000). *Knowledge and Its Limits*. Oxford: Oxford University Press.

Zagzebski, Linda (1994). "The Inescapability of Gettier Problems." *Philosophical Quarterly* 44(174): 65–73.

NOTES

1. I thank Alvin Goldman for extremely useful advice on the organization and content of this chapter, especially Section 3.4. His influence will be evident to epistemologists.

2. The findings are available here: http://www.oxforddictionaries.com/words/the-oec-facts-about-the-language

3. For more on the importance of questions about the value of knowledge, see Jonathan Kvanvig (2003).

4. It is worth noting that some languages, including French, have distinct words for knowledge of persons or things vs. knowing of facts (*connaître* vs. *savoir*). See Stanley (2011) for a defense of the view that knowledge-how is a species of knowledge of facts.

5. For a powerful influential account of the distinction between what is strictly said and what is implied or implicated, see H. P. Grice (1967). Often, in saying "I believe," we imply or implicate that we don't bear a stronger cognitive relation to the proposition in question—that is, that we don't know.

6. This is an example from the philosophical lore. Whether it is an accurate account of chicken-sexers is doubtful. See the Wikipedia page on chicken-sexing. The two methods described, vent sexing and feather sexing, apparently involve looking for very specific indicators rather than a general overall gestalt as the lore suggests. Here we play along with the lore.

7. Our formulation retains Gettier's wording except for the addition of "competently" to rule out cases in which someone deduces in accordance with silly rules, such as the rule from "P or Q" deduce "P and Q." We should admit that, even apart from issues concerning question-begging deductions, further tweaks are needed. Suppose that as you do the deduction, you gain reasons to doubt the truth of P. Then you wouldn't arrive at a justified belief in Q through the deduction. So, we would need to add a qualification to this effect: As you do the deduction, your belief in P doesn't cease to be justified. Finally, we, like Gettier, won't worry much about doxastic vs. propositional justification. This distinction is not particularly relevant to the Gettier problem.

8. Some philosophers use "Gettier case" to refer only to cases like Gettier's original cases in which the subject arrives at JTB without K because of inference from a false premise. Our usage in this chapter is broader: Any JTB without K is a Gettier case.

9. See Chapter 7, Section 7.3.2, for discussion of the empirical study of intuitions about Gettier cases.

10. Again, more fine-tuning is needed, just as we saw with Gettier's Assumption 2. (See note 7.)

11. Our use of "defeater" here is distinct from but related to that of Chapter 1, Section 1.8. Chapter 1 discusses defeaters of justification. Defeaters of justification are evidence the subject has that reduce or eliminate his or her justification for a belief. Using this notion of defeat, we can define the notion that defeasibility theorists use: that of a fact that the subject isn't aware of but that, if he or she were aware of it, would defeat his or her justification. If the existence of such a fact guaranteed that the subject lacked knowledge, we might well call such facts *defeaters of knowledge*. It is controversial whether such facts guarantee that the subject lacks knowledge, as we'll see. Still, the term "defeater" is standardly used for such facts. Thus, the terminology can confuse. The basic rule is: If we're talking about justification, defeaters are evidence the subject has that undermine his or her justification for a belief; if we're talking about knowledge, defeaters are facts that if the subject were aware of them would undermine his or her justification for a belief.

    One subtle but key distinction that defeasibility theorists sometimes make is between facts such that knowing about them would make you unjustified in believing that P and facts such that knowing about them would deprive you of your particular grounds for believing that P. All facts of the second kind are facts of the first kind but not vice versa. One way learning a fact might make you unjustified in believing that P is by giving you a new ground to believe not-P, one that outweighs your grounds for believing P but doesn't deprive you of those grounds.

12. The interested reader might consult Kent Bach (1984)'s examination of what it is to take something for granted. Such a notion might be of use to those defending the no-false-assumptions account.

13. As we'll see in Section 3.6, there is both a local and a global notion of reliability. The local one, which concerns nonaccidentality, is relevant to knowledge but clearly not relevant to justification. (Gettiered subjects are justified, for instance.) The global one, which concerns the general truth-conduciveness of the process or method used to form the belief, is arguably relevant to justification. The discussion of reliabilism about justification in Chapter 2 concerns global, not local, reliabilism.

14. The counterexamples here are counterexamples to the claim that sensitivity is necessary for knowledge. Are there reasons to think that it—together with TB (or JTB)—is insufficient for knowledge? Nozick (1981, 175–176) gives a clever example. Consider a person who is in a tank being fed experiences that are completely out of keeping with his outside surroundings (i.e., being in the tank). For one brief moment, he is fed experiences of being in a tank. He is fed those experiences; they are not caused by interaction with the surrounding water. He believes he is in a tank. Were he not in a tank, he wouldn't of course believe he was in the tank. Yet he still doesn't know he's in the tank. This looks like a Gettier case in which a subject's belief is sensitive. Because of cases like this, Nozick adds a further condition to his account, which he calls *adherence*. Your belief in P is adherent just if the following holds: were P true and were you to use the method you in fact use to determine whether P, you would believe P. We do not have space to consider whether this is a plausible condition on knowledge.

15. Saul Kripke argued in lectures in the 1980s that on Nozick's account a person might know she sees a red barn without knowing (or being positioned to know) that she sees a barn. Suppose the red barns were left standing but all yellow barns were replaced with yellow façades. Suppose Peg knows nothing of this. Peg sees a red barn. It seems her belief that she sees a red barn is sensitive: Had it been false, she wouldn't have believed she sees a red barn, because it would either have been a yellow façade or an object that looks very much different than a barn (e.g., a silo). But her belief that she sees a barn is insensitive: Had she not been looking at a barn, she might have been looking at a yellow barn façade and so believed it was a barn. Defenders of the sensitivity account, such as Adams and Clarke (2005), reply that Kripke's example ignores methods. Kripke's lecture is now published (see Kripke 2011).

16. Here is an example. Suppose only a very serious illness would prevent the work-obsessed John from coming to work. The most common and typical mild illnesses wouldn't keep him at home. So it's true that if John were ill, he'd come to work. However, still it needn't be true that if John didn't come to work, he wouldn't be ill. After all, the only way John wouldn't come to work is if he was very seriously ill, and this is a way of being ill. In general, when there are several ways A could conceivably happen, some very ordinary and others extraordinary, it can be that were A to happen, it would happen in the ordinary way, ensuring that result B would take place. Yet, were B not to take place, this would have to be because an extraordinary A-possibility took place.

17. Timothy Williamson (2000) argues that knowledge requires safety. He would not accept the safety account of knowledge, however, because he thinks knowledge is undefinable (see Section 3.7.2). Ernest Sosa (1999) endorsed the safety account but has since abandoned it. See the discussion of the competence view in Section 3.6.

18 Stewart Cohen claims (reported by Jonathan Kvanvig) that the safety account runs into trouble with Kripke's red barn examples (see note 15). Suppose the only real barn in the area is a red barn. The others, all yellow, are fakes. Were Peg to believe she sees a red barn, she would be right. Were she to believe she sees a barn, she might be looking at one of the fakes and so be wrong. (These issues are further complicated if the safety theorist, like the sensitivity theorist, appeals to methods.)

19. Suppose you find the relevant alternatives framework appealing. You might then want to consider basic ground rules to follow in trying to explain what ruling out and relevance amount to. One ground rule, of course, is not to explain these notions in terms of knowledge. However, there are others. To have an account to be compatible with the deductive closure of knowledge, you want to be sure that where Q is known by deduction from one's knowledge of P, if one has evidence that rules out all relevant alternatives to P, one will also have evidence that rules out all relevant alternatives to Q. The interested reader should consult the classic paper by Gail Stine (1976) on these issues.

20. Goldman (1986) defends a view of this kind, spelling out the local requirement in terms of relevant alternatives.

21. An important twist emerges when we consider the possibility that the word "know" doesn't always mean the same thing in every conversational context. See the discussion of contextualism in Chapter 5.

22. Knowledge-first epistemology isn't limited to the defense of E = K. Williamson (2000) argues knowledge is the norm of assertion. We discuss norms of assertion in Chapter 5, Section 5.3.

23. For further discussion, see Schroeder (2008) and Comesaña and McGrath (2014).

24. The safety theorist might reply that these beliefs are safe because by the time they are formed the belief couldn't easily be false. At the last minute, in Comesaña's example, the subject decides not to disguise himself as Michael, and we might think, given that fact, the subject wouldn't easily go wrong in taking Judy's word about the route to the party. However, this sort of reply is a double-edged sword. Consider Henry in the barn case. Given the fact that he is looking at the (lone) barn, could he easily go wrong? If the safety theorist wants to appeal to safety to explain why Henry doesn't know, it seems he can't reply to Comesaña by this sort of "by the time the belief is formed" gambit.

25. For a recent argument that one can know something while believing it unreasonably, see Lasonen-Aarnio (2010).

Skepticism About Knowledge
Matthew McGrath

The skeptic claims we lack knowledge, or justified belief, or both, across some important domain. In the extreme case, the domain is universal—that is, we lack any knowledge at all, or any justified belief at all. Such skepticism is sometimes called *global skepticism*. For instance, the regress argument from Chapter 1 is an argument that no one is ever justified in believing anything. But there are local skepticisms as well, such as skepticism about knowledge of other minds, about the future, about the external world (the world outside your own mind).[1] These skepticisms are certainly radical, even if they do not question all our knowledge. Out in the street or in the coffeehouse, all of us claim we know things about other minds, about the future, and certainly about the external world. Think of what we say: "I know the waiter recognized me from last week" (implying knowledge of another mind) or "I know Beth will get to the restaurant before us" (implying knowledge of the future), and of course both of these imply knowledge of an external world, the world outside your own mind. Could all of these statements, and the beliefs they express, be *wrong*? It seems ludicrous to think so. What makes the issue of skepticism interesting, though, is not the plausibility of skeptical claims about lack of knowledge but the compelling arguments in favor of those claims.

In this chapter, we will focus on what is probably the most widely discussed sort of skeptical argument since Descartes: arguments that we lack knowledge of the external world, based on our inability to rule out "skeptical possibilities." We'll call these *skeptical possibility arguments*. Such arguments can be given for skepticism about justified belief, but they are particularly powerful for skepticism about knowledge. There is something about the concept of knowledge that makes this sort of argument compelling. After illustrating how these arguments go in more detail, we will examine a number of traditional responses to them.

4.1 DESCARTES AND SKEPTICAL POSSIBILITY ARGUMENTS

To get the flavor of skeptical possibility arguments, let us begin with the master, René Descartes, in his *Meditations on First Philosophy* (first published 1641). Descartes begins Meditation I by resolving to rid himself of all the opinions he had adopted. Having observed so many of his previous opinions to be in error, he set about "commencing anew the work of building from the foundation" in order to "establish a firm and abiding superstructure in the sciences." He tells us that reason has convinced him that he ought to withhold belief from what is not entirely certain no less than from what is manifestly false. His strategy is to try his best to doubt as many of his former beliefs as he can, striking at the foundations of these beliefs.

You might wonder about the wisdom of Descartes' search for certainty, or whether his method of doubt would help establish a firm basis for the sciences. However, you need not agree with him on these matters in order to find what comes next very compelling.

We now will quote one of the most powerful paragraphs in all of Western philosophy. Descartes has just suggested that perhaps because the senses sometimes deceive (e.g., about distant objects or minute objects) we can never trust them, even in the best cases (e.g., about whether Descartes is now before a fire holding a piece of paper). He proceeds to mock this suggestion by comparing such doubts to those of a madman. And yet he continues . . .

> Though this be true, I must nevertheless here consider that I am a man, and that, consequently, I am in the habit of sleeping, and representing to myself in dreams those same things, or even sometimes others less probable, which the insane think are presented to them in their waking moments. How often have I dreamt that I was in these familiar circumstances, that I was dressed, and occupied this place by the fire, when I was lying undressed in bed? At the present moment, however, I certainly look upon this paper with eyes wide awake; the head which I now move is not asleep; I extend this hand consciously and with express purpose, and I perceive it; the occurrences in sleep are not so distinct as all this. But I cannot forget that, at other times I have been deceived in sleep by similar illusions; and, attentively considering those cases, I perceive so clearly that there exist no certain marks by which the state of waking can ever be distinguished from sleep, that I feel greatly astonished; and in amazement I almost persuade myself that I am now dreaming.

Let us look at the structure of Descartes' argument a bit more carefully. Descartes raises a *skeptical possibility*, a possibility in which all his experiences systematically mislead him about the world around him. The possibility he raises is that he is now dreaming. If he were now dreaming, his beliefs about his surroundings would be badly mistaken. In order to be certain about his surroundings based on his sensory experiences, it seems, he must rule out the possibility that he is now dreaming. And yet there are "no certain marks by which the state of waking can ever be distinguished from sleep." So, how can he be certain he is sitting before the fire, with a piece of paper in his hand? He can't. He has found a reason to doubt even his present perceptual beliefs.

Descartes seems to intend his argument to concern certainty. But we can recast it in terms of knowledge. The argument goes as follows:

The Dream Argument

1. You don't know you're not now dreaming.
2. Unless you know you're not now dreaming, you cannot know anything about the world around you based on your current sensory experiences.
3. Therefore, you cannot know anything about the world around you based on your current sensory experiences.

The argument for (1) might proceed much as Descartes' does. How can you know you're not dreaming unless you have a test that you could apply to distinguish waking from sleeping? But you don't have any such test.

If you're like the author of this chapter, you'll feel that clearly you *do* know much about things around you and that you *do* know you're not dreaming. But you'll worry about exactly *how* you know these things. Most epistemologists, starting with Descartes himself, see the problem this way. The final goal is not to convince people they don't know much; rather, it is to explain how it is possible that we do know, given these powerful arguments to the contrary.

You might hope for an easy victory over the skeptic. Couldn't we question the argument for step (1) once we quit certainty for knowledge? Why can't you know you're not now dreaming? You know dreams rarely are so orderly, coherent, what we call "realistic." Some are, but comparatively few. So, isn't it very likely that you're not dreaming? If we don't require absolute certainty for knowledge, isn't this enough for knowledge, assuming your belief is true and you are not right by the sort of luck found in Gettier cases (see Chapter 3, Section 3.2)?

There are several argumentative strategies the skeptic might use in response. We'll consider two. First, the skeptic might point out that dreaming could affect memories, too, so that what appears to be a genuine memory in a dream might well not be. Given this, how do you know that what you call your "knowledge" of what dreams are typically like isn't just a dream-memory and not knowledge at all? A second strategy, perhaps more compelling, is to argue that unless you know now that you weren't dreaming in the past when you acquired beliefs about what dreams were like, you don't know what dreams are typically like and so don't have information that would allow you to know you're not now dreaming. How do you know you weren't dreaming on these past occasions? In fact, we might push the dreaming hypothesis further: How do you know your entire life hasn't been spent dreaming? If you don't know you haven't spent your life this way, how can you know anything based on sensory experience either in the past or present?

Descartes himself didn't stop with the dreaming argument. He raised the skeptical stakes higher, with his evil genius possibility. The argument, transformed into an argument about knowledge, is this:

The Evil Genius Argument

1. You do not know you haven't spent your life being deceived by an evil genius.
2. Unless you know you haven't spent your life being deceived by an evil genius, you cannot know anything about the world around you (or even about mathematics or logic).
3. So, you cannot know anything about the world around you (or even about mathematics or logic).

This is a very powerful skeptical argument. Indeed, early in Meditation II, Descartes suggests that only knowledge of his current thoughts—of the fact that he thinks, that he seems to see things, etc.—can elude it.[2]

Let's sketch the general plan of a skeptical possibility argument. The person giving the argument—call him or her the "skeptic"—targets some ordinary belief or class of beliefs that we ordinarily think we know. Call this belief or class of beliefs O (short for "ordinary"). The skeptic then formulates a skeptical possibility (SK)—that is, a possibility in which everything is the same as far as you can tell from the inside (you have the same experiences, apparent memories, beliefs, etc.) but in which the target beliefs are false. The skeptic then argues as follows:

Premise 1: You do not know that not-SK.
Premise 2: Unless you know that not-SK fails, you do not know O.
Conclusion: You don't know O.

4.2 RESPONDING TO SKEPTICAL POSSIBILITY ARGUMENTS: REJECTING PREMISE 2

One way to respond to such arguments is to insist that you don't need to know not-SK in order to know O. To respond in this way is to reject Premise 2. It might be asked: Why exactly must you know you're not dreaming or not a brain in a vat (BIV) in order to know that there is a desk over there, a tree out the window, and so forth? If accounts of knowledge such as those discussed in Chapter 3 are on the right track, all you need to have knowledge is to have a justified true belief that isn't right by luck. Call the no-luck condition, whatever it is, X. Couldn't you have such JTB + X for the proposition that there is a desk over there without knowing much of anything about skeptical scenarios?

It can't be this simple, though. For one thing, some skeptical possibilities are incompatible with some ordinary propositions that we believe. Consider the skeptical possibility that you are a (handless) BIV. This skeptical possibility can't obtain if you have hands, because having hands entails that it's false that you are a BIV. Moreover, you can see the entailment. How, then, can you know that you have hands but not know that you are not a BIV, when you can plainly see that if you have hands, you're not a BIV?

The point just made seems to depend on a principle like that of "deductive closure" from Chapter 3. According to the deductive closure principle, if you know P, then if you competently deduce Q from P, believing Q as a result of this deduction, then you know Q. Applied to the case at hand, deductive closure would tell us that if you know that you have hands and you deduce from this that you aren't a BIV believing you aren't a BIV as a result, you end up knowing you aren't a BIV.

However, as we noted in Chapter 3, deductive closure is controversial when the relevant deduction is question-begging. It was fine to appeal to it in Chapter 3, where we were concerned only with ordinary cases in which we expand our knowledge through deduction (e.g., "*my* 1983 Toyota Celica has a timing chain problem, so *some* do"). As we noted, if you deduce Q from P where this deduction is question-begging or circular, it's not clear that you could thereby come to know Q. And the deduction from having hands to not being a BIV seems question-begging or circular. We need to formulate a closure principle designed to be neutral about these issues. Let us pause to try to get straight on just what the needed closure principle looks like.

4.2.1 Formulating a Closure Principle for Knowledge

Instead of supposing one has deduced something from something else one knows and asking about the epistemic status of the resulting belief, let's ask about the implications of knowing a proposition with respect to knowing further things that it entails. In some cases, you won't be able to *come to know* something entailed because you *already* know it. Suppose you haven't measured your little brother's height in a few years. He's nine years old. You measure it and so come to know that he is a certain height, say four feet five inches tall (135 cm). But there is no question of your coming to know by deduction from this piece of information that he is less than seven feet tall. You *already* knew, prior to finding out about his exact height, that he isn't anywhere near seven feet tall, based on looking at him.

In other cases, it's not merely that you happen already to know Q based on grounds independent of P; it's that you *need* to already know Q *in order* to know P in the first place. For instance, to use an example of Crispin Wright's (2002, 333), suppose, when watching people mark an X on a sheet of paper, that you can know on the basis of seeing them do this that they are voting only if you already know that an election is taking place. We might well think that this applies to the skeptical case. In order to know I have hands, I have to already know—so it is plausible to think—that I am not a BIV. That's why I can't come to know I'm not a BIV by deducing it from my knowledge that I have hands.

Notice, though, that in both sorts of cases mentioned (where you happen already to know the conclusion and where you had to already know it in order to know the premise), although you can't come to know the entailed proposition Q from the original proposition P, it is nevertheless true that if you know P then you also do know Q. Even if you already knew Q before knowing P (as in the little brother's height case), it's still true that if you know P, you know Q. Similarly, if you had to already know Q in order to know P, again it's still true that if you know P, you know Q (as in the voting case). Given that these seem to be the only ways you might know P, know that P entails Q, but not be able to come to knowledge of Q through deduction from P, and given that in all of them you do know Q, we can propose a closure principle:

If you know P, and you know that P entails Q, then you know Q.

One further tweak is needed before we continue. Closure, as we've formulated it, seems not to allow for failing to "put two and two together." But I might know that *bazaar* is a word that has a *zaa* in the middle. And I might know that if *bazaar* is such a word, then some English word has *zaa* in the middle. But if I don't put these together, I might not believe and so not know that some English word has *zaa* in the middle. We don't want our closure principle to declare otherwise. Something similar might well be true of skeptical hypotheses. Perhaps we have strong grounds to believe them false, but we might never have assembled those grounds and "put two and two together." To avoid this implication, we'll use this formulation:

(Closure): If you know P, and you know that P entails Q, then you are in a position to know Q.

We call this *closure*, as distinguished from the principle of Chapter 3 we called *deductive closure*. The difference between the principles is irrelevant except when we are considering question-begging or circular deductions.

We now have a closure principle suitable for use in our discussion of skepticism. The principle still has real bite to it. We can appeal to it to defend Premise 2 in skeptical possibilities in which the skeptical possibility (SK) is incompatible with the target ordinary proposition (O). So, for instance, consider this skeptical possibility argument:

   i. You are not in a position to know you're not a BIV.
   ii. In order to know you have hands, you must be in a position to know that you're not a BIV.
   iii. So, you don't know you have hands.

The closure principle is used to defend (ii), thus blocking the sort of response to skeptical possibility arguments that we have been considering. For, if you know you have hands, then one of three situations is the case: (A) you can deduce and come to know that you're not a BIV; (B) you already knew you aren't a BIV; or (C) you were already in a position to know you're not a BIV from grounds independent of any deduction from *I have hands* but hadn't put two and two together. Whichever of the three situations obtains, if you do know you have hands, you are also in a position to know you are not a BIV. And this is what (ii) says.

What about the original thought behind rejecting Premise 2 of skeptical possibilities arguments—the thought that JTB + X is enough for knowledge of ordinary propositions such as *I have hands* regardless of whether one has any idea of what to think about skeptical possibilities? Appealing as this thought is, we can see that closure makes it doubtful. For, if closure is true for knowledge, and K is JTB + X, then JTB + X itself obeys closure as well: If you have JTB + X for P and you have JTB + X for the proposition that P entails Q, then you're in a position to have JTB + X for Q. But then we can see that we can't happily claim we have JTB + X for ordinary propositions while not worrying much about whether we have JTB + X for claims that we are not in skeptical scenarios. Closure disturbs the consoling thought that "philosophical" worries about skeptical scenarios have nothing to do with whether we know ordinary facts. This is one reason it is such an interesting principle.

One small matter deserves attention before turning to ways one might reject closure. You might notice that argument (i)–(iii) differs from the skeptical possibility arguments discussed above, and from the general schema for them, by including "in a position to know" instead of "know" in several places. That substitution was needed in order to make use of the closure principle to justify (ii). This substitution requires the skeptic to defend the claim—(i) here—that you aren't in a position to know the relevant skeptical possibility fails to obtain. A question arises here: Is it harder for the skeptic to defend this claim than to defend the weaker claim that you simply don't know that possibility fails to obtain? If so, appealing to closure would come at a cost to the skeptic.

Fortunately for the skeptic, substituting "position to know" for "know" in the first premise doesn't make that premise any harder to defend. The guiding idea behind the skeptic's claim that you don't know that you're not dreaming, that you're not a BIV, and so forth was always that you don't have the materials to know, and never merely that you don't know. A person might fail to know something simply because he hasn't put two and two together. For example, suppose it's Sunday. You know the library is closed on Sundays, and you know that today is Sunday. But you fail to put two and two together and so, failing to realize it's closed today, you head off to the library. In this case, you don't know it's closed today, but you *would* know this if only you would put these other pieces of information together in your mind. You're in a position to know it's closed today. However, according to the skeptic, given what you have to go on, you can put all your evidence together all you like and you still won't end up knowing you're not a BIV. For the skeptic, you're not in a position to know such things. The switch from "knows" to "position to know" if anything *better* expresses what the skeptic is trying to say.

main point — use in Descartes Argument

Recall the skeptical argument:

i. You are not in a position to know you're not a BIV.
ii. In order to know you have hands, you must be in a position to know that you're not a BIV.
iii. So, you don't know you have hands.

From this discussion, we may conclude that in order to block the second premise of arguments like (i) – (iii), one would need to reject closure. We need to see whether there is a plausible way to do this.

4.2.2 Nozick on Skepticism: A Way to Reject Closure?

Robert Nozick doesn't simply declare closure false when applied to these cases. Rather, independently of concerns about skepticism, he defends an account of knowledge under which it turns out that closure fails exactly in these sorts of cases. On his account, which we discussed in Chapter 3 (Section 3.4.2), in order to know P, your true belief in P must be sensitive—that is, if P were false, you wouldn't believe P. (We can ignore methods for the purposes of this discussion.)

Working with this account of knowledge, Nozick gives a clever response to skeptical possibility arguments. Such arguments are appealing because the first premises are true: You don't know, and you're not in a position to know, that you're not a BIV, that you're not dreaming, and so forth. Were you in one of these skeptical scenarios, you would still think you weren't. That's why you don't know. (He thinks, moreover, this captures our sense of why it seems we don't know these things.) So, for Nozick, the skeptic is right about that much. However, the skeptic is wrong to conclude from this that you lack knowledge of ordinary matters, such as that you have hands. Just because your belief that you're not a BIV isn't sensitive, it doesn't follow that your beliefs in ordinary propositions that entail this proposition are not sensitive. Sensitivity isn't closed under known entailment. You can know P, know P entails Q but not know Q, and yet not be in a position to know Q. The closure principle for knowledge, on Nozick's account of knowledge, has many true instances, but it fails in precisely these sorts of cases. Premise (ii) above and all Premise 2's in skeptical possibilities arguments are therefore false. So Nozick argues.

How could one sensitively believe *I have hands* without sensitively believing *I am not a BIV?* Let's say that the actual world is "normal" just if it is roughly what you think it is—that is, a world in which you perceive tables, chairs, and so forth in all the normal ways. If the actual world is normal, then the BIV world is very remote from actuality, unlike, say, worlds in which Mitt Romney won the 2012 U.S. election. Now, a statement of the form "had A not been the case, C wouldn't be the case" is true in a world W if and only if in the closest worlds to W in which A is false, C is also false. Assume the actual world is a normal one. Then the closest worlds in which you don't have hands are ones in which you lost them in an accident, say. In such worlds you can plainly see and feel that you don't have hands and so you wouldn't believe you do have hands. Thus, if the actual world is normal, your belief that you have hands is sensitive. However, whatever the character of the actual world, your belief that you're not a BIV is insensitive: If you were a BIV, you'd still think you weren't a BIV. So, if the actual world is normal, your belief that you have hands is sensitive, whereas your belief that you aren't a BIV is insensitive. Putting this together with Nozick's account of knowledge, it follows that if the actual world is normal, you know you have hands but don't know you're not a BIV.

Is Nozick begging the question against the skeptic by appealing to the fact that our world is a normal one? No. His point is that it is not a necessary condition of having knowledge of ordinary matters that you know or are in a position to know that you're not in skeptical scenarios, contrary to what Premise 2 in skeptical possibility arguments asserts. To show one thing, A, isn't a necessary condition of another, B, it's enough to give a possibility in which B obtains but A doesn't. This is what he does. His claim is not that ours is a normal world (although he of course believes this to be true), but that normal worlds are possible, and that if ours is a normal one, then ordinary beliefs such as your belief that you have hands would be sensitive, even though the belief that you aren't a BIV wouldn't be sensitive. Given his theory of knowledge, this would show that it is possible for you to know that you have hands but not know or be in a position to know that you are not a BIV. Thus, Premise (ii) is false in the above skeptical possibility argument, and generally whatever the skeptic chooses for Premise 2 will be false. Thus, skeptical possibility arguments fail—all of them.

As we saw in Chapter 3 (Section 3.4.2), there are apparent counterexamples to the sensitivity requirement on knowledge that have nothing to do with closure. So anyone following Nozick will need to find something plausible to say in response to these counterexamples.

But even putting such counterexamples aside, it seems impossible to limit counterexamples to closure to skeptical cases. In Chapter 3, we noted that on Nozick's account, you could know P but not be in a position to know through deduction that *you do not falsely believe P.* This was a violation of the deductive closure of knowledge. The same example can be used to show that Nozick's account violates the closure principle more appropriate to theorizing about skepticism, the principle we are calling "closure." You do know that P is true (for some P, such as *there is a chair over there*), and you do know that this entails that you don't falsely believe P. But you do not sensitively believe the latter. There are also other counterexamples that link the ordinary to mildly skeptical propositions. Consider this one: I know there is a maple tree standing in my front yard. I'm at my office now, several miles from home, but I still know this. Had it been false, I would have known about it, it seems, because in the closest worlds in which it is false I would have arranged to have the tree cut down or I would have witnessed the fallen tree in the morning after a storm. Now consider the possibility that the maple tree hasn't been cut down moments ago by rampaging hooligans. This proposition is entailed by *there is a maple tree standing in my front yard.* But my belief in it is not sensitive.

Had the maple just been cut down moments ago, I wouldn't have known about it (yet). So while I know there is a maple tree standing in my front yard, Nozick must say that I don't know that rampaging hooligans haven't cut it down moments ago. You can invent many other similar examples (e.g., you know your car is parked in such and such lot, but you aren't in a position to know it hasn't been stolen and driven away).

Stemming the tide of counterexamples to closure is one problem for Nozick's account of knowledge. Another is the puzzle of why, if the instances of the closure principle involving skeptical scenarios are false, we feel a pressure to retract our claim that we know ordinary matters such that we have hands after we concede we don't know we're not BIVs. Why does conceding you don't know you aren't a mere BIV make you feel you really can't just continue to maintain that you know that you have hands, feet, and so forth? The truth of the closure principle would explain why we feel this pressure: We feel it because we sense that knowing something (P) that one can see entails something else (Q) isn't possible unless one in a position to know Q.[3]

We have seen there are serious problems with the attempt to block skeptical possibilities arguments at Premise 2, that is, the premise that unless one knows (or is in a position to know) ~SK, then one does not know O. At least when the ordinary propositions (O) entail the falsity of the skeptical hypothesis SK, it seems Premise 2 is in good shape. In this author's view, a more promising line of response is to grant Premise 2 to the skeptic but to reject Premise 1—that is, to insist that we *do* know that the various skeptical hypotheses are false. We *do* know that we're not BIVs. We *do* know that we're not dreaming and so forth.

4.3 REJECTING PREMISE 1: YOU KNOW YOU'RE NOT A BIV!

Fine, you might say, but *how* do we know these things? Notice what this question seems to be asking for: a reason, a justification. We might hope to reply dismissively by claiming that the issue of justification is irrelevant, because justification is not necessary for knowledge. So long as you have true belief that is not true by sheer luck, then you know. In Chapter 3, we discussed various proposals that might justify this sort of reply, in particular proposals featuring reliability conditions of one sort or other on knowledge (though not the sensitivity proposal!). The idea, in general, would be to eliminate the justification condition on knowledge and think instead of knowledge as requiring only true reliable belief, and then claim that we can know the skeptical possibilities are false without having any reason or justification.

Yet it has seemed to many philosophers, including this author, that this is not enough. If all we can justifiably say in reply to the skeptic is that maybe we're hooked up nonaccidentally to the truth in this way, then all we can justifiably say is "maybe we know." But this seems problematic in at least two ways. First, it's an awfully weak answer. I think I'm justified in thinking that I do know, not only that maybe I do. Second, it's an awfully odd answer to the skeptic. It is the sort of answer that we might think relies on a false theory of knowledge. Knowledge and justification are not so cleanly separable as this response would have it. To see this, imagine a team of detectives working on a murder case. They have some good evidence, let's suppose, that the suspect did it. They might say, "We have some reason to believe he did it, but we don't know yet that he did it." Later, after much stronger evidence comes in, they might say, "Now we don't merely have reason to believe he did it; we know it." It seems the detectives are treating degrees of justification as a kind of scale with knowledge on top or at least at the upper end. This way of thinking about knowledge cannot simply be dismissed by saying that knowledge is one thing, justification is something very different. They seem importantly related, and the skeptic is drawing on this relationship.

Well, then, how do we know we're not living in a skeptical scenario? Here are three traditional proposals for explaining how we pull this off:

1. We know such things a priori; that is, our knowledge is not based on experience.[4] Call this the *a priori proposal*.
2. We know them a posteriori, but not based on knowledge of the world we've gained through experience, only based on knowledge of what our experience is like together with our apparent memories. Call this the *straightforward a posteriori proposal*. It is straightforward because it doesn't seem to beg any questions against the skeptic, unlike the next proposal.
3. We know them a posteriori, based on knowledge of the world we've gained through perception. Call this the *bold a posteriori proposal*.

The remainder of the chapter will consider each of these three proposals in turn. We postpone to the following chapter a fourth relatively new proposal concerning the semantics of "know."

4.4 THE A PRIORI PROPOSAL

The eighteenth-century Scottish philosopher Thomas Reid argues that we are justified in believing and presumably know certain "first principles" concerning contingent matters of fact. The justification is a priori because it is based on the self-evidentness of the principles rather than experience.

Some of the first principles Reid lists concern a person's own mental life, but most on his list concern the world outside one's mind. Consider these examples (Reid 1785, Essay 6, Chapter 5):

First Principle Concerning Memory

That those things did really happen which I distinctly remember.

Concerning Perception

That those things do really exist which we distinctly perceive by our senses, and are what we perceive them to be.

Concerning Reasoning

That the natural faculties, by which we distinguish truth from error, are not fallacious.

Concerning Other Minds

That there is life and intelligence in our fellow-men with whom we converse . . . That certain features of the countenance, sounds of the voice, and gestures of the body, indicate certain thoughts and dispositions of mind.

None of these propositions is true as a matter of necessity. There are possible worlds in which what we distinctly remember (i.e., distinctly seem to remember) didn't really happen; worlds in which what we distinctly perceive (what we experience) isn't reflective of what there is; and so forth. Reid claims, nevertheless, that we are justified in believing that memory and perception are reliable.[5] So, Reid claims our beliefs in first principles are justified; and if they turn out to be true nonaccidentally, they constitute knowledge, at least according to the sorts of views of knowledge discussed in Chapter 3. The knowledge would be a priori because it is not based on experience, but rather on the self-evidentness of the principles.[6] Using this knowledge, we could clearly rule out a great many skeptical hypotheses. If your senses are reliable, you are not a BIV, for instance. If your reason and memory are reliable, a Cartesian demon is not constantly deceiving you in your reasoning about mathematics and logic.

Reid's claims stand in stark contrast to the traditional view of the a priori going back at least to Kant. On the traditional view, only necessary truths can be known a priori and contingent truths can only be known with the help of experience (understood broadly to include introspection of one's own mind). One reason for thinking contingent truths cannot be known a priori is that when we put aside experience, all that remains as a source of knowledge is pure reason—and pure reason by itself can't tell you that you are in one possible world rather than another. It can only tell you about what is true in all possible worlds or none. You have to, so to speak, "look to see" what is *specially* the case in the possible world that is actual.[7]

Although Reid maintains there is no way to prove a first principle via "direct or apodictical proof," he does offer some suggestive remarks about how we might, as he says, "reason even about them." He gives us some marks by which we might decide what is a first principle and what isn't. Such marks would be quite useful, for if we could determine that a proposition P is a first principle, then since first principles are true, we could conclude that P is true. Some of the marks Reid lists could only be verified a posteriori, such as the "consent of ages and nations" or the appearance of certain beliefs early in our lives before education, as well as the agreement in the testimonies our faculties give us. You can't know a priori what the consent of ages and nations is, nor when beliefs appear in normal development; and you must use knowledge of what your experiences are over time to know about the agreement of our faculties' testimonies. However, two of the marks he mentions are things we can arguably know a priori, and we will focus on these.

First, Reid suggests that first principles might "admit of proof by reductio ad absurdum." To prove something by reductio ad absurdum, we assume the proposition is false and derive an absurdity from it; we then conclude, from the fact that the assumption led to absurdity that the proposition must be true. Here is an example from elementary logic. How can we prove the following is true: "If P&Q, then P"? Like this: Assume it is false. Then P&Q is true and so P is true; but P is also false. But that is absurd. Therefore, the statement "If P&Q, then P" is true. This strategy seems appropriate for proving *necessary* first principles, such as those of logic, but the ones important for us at the moment (e.g., the first principle concerning perception) are contingent. If we assume them to be false, how can we derive an absurdity?

The second consideration concerns consistency. Reid writes:

> . . . [it] is a good argument ad hominem, if it can be shewn that a first principle which a man rejects, stands upon the same footing with others which he admits: for, when this is the case, he must be guilty of an inconsistency who holds the one and rejects the other.
>
> Thus, the faculties of consciousness, of memory, of external sense, and of reason, are all equally the gifts of nature. No good reason can be assigned for receiving the testimony of one of them, which is not of equal force with regard to the others. The greatest sceptics admit the testimony of one of them, and allow that what it testifies is to be held as a first principle. If, therefore, they reject the immediate testimony of sense or of memory, they are guilty of an inconsistency." (Reid 1785, Essay 6, Chapter 4)

It is a striking argument, but the skeptic has a number of replies available.

On the one hand, the skeptic might heartily agree that consciousness (which for Reid amounts to introspective beliefs about one's mental life) is in the same boat as sense experience: We can devise Cartesian-style skeptical arguments that attack it, too. For instance, perhaps the Cartesian demon can make it seem that you have certain experiences, beliefs, desires, and so forth when you don't. If this is possible (an interesting topic in itself), then the skeptic will argue as follows: You don't know there isn't a demon deceiving you about these things, and therefore your introspective beliefs aren't knowledge.

On the other hand, the skeptic might reply that Descartes was right that skeptical possibilities must include stipulations about aspects of our mental lives—for example, that things at least seem certain ways to us—and these aspects therefore can't be targeted by skeptical possibility arguments. If so, then we have a good basis for treating consciousness differently than perception ("external sense") or memory, contrary to what Reid claims.[8]

Finally, as Reid acknowledges, he proposes consistency only as a basis for an ad hominem argument (i.e., only to point out irrationalities on the part of certain philosophers). If we tried to turn his remarks into a defense of the principles about sense perception, consciousness, memory, and so forth, by suggesting that they concern natural faculties and that natural faculties are all reliable, we would face a suite of difficult questions: What is naturalness? Can we know a priori what is natural? Even if we can know this a priori, what basis could we have a priori for thinking that naturalness conduces to reliability rather than unreliability?

The a priori strategy is by no means ruled out, but its proponents have much work to do.[9]

4.5 THE STRAIGHTFORWARD A POSTERIORI PROPOSAL

We next turn to the *straightforward a posteriori* strategy, which appeals to facts about what our experiences and apparent memories are like. This strategy attempts to do just what the skeptic thinks we must do: to argue, based on the character of how things seem from the inside, to the conclusion that we're not in the various skeptical scenarios. The main worry about this strategy is that this is just too meager a set of data from which to draw the desired conclusion.

How might the argument from our experiences and apparent memories to the conclusion that we're not BIVs go? There seems no way to deduce from the fact that you have certain experiences and apparent memories that you are not a BIV. To deduce is to draw a conclusion that *must* be true if the premises one uses in the deduction are true. But the truth of premises about your experience and apparent memory does not guarantee you are not a BIV, for BIVs, too, can enjoy the very same experiences and memories you have (this is how the BIV hypothesis is specified.) We might do better to appeal to *inference to the best explanation*.[10] Inference to the best explanation is a mode of inductive inference whereby one infers the truth of the best explanation of the data. The best explanation isn't strictly deducible from the data. There might well be rival explanations that are compatible with the data (but not with the best explanation). But still these rival explanations may well not explain the data as well. Indeed, when, in the Sherlock Holmes stories, Holmes "deduces" things, he doesn't use what philosophers call deduction; he uses inference to the best explanation. Of course, it's not only detectives who use this mode of argument. We use it when we try to figure out what's wrong with our cars or why the soup we cooked for dinner turned out so bland.[11] The claim we want to consider, then, is that your experience and apparent memories are better explained by the hypothesis that you have a body and interact perceptually and agentially with a real world in much the way you think we do (call this the *Real World Hypothesis* [RWH]) than by any skeptical hypothesis, and therefore that you can know the skeptical hypothesis to be false.

In Chapter 1 (Section 1.9), we considered a principle about inference to the best explanation.

(JEI) Justification by Explanatory Inference

If hypothesis H purports to explain S's evidence E, and there is no incompatible hypothesis H' that provides a better or equally good explanation of E, then S is justified in believing H on the basis of E.

Numerous questions arise concerning JEI. How should we understand "no incompatible hypothesis"? Should we take this to subsume all hypotheses, whether anyone has ever formulated them or not? If so, it could be difficult to know in many cases whether we are justified in believing H on the basis of E; perhaps there is some incompatible hypothesis out there that we haven't thought of that better explains E. If, instead, we take "no incompatible hypothesis" to subsume only those incompatible hypotheses we know about, only those available to us, we face a different problem. Couldn't H be the "best of a bad lot," as Bas Van Fraassen puts it (1989), so that it provides the best explanation compared with the available rival hypotheses, but still not a particularly good one, with the consequence that we aren't justified in believing H? Suppose there are ten possible suspects for a burglary. One of these ten had to do it, because they were the only ones with opportunity. We don't have any good explanation, for any of them, though, why they committed the burglary. There presumably is some excellent explanation out there, but it isn't available to us ready to hand. However, we do know that one of the ten suspects, Scott, once shoplifted. The proposition *Scott committed the burglary* therefore offers a slightly better but still weak explanation of burglary. Are we therefore justified in believing that poor Scott did it? That seems far too strong.

There are further difficulties. What if H is in fact the best explanation of E, but the subject S has no idea this is so? The best explanation for the observation of rainbows is one appealing to refraction and reflection of light within water molecules at a certain angle to the observer. But human beings haven't always been justified in believing this hypothesis! It took major developments in science to discover it. We could revise JEI by adding a qualification to the effect that the subject S know or justifiably believe that H better explains E than the competing hypotheses. But this is asking a lot, in the skeptical case. Must an ordinary person, to be justified in believing RWH, let alone ordinary propositions like *this is a tree*, know that these provide the best explanations of the evidence? Is an ordinary person even in a position to construct such explanations?

Aside from these reservations, we have to ask whether RWH is a better explanation than any of the competing hypotheses, including skeptical hypotheses. If we could help ourselves to our accumulated scientific knowledge, the answer would be easy. But to do this is to beg the question against the skeptic; it is to appeal to knowledge that the skeptic calls into question. What makes the straightforward a posteriori approach straightforward is that it plays fair with the skeptic and thus disallows such question-begging argumentation. Suppose, though, we limit ourselves to the character of our experiences and apparent memories and whatever else we know a priori. Within these constraints, does RWH provide a better explanation of our experiences and memories than skeptical hypotheses? Many philosophers, going back at least to John Locke, have argued in the affirmative.[12] Reid, too, although he says that first principles are beyond evidence, speaks of memory and "external sense" as confirming one another. Here are some of the regularities these philosophers cite:

- Regularities within any sense-experience modality (e.g., if you seem to see someone pick up a rock and make a throwing motion, you can expect to seem to see it flying through the air toward the window)

- The cross-modal regularities of sense-experiences (e.g., if you seem to see a rock heading in the direction of glass, you can expect to seem to hear a sound of the glass breaking)
- Regularities in the connection between decision, effort, and sense-experience (e.g., if you decide to throw the rock, you can expect to feel as if your muscles contract and then release with the rock seeming to leave your hand, and then as an apparent result to seem to see it flying through the air, hear it strike the window, etc.)
- Regularities between apparent memories, effort, and current experience (e.g., if you have an apparent memory of having placed your keys on the mantel, you can expect that, upon seeming to walk over to the mantel and seeming to look at it, you will seem to see keys on it)

Such regularities seem well explained by RWH. This is because they seem to be just what we would expect if there were real objects we perceived and which had at least roughly the character we believed them to have. By contrast, consider the hypothesis that your experiences and memories are simply "random" (i.e., that they have no explanation at all). How likely would it be that they take this coherent form?

But this "random" hypothesis is not the skeptic's; the skeptic appeals to lifelong dreams, evil geniuses, and super-neuroscientists. We can distinguish versions of skeptical hypotheses, weaker and stronger versions. Strong versions build into the hypothesis assumptions about the character of your experience and memories. The weakest versions don't. An example of a strong version is the hypothesis that you are a BIV with these very experiences and memories. An example of a weaker version is that you are a BIV stimulated by a neuroscientist of some sort or other. Where not otherwise noted, in this book we have in mind strong versions of skeptical hypotheses.

With this strong/weak distinction in mind, let's ask: Could we make sense of the coherence of your experiences and memories assuming stronger or weaker variants of the BIV possibility? Start with the weak hypothesis that you are simply a BIV. Being a BIV seems compatible with just about any run of experience, coherent or incoherent. Why think your experiences would be coherent if you were simply a BIV? Suppose we strengthen the hypothesis by adding to it that the scientists give you orderly experiences of a kind that make it seem that you perceive tables, trees, people, and so forth. Still, there are many sorts of coherent regularities involving tables, trees, and people that a priori possible. Why does your experience exhibit these particular coherent regularities rather than others? Suppose we strengthen the hypothesis further so that it builds in that you have the very experiences and memories you have. Then we have no difficulty seeing that if that hypothesis were true, your experiences and memories would exhibit the sorts of regularities they do. The hypothesis clearly predicts the regularities. But are they explained by the hypothesis? It seems they aren't.

The skeptic can point out that the evil neuroscientists themselves have plans and execute these plans. Could this provide the materials for an equally good explanation of the particular sorts of coherence exhibited in our experience and memory? The skeptic's general strategy might be to create a mapping between the supposed real-world objects and a realm of "substitute" entities that preserves properties and relations (Vogel 2005), or to use a term from mathematics to create an *isomorphism*. Thus, just as there are rocks and windows, with their particular properties and modes of interaction, the skeptic would posit as part of her hypothesis ideas in the mind of the deceiver with corresponding properties and relations; or perhaps instead of ideas she might choose files in a supercomputer, or what have you. The idea is to piggyback off the RWH but in a way that would make our experiences and memories very much inaccurate.

Is the RWH better than such a complex skeptical hypothesis? You might think the latter is ad hoc, complicated, forced, and so forth, and so a worse explanation. But supposing all this is true, are such factors epistemically relevant? Do they make the hypothesis less credible for us? Or are these features of explanation merely ones we find pragmatically useful—we can work better with theories with these "virtues," we can better understand them, and so forth?

The explanationist response to skepticism is by no means hopeless, but it is fair to say that making the case that the response succeeds is not a straightforward matter. And we need more than just a reason to think the evidence tips in favor of RWH over skeptical hypotheses. We are looking for a reason good enough to provide us with knowledge of the external world, and it is not clear that the explanationist response gives us this.

4.6 THE BOLD A POSTERIORI PROPOSAL

Finally, consider the bold a posteriori proposal. On this view, you can use information about the world gained through present and past sensory experience to know skeptical hypotheses are false. Here is one way the argument that we're not BIVs might go:

1. I have hands.
2. So, I'm not a (handless) brain in a vat.

(You might find this reasoning humorous: Is it a joke? It's interesting to ask why it seems humorous.) Can I know (2) through this reasoning from (1)? This example borrows from early-twentieth-century philosopher G. E. Moore's famous "proof of an external world." In his 1939 lecture to the British Academy, Moore told the audience:

> It seems to me that, so far from its being true, as Kant declares to be his opinion, that there is only one possible proof of the existence of things outside of us, namely the one which he has given, I can now give a large number of different proofs, each of which is a perfectly rigorous proof. I can prove now, for instance, that two human hands exist. How? By holding up my two hands, and saying, as I make a certain gesture with the right hand, "Here is one hand," and adding, as I make a certain gesture with the left, "and here is another." (1959, 145–146)

Moore addressed his proof to idealists—that is, philosophers who think there are nothing but minds and ideas (and so no physical mind-independent world). It would take us too far afoot to discuss its merits against idealists. But his argument, his "proof," inspires the reasoning (1)–(2) above.

Such Moorean reasoning (reasoning via Moore-style proofs) clearly begs the question if given in response to the skeptic. The skeptic argues that you don't know (1) because you don't know (2). If, following Moore, you respond by arguing from (1) to (2), you'll be using a premise the skeptic has just claimed you can't know unless you already know (2)! In arguing from (1) to (2), you're simply ignoring his arguments, not engaging with them. To the extent that someone found the skeptic's arguments compelling, that person could not be convinced out of them by your reasoning. Your reasoning from (1) to (2) is thus dialectically useless.

However, think about arguing against a determined flat-earther. The flat-earther claims the earth is flat and explains to you how there is a massive conspiracy afoot that extends to satellite photography. Suppose you reply to him by citing satellite photography, without explaining how it is that this photography in fact isn't a hoax. You simply appeal to the photography. Clearly you beg the question against this flat-earther. To the extent that someone found the flat-earther's arguments compelling, that person couldn't be convinced by your merely appealing to the satellite photography. Still, such photography can help a person come to know the earth isn't flat.[13] Might it be similar with Moorean reasoning? When we discussed closure in Section 4.2.1, we put aside questions about whether deductions that beg the question can be ways of expanding our knowledge. We wanted closure to be neutral on that matter. Here we return to those questions. Might Moorean reasoning, despite its question-begging character, still be a way of giving us knowledge that we're not in skeptical scenarios? It might be speculated that the historical Moore had something like this in mind. He surely knew his "proof" wouldn't satisfy idealists, because it begged the question, but perhaps he thought it was a perfectly good proof nevertheless, one through which a person could know that idealism is false.

So, in evaluating the Moorean reply to the skeptic (i.e., the bold a posteriori reply), we must distinguish dialectical issues from epistemic ones.[14] The key question is whether Moorean reasoning could give us knowledge that we are not in skeptical scenarios, or whether, instead, we'd have to already know we're not in skeptical scenarios in order to know the premises of that reasoning. If one already has to know or be in a position to know the truth of the conclusion of a piece of Moorean reasoning like (1)–(2), then such reasoning couldn't enable us to know we're not in a skeptical scenario.

Let's try to get clearer on just how the Moorean reasoning is supposed to give us knowledge we're not in skeptical scenarios. The Moorean claims that reasoning from (1) to (2) is a way of coming to know that one isn't a BIV. So far, so good. But how is it that the reasoning is supposed to pull off this feat? Let's ask the Moorean: Does the fact that one has the experience of having hands by itself provide sufficient grounds for knowing the conclusion that one isn't a BIV, without going through the Moorean reasoning? If the Moorean answers "yes," it seems the Moorean is sliding back to the straightforward a posteriori proposal. We would have to explain how it is that facts about experience could provide strong reasons to think skeptical hypotheses are false. The Moorean proposal is supposed to be distinct from this. It is supposed to be bold in a way that the straightforward proposal isn't. So, the Moorean's answer should instead be: No, the experience by itself isn't strong evidence that one isn't a BIV, but nonetheless if one begins with the experience and goes through Moorean reasoning, one gains and relies on strong evidence that one isn't a BIV and so comes to know that one isn't a BIV.

So, the truly novel idea in the Moorean proposal is that what the experience can't do by itself can be done when one goes through the Moorean reasoning. You might ask: How does this work? How, by going through the Moorean reasoning, does one gain more evidence for believing one isn't a BIV—more empirical evidence, not a priori evidence (for recall this is the bold a posteriori proposal)?

This might seem like magic. It might seem too easy a way of acquiring knowledge that one isn't a BIV if one didn't have it before. It's as if one begins with weak evidence (the experience) and somehow bootstraps one's way up to strong evidence simply by reasoning, without any further information coming in.

Here is one way the Moorean might attempt to explain the power of Moorean reasoning. Your experience by itself is sufficient to give you justification that you have hands and, when all goes right (you do have hands, you're not in a Gettier case), knowledge that you have hands. You don't need already to know that you aren't in a skeptical scenario. Then, once you have the knowledge that you have hands, you have a new reason, beyond the mere experience, to believe that you are not a BIV. This new reason is that you have hands. This is very strong support indeed for the conclusion that you are not a BIV. That you have hands entails that you aren't a BIV, whereas that you have an experience doesn't.

What the Moorean might suggest, then, is a two-part proposal. First, experience gives us grounds for knowledge of ordinary propositions about the world, regardless of whether we are already justified or know that we are not in skeptical scenarios. Second, once we do have this knowledge, we have evidence that we know entails that we are not BIVs. We can then deduce and come to know—if we didn't already know it—that we are not BIVs. In Chapter 6, we will examine in detail whether this two-part proposal is too good to be true.

So, we have reached some tentative conclusions about what the bold a posteriori proposal must look like and what problems it faces. We have found that if it is to distinguish itself from the straightforward a posteriori proposal, it must attribute some epistemic power to Moorean reasoning: Experience alone isn't a sufficient basis for knowing one isn't a BIV, but the Moorean reasoning somehow gives one a sufficient basis. The key question about it is how Moorean reasoning could have this epistemic power.

4.7 CONCLUSION

We have examined a number of traditional responses to skepticism and found none clearly correct. This does not mean we ought to be skeptics. As the historical Moore is also famous for remarking, it would not be rational to be as confident of the premises of any skeptical argument as we are that we know a lot about the world around us. In response to a skeptical argument of Bertrand Russell's based on four assumptions, Moore writes:

> I cannot help answering: It seems to me *more* certain that I *do* know that this is a pencil . . . than that any single one of these four assumptions is true, let alone all four . . . Nay, more: I do not think it is *rational* to be as certain of any one of these four propositions, as of the proposition that I do know that this is a pencil. (Moore 1959, 226)

Moore is exactly right here, in the view of this author. We should not give up our belief in our knowledge of the external world in the face of skeptical arguments. Similarly, when we read about the liar paradox or Zeno's paradoxes of motion, the right reaction to take when we can't see exactly what goes wrong is not to stop believing in truth or motion; rather, it is to hold on to those beliefs and think there must be something wrong in the arguments. For example, consider the following argument from Zeno:

> For any two places, A and B, which are not right next to one another, to move from A to B, a thing must first go halfway from A to B. But to go halfway from A to B, one must first go halfway from A to the halfway point between A and B—that is, one must go a quarter of the way from A to B. Similarly, to go a quarter of the way from A to B, one must go an eighth of the way. This series is infinite. Each distance corresponding to an element in the series takes some finite amount of time to cover in one's motion. An infinite sum of finite amounts of time is itself an infinite amount of time. Thus, in order to move from any place A to another separated place B, it takes an infinite amount of time!

It takes the concepts of calculus to see where and why precisely it goes wrong. If you aren't a calculus pro, still you shouldn't be taken in by the argument. You *know* there is motion. The rational thing to conclude, even if you don't know where the argument goes wrong, is that it does go wrong somewhere. This is exactly what Moore thinks we should think in response to skeptical arguments like the ones we have considered in this chapter.

Of course, such a response is not all that we want. We want to know what goes wrong in the skeptical arguments and more important how and why it goes wrong. In this chapter, we focused on attempts to explain why Premise 1 of the skeptical possibility arguments goes wrong. (Recall that Premise 1 is the step that denies that we know that the skeptical possibility fails to obtain.) We discussed in some detail three strategies for explaining how we know we're not in skeptical scenarios: the a priori strategy, the straightforward a posteriori strategy, and the bold a posteriori strategy. But, speaking for myself, I can say that, like Moore, I am much more confident, and I think rationally so, that I do know about the external world than I am that any particular one of these strategies succeeds. (Easy to say, you might think! But consider your own case. What would *you* say?)

This chapter has discussed the problem of skepticism about knowledge from a traditional perspective. It has not brought to bear any of the innovations of recent years. In the next chapter, we will discuss the antiskeptical potential of one such innovation, viz. contextualism about "knows."

QUESTIONS

1. Play the part of the skeptic. What would you, as skeptic, say in response to the following argument that you know you are not dreaming?

   > Dreams typically are disjointed and don't make use of memories of events the day before. Waking life is typically not like this. So, it's very likely that right now, I'm not dreaming, because my experience right now is coherent and I'm recalling events the day before. Maybe I can't be absolutely certain on this basis that I'm not dreaming, but I can be very justified—enough to know I'm not dreaming.

2. Nozick argues that if our world is normal, then we know we have hands but don't know we're not BIVs. This is because the BIV world is so very far removed from actuality. But some skeptical hypotheses aren't so far removed, it would seem. Consider the possibility that you're having a very realistic dream right now that you're reading a book. Is this at all "abnormal"? If it isn't abnormal, does Nozick have to concede that you don't know you're reading a book unless you know you're not merely having a realistic dream that you're reading a book? Or is there a way Nozick could apply his general strategy to the dreaming possibility as he does to the BIV one? If so, explain how he might do this.

3. Is it inconsistent, as Thomas Reid claimed, to think introspection delivers us knowledge of our minds while thinking that skeptical arguments show that perception cannot deliver us knowledge of the world outside our minds? Try to devise a skeptical possibility argument against introspection. Can you do it?

4. In his "Proof of an External World," Moore (1959, 146) gives three conditions he takes to be individually necessary and jointly sufficient for a proof: (i) the conclusion must be different from the premises; (ii) the conclusion must follow from the premises; and (iii) the premises must be known to be true. Do you think these conditions are indeed individually necessary for a proof? Do you think they are jointly sufficient? Explain.

5. Moore claimed that his "proof of an external world," which you recall took the form of holding up his hands and arguing "here is one hand, and here is another, therefore there are external objects" is exactly analogous to a perfectly good proof that there are three misprints in a manuscript that one might offer by pointing to each of the three and remarking "here is a misprint, here's another, and here's a third" (Moore 1959, 147). Citing the three misprints settles the

question of whether there are any misprints in the manuscript; it proves that there are some. Does the proof of an external world, by the same measure, prove that there are external objects? Why or why not? What is the relevant difference between the two "proofs" if there is any?

6. One might argue that it doesn't matter to you whether you're a BIV; all that counts is your psychological state (i.e., your experiences, feelings, and apparent memories). That's what makes life worth living. Since, by stipulation, you're in the same psychological state if you're a BIV, who cares? Consider the following response. You *do* care about things other than your psychological state; you care about having real friends, not just "virtual" ones. You care about being in good physical shape, not just "seeming" to be in good physical shape from the inside. And so on. If the Real World Hypothesis is true, you're achieving some things you care about that you wouldn't be achieving if the BIV hypothesis were true. Thus, it does matter whether you're a BIV. Do you agree with this response? Why or why not?

7. For the sake of argument, assume that it does matter whether you're a BIV. It's better not to be a BIV than a BIV, other things equal at least. Even still, does it matter whether you *know* you're not a BIV? Try to give the best case you can for answering yes, and then try the same for answering no. Which is the better case? Why?

8. We focused in this chapter on skeptical possibility arguments for skepticism. There is another sort of skeptical argument called an "underdetermination" argument. The argument goes like this. We do not know that the Real World Hypothesis (RWH) is true unless we have evidence that favors it over its rivals, such as the BIV hypothesis. But our evidence does not favor RWH over BIV. Our evidence "underdetermines" which of these two hypotheses is correct. Therefore, we do not know the RWH hypothesis is true. Where is the weakest point in this argument?

FURTHER READING

Blumenfeld, David, and Jean Beer Blumenfeld (1978). "Can I Know I Am Not Dreaming?" In Michael Hooker (ed.), *Descartes: Critical and Interpretive Essays*. Baltimore: Johns Hopkins University Press.

Descartes, René [1641] (1996). *Meditations on First Philosophy*. In J. Cottingham and B. Williams, eds., *Meditations on First Philosophy and Selections from the Objections and Replies*. Cambridge: Cambridge University Press.

Logue, Heather (2011). "The Skeptic and the Naïve Realist." *Philosophical Issues* 21(1): 268–288.

Moore, G. E. (1959). *Philosophical Papers*. London: George Allen and Unwin. This volume includes the key epistemological papers by Moore: "Proof of an External World," pp. 127–150; "Four Forms of Skepticism," pp. 196–225; and "Certainty," pp. 226–251. Key excerpts are reprinted in Kim, Sosa, Fantl, and McGrath (eds.), *Epistemology: An Anthology*. Oxford: Blackwell.

Nozick, Robert (1981). *Philosophical Explanations*. Cambridge, MA: Harvard University Press.

Reid, Thomas [1785] (1983). *Essays on the Intellectual Powers of Man*. In R. E. Beanblossom and K. Lehrer, *Reid: Inquiry and Essays*. Indianapolis: Hackett Publishing.

Stroud, Barry (1984). *The Significance of Philosophical Skepticism*. Oxford: Oxford University Press.

NOTES

1. It's important to recognize that skepticism about knowledge concerning some domain is not the same as the denial of the existence of that domain. To be a skeptic about our knowledge of other minds is to think that we cannot know that there are minds other than our own. This is consistent with not denying their existence.

2. This is the point of the cogito, his famous "I think, therefore I am." Even if you are in a skeptical scenario, and so you are being deceived about many matters, you are still thinking and indeed you *are* (i.e., you *exist*). Thus, Descartes thinks he finds his Archimedean point, one from which he can "move the earth" and build his foundation for firm knowledge.

3. To admit that you don't know you aren't a BIV while insisting that you do know you have hands, feet, and a body is to affirm what Keith DeRose calls the "abominable conjunction" (1995, 27–29): "Yes, I know that I have hands, feet, and body; but no, I don't know that I'm not a brain in a vat." This isn't merely an odd thing to say; it seems absurd.

4. A priori knowledge, going back at least to Kant, is traditionally defined negatively as knowledge that is "independent" of experience.

   You may naturally ask, "What is meant by 'independent' and what is meant by 'experience'?" "Independent" should be understood to concern epistemic independence, not causal independence. Perhaps you couldn't know this proposition (call it T)—if one thing x is taller than another y, then y isn't taller than x—without having had some experiences to give you concept of *taller than*. So, your knowledge that T is true isn't causally independent of experience. But the source of your knowledge—the epistemic basis—is not experience. Given that you have the experience necessary to think about whether T is true, it isn't experience that helps make this knowledge.

   How broadly we understand "experience" is to some extent a matter of choice. Do you know a priori that you're thinking right now? If we understand "experience" to include introspection of thoughts, then *yes*. If we understand it to refer exclusively to perceptual experience, then we might conclude that it is a priori (assuming that we don't literally perceive our thoughts). Here we understand "experience" to include not only perceptual experience but also introspection.

   For a more thorough introduction to the a priori/a posteriori distinction, see Bruce Russell (2013).

5. The justification is prima facie only. It can be defeated if you acquire special evidence that your senses, in a particular situation, or perhaps even in general, are unreliable. See Chapter 1 (Section 1.8).

6. There is debate among interpreters of Reid just how his first principles are to be understood. William Alston (1985) and Keith Lehrer (1989) maintain that they are general truths, and we, too, adopt this interpretation. However, Van Cleve (1999) argues that they are rather principles of evidence. To give an example, Van Cleve understands the case concerning memory as follows: If you distinctly remember that p, then it is a first principle for you that p. As Van Cleve puts it, his interpretation posits indefinitely many first principles of memory, one for each of the testimonies of memory. He then understands "It is a first principle for you that p" as meaning that you are immediately justified in believing that p (in the

sense of "immediately justified" discussed in Chapter 2 [Section 2.1]). If Van Cleve's interpretation is correct, Reidian first principles do not provide an a priori way to know that skeptical hypotheses are false. I thank Marina Folescu and Patrick Rysiew for advice on the interpretation of Reid.

7. Saul Kripke (1980) argued that contingent a priori knowledge is possible, indeed actual. He claimed that we have a priori knowledge of such matters as "the standard meter bar in Paris is one meter long." The thought is that the definite description "the length of the standard meter bar in Paris" fixes the reference of "one meter." But is this a case of a priori knowledge of a contingent truth? Or is the most we can say this: Merely by knowing what you mean, you can know that the sentence above expresses something true? But knowledge of what you mean seems to depend on introspection of your intentions and so not to be a priori. See note 4.

8. Can the skeptic give a similar response for reason? Can she say that we have a good basis for treating reason differently than perception?

9. See Chapter 11 (Section 11.4.2) for a ray of hope for the a priori approach. The ray of hope is not of the sort Reid had in mind, however, but rather one concerning probability. Essentially, the thought is that building so much about one's actual experiences and memories into the skeptical hypothesis reduces its prior probability severely. This prior probability, a probability not grounded in empirical information, is an a priori probability.

10. The discussion to follow overlaps with Chapter 1 (Section 1.9).

11. For more on how exactly to spell out what inference to the best explanation amounts to, see Peter Lipton (2004).

12. Their ranks include Bertrand Russell, C. D. Broad, and A. J. Ayer, as well as the contemporary philosophers Laurence Bonjour and Jonathan Vogel. The eighteenth-century philosopher George Berkeley famously appealed to something like inference to the best explanation in favor of an idealist version of RWH.

13. In fact, for a naïve flat-earther, one simply going on how things look from Earth or from the fact that we don't "fall off" Earth, satellite photography is a way to learn the earth is round.

14. Relatedly, we should distinguish questions about whether one could resolve one's doubts by going through a piece of reasoning from the epistemic question of whether the reasoning could be a way of coming to expand one's knowledge if one lacked the relevant doubts. In some cases, one cannot resolve one's doubts with a piece of reasoning even though that piece of reasoning if you lacked those doubts could give you knowledge. Suppose I doubt whether there were 250 years of relative peace during the Ming Dynasty. However, my reasons for doubt are not the usual ones. I doubt this, suppose, because I, quite irrationally, doubt current historical methods are at all reliable. I cannot then resolve this doubt by reasoning in accord with an argument appealing to premises justified by those very historical methods. However, this isn't to say that someone reading a book on the Ming Dynasty couldn't expand his or her knowledge by reasoning from those very premises to the conclusion that there were 250 years of relative peace during the Ming Dynasty. An argument's being incapable of resolving one's doubts about the conclusion seems to be an intrapersonal counterpart of an argument's begging the question against an opponent. See Pryor (2004), Section 5, for a clear and detailed account of these matters.

PART II

Justification and Knowledge: Special Topics

Contextualism, Pragmatic Encroachment, and the Knowledge Norm of Assertion

Matthew McGrath

One of the notable recent developments in epistemology is the increased attention to the workings of the language we use to talk about epistemic matters. Fueling this increased attention is a suspicion that some of the traditional problems in the study of knowledge arise because we fail to appreciate how "know" and related words work. Maybe it isn't as simple as "knows" means knowledge. So-called *contextualists* claim that what you say when you say a person "knows" varies with the context in which you say it. Contextualists often claim that the problem of skepticism about knowledge, in particular, arises because we neglect this context-variability.

However, this chapter isn't solely about the use and semantics of "know." As we'll see, in the course of examining the semantics of "know," new questions arise about knowledge itself and its relationship to phenomena not traditionally thought to fall under the purview of epistemology, including in particular *action* and *assertion*. The second and third parts of the chapter consider, respectively, the relation between knowledge and action and between knowledge and assertion. In these sections, we consider how knowledge–action and knowledge–assertion relationships lend support to the surprising thesis of *pragmatic encroachment*, which holds that differences in pragmatic factors (e.g., practical stakes) can make a difference to whether a person knows.

5.1 CONTEXTUALISM

Context-sensitivity is a familiar phenomenon. Take the first-person pronoun "I." This word has no reference independently of its use on a particular occasion. In one *context of speech* it refers to Matthew McGrath, whereas in another it refers to Alvin Goldman. Given a context of speech, "I" refers to the speaker of that context. "I" is therefore context-sensitive: Its reference varies across contexts of speech. The same goes for "you," "we," "now," "last week," "here," "nearby," and other indexicals.

The contextualist maintains that "knows" is similarly context-sensitive. Thus, we have the thesis of contextualism:

> "Knows" varies in its sense across contexts of speech in such a way that "S knows P" can have one sense in one context of use and another in another context.

If these senses of "know" vary by demandingness, so that there are stronger and weaker senses, then we can see how "S knows P" could be true uttered in one context (a lax context in which a weak sense is expressed) and false uttered in another context (a demanding context in which a strong sense is expressed). This shiftiness in "knows" plays tricks on us if we don't recognize it. We might find ourselves faced with unsoluble problems. We do best not to try, futilely, to solve these problems but rather to diagnose them by showing how they arise from our ignoring the shiftiness of "know."

Might the skeptic's arguments somehow be playing tricks with the word "know"? Does the skeptic somehow pressure us to use "know" in a strong sense rather than in the ordinary weak sense? When you concede, "OK, I guess I don't know I'm not a brain in a vat," are you giving in to the skeptic's pressure to use "know" in this way, even if you don't realize it?

Compare "empty." If I say that the refrigerator is empty, when it only has ketchup and baking soda in it, usually all will agree, "Yes, it's empty." However, if someone really wanted to be a pest, he or she could say, "If something is empty, it doesn't have *anything* in it, and ketchup is *something*, isn't it? So the refrigerator really isn't empty." Here the emptiness-skeptic (if you will) is pressuring you to use "empty" in a strict sense. But it's hardly some great victory; it's just playing on the shiftiness of "empty" (i.e., its context-sensitivity). Is the skeptic about knowledge doing something similar?

Let's see how the contextualist diagnosis of skepticism works. Suppose the skeptic gives the Dreaming Argument: "You don't know you're not dreaming; if you don't know you're not dreaming, you don't know anything about the external world; and so you don't know anything about the external world." Where does this argument go wrong, according to the contextualist? The answer is surprising: It *doesn't* go wrong. When the skeptic gives the argument, its premises are true and its conclusion follows from its premises. So it is a sound argument . . . *when* it is given![1] What goes wrong is the lesson we draw from it. We assume that if the argument is sound when given by the skeptic then it is always sound, and thus its conclusion is always true (i.e., true in every context of speech), so that whenever people say they "know" things about the external world they are wrong. But this is an overgeneralization: Just because the argument is sound when the skeptic gives it doesn't mean it is always sound and so doesn't mean its conclusion is always true.

To better appreciate the overgeneralization, compare the following argument, for "flat" this time rather than "empty":

1. All tabletops have some bumps on them.
2. If something has some bumps on it, it isn't flat.
3. So, no tabletops are flat.

When someone asserts (1) and (2), a strong sense of "flat" is used. (1) and (2) do entail (3). So, when someone asserts (1) and (2), (3) will be true. This doesn't mean it is always true. In ordinary contexts, we use a weak sense of "flat," one on which not both of (1) and (2) are true. If all this is right, then it would be an overgeneralization to conclude that because this argument, when given, is sound, (3) is *always true*. The same sort of thing is going on, says the contextualist, in the case of skepticism.

Let's consider the analogue in the case of knowledge. Suppose after I taste the broccoli I boiled, I say, "I know, I overcooked the broccoli." This is an ordinary, low-standards context. Later the skeptic presses me, asking, "Do you know you're not dreaming? If you were dreaming, there wouldn't be actually tasting broccoli at all, but it would seem just like you were tasting broccoli." Suppose I concede, "No, I guess I don't know I'm not dreaming all this." The skeptic then says, "So, you didn't know you overcooked the broccoli." I concede: "I guess that's right." The skeptic follows up: "So you were wrong before when you said that you knew you overcooked the broccoli." It's tempting for me to concede, "It appears so." But it's in this final remark that I overgeneralize. The contextualist might put it this way:

You were right when you said in the ordinary context, "I know I overcooked the broccoli." And the skeptic is right when *she* says in her later context of speech, "You didn't know you overcooked the broccoli." Those might *seem* incompatible, but there is no conflict because what the skeptic is denying is not the same as what you are asserting. When you said "I know I overcooked the broccoli," all that you were saying is that—roughly—you were in at least a *fairly good* epistemic state; and that's true. What the skeptic says when she says, "You didn't know you overcooked the broccoli" is that you weren't in an *extremely good* epistemic state. Both are true. Thus, when you concede "it appears so" at the end, you overgeneralize. You assume that "knows that . . ." doesn't change in its sense across contexts, but it does. If it didn't change, your generalization would be correct. But it does, and so your generalization isn't correct.

You can see why this might be called a *diagnosis* of skepticism rather than a *solution* to the skeptical problem. It doesn't solve the skeptical problem by showing where the skeptic's argument goes wrong. For the contextualist, the argument doesn't go wrong. *We* go wrong in assuming that if it works when it is given, it always works! The skeptical "problem" arises simply because language bewitches us, to put it in Wittgenstein's way.

A couple of clarifications are in order about contextualism. First, to say that the sense of "knows that . . ." varies with the context of speech is not to say that knowledge itself varies with the context of speech. Although "know" has a different sense in a conversation about skepticism than it does in a normal conversation around the office, this doesn't mean that you go from knowing to not knowing as you go from context to context (although we will consider a view that does hold something like this claim below). Nor does it mean—even more strangely—that whether *you* know can be affected by how other people in other contexts of speech use the word "know." Compare "flat." Whether a particular stretch of ground is flat is just a matter of what it's like in and of itself, not a matter of what people say in different contexts. Of course, what you say in using the world "flat" will vary with context; but holding the context fixed, whether "flat" applies to something depends only on what that thing is like in and of itself. The contextualist says the same about "knows." What you say in using "know" varies with the context in which you say it, but holding fixed the context in which you use "know," whether "know" applies to a person depends only on that person's situation (her evidence, justification, and the like) and not on other people who might be talking about her.

Second, to say that the sense of "knows that . . ." varies with context isn't to say that "knows" is lexically ambiguous in the way that "bank" is (financial institution vs. river bank) or "pen" is (pig pen vs. fountain pen).[2] If you translate lexically ambiguous words into another language, you'll usually find that the other language contains two words spelled and pronounced differently that express the two senses. This is true for "bank" but not for "know," "empty," and "flat." There is a core meaning of "knows," according to the contextualist, that determines how its sense varies across contexts. The same goes for indexicals like "I," "now," and "here." Who gets referred to by "I" varies with the context (varies with who is speaking), and similarly for "now" and "here." There is a common core meaning, though, that determines different referents or senses depending on features of the context in which it is used.[3]

So far, we have considered only the general scheme for giving a contextualist diagnosis of skepticism. To put a bit more flesh on these bones, we'll consider two ways of implementing the contextualist story. What exactly shifts from context to context, and why does it shift when the skeptic presents her argument? We'll discuss two possible implementations, the *relevant alternatives* approach and the *epistemic standards* approach.

5.1.1 The Relevant Alternatives Implementation

Recall the relevant alternatives approach to defining knowledge, considered in Chapter 3. To know P, you must have evidence that rules out all relevant alternatives to P. Irrelevant alternatives to P don't need to be ruled out. In the land of fake barns, in order to know from the road that what you see is a barn you have to rule out the alternative *I'm looking at a fake barn*. But in ordinary farmland, this alternative is irrelevant and so doesn't need to be ruled out.

This approach might seem custom-made to handle skepticism. Couldn't we say that alternatives such as *I'm a brain in a vat* (BIV) are irrelevant and so don't have to be ruled out in order to know propositions such as *I have hands?* This would be a noncontextualist relevant alternatives theory. However, it wouldn't by itself do much to explain the apparent power of skeptical arguments. It would purport to show us where the arguments go wrong: They treat certain irrelevant alternatives as relevant. However, we want an explanation of why we are taken in by them, why we feel pressure from them to concede ignorance.

Perhaps if we combine the relevant alternatives approach with contextualism, thereby allowing the same alternatives to count as sometimes relevant and sometimes irrelevant *depending on the context of speech,* we will have the makings of a promising diagnosis of skepticism. (For an example of such an account, see Lewis 1996.)

We'll give an illustration, using a case from ordinary life that has the flavor of mild skepticism. Suppose I say in an ordinary context, "I know the car is parked in Lot A." In a normal context in which I say this (in a conversation I'm having with my spouse as we deplane), this statement is true if I can rule out possibilities such as that it is parked in Lot B or Lot C, or that we actually didn't drive to the airport but took the airport shuttle from our house. Suppose I can rule those alternatives out, so my statement "I know the car is in Lot A" is true. However, in a context in which someone argues, "You don't know your car hasn't been stolen and driven away, and so you don't know it is parked in Lot A, do you?" other alternatives become relevant, ones that were irrelevant in the normal context, and ones that I can't rule out, such as the possibility explicitly mentioned, namely that my car isn't in Lot A because it was stolen and driven away.

The general scheme for the account is this:

Relevant Alternatives Implementation

A claim "S knows P" is true in a context of speech C if and only if S's evidence rules out all alternatives to P that C determines as relevant.

Different contexts determine different alternatives as relevant, and so whether a knowledge attribution[4] is true varies from context to context. We can think of the senses of "knows that . . ." as taking this form: *has evidence that rules out class X of alternatives.* The X's differ from context to context, sometimes including more alternatives, sometimes fewer, sometimes overlapping.

How does the skeptic make far-fetched alternatives like the BIV scenario relevant? She doesn't give us evidence that these scenarios obtain. What she does is get us to consider them, to stop ignoring them as we usually do. There is a parallel here for "empty" and "flat." We normally ignore microscopic particles or bumps in saying things are empty or flat. But the scientist or the skeptic can make us attend to them by bringing them to the fore, and then we can't ignore them.

We can't ignore them once they're pointed out, fine: But why does this make them relevant? One popular explanation is that "empty," "flat," and "knows" are absolute terms (Unger 1975). If something is empty, it has *nothing* in it; if something is flat, it has *no* bumps; and similarly, if you know something, you can rule out *all* alternatives to it. But what counts as "all" depends on what we're considering and what we're ignoring. If I say, "Everyone is here today" at the beginning of a class, the students might well agree. But obviously President Obama wouldn't be there, nor the Pope. My use of "everyone" ranges only over the class of people I'm considering, not those I'm ignoring. But suppose a clever student says, "Obama is someone and he's not here today." I can't say in reply, "No, everyone is here today, even though Obama is someone who is not here today." Rather, I have to say something like, "Well, everyone enrolled in the class is here today."

5.1.2 The Standards Implementation

One notable feature (some would say *bug*) of the relevant alternatives implementation is that, in a certain context, it might be true to say that a person knows P but doesn't know Q, where the person's epistemic situation seems to be as good for Q as it is for P—that is, the person is just as justified in believing Q, just as reliable in that belief, and so forth as she is in believing P. This can seem odd.

Consider the car theft example again. If my skeptically minded spouse starts raising possibilities about the car being stolen from Lot A and driven away, it will be false in that context for me to say that I "know" that the car is in Lot A. In that context, my spouse isn't raising any questions about whether my bike at home is still in my garage or is instead stolen. She hasn't called attention to *that* possibility. So that possibility would seem to be irrelevant with respect to whether I can be said to "know" that my bike is still there. So, in our context of speech, it looks like—on the relevant alternatives implementation—the statement "I know my bike is in my garage" is true, even though the statement "I know my car is in Lot A" is false. This seems counterintuitive because my epistemic situation with respect to my bike being in the garage is no better than my epistemic situation with respect to my car being in the lot where I parked it.

The reason for this feature (or bug) is that all that matters for a knowledge-attribution to be true on a relevant alternatives approach is that the subject has evidence to rule out a certain set of alternatives. It really doesn't matter how *big* that set is, it matters only whether the subject's evidence rules out all the members of the set. So, it can happen that I can rule out exactly the same size set of alternatives to *my car is in Lot A* as I can to *my bike is in my garage*, but because my wife has mentioned the car theft possibility (and not the bike theft possibility) I don't "know" the former, though I still "know" the latter. The relevant alternatives implementation doesn't set up a *standard* of goodness of epistemic position and declare that a subject can't know anything unless the subject meets that standard for the proposition. If we want an implementation of contextualism that does that, we need to look elsewhere.

In particular, we might look to:

Standards Implementation
An attribution "S knows P" is true in a context of speech C if and only if S's belief in P satisfies the epistemic standard determined by C.

An epistemic standard might demand a certain degree of justification, degree of reliability, and so forth, and if and only if a person's belief— regardless of the proposition believed—clears all those hurdles, it is counted as "knowledge." All beliefs are held to this same standard.

Returning to the example of my conversation with my wife about the car, the idea would be that my wife's mentioning the possibility that someone has stolen our car raises the standards that *any* belief must meet if we are to describe it correctly as "knowledge." So, the sentence "I know my bike is in the garage" wouldn't be true in this context.[5]

Whether the contextualist diagnosis of skepticism succeeds is a matter of continuing debate. You can explore some objections to it in the questions section at the end of the chapter (see especially Question 2).

5.1.3 Contextualism Apart from Skepticism: The Stakes-Shifting Cases

If there was no reason to think contextualism about "knows that" is true apart from the prospects of using contextualism to diagnose skepticism, you might think its diagnosis of skepticism is ad hoc or forced. Is there any good argument for contextualism, other than its diagnosis of skepticism? Contextualists think so. They commonly turn to pairs of cases across which the practical stakes vary dramatically, a low-stakes case and a high-stakes case. Here are two prominent cases in the literature, invented by Keith DeRose (1992):

> *Bank Case A.* My wife and I are driving home on a Friday afternoon. We plan to stop at the bank on the way home to deposit our paychecks. But as we drive past the bank, we notice that the lines inside are very long, as they often are on Friday afternoons. Although we generally like to deposit our paychecks as soon as possible, it is not especially important in this case that they be deposited right away, so I suggest that we drive straight home and deposit our paychecks on Saturday morning. My wife says, "Maybe the bank won't be open tomorrow. Lots of banks are closed on Saturdays." I reply, "No, I know it'll be open. I was just there two weeks ago on Saturday. It's open until noon."
>
> *Bank Case B.* [the same as Case A but . . .] in this case, we have just written a very large and important check. If our paychecks are not deposited into our checking account before Monday morning, the important check we wrote will bounce, leaving us in a *very* bad situation. And, of course, the bank is not open on Sunday. My wife reminds me of these facts. She then says, "Banks do change their hours. Do you know the bank will be open tomorrow?" Remaining as confident as I was before that the bank will be open then, still, I reply, "Well, no. I'd better go in and make sure." (1992, 913)

Let's pretend bank deposits still work this way: One physically takes the check to the bank. Now, the contextualist might argue as follows:

1. In Bank Case A, you speak the truth when you say, "I know it'll be open."
2. In Bank Case B, you speak the truth when you say, "Well, no, [I don't know it'll be open]."
3. Your epistemic position—which standards you meet, which possibilities you can rule out, how strong your justification is, how reliable you are, and so forth—is the same across Cases A and B.
4. If your epistemic position across the cases is the same, then if "know" had the same sense in the two contexts (the contexts of the two cases), then you couldn't speak the truth in both cases in saying what you do.
5. So, "know" must have a different sense in the two contexts. That is: Contextualism about "know" is true.

Premises (1) and (2) seem plausible for two reasons. First, ordinary people *do* say things like this in a perfectly serious way without relying on mistaken factual assumptions in doing so. This doesn't *entail* that they speak truly, but we might think it is good evidence that they do. Second, don't these statements seem intuitively correct? That, again, isn't decisive, but it is evidence.

Premise (3) is presumably guaranteed by the description of the cases. And (4) seems very plausible, insofar as it seems that whether a subject knows is a matter of how strong the subject's epistemic position is, which epistemic standards he or she meets, and so forth. It is *not* a matter of practical stakes, nor is it a matter of whether the conversation has taken a certain shape, and practical stakes and conversational context are the only difference between Case A and Case B.

Lively debate continues about whether arguments like (1)–(5) provide good grounds for contextualism.[6] Here we only scratch the surface. We'll consider possible replies to steps in the argument. A piece of terminology is useful in what follows: Someone who isn't a contextualist about "knows" we'll call an *invariantist*.

Reject Premise 1

One way the invariantist could reject Premise 1 is by appealing to the phenomenon of *loose use* (Davis 2006). We all know that if a softball game has one out left in the final inning, it isn't over, even if the score is 22–0. But it's as good as over in some sense, and players and fans might say, "This game is over." Here it seems that the game *isn't* over, strictly speaking, but it's close enough to over. We speak loosely when we say something that isn't strictly true but is close enough for present purposes to the truth. Arguably, we speak loosely when we say that a test took two hours (when it took one hour and fifty minutes), when we say that we're out of milk (when there is only enough left for one more bowl of cereal), and in many other cases. Isn't it plausible you'd be speaking loosely in Bank Case A? You don't know, but your epistemic state is close enough to knowledge for the purposes at hand. Could that be why you say you know, and why it seems appropriate for you to say this, even though you really don't know?

The main worry associated with this line of response is that the resulting invariantist view will collapse into a fairly robust form of skepticism. But suppose the "loose talk" invariantist studiously avoids skepticism. Suppose he or she allows that we do have much of the knowledge we think we have, including for instance the knowledge of our birth name. Now, this knowledge isn't knowledge with absolute certainty. Indeed, we know some things better than what our birth name was—we know what we are normally called today better, for instance. And we know that we exist better still. So, the knowledge that one's birth name was such-and-such is knowledge but not maximally certain knowledge. But then why couldn't we devise a high-stakes case similar to Bank Case B in which the costs of relying on your belief about your birth name are very high indeed? If so, suppose you said in such a high-stakes case "Hmm. Maybe I should check with the authorities. I don't know this was my birth name." If we could devise a case like this, the contextualist could rerun the argument, without fear that the "loose use" invariantist would block the first step.

Reject Premise 2[7]

Perhaps in Bank Case B, you *do* know, even though you say you don't. But why would you say you knew when you didn't? Do we have to suppose that you'd be mistaken in your *belief* about whether you know? Or is the idea that you know you know but for some reason say you didn't know anyway?

One invariantist proposal, due to Brown (2006) and Rysiew (2008), takes the latter route. The proposal is that you do know, and you know you know, but you don't say you know because saying you know would be misleading. Saying you know in Bank Case B would suggest that you can act on the belief that the bank is open by just skipping the lines and coming back tomorrow, but this is false: You can't just skip the lines today, given the need to deposit the check before Monday.

Two questions arise. First, why is it that by saying you know in Case B you'd be implying that you can act on your belief? One natural explanation is that *knowing P* entails that you can act on your belief in P. But since you can't act on *the bank is open tomorrow* in Bank Case B, if knowing entailed that you could act on your belief, it would follow that you don't know. However, on the response we're considering, you do know. So, this natural explanation is unavailable.

But even supposing we could come up with an explanation of why it is that saying you know the bank is open tomorrow in Case B would imply something false, this would not explain all that needs to be explained, as DeRose (2009) notes. In Case B you don't merely refrain from saying, "I know," you say, "I don't know." So, assuming you do know, you don't merely refrain from saying something true; you assert something false. We typically try not to speak falsely, although we often don't assert misleading truths. Suppose a woman had dinner with her father, who is a handsome man. She wouldn't say to her husband, who didn't know the identity of her dinner companion, "I had dinner with a handsome man"; this would be misleading. But she wouldn't assert the falsehood, "I didn't have dinner with a handsome man."

The two invariantist objections we considered so far, the loose use objection to Premise 1 and the current objection to Premise 2, are similar in nature. They both maintain that a certain statement can be appropriately made without being true, and they both try to explain what makes the statement appropriate despite being false.

Rejecting Premise 4

To reject Premise 4 is to think that whether you know something could depend on more than your epistemic position, on more than just which epistemic standards you meet, which alternatives you can rule out, how justified you are, how reliable you are, and the like. Now if it were only a matter of variations in knowing because of variations in whether you *believe*, this would not be particularly surprising (cf. Nagel 2008). However, perhaps there can be variations in knowing that do not trace to variations in belief but rather to the practical stakes.[8] The claim that practical stakes can make a difference to knowledge, holding fixed belief and strength of epistemic position, is certainly surprising. In the literature it is called the thesis of *pragmatic encroachment*. The term "pragmatic encroachment," invented by an opponent, suggests something sinister, the "encroachment" on a pure domain by something somehow tainted. But advocates have adopted the term as well (as commonly happens!). We will discuss pragmatic encroachment in detail in the next section. Here we examine the plausibility of rejecting Premise 4 on the grounds that you believe in Case A but don't believe in Case B.

Couldn't we stipulate that you believe in Case B but not in Case A? This would secure Premise 4. However, it would make it odd that you said, "I don't know" in Case B. Why are you saying you don't know if you believe? Of course, we could change Case B so that it's not you but your spouse who says to you that you "don't know." Would that make Premise 2 less plausible? If not, it looks like considerations about belief will not block an argument from contextualism from the revised versions of Case A and Case B.

5.2 KNOWLEDGE, ACTION, AND PRAGMATIC ENCROACHMENT

Pragmatic encroachment, again, is the thesis that differences in pragmatic factors—factors broadly related to the "practical" sphere, such as stakes—can make a difference to knowledge. Why believe this thesis?

One sort of argument simply appeals to cases like the bank cases. Doesn't it seem that you *don't* know in Case B? And doesn't it seem that you *do* know in Case A? If so, this is evidence that knowledge varies across these cases alike except for variations in pragmatic factors, and in particular the stakes.

This by itself is not an impressive basis for pragmatic encroachment. After all, it is plausible that knowledge doesn't depend on the stakes. As the stakes go down, you don't normally think that you know something that you previously didn't. And you don't think that if the stakes were much higher right now, you would know a lot less than you do. It seems, rather, that whether you know is solely a matter of how strong your epistemic position is (i.e., how justified you are, how reliable, etc.).

A better basis for pragmatic encroachment appeals to links between knowledge and reasons for action, as we'll next explore.[9]

5.2.1 The Case for Pragmatic Encroachment

As we suggested in Chapter 3 (Section 3.1.3), knowledge seems to mark things we can appropriately *reason from* both in reasoning about what to do as well as what to think. It gives us starting points for further inquiry of any kind. We can formulate the basic idea more precisely as so:

Knowledge-Reasons (KR)

If you know P, then P is sufficiently warranted to be a reason you have to believe and do other things.

We include the qualification "sufficiently warranted" in order to cover the many cases in which something you know isn't a reason to do random unrelated things (you know that Mercury is a planet, but this doesn't give you a reason to do jumping jacks). The idea behind KR is that knowing something is enough epistemically to qualify it as a reason you have, a practical as well as a theoretical reason.

Suppose we grant that this principle is correct. Now, *the bank is open tomorrow* looks like an extremely good reason (given the long lines today and no lines tomorrow) to come back tomorrow to deposit the check. So, if you know the bank is open tomorrow in Bank Case B, it seems you have an excellent reason to come back tomorrow and skip the long lines today. But, given how we've set up the case, you shouldn't come back tomorrow (it's too risky). So if you do have this excellent reason to come back, it must somehow be defeated or outweighed by other reasons you have. But what would these defeating reasons be? The best candidate is the serious risk that if you waited to come back tomorrow the bank might be closed and you might not get the check deposited. But does it make sense to think that you can simultaneously have the following two reasons?

- Reason 1 (in favor of coming back tomorrow): *The bank will be open tomorrow.*
- Reason 2 (against coming back tomorrow): *The bank might not be open tomorrow, and if it isn't and we come back, then that would be disastrous.*

If you have these reasons, you ought to be able to weigh them. But can you weigh "the bank will be open tomorrow" with "the bank might not be"? Consider how you weigh reasons in everyday cases:

- "On the one hand, adding cream to my coffee makes it delicious. On the other hand, it's fattening. Which is more important, the deliciousness or avoiding the extra fat?"
- "On the one hand, we could vacation nearby, saving the gas money and time driving, enjoy swimming in a manmade lake. On the other hand, we could drive to the mountains, enjoy hiking, beauty, and cool temps. Which is more important, saving time and money on a local swimming vacation, or spending time and money to enjoy all the mountains offer?"

Compare:

"On the one hand, the bank will be open tomorrow. So, if I wait until then, I'll deposit the check without having to wait in the long lines. So, that's a reason to come back to the bank tomorrow. On the other hand, the bank might not be open then, and if I come back and it isn't open then I won't deposit the check before Monday, which would be disastrous. Which is more important, the fact that it will be open tomorrow or the serious risk that it won't?"

Doesn't this last weighing sound decidedly odd, even irrational? A more natural weighing in Bank Case B is:

"On the one hand, the bank *probably* is open tomorrow . . . On the other hand, the bank *might not* be open tomorrow, and if I came back when it wasn't open, it would be a disaster. Which is more important, the good chance that it will be open tomorrow or the small but serious risk that it won't?"

When we start weighing reasons relating to the serious risk that P is false, we seem automatically to pull back from employing P itself as an opposing reason. This supports the conclusion that if you have P as a reason for action or belief, then you don't have, as opposing reasons, considerations related to the possibility that P is false. This is a kind of "safe reasons" principle:

Safe Reasons (first version): If you have P as a reason to do or believe something, then P is sufficiently warranted to justify you in that action or belief.

In fact, it doesn't seem to matter that P is a reason you have; it only matters that it is sufficiently warranted. And so we can strengthen the above to reach:

Safe Reasons
If P is sufficiently warranted to be a reason you have to do or believe something, then P is sufficiently warranted to justify you in that action or belief.

If we put KR and Safe Reasons together, we can draw the following conclusion:

Knowledge-Justification Principle (KJ)

If you know P, then P is sufficiently warranted to justify you in actions or beliefs.

Given KJ, the pragmatic encroachment theorist can argue as follows: If you have knowledge in Bank Case B, then you'd be justified in coming back tomorrow to deposit the checks; but you're *not* justified in coming back tomorrow to deposit the checks in Bank Case B; therefore, you don't have knowledge.

To derive pragmatic encroachment, we need only one more step: the premise that you do have knowledge in Bank Case A. Do you? Here one option for the pragmatic encroachment theorist is go along with the contextualist, appealing to the fact that this is what competent speakers would say, not relying on factual errors.

An alternative approach, one favored by this author, is again to appeal to an epistemic principle:

Fallibilism (about knowledge)

Knowledge does not require absolute epistemic certainty: that is, you can know something even if you aren't justified in being absolutely sure it is the case.

Just to be clear: This is a technical use of the term *fallibilism*. In an ordinary use, *fallible* means something like *can be wrong*. Of course, assuming knowledge implies truth: If you know something, it is not wrong. So knowledge isn't fallible in this ordinary sense. *Fallibilism* as we use it here is compatible with knowledge implying truth.

An example can make fallibilism about knowledge plausible: You know that if the American major league baseball season isn't cancelled next year, then at least one player will strike out in at least one game. (There are 162 games per year and in each over 50 opportunities to strike out. There are very few games, generally, in which there are no strikeouts.) But is this absolutely certain? You can calculate the frequency-based probability that no one will strike out in any game in a 162-game season, based on past data, and it is very close to 100%, but it isn't *quite* there! Now: Do you know? This author is strongly tempted to say: *yes*.

We can't argue that if fallibilism is true then you know in Bank Case A. But we can give a more abstract argument for the conclusion there will be some case like Bank Case A in which you know but aren't justified in being absolutely certain. Perhaps Bank Case A isn't the right case, but there are cases to fit the bill.

Given all this, here's how the abstract argument for pragmatic encroachment goes:

Suppose fallibilism and the KJ are both true. Given fallibilism, there is some case—call it LOW—in which you are justified in acting on a proposition P (i.e., in performing the action that P is a reason to perform). In LOW, the difference between the level of warrant you have for P and the warrant needed for absolute certainty in P doesn't make a difference to what you are justified in doing. But now imagine a different case, HIGH. In HIGH, you're in an identical epistemic position, as far as how warranted you are in P. However, in HIGH, because of the stakes involved, the difference between the level of warrant you have for P and the warrant needed for absolute certainty in P *does* make a difference to what you are justified in doing. In particular, you're not justified in HIGH in acting on P. Thus, by KJ, you don't know P in HIGH. But you do know P in LOW. It follows that knowledge can vary across cases alike except for the variation in a pragmatic factor, namely the practical stakes. That is, it follows that pragmatic encroachment is true.

The pragmatic encroachment theorist can see the bank cases and this abstract argument as mutually supporting considerations. The abstract argument helps explain why it seems plausible that you don't know in Case B and why it's plausible to think you do know in Case A. Given the abstract argument, not all is left to intuitions about these cases. General principles about how knowledge, reasons, and justified action are related provide further and mutually reinforcing support.

5.2.2 Implications of Pragmatic Encroachment for Epistemology

Before we consider objections to pragmatic encroachment and to the steps in the argument for it, we should pause to consider the ramifications of pragmatic encroachment for epistemology. We will mention two noteworthy ramifications.

An old puzzle for epistemologists of a fallibilist bent concerns the level of warrant needed for knowledge. Knowledge, fallibilists say, doesn't require warrant sufficient for absolute certainty, but it does require some strong warrant. You don't know a six-sided die isn't going to come up 6 before you roll it, even though there's 5/6 chance it won't come up 6. Just what level of warrant is needed for knowledge? Given pragmatic encroachment, we can at least provide an informative lower bound for the warrant needed for knowledge: If your warrant isn't sufficient enough to justify you in acting on P, then you don't know P. If pragmatic encroachment is correct, just which level of warrant is necessary varies with practical factors. In Bank Case A, the lower bound for knowledge is lower than it is in Bank Case B.

A second ramification concerns the importance of the concept of knowledge. Why is it that the concept of knowledge is such an important tool in ordinary life? If knowing P is enough to make P a suitable basis for action and belief, as the Knowledge-Justification Principle dictates, then this helps answer this question. When you know something, this marks the reaching of an important threshold: You can use P as a reason in your actions and beliefs. This is obviously the sort of threshold we care about; we care about whether we can plug in considerations and base our practical and theoretical reasoning on them.[10]

5.2.3 Objections

There is no shortage of objections to pragmatic encroachment. We'll discuss objections to the thesis itself as well as objections to the abstract argument for it (from KR, etc.).

One sort of objection simply declares the thesis of pragmatic encroachment implausible. This objection certainly has some force: Even proponents admit that pragmatic encroachment is highly surprising and counterintuitive. It doesn't seem that whether a subject knows can depend on the stakes or any practical factors. It seems knowledge is only a matter of strength of epistemic position or warrant. Let's simply grant this. It is a factor. But the argument for pragmatic encroachment might be strong enough to outweigh it.

A different but related objection points out odd-sounding implications of pragmatic encroachment. As we've noted above, if knowledge can vary with changes in practical factors, statements like the following can be true:

- John doesn't know P, but if the stakes were lower, he would know P.
- John used to know P, but now, because the stakes are higher, he doesn't know P anymore. But he hasn't lost any evidence.

Such statements do sound odd, to say the least. They might seem fairly clearly false. Proponents often point out that many epistemologists face similar problems. Contextualists, for instance, seem committed to allowing that the following can be true:

- It's true to say, "John knows P," but if the stakes salient in our context of speech were higher, it wouldn't be true to say, "John knows P."
- It used to be true to say, "John knows P," but now, because the stakes salient to us are higher, it isn't true to say, "John knows P" anymore. But John hasn't lost any evidence.

Perhaps these aren't *as* odd, but they are odd. Even orthodox invariantists might seem committed to acknowledging oddities somewhat like those above. Consider the barn façade case from Chapter 3. "John knows he sees a barn but he wouldn't if there were lots of barn façades around," too, sounds odd but comes out true on most orthodox theories of knowledge such as those considered in Chapter 3.[11]

Even if proponents of pragmatic encroachment are correct in thinking we're stuck with oddities like these, they need to explain *why* they seem so odd if they are sometimes true. We can arguably do this for the barn façade case.[12]

No proponents of pragmatic encroachment accept it because it is intuitive. They accept it because of arguments for it, arguments from examples like the bank cases, as well as from more general principles, like the abstract argument considered above. Because the dialectic for arguments based solely on the bank cases (or similar pairs of cases) proceeds in the same fashion as it does for contextualism (see Section 5.1.3), we will consider only objections to the abstract argument for pragmatic encroachment given in Section 5.2.1.

The crucial steps of the abstract argument were these:

- KR (i.e., the Knowledge-Reason Principle)
- Safe Reasons
- Fallibilism

KR + Safe Reasons gave us KJ, which together with fallibilism gave us pragmatic encroachment. Let's put aside objections to fallibilism. Most epistemologists want to retain fallibilism, and giving it up to avoid pragmatic encroachment would seem to be a cure worse than the disease.

What about the other principles? Some philosophers offer counterexamples to KJ, which follows from the KR and Safe Reasons. Here is one example due to Jessica Brown:

Surgeon

A student is spending the day shadowing a surgeon. In the morning he observes her in clinic examining patient A who has a diseased left kidney. The decision is taken to remove it that afternoon. Later the student observes the surgeon in theater where patient A is lying anaesthetized on the operating table. The operation hasn't started as the surgeon is consulting the patient's notes. The student is puzzled and asks one of the nurses what's going on:

> *Student*: I don't understand. Why is she looking at the patient's records? She was in clinic with the patient this morning. Doesn't she even know which kidney it is?
>
> *Nurse*: Of course, she knows which kidney it is. But imagine what it would be like if she removed the wrong kidney. She shouldn't operate before checking the patient's records. (Brown 2008, 176)

This might seem to be a case in which the surgeon knows that the left kidney is diseased but isn't sufficiently warranted to act on that belief. Against this, the pragmatic encroachment theorist might note that there still seems to be a clash between "she knows which kidney it is" and "she needs to check the patient's records before operating." We could revise the example so that "she doesn't know" might seem quite acceptable. Imagine the student making the same remarks except *without* adding at the end, "Doesn't she even know?" Then the nurse might respond, "People forget things. She needs to know which kidney it is before operating. That's why she's checking the charts." Now, given that we can set up the conversation in a way that makes it sound intuitively correct to say, "She doesn't know," it isn't clear how strong this putative counterexample is.

One might hope to reinforce the example by supplying an account of where and why the argument for KJ goes wrong. Is KR false? Is Safe Reasons false? We will consider one natural objection to the former.

Knowing P, the objection goes, ensures only that P can be used as a reason for other beliefs, not necessarily as a reason for action. Generally, what can be used as a reason for belief can also be used as a reason for action, but not when the stakes are high. So, the idea would be that when we find KR plausible, we're thinking only about ordinary low-stakes situations. It is true when restricted to those situations. But of course if restricted to those situations, it can't be used in the argument for pragmatic encroachment.

Think, though, about what it would mean for KR to be false for action but true for belief. It would mean that there was a case in which you knew something, say *the bank is open tomorrow,* which was a reason to *believe* things like *I'll be fine if I wait till tomorrow to deposit the check* and *nothing bad will happen if I wait till tomorrow to deposit the check*—and indeed would justify you in believing these things. Yet, in this case, the fact that the bank was open tomorrow wouldn't be even *a reason* you have to come back tomorrow. It would be a reason you have to believe that plan of action would work out without a hitch but not a reason to do that course of action. It's as if it would be OK to load *the bank is open tomorrow* into your reasoning about what is the case but not OK to load it into your reasoning about what to do. We would therefore expect it to be perfectly reasonable for you to think, "Well, it is open tomorrow, but I can't consider that in deliberating about whether to come back tomorrow or wait in line today." Is this thought reasonable, though?

The debate over pragmatic encroachment continues to engage the attention of epistemologists. At the very least, proponents of pragmatic encroachment have opened up for discussion questions about how exactly reasons for action relate to reasons for belief and how both relate to knowledge: Does it take more warrant in some (all?) cases for a proposition to be among your reasons for action than it takes for it to be among your reasons for belief? What does it take: Knowledge? Justified belief? Certainty? Different epistemic states depending on the practical situation?[13]

5.3 KNOWLEDGE AND ASSERTION

There is a good prima facie case for supposing that knowledge is intimately related to assertion. Here are three lines of evidence for a tight relationship, due to Timothy Williamson (2000, Chapter 11).

Conversational patterns. It is an interesting fact that in making an assertion the content of which isn't at all about knowledge, such as "Tea has more health benefits than coffee," our interlocutors should take us to be somehow presenting ourselves as knowing the truth of what we say. We say the likes of "You know that?" or, more politely, "That's interesting; how did you come to know that?" We also use "can't say" interchangeably with "don't know." If a friend asks me, "Do you know whether you'll be in town next Saturday?" You might reply, "At this point, I can't say." Why would this address the question asked? The question asked was about knowledge. The answer given was about what one "can say."

Lottery cases. We hold back from asserting flat-out that our lottery ticket will lose. Why? We do say, "It will very likely lose" and even, "I believe it will lose." Why not simply *it will lose*? One story: We hold back from asserting this, and rightly so, because we don't know the ticket will lose. Once we see the report of the winner, we do assert, "My ticket lost." Why is this OK at this point? Because we know it lost.

Moore Paradoxes. In 1913, G. E. Moore discussed what he called a paradox. Why is "it's raining but I don't believe that it's raining" such an absurd thing to say? The sentence "it's raining but I don't believe that it's raining" is sometimes true. Generally, there are many truths of the form "p but I don't believe that p." Why can't you intelligibly assert such a statement, then? This is the "paradox," or at least the puzzle. A version of the puzzle arises when "don't know" replaces "don't believe." Consider "it's raining but I don't know that it's raining." Here again, this could well be true, but it sounds absurd. Why would this be? One story is this. We shouldn't assert something if we don't know it. In asserting "it's raining but I don't know that it's raining," you'd be asserting something you shouldn't do unless you know that it's raining. Thus, you'd be implying that you know that it's raining. But then you add in the second part of your statement that you *don't* know that it's raining. You'd be implying something and then explicitly denying it all in the same statement![14]

These considerations have led Williamson and other philosophers to posit a "knowledge norm of assertion." There are disputes about exactly how to formulate the norm and what the nature of the norm is. For our purposes, we can think of the norms as norms of conversational propriety. Many norms bear on conversation: Be relevant, be orderly, be polite. The data above might lead us to think that, in addition to these, there is the following knowledge norm on assertion:

Knowledge Norm of Assertion

There is a norm of conversation according to which you shouldn't assert P unless you know P.

This norm is outweighed by other norms in many situations. If you don't believe the meatloaf your uncle serves you is tasty, and so don't know it is, a politeness norm might still make it acceptable to assert, "This is tasty" if he asks you. But there is still a defect to the assertion, one that your uncle will not look favorably upon if he finds out your true opinion.

You might agree that there is an epistemic norm of conversation but disagree about whether it requires knowledge, or justified belief, or truth, or certain knowledge, and the like. Supposing there is such an epistemic norm on assertion, we can consider the following principle:

Knowledge-Assertion Principle

You satisfy the epistemic norm on assertion with respect to P if and only if you know P.

This principle has an "if and only if," unlike the "knowledge norm" above. So it doesn't merely imply that you violate a norm in asserting what you don't know; it also implies that you don't violate the epistemic norm on assertion if you assert something you do know. Of course, you could well violate any number of *other* norms in asserting what you know. What you say might be irrelevant to the conversation at hand, trivial, etc., but epistemically it would be in the clear, according to the principle.

If the Knowledge-Assertion Principle were true, this would be a surprising discovery. We would learn that knowledge is centrally related to a pervasive phenomenon not traditionally considered epistemic: assertion. In this respect, it is like the Knowledge-Justification Principle, KJ, above. Like that principle, if true, it might help explain the importance of the concept of knowledge: why it is so commonly deployed, and why it matters whether someone has knowledge in a particular case as opposed to something less than knowledge.[15]

The Knowledge-Assertion Principle, finally, bears on the question of pragmatic encroachment. If it is true, then if sufficient warrant to satisfy the epistemic norm on assertion varies with the practical stakes, we have the materials for a different argument for pragmatic encroachment, an argument that isn't about action in general but only about a particular kind of action, assertion. In effect, we could substitute the Knowledge-Assertion Principle for the Knowledge-Justification Principle in the argument for pragmatic encroachment above. By fallibilism, there would be some LOW case in which you know that P without being justified in being absolutely certain that P. In LOW, you satisfy the epistemic norm on assertion with respect to P. Next, holding fixed the strength of your epistemic position, vary the practical stakes, creating a HIGH case, like Bank Case B, in which aren't sufficiently warranted to assert that the bank is open tomorrow. In this HIGH case, you don't satisfy the epistemic norm on assertion. By the Knowledge-Assertion Principle, you don't know the bank is open tomorrow in this case, either. Thus, we have a variation in knowledge across cases that different only in practical stakes. That's pragmatic encroachment.

Contextualists, too, have used knowledge norms of assertion in supporting their views. You can imagine how this would go. The contextualist doesn't conclude that *knowledge* varies across the cases; rather, she concludes that what's expressed by "know" in the two contexts varies. For the contextualist, it's not the Knowledge-Assertion Principle that's true; it's rather:

Contextualist Knowledge-Assertion
You satisfy the epistemic norm on asserting P if and only if in your context "know P" applies to you.

This can be used, together with the premises that you satisfy the norm for *the bank is open tomorrow* in Bank Case A but not in Bank Case B, to derive contextualism (DeRose 2002).

To decide between the original Knowledge-Assertion Principle and this contextualist version, we would need some reason to think that assertion is connected importantly to knowledge itself (or *to all* the various senses expressed by "knows"). It is not clear, however, that appealing to connections between knowledge and reasons for assertion will do much good in defending the Knowledge-Assertion Principle. Does knowing that $2 + 2 = 4$ give you a reason to assert it? Think of the millions of boring propositions you know. Do you have reasons to assert each of them? It is hard to believe this. If we want a defense of the Knowledge-Assertion Principle, over and above the contextualist version of it, we need to turn elsewhere.

One natural way to go here is to try to explain assertion in terms of knowledge. Suppose asserting something constitutively involves—this is part of what assertion is—presenting oneself as knowing it. On the assumption that your asserting something is improper if you present yourself as knowing it when you don't (and epistemically proper if you do know it), we would have an account of why the Knowledge-Assertion Principle holds. But much remains to be explained here: What is it to present oneself as knowing? What is it, moreover, to *present* oneself as being such-and-such in the first place?[16]

As we hope is clear, questions about the relation between knowledge and assertion connect epistemology with the philosophy of language and linguistics in fruitful ways, just as questions about the relation between knowledge and action connect epistemology fruitfully with ethics and decision theory.

QUESTIONS

1. In the high-stakes Bank Case B, when you say, "I don't know the bank will be open tomorrow," is what you say true? Why or why not? If you say it is not true, why might it seem true?

2. One response to the contextualist diagnosis of skepticism is that it, at best, is of limited scope. Suppose the skeptic revises the BIV argument, for instance, by replacing "knows" with "meets ordinary epistemic standards." Thus, the argument becomes:

   a. You don't meet ordinary epistemic standards for *I am not a BIV.*
   b. If you don't meet ordinary epistemic standards for *I am not a BIV,* you don't meet ordinary epistemic standards for any proposition about the external world.
   c. So, you don't meet ordinary epistemic standards for any proposition about the external world.

   (c) is a radical skeptical claim, even if it doesn't use the term "know." Is this argument (a)–(c) clearly worse than the usual BIV skeptical argument, which uses "know" throughout? If not, can contextualism about "knows that . . ." help in diagnosing it?

3. When explicitly talking about your ticket in a fair lottery, it can seem true to say, "I don't know my ticket will lose." Later in the day, thinking about whether next year you'll have enough money to buy a yacht, it might seem true to say, "I know I won't have enough money to buy a yacht next year." And yet if you did win the lottery, you would have enough money to buy the yacht next year. Moreover, it always seems false to say, "I don't know my ticket will lose, but I do know I won't have enough money to buy a yacht next year." Contextualists think they explain how all of these intuitions are correct. How? Do they succeed?

4. Contextualists distinguish between subject factors and speaker factors. Subject factors are factors bearing on the truth of a knowledge-attribution that concern the subject, not the speaker (unless the speaker is self-attributing knowledge, in which case the subject is the same as the speaker). Most contextualists take *true belief* to be among the subject factors. A consequence of this is that if you have a false belief, then regardless of what a speaker thinks or says, a speaker can't truly say that you "know." Salience of error possibilities is typically taken to be a speaker factor. If a possibility in which a subject is in error is salient to a speaker, this doesn't automatically mean that the subject can't truly be said to "know" by other speakers. It only means that the subject can't truly be said to "know" by *speakers who finds the error possibility salient*, including the subject herself if she is speaking about herself.

   The question for you is whether contextualists ought to take *not being the victim of Gettier-like lucky true belief* as a subject or a speaker factor. If it is a subject factor, then it doesn't matter what happens in various speaker contexts: The attribution of knowledge to the subject would be false. If it is a speaker factor, the speaker's context matters, because depending on what the speaker is thinking about, finding important, and so forth, "knows" might have a stronger or weaker sense when the speaker ascribes "knowledge." Which is it, a subject or a speaker factor? Why?[17]

5. William James (1896) famously declared that there are two great precepts of belief, "Know the truth" and "Avoid error." Let's think of the first as "believe the truth." James thought that we need to balance these two aims and that we might balance them differently for different beliefs. For instance, James thought we should weight "believe the truth" higher in asking whether to believe in God, but that we should weight "avoid error" higher in asking about whether to believe scientific hypotheses. How does the question of balancing these two precepts bear on the question of pragmatic encroachment?

6. Statements of the form "I know that p but it might be that not-p" sound odd, even contradictory. In the epistemology literature, these are called "concessive knowledge attributions" (the term is from Rysiew 2001). Is the fact that concessive knowledge-attributions seem contradictory a problem for fallibilism about knowledge? Why or why not? If it is a problem, how can fallibilists address it?

7. Suppose you reject the knowledge norm of assertion, along with the Knowledge-Assertion Principle. How could you explain the three sorts of data for it (i.e., from conversational patterns, from lotteries, and from Moore's Paradox)?

8. It can seem reasonable to take out life insurance policies. It can also seem, at least for people with good health and under forty, that you know you will be alive next year. Is there a problem for the Knowledge-Justification Principle here? If so, how could a defender of the principle best reply? Is the reply sufficient?

FURTHER READING

Brown, Jessica (2008). "Subject-Sensitive Invariantism and the Knowledge Norm for Practical Reasoning." *Noûs* 42(2): 167–189.

DeRose, Keith (2009). *The Case for Contextualism, Volume 1.* Oxford: Oxford University Press.

Fantl, Jeremy, and Matthew McGrath (2009). *Knowledge in an Uncertain World.* Oxford: Oxford University Press.

Hawthorne, John (2004). *Knowledge and Lotteries.* Oxford: Oxford University Press.

Lewis, David (1996). "Elusive Knowledge." *Australasian Journal of Philosophy* 74(4): 549–567.

Nagel, Jennifer (2008). "Knowledge Ascriptions and the Psychological Consequences of Changing Stakes." *Australasian Journal of Philosophy* 86: 279–294.

Stanley, Jason (2005). *Knowledge and Practical Interests.* Oxford: Clarendon Press.

Unger, Peter (1975). *Ignorance.* Oxford: Oxford University Press.

Williamson, Timothy (2000). *Knowledge and Its Limits.* Oxford: Oxford University Press.

NOTES

1. A reminder: a sound argument is a valid argument with all true premises. A valid argument is one in which the conclusion follows from the premises. Thus, in a sound argument, the conclusion is true as well.

2. It's called "lexical" ambiguity to emphasize that there are two entries in the lexicon for it: two words spelled and pronounced the same but nonetheless distinct, with different etymologies and meanings.

3. In the literature on contextualism, contextualism is usually explained in terms of "semantic content," in particular as the view that "knows that . . ." expresses different semantic contents in different contexts of speech but has a single "character," where a character is what a speaker must know to be competent with a term. The terms "content" and "character" come from David Kaplan (1989). Here our use of the more ordinary word "sense" picks out what in the literature is referred to as content, rather than character.

4. We here follow the usual practice of using the term 'knowledge attribution' when referring to utterances of sentences of the form "S knows P."

5. For standards contextualism, see Cohen (1999) and DeRose (2009).

6. The issue at hand is whether contextualism is true, not whether it diagnoses skepticism successfully. One might be a contextualist but deny that it diagnoses skepticism.

7. A number of studies by experimental philosophers might seem to cast doubt on the claim that we find it intuitive to say that the protagonist in Bank Case B knows or speaks the truth in saying he or she doesn't know. However, others seem to provide support. These matters are discussed in Chapter 7 (Section 7.3.3).

8. We operate with a fairly rough-and-ready notion of stakes. Think of stakes as encompassing both the cost of being wrong and the availability of options such as playing it safe or taking a risk. The important point is that stakes are pragmatic factors that have nothing to do with how strong a subject's epistemic position is. They have nothing to do with how strong the subject's evidence is for the proposition in question, how reliable her processes are, and so forth.

9. The case below is taken from Fantl and McGrath (2009), with minor revisions. For other arguments for pragmatic encroachment, see Hawthorne (2004) and Stanley (2005).

10. For doubts about how pragmatic encroachment theorists can set this threshold, see Jessica Brown (2014).

11. Indeed, there is something decidedly odd about the claim, accepted by many orthodox invariantists, that whether one is sufficiently warranted to use a premise P in practical reasoning varies with the stakes. To think "Yes, the bank is open tomorrow," and then receive new information about high stakes and back off to "Hmm, maybe the bank isn't open tomorrow" is peculiar. Why did you stop affirming this despite gaining no evidence bearing on its truth? It is even more peculiar when one starts in a high-stakes case and then, after the stakes go down, begins to judge "Yes, the bank is open tomorrow." To go from "Hmm, maybe it's not open tomorrow" to "Yes, it is open tomorrow"—in practical reasoning or any sort of reasoning—it seems one needs to gain new evidence bearing on whether it is open tomorrow. But learning the stakes are low is not acquiring evidence bearing on whether the bank is open tomorrow. It is harder to avoid the difficulties associated with pragmatic encroachment, in this author's view, than it might initially seem! (See Fantl and McGrath [manuscript].)

12. For partial attempts, see Hawthorne (2004, Chapter 4), Stanley (2005, Chapter 5), and Fantl and McGrath (2009, Chapter 7). For doubts about the success of such attempts, see Nagel (2008).

13. One prominent account of knowledge-attributions omitted here is assessment relativism. We can explain one key rationale for relativism by pointing out a weakness of contextualism that relativism avoids. If the contextualist is right, then when the stakes go up (or the skeptic makes her argument), it becomes false to say, "I knew P" even though, according to the contextualist, knew what you said earlier when you uttered "I know P" was true. Why, then, do we retract our earlier knowledge claims at the later time? If contextualism were true, shouldn't we say, "What I said earlier was perfectly correct. The stakes were lower then"? But we don't. The assessment relativist avoids this awkward consequence by dropping contextualism and making knowledge relative to a context of *assessment* rather than of speech. A context of assessment is a context in which someone is assessing whether someone knows or whether a claim to knowledge is true. So, why do we not retract our earlier knowledge-claims when the stakes go up? Answer: because those knowledge-attributions are false relative to our context of assessment. Relative to our HIGH context of assessment, both "I knew P" and "What I said earlier in uttering 'I know P' was true" are false. One significant consequence of this approach is that it relativizes truth to a new sort of parameter, contexts of assessment. The interested reader should consult MacFarlane (2005).

14. Williamson (2000, 253) points out that one cannot know a proposition of the form: *p and I don't know that p*. To know it would require knowing both conjuncts, that is, knowing that p and knowing that one doesn't know that p. But you can't know that you don't know that p while also knowing that p! For, if you know that you don't know that p, then you don't know that p! Knowledge requires truth, after all.

15. The Knowledge-Assertion Principle entails that if you know P, then you satisfy the epistemic norm on assertion with respect to P. This claim might require refinement. If I say something I do know to be true but which I know would mislead my audience, do I thereby violate a norm of assertion? If so, do I violate the *epistemic* norm on assertion? If we think the answer is yes to both questions, we might want to revise the principle so that it takes more than merely knowing P

to satisfy the epistemic norm on assertion. It's not that it takes some epistemic position better or more secure with respect to P. Rather, the suggestion would be that it takes knowledge (or reasonable belief?) that the assertion would not mislead one's audience, assuming they are reasonable. Misleading an audience needn't have a moral flavor. If someone asks me a piece of trivia, for example, about where Brad Pitt attended college, and I reply, "somewhere in Missouri," I would be asserting something I know but at the same time misleading my interlocutor into thinking I didn't have more detailed information about just where he attended college, which I do.

One way to avoid worries about misleading implications is to maintain that the epistemic norm is merely a norm of how strong one's epistemic position must be with respect to P to assert P. One might then claim that knowing P is good enough.

16. See Williamson (2000, Chapter 9) for a thorough defense of the knowledge norm of assertion. Before him, Unger (1975) also gave a compelling defense. Unger noted that we sense that global skepticism, the view that no one knows anything at all, is somehow self-defeating. If you say, "No one knows anything," you're somehow defeating your purposes. Why do we sense this? The knowledge norm of assertion gives us an explanation: You shouldn't assert something unless you know it; but in asserting "no one knows anything" what you assert entails that you don't know it; so by asserting it you guarantee the impropriety of your asserting it. What you assert, in other words, guarantees the impropriety of your asserting it! That's a kind of self-defeat.

17. After trying to answer this yourself, you might consult Stewart Cohen (1998) for an argument that we can't solve the Gettier problem this way.

Perceptual Justification

Matthew McGrath

Perception is a source of knowledge. When you walk out your door and see a squirrel on the porch railing or hear a chickadee's *dee dee dee*, you come to know things about your surroundings: that there's a squirrel on the railing, that there's a bird calling in the yard, and so forth. In fact, it is hard to see how we could know much about the world around us if we could not perceive how things are. Perception is also a source of justified belief. You are justified in believing a squirrel is on the railing when you see it there, and justified in believing that a bird is calling in the yard when you hear the *dee dee dee*.

So far, we are merely stating the obvious. However, when we ask how perception provides us with knowledge and justified belief, difficult questions arise. This chapter focuses primarily on justified perceptual belief, rather than perceptual knowledge. If knowledge requires justified belief, these questions will arise derivatively for knowledge as well. As we'll see, many of the issues discussed in the earlier chapters of this book—internalism vs. externalism, foundationalism vs. coherentism, and skepticism—come to the fore when we explore perceptual justification.

We begin with a brief discussion of perceptual experience.

6.1 PRELIMINARIES ON PERCEPTUAL EXPERIENCE

Perception, at least in paradigm cases, involves *perceptual experience* ("experience" for short). You have an experience when you look at a Fuji apple in normal daylight, distinct from the one you have when you look at a Granny Smith apple. You have an experience when you hear a C-major chord played on a piano, distinct from the one you have when you hear a C-minor chord.

When you have such experiences, things and their properties seem *present* to you in a way they don't in nonperceptual thought. Compare seeing a Granny Smith apple on a table with being told, when your eyes are closed, that there is a Granny Smith apple sitting on the table. In both cases, you know there is an apple on the table, but when you see it, the apple, its green-ness, its waxiness, its plumpness are present to you in a way that they are not when you sit before the table with your eyes closed. In having this and other paradigm perceptual experiences, the properties are not merely present, they are present as qualifying things—the greenness isn't simply present when you see the apple; it is present as qualifying the apple. As some philosophers (e.g., Siegel 2010) put it, properties are present "as instantiated by" things.

The term *perceptual experience* isn't part of common parlance, but it is con-nected to talk of how things look, sound, feel, and so forth to us. When we have a visual experience, things *look certain ways* to us; when we have an au-ditory experience, things *sound certain ways* to us, and so forth. The "ways" things look, feel, sound, correspond to the properties present to us when we undergo these experiences.[1]

6.2 CAN EXPERIENCES JUSTIFY BELIEFS?

When you see the Granny Smith apple, it looks plump and green to you, and you'll justifiably believe it has these properties. What is the role of experience in the justification of beliefs like this? Can experiences be *justifiers* of such beliefs? That is, can having an experience make it the case that you are justi-fied in such beliefs?

Epistemologists disagree about how to answer this question. The domi-nant view among epistemologists today is that experiences can and do jus-tify beliefs. However, there are philosophers who think that experiences cannot justify any beliefs; but can only cause beliefs (cf. Davidson 1986 and Rorty 1980). For instance, an apple's looking green to you might cause you to believe that it is green. The green-belief will in turn justify you in holding other beliefs, so long as it fits with your other beliefs (notice the *coherentism* involved here). But the apple's looking green to you, on this view, wouldn't justify you in believing anything. In the next section, which is marked op-tional, we consider an influential and complex argument for this view. The argument is worth considering even if, as this author believes, it fails to es-tablish its conclusion. Most of this chapter focuses on how experiences do justify beliefs, not whether they can at all. Readers wanting to proceed to the "how" question as opposed to the "whether" question may skip ahead to Section 6.2.2.

6.2.1 The Sellarsian Dilemma (Optional)

The argument we discuss in this section for the conclusion that experiences cannot justify beliefs is called the *Sellarsian Dilemma* after the philosopher Wilfrid Sellars.[2] In the version we will discuss, a certain technical term ap-pears, "assertive propositional content." We need to explain it upfront. Let's start with "propositional content." The meaning of this term is best explained by examples. Beliefs have propositional content: They are beliefs *that such and perception is neither True or False* [handwritten marginalia]

such, where *that such and such* is a proposition, something true or false. The belief that the squirrel is on the railing has the propositional content *that the squirrel is on the railing.* Similarly, hopes and intentions have propositional content. When you hope, you always hope *that such and such.* Next, "assertive." A belief represents its propositional content as being *true.* A hope instead represents its propositional content as something *that would be good to be true,* an intention as something *to make true.* A mental state has assertive propositional content just in case it has propositional content and it represents that content as true. Such mental states are not neutral with respect to their contents. They "assert" the truth of those contents, so that if the content is true, the mental state is *correct* or *veridical*, and if the content is false, the mental state is *incorrect* or *unveridical.* We don't call a hope for something that isn't the case false or incorrect; we do call beliefs in false propositions by these terms.[3]

Here, then, is the argument:

The Sellarsian Dilemma   *2 options* [handwritten marginalia]
1. Either experiences have assertive propositional content or they do not.
2. If experiences lack assertive propositional content, they cannot justify beliefs. *→ B/c Belief is an Assertive Proposition* [handwritten marginalia]
3. If experiences have assertive propositional content, they cannot justify beliefs. *become more Then Experiences → saying statement* [handwritten marginalia]
4. So, experiences cannot justify beliefs. *↳ can be wrong* [handwritten marginalia]
   •Judgements require more The Sense data [handwritten marginalia]

We will consider what can be said in favor of each of the "horns" of the dilemma, (2) and (3), beginning with (2).

Why think lacking assertive propositional content would disqualify experiences from justifying beliefs? One powerful line of thinking is as follows. Justification of beliefs is a matter of having reasons. So, if something X justifies a belief that P, this X must amount to having a reason to believe that P. However, merely being in a state without assertive propositional content can't amount to having a reason to believe anything. So, if experiences lack assertive propositional content, they cannot justify beliefs. This reasoning depends on two crucial ideas. The first connects justification to having reasons:

The Justification-from-Reasons View (J-from-R)

If you are justified in believing that P, you are so justified in virtue of your having a reason to believe that P.

The second tells us what reasons are and what is required to have one:

The Propositional View of Reasons (PV)

(i) a reason for belief is a proposition and (ii) to have a proposition P as a reason is to be in a mental state that assertively represents that P.

(2) follows from (J-from-R) and PV. For, if experiences lack assertive representational content, experiences are not states in which one has a reason for

a belief (according to PV), and so experiences can't justify beliefs (according to (J-from-R)).

The claim that justification always comes from having reasons certainly sounds plausible. How could you be justified in believing, say, that the Winter 2014 Olympics were held in Russia unless you have a reason to believe this? The same seems true about perceptual beliefs. If you are justified through perception in believing the wall in front of you is beige, don't you need to have a reason to back up this belief? We can debate what exactly the reason is, but it seems plausible that you must have one. We will return to (J-from-R) below, but initially at least, it seems very plausible.

The propositional view of reasons, or (PV), however, seems less obvious on its face, given that it is a highly theoretical view. However, examples seem to confirm it.[4] Suppose you have a book in front of you. You haven't opened it yet. It is called *Introduction to Statistics*. Do you have a reason to believe it has formulas inside? Clearly yes! What is this reason? Well, it is something like this: *Statistics involves the use of formulas and this is a book of statistics*. Your reason is thus a proposition. It is *that such and such*. This case is not a one-off case. Take anything you think is a reason. Can't you formulate it as a statement that is capable of being true or false—as a proposition?

Moreover, we can give a general argument that a reason must be a proposition. Reasons to believe a proposition P must *support* or *confirm* P. But only propositions can confirm propositions. We talk, loosely, of bloody knives found in the accused's home confirming that he is guilty. But the knife itself doesn't confirm anything; it's the fact that the knife is bloody and was found in the accused's home that confirms the proposition that the accused is guilty. And facts, broadly speaking, are propositions (i.e., true propositions).

So far, we have a defense of the first clause, (i), of the propositional view of reasons. What about the second clause, (ii), which concerns *having* a reason? *Having* reasons makes reasons available to justify your beliefs. The question is therefore how a reason becomes available to do this. In general, a proposition being true won't suffice. If the gym is closed on Sundays but I don't have any idea that this is so, the proposition that *the gym is closed on Sundays* isn't available to justify further beliefs such as *I can't exercise there today*. Plausibly, having a reason requires being in some mental state with that reason as content. But not just any mental state will do. Hoping that P is true doesn't make P my reason. If I hope that my car doesn't break down on my trip, I certainly don't thereby have *my car won't break down on my trip* as a reason to believe other things! The same goes for intention, fear, and the like. The mental state must involve some sort of "assertion" of the proposition as true. The prime candidate for this sort of assertive representation is *belief*. But perhaps there are other candidates, including experience. In experience, a property is presented to you as instantiated by the object—the greenness is presented as instantiated by the apple. This seems a good candidate for assertive representation. Your experience is *veridical* if the apple is green and *unveridical* if it isn't.

The propositional view of reasons thus seems to hold up fairly well so far. Assuming that justification amounts to having reasons, it looks like the

Sellarsian is in good shape as far as the first horn of the dilemma is concerned. Let's turn to the second horn:

3. If experiences have assertive propositional content, they cannot justify beliefs.

Why think this is true? The argument goes as follows: States that have assertive propositional content can justify beliefs only if they themselves are justified; but experiences cannot be justified; and so even if they have assertive propositional content, they cannot justify beliefs.

Let's grant that experiences cannot be justified (something you might want to think about again after reading Section 6.4). Experiences usually are understood as "givens" received from the world, rather than our "takes" on the world. Only our "takes" on the world are assessable for justification.

The case for (3), then, turns on whether the mental states with assertive propositional content must be justified in order for them to justify the subject in having certain beliefs. Why think that? The best argument for this claim relies on the principles we saw above—(J-from-R) and (PV)—but it makes a crucial addition to (PV), viz. that the relevant assertive mental state be itself justified. So, the argument would be that justification amounts to having reasons, as (J-from-R) says, and that having a reason amounts to having a mental state that is a *justified* assertive representation of the proposition or fact that is one's reason. (PV) is expanded to:

Expanded Propositional View of Reasons

(i) a reason for belief is a proposition and (ii) to have a proposition P as a reason is to be in a mental state M that assertively represents P; and (iii) this mental state M is itself justified.

(iii) is surely a *major* addition. Why is it needed?

Again, we can give mundane examples in support of adding (iii). (PV) with only (i) and (ii), it seems, is false. Not just any old belief—or any old assertive representation—turns a proposition into a reason you have. Suppose I just believe on a whim that I will win the Missouri Lottery. Do I acquire a reason to believe I'll be rich? No. (Remember, having reasons is supposed to help make a person justified.) My belief that I'll win the lottery would need itself to be justified for me to acquire a reason to believe I'll be rich. What goes for belief—one might generalize—goes for all other assertive mental states. You don't have P as a reason unless you are in a mental state that both assertively represents P and is itself a justified mental state.

At this point, looking back over our discussion, you might start to worry about the combination of (J-from-R) and the expanded (PV). Together they entail that only an infinite chain of justification or else a circle of justification could give us a justified belief! What they rule out is any sort of *immediate* justification, whether by experiences or not. Given the negative conclusions of Chapters 1 and 2 about the alternatives to immediate justification, we ought to explore ways to resist the conjunction of (J-from-R) and (PV). There does seem to be a viable option. It is to say: Some beliefs are immediately justified; and insofar as they are immediately justified, they aren't justified because one has reasons for them; it's only in the case of mediately justified beliefs that the justification must come from the having of reasons. That is to say: (J-from-R) is false for immediate justification but true for mediate justification.[5]

If we have to back off from (J-from-R) in this way, the Sellarsian Dilemma collapses. Experiences would seem to be exactly the sorts of mental states that gave us immediate justification, and so justification not by virtue of having reasons. Depending on just how one thinks of experiences—whether one thinks of them as having assertive propositional content or not—one would reject the corresponding horn of the dilemma.[6]

The Sellarsian might now demand an explanation of how one could be justified if not through the having of a reason. That is a very good question. But perhaps the best way to approach it is not to impose principles from on high but to try out the hypothesis that experiences can justify and see how it fares. Perhaps after making these attempts, we might find ourselves wondering if the Sellarsian is right after all and so find ourselves skeptical of immediate justification. Perhaps not. There is no substitute, though, for trying our hands at it.

6.3 ASSUMING EXPERIENCES CAN JUSTIFY BELIEFS, HOW DO THEY DO SO?

We will assume as a working hypothesis, then, that experiences can and do justify beliefs. When it comes to the question of *how* they do this, we can divide theories into two categories. Some theories take experiences in which things look a certain way *directly* to justify us in believing propositions about things in the external world. On such views, we have immediately justified perceptual beliefs about the external world. (In the terminology of Chapter 1, some perceptual beliefs about the external world are *basic* beliefs.) Other theories take the justification to be indirect: Experiences directly justify us in beliefs in propositions about our experiences (propositions such *as it looks to me like there is something green here*) and these beliefs in turn justify us in believing propositions about how things are in the world around us (propositions such as *this thing is green*). On these views, beliefs about our experiences are immediately justified by experience and beliefs about how things are in the external world are only mediately justified. Let's call theories of the first sort *direct theories* and theories of the second sort *indirect theories*.

6.3.1 Indirect Theories

How could the experience in which an apple looks green to you justify you in believing propositions about the world outside you (e.g., that the apple is green)? Don't you first have to notice the apple looks green to you and then to conclude that it is green on that basis? According to indirect theories, *yes*.[7]

However, indirect theories face a number of problems. First, it seems difficult to reach the conclusion that the apple is green if all you have to start with is the justified belief that it looks green to you. After all, this inference is hardly conclusive. How serious this problem is for indirect theories depends on how strong the *looks-F-to-me/is F* inferential connection is and on questions about the justification of background beliefs that might help close the gap.

A second worry concerns psychology. Before spelling out the worry, we need to review the distinction from Chapter 2 (Section 2.1) between *propositional* and *doxastic justification*. The first is a matter of our having justification *to* believe a proposition, whether you do believe it or not. The second is a matter of having a belief that is justified. As we saw in Chapter 2, to have a justified belief that P, you have to believe P *on the right basis*. Thus, we have:

Basing Requirement on Doxastic Justification

Your belief in P is justified only if you are justified in believing P and you believe P on the basis of the factors that make you justified in believing P.[8]

The psychological worry about indirect theories is that they cannot explain our doxastic justification for perceptual beliefs about things in the external world. Do we really base our perceptual beliefs such as *this apple is green* on beliefs about our experience? Arguably, we don't. Suppose a person believed the apple in front of her was green upon its looking green to her. Suppose, though, she believed this *without* first believing that it looked green to her and then inferring that it must be green because it looks green to her. On indirect theories, what makes her justified in believing it is green (what provides propositional justification) is not merely the experience but the inferential relations between its looking green to her to its being green. But the person in the example didn't go through that reasoning based on these factors, even implicitly. Do we want to say that the person's belief that the apple before her is green is not justified in this case?

A final observation about indirect theories. Anyone who accepts such a theory needs to be able to explain *why* experiences can directly justify us only in beliefs about our experience and not also beliefs about how things are in the world outside us. We might be tempted to try to explain this by saying that, although we can be wrong about how things are outside us, we can't be wrong about our experience, and that only when we can't be wrong do we have direct justification. However, we should resist this temptation. Can't we be wrong even about how things look, sound, and so forth to us? Couldn't I get my experience wrong despite my best attempts to get it right? (Think of the look of snow in shadow: Does it look gray to you? Or blue?) Also, why exactly is direct justification possible only in a way that makes error impossible?

The remainder of this chapter focuses on direct theories.[9]

6.4 DOGMATISM

The simplest version of a direct theory, and the one we consider below, holds
that when you have an experience in which something looks, sounds, and so
forth a certain way to you, this experience alone is enough to justify you in believing it is *that very way*. The experience justifies you in this belief immediately—
that is, not in virtue of your being justified in believing other propositions. The
justification provided is nonetheless prima facie, however, insofar as it is defea-
sible; it can be opposed or undermined by defeaters (on defeat, see Chapter 1,
Section 1.8). In the literature, this popular view is referred to as *dogmatism*.[10]
We'll see why it earns this name below (see Section 6.6).
    Here is a simple formulation of the view:

Dogmatism (simple version)

Whenever you have an experience in which a thing appears (i.e., looks, sounds,
etc.) a certain way, F, to you, then you thereby have immediate prima facie justification to believe that it is F.

This formulation needs revision if it is to apply to cases such as hallucina-
tion in which nothing in fact appears to you. We might expand dogmatism
to apply to these cases by using the concept of experience *as of* a thing appearing a certain way, a concept that includes the normal case of a thing appearing a certain way to you but also includes abnormal cases in which it
seems like something appears to you even though there is nothing you are
perceiving. We then have:

Dogmatism (expanded version)

Whenever you have an experience as of something being a certain way, F, to
you, then you thereby have immediate prima facie justification to believe that it
is F.

For the most part, therefore, we will not worry too much about the difference between these two versions of dogmatism. To have a convenient general
expression, we will use "experience as of P."
    Dogmatism has strong antiskeptical implications. This is because if it is
true, then prominent skeptical arguments have false premises. As we saw in
Chapter 4, "skeptical possibility" arguments rely on claims such as this:

In order for an experience as of P to justify you in believing P, where P is some
proposition about the external world, you have to be justified in believing that
you aren't a brain in a vat (aren't dreaming, etc.), and your justification for believing you aren't a brain in a vat (dreaming, etc.) can't come from inference
from P. That is to say: Your justification to believe you aren't in the skeptical
scenario must be *independent* of your justification to believe P.

If dogmatism is true, it seems this skeptical assumption is false. For, if
dogmatism is true, all you need is the experience as of P to be justified in

believing P, absent defeaters. The experience is enough. You don't need to be independently justified in believing you aren't in skeptical scenarios.

Dogmatism is a simple and attractive theory. It allows that we can enjoy justified perceptual beliefs without having in our possession complicated skeptic-proof arguments. Dogmatism has the merit of fitting well with how our perceptual beliefs seem to us: They seem justified but not justified by complex arguments.

So, there are real attractions to dogmatism. Nonetheless, there are challenges the view must answer. The two challenges that we will consider below are these:

> *Will just any experience do?* That is, does any experience provide immediate justification, or must an experience satisfy certain further conditions in order to provide immediate justification?

> *Is an experience all it takes?* That is, is all it takes to make a belief justified that one has an experience? Or do you need, in addition to your experience, background evidence that your experience is reliable, or that conditions making it unreliable don't obtain? If it takes background evidence, then experiences as of P do not immediately justify us in believing that P, contrary to dogmatism.

6.5 WILL JUST ANY EXPERIENCE DO?

In recent work on dogmatism, several philosophers have raised objections to the claim that just any experience will do. They agree that *some* experiences do make the corresponding beliefs prima facie justified, and do so immediately; they just think not every experience does so. They therefore think we need to restrict dogmatism to certain sorts of experience. We will consider two objections aiming to show that dogmatism requires restriction: the *cognitive penetrability objection* and the *speckled hen objection*.

6.5.1 The Cognitive Penetrability Objection

A number of decades ago, a lively debate took place within the philosophy of science about whether observation is "theory-laden" (cf. Fodor 1983, Pylyshyn 1999). Do we "see" different things depending on which theories we accept? If we do, then if we use what we see to justify those theories, aren't we going in a circle?

More specifically, suppose that your acceptance of a theory leads you to expect that a certain experiment will turn out in a certain way, and suppose this expectation influences your experience when you observe the experimental results (when you look in the microscope). This does seem problematic. Here is an example (due to Susanna Siegel 2012). In the nineteenth century some biologists were preformationists. They believed that each cell in the human body contained a very small embryo that, when given the right circumstances, could grow into a human being. Suppose a preformationist peers through a microscope, expecting to see a tiny embryo. As it turns out, there is something there that looks only a little bit like an embryo. However, suppose that, because of the expectation, the preformationist "sees it" as an embryo. We can assume, moreover, that he doesn't have any special reason to doubt the veridicality of his experience. According to dogmatism, the preformationist is justified in believing that what he sees under the microscope is an embryo. This seems problematic.[11]

The key factor here is not so much *theory*-ladenness per se but the influence of our cognitive attitudes on our experiences (i.e., cognitive penetration). Such penetration isn't always by theoretical beliefs: Desires, moods, and other nondoxastic attitudes might influence experience as well. ("Cognitive" is used very broadly in this literature, referring to any mental state of the person beyond experiences.) Consider another example, due to Markie (2006), raising the same problems for dogmatism as the preformationist case but without any sort of theory-ladenness. (Similar cases are also found in Siegel 2012 and Goldman 2009.) Suppose Gus, a novice gold prospector, wants to find gold, and this desire, rather than any gold-identification skills, makes him see the dusty nugget in his pan as gold. He believes it is gold on this basis. Had he used only his (rather meager) gold-identification skills, he wouldn't have believed the nugget was gold. Does Gus get to be justified because of the desire to find gold? This seems no better than wishful thinking. Here the wish affects experience first and only indirectly the belief formed on the basis of it, but does the indirectness of the effect make any epistemic difference?

Do such cases refute dogmatism? Perhaps not. If something looks clearly like a gold nugget to you, what are you supposed to think? That it *isn't* one? Justification is a matter of what is reasonable for you to believe given what you have to go on. The experience is what Gus has to go on, and given this experience the only reasonable doxastic attitude for him to take toward the proposition *this is a nugget of gold* is belief. So, the gold-digger is justified in believing it is gold, despite the cognitive penetration of his experience by desire.

Yet it does seem like there is something suspect about this line of defense—the "what am I supposed to think?" response to the examples. Why think that the pebble's looking like gold to Gus is part of "what he has to go on" rather than something he *adds* to what he has to go on, because of his wish to find gold? At least this could be the correct psychological story in certain cases. It does seem to be suggested by the example. Suppose this is what is going on: Gus has certain experiences, and through wish-motivated "enhancements," facilitated by focusing on particular aspects of the experience, exaggerating them, and ignoring others, Gus comes to have the experience of the pebble looking like gold. Isn't this something like *jumping to conclusions*? It would literally be jumping to conclusions if Gus inferred the *belief* that the pebble was gold based on a *belief* about its color and shape, where the color and shape, given Gus's information, didn't adequately support the conclusion that it was a gold nugget. But if the "jumping" takes place within experience, so that one experience is based on another, is this any better epistemically?[12]

Maybe so, the dogmatist might say, but we should be clearer about just what is included in *experience* and what isn't. The dogmatist might say that experience leaves off at "lower-level" features (i.e., colors, shapes, sounds, textures, and the like); it doesn't extend to *being a nugget of gold, being an embryo,* and other "higher-level" features.[13] Thus, you don't really experience things as *nuggets of gold,* as *trees, cars,* and so forth. You might say, "This looks like a tree," but really your experience is at best of the spatial and color properties—a "look" that trees present. When something looks to you to be a tree, this is a matter of postexperiential thought (beliefs, or inclinations to believe, for instance), which like all forms of thought is penetrable by epistemically bad cognitive states. The epistemic faultiness lies with postexperiential thought rather than experience itself. It is in thought rather than experience that the jumping to conclusions occurs. Thus, dogmatism is not touched by the cognitive penetration cases, because it is about *experience,* not postexperiential thought. So, at least, the dogmatist might argue.

The persuasiveness of this defense of dogmatism turns on debates over whether we experience "higher-level" features such as kind properties (e.g., "nugget of gold"). The issue is an old one. Thus, George Berkeley in the eighteenth century claimed we don't hear a coach, when the horses and carriage go by:

> Sitting in my Study I hear a Coach drive along the Street; I look through the Casement and see it; I walk out and enter into it; thus, common Speech would incline one to think, I heard, saw, and touch'd the same thing, to wit, the Coach. It is nevertheless certain, the Ideas intromitted by each Sense are widely different, and distinct from each other; but having been observed constantly to go together, they are spoken of as one and the same thing. (1732, section 46)

For Berkeley, auditory perception is limited to sounds and doesn't extend to object kind properties like *coach.* By contrast, Thomas Reid (1764, 1785) distinguishes original from acquired perception, allowing that we can hear a coach (as a coach) through acquired perception. (For a discussion of Reid's subtle views of these matters, see Copenhaver 2010.)

Today, philosophers make use of the rich set of experimental results from psychology and neuroscience in the debate over the "levels" of experience.[14] Evidence from a variety of psychological experiments seems potentially relevant, including studies of reaction times (comparing reaction times for classification of higher-level features like kinds vs. classification of colors and shapes) and fMRI scans (examining the regions of the brain active during classificatory and other tasks). Of particular interest are studies of patients with *associative agnosia,* a deficit in which subjects' "early" visual areas operate normally or nearly normally, enabling them to draw by hand accurate pictures of what they see, but in which they are mystified as to how to classify the object. A subject seeing a banana might be able to draw it accurately but be perplexed as to what it could be. If associative agnosics have *experiential* deficits, then it appears that the higher-level feature view is correct: Those of us without the deficit have experience of higher-level features. It should be noted that the deficits are not due to loss of "semantic memory" (i.e., to a loss of knowledge of what, say, a banana is). The associative agnostic who can't classify a banana can tell you about bananas (they're fruit, often eaten at breakfast, they're sweet, etc.). However, it is not obvious we have to see their deficits as experiential. As it is sometimes put, vaguely, perhaps their deficit is an inability to link such semantic memory to experience in a way necessary for classification.[15]

There is a further problem for this "low-level experience" response to the cognitive penetration cases. In principle, it seems lower-level experience could itself be cognitively penetrated. Perhaps, as some psychologists have argued (e.g., Hansen et al. 2006), we can in some cases see grayish bananas as yellower than they are because we expect them to look yellow. In principle, and arguably in actual fact, it seems possible for desires, fears, and biases to intervene in the processing that leads to experience, affecting its final character. Might a white subject who categorizes a face as belonging to a "black" person see the face as darker than it is? Yes, according to a study by Levin and Banaji (2006).

If cognitive states penetrate experience of lower-level features like color and shape, what is the epistemic upshot? If you and I have the same sorts of color experiences, mine being influenced by an expectation that bananas look yellow and yours not, am I less justified than you are to believe the banana I see is yellow?

Let's push the question further: What if (hypothetically) my desires affect even earlier processing leading up to the experience—say, in the signals leaving the retinal cells through the optic nerve? Could this have an effect on my justification? If you think, with this author, that the brain in a vat (BIV) is justified just as much as we are in its perceptual beliefs, you will want to say that the fact that the neuroscientist's desires affect the BIV's experience doesn't reduce the justification of the BIV's justification. Does it matter that the desires are someone else's and not the subject's? If so, why?

We've seen, then, that there are ways a dogmatist can attempt to retain dogmatism fully intact in the face of cognitive penetration cases like the preformationist and Gus the gold-digger. But suppose the dogmatist concedes that some of these cases do refute dogmatism. Is there a way she can restrict the scope of dogmatism to avoid these counterexamples, while preserving the heart of the view? Of course, she doesn't want to throw out the baby with the bath water. Perhaps some cognitive penetration isn't epistemically bad. Suppose the birder's current knowledge of the visual features of flycatchers influences her experience when she sees one, so that the distinctive features stand out. This wouldn't seem epistemically problematic. What is the difference between good and bad cognitive penetration?

Can we at least say that penetration by desires always makes for bad cognitive penetration? Well, if by "penetration" we mean *causation*, then clearly no. Suppose you want to see something indigo (say, to compare it to the color of the sky that day), and so you open your guide to birds to see an indigo bunting. We don't want to say there is anything bad about your believing the bird's color is indigo based on your experience. Of course, "penetration" doesn't simply mean causation of any old sort; we mean causation after the initial stimulation of sensory receptors occurs.

Can we say, then, that any influence of desires in processing after the initial sensory stimulation leads to bad cognitive penetration? Again, no. Fear of snakes can cause snake-shapes to "pop out" in experience, drawing our attention, leading us to spot snakes we wouldn't otherwise spot (see Lyons 2011a). This "pop out" occurs after initial stimulation of sensory receptors. It needn't be epistemically bad (let's suppose it doesn't lead to a greater number of false positives). We should define cognitive penetration in such a way as to rule this out, too.

According to one promising definition given in the literature, an experience is cognitively penetrated if and only if a cognitive state of the person penetrates (i.e., causally influences) the postattentional processing of sensory input (Siegel 2012). Still, it isn't *obvious* from this definition that all cognitive penetration by desires is epistemically bad. (If you think it is, why?) At this point, we could either attempt to sift through more cases or instead seek a theoretical basis for distinguishing the good cognitive penetration from the bad. We'll pursue the latter option.

One proposal for distinguishing good from bad cognitive penetration, however the latter is exactly defined, is to appeal to *reliabilism* or some other form of *externalism* about justification.[16] Reliabilism, in its simplest form, holds that a belief's being justified is a matter of its being formed in a reliable way, where this means being formed using a belief-forming process that generally produces true rather than false beliefs. On reliabilism, the fearful snake-detector's experience justifies his belief because the process of believing there's a snake based on the fear-attuned "snake"-experience is reliable. The process of believing there is an embryo based on the expectation-based "embryo"-experience, however, is not reliable, and so that experience doesn't justify the preformationist's belief. The same goes for Gus, the wishful gold-digger.

However, one might wonder if this reliabilist account can go the full distance. Consider, fancifully, two people who are completely wrong about their environments, two BIVs. Imagine BIV-Gus. BIV-Gus is just like Gus, except of course that he is a brain in a vat. His desire penetrates his experience in exactly the way Gus's does. Now, consider Grace, a reliable gold-digger whose desires don't penetrate her experiences in the actual world. She has a counterpart, BIV-Grace, whose experience as of gold isn't penetrated by her desires. Compare BIV-Gus to BIV-Grace. BIV-Gus seems just as unjustified as Gus, but BIV-Grace seems much better epistemically. BIV-Grace (to this author at least) seems just as justified as a real expert gold-digger would be. So, the two BIVs (BIV-Gus and BIV-Grace) differ crucially in justification, but neither is reliable in his or her belief-forming process—they're BIVs, after all, and so the truth-ratio of processes delivering beliefs about things outside their minds is *very low*. So there is a difference in justification but no difference in reliability. Quite possibly, some further variety of externalism might fare better here, but simple reliabilism seems not to do the job.[17]

Suppose you aren't an externalist. What can you say? One proposal is to restrict dogmatism to experiences that lack an *irrational etiology* (see Siegel 2013a). What constitutes an irrational etiology, though? One way to get at this issue is to ask whether the same etiology, if it involved beliefs rather than experiences, would count as irrational. Suppose I believe the thing I see is an embryo on the basis of a belief that it has such-and-such a shape (where this is not clearly that of an embryo), and I form the belief it is an embryo on the basis of this belief only because I want to see an embryo. Then my embryo-belief has an irrational etiology: It's a case of jumping to conclusions. (Thus, it is an unjustified belief.) Similarly, if it looked like an embryo because it looked such and such (the same shape features as before), then this would be an irrational etiology for the experience—jumping to conclusions within experiences. Even if they cannot be justified or unjustified, experiences can fail to make the corresponding beliefs justified, when they have irrational etiologies. Of course, "jumping to conclusions" because of the influence of cognitive states is only one way beliefs can have irrational etiologies due to "cognitive penetration." There are others. If every etiology that is irrational for beliefs is also irrational for experiences, then so long as we have a good grasp on irrational etiologies for belief, we have a program for separating good from bad cognitive penetration.

Just what the upshot of cognitive penetration for dogmatism is continues to be a matter of lively current debate, engaging epistemology, philosophy of mind, and empirical psychology.

6.5.2 The Speckled Hen Objection

We now turn to a second worry about whether *any old* experience in which something looks a certain way can immediately justify a person to believe the thing is that way. This is the so-called *speckled hen problem*, made prominent by Ernest Sosa (cf. BonJour and Sosa 2003).

Imagine seeing two hens, one with 48 speckles and the other 3. Before you count, you are not justified in thinking the first has 48 speckles, but you are justified without counting in thinking the second one has 3 speckles. The problem for dogmatism is that it seems that 48-speckledness is present in your experience when you look at the first hen, just as 3-speckledness is present in your experience when you look at the second hen. But if it looks 48-speckled to you, then by dogmatism, wouldn't you be justified in thinking it is 48-speckled? But you aren't. So we have a problem for dogmatism.

The dogmatist might complain that this isn't a counterexample at all. Dogmatism claims that experiences in which an object appears a certain way immediately prima facie justify you in believing the object is that way. But, she might say, in the speckled hen case, the hen doesn't appear 48-speckled, but only *many-speckled*, say. The hen may be in reality be 48-speckled, but this feature is not present to the subject experiencing the hen.

However, consider the following case (cf. Davis 2006 and Pace 2010). Suppose you hear a middle C played on the piano. Suppose a friend plays the note and you can't see which key is pressed. If you lack perfect pitch, you'll hear the note and perceive the pitch clearly. But you won't be justified in believing it's a C; it could easily be a D, E, or any other pitch as far as you can tell. Next, imagine you go over to the piano and play a middle C. You might think, "Ah, yes, that's it—that's the pitch I heard a minute ago." It seems you will be right. You *did* hear the C pitch. This property was present to you in your auditory experience. But you weren't justified in believing the note had a C pitch. Thus, it seems we have a counterexample to dogmatism: You have an auditory experience of a note being a C, but you aren't immediately prima facie justified in believing it is a C. This case can substitute for the speckled hen case if necessary. Because of the availability of this sort of reply to doubts about the hen cases, we can stick with the original speckled hen case, inviting those skeptical of whether 48-ness is present in experience to substitute the middle C case. The middle C case makes it clear that the core of the speckled hen problem doesn't have to do with numerosity or even complexity.

Here again, as with the cognitive penetration objection, reliabilism offers a possible response. This is similar to Sosa's favored response. We are justified in believing that there are 3 speckles because we are reliable at detecting 3-speckledness. We are *not* justified in believing, before counting, that there are 48 speckles because we are not reliable at detecting 48-speckledness without counting. The reliabilist might point out a further advantage of her view on these matters: Given reliabilism, we can see not just why 48-speckledness experiences don't justify but also why they *could* justify more powerful perceivers than us. If someone could reliably believe, based on experiences involving large numbers of scattered speckles, this person would be justified by those experiences, even though we aren't. There is no logical problem with a 48-speckled experience justifying; it doesn't justify us, but that is only because we lack the relevant reliable belief-forming process; other possible beings could have it and so be justified.

Just as with the cognitive penetration objection, though, we can devise BIV cases to raise questions about whether simple reliabilism covers all cases. Consider a BIV with the sort of experience we have when we see a 48-speckled hen. The BIV isn't justified in believing it has 48 speckles. But when the BIV has the sort of experience we have when we see a 3-speckled hen, the BIV is justified. There is no difference in reliability, but there is a difference in justification. Simple reliabilism fails to distinguish all the cases that need distinguishing.

Is there an internalistically acceptable way to solve the speckled hen problem? What is needed is some internalist way to carve out a class of experiences that, for us, excludes experiences of 48-speckledness but includes 3-speckledness. And we would want our carving principle to allow the person with perfect pitch to have justification to believe a note is a C but the person without not to lack it. How can we do this?

In trying to give an internalist solution, the dogmatist needs to take care that she doesn't treat experiences as if they were beliefs. The dogmatist cannot say: The experiences that are included are ones in which people are *aware* that a thing has a property. Being aware that a thing has a property consists in having knowledge or justified (true) belief, and so brings us back to belief. But then experiences, to justify beliefs, would themselves have to be justified, because experiences would be beliefs, and beliefs justify other beliefs only if *they* are justified.

The dogmatist therefore needs to walk a fine line in responding to the speckled hen objection. There are a number of ways of trying to walk this line in an internalist-friendly way. We will mention three. You can judge for yourself their prospects.

The first is the *seemings response.* The dogmatist should understand experiences in the relevant sense as mental states in which it seems to the subject that a thing is F; only such seemings can justify. In the speckled hen case, it doesn't seem to the subject that the hen is 48-speckled, and so that's why he isn't justified. (This is the so-called "phenomenal conservatism" of Michael Huemer [2000].)

Questions to Consider

What are these seemings? Are they different from beliefs and from inclinations to believe? Would any seeming, however formed, provide prima facie justification? Or would only some seemings suffice? Of what sort?

The second is the *mode of presentation response.* The dogmatist might claim that only experiences in which a property is present in a certain mode or way provide prima facie justification. In the speckled hen case, 48-ness is present but not present *as 48-ness.* When you see a three-speckled hen, 3-ness is present *as 3-ness.*

Questions to Consider

What is it to be present *as* such and such? Is this any different than the seemings response?

The third is the *demonstrative response.* The dogmatist might severely restrict her dogmatism so that it only applies to beliefs such as *this thing is that way.* So, if an object looks a certain way to you, you are prima facie immediately justified only in believing that it is *that way.* This has some appeal for the case of the person without perfect pitch hearing the middle C. You hear the sound. You are immediately justified in believing that the note is *like that.* You go to the piano and play the middle C and then learn that *that sound* was a Č. You can of course come to have further *mediately* justified beliefs by building from your immediately justified beliefs, but the idea would be that experience only gives immediate justification for such demonstrative beliefs.[18]

Question to Consider

Does this deprive dogmatism of the advantages it has over indirect theories?

6.6 SECOND CHALLENGE TO DOGMATISM: IS AN EXPERIENCE ENOUGH?[19]

Recall the Moore-style proof we discussed in Chapter 4:

1. I have hands.
2. So, I am not a (handless) BIV.

On first blush, it seems you can't *get* to be justified in (2) via this reasoning because in order to be justified in believing (1) you have to already be justified in believing (2). However, if dogmatism is true, isn't this "first blush" intuition incorrect? According to dogmatism, all it takes to be justified in believing that you have hands, (1), is an experience as of having hands. You don't need already to have justification to think you aren't in a skeptical scenario like the BIV scenario. So, suppose you don't have such justification. Then Moorean reasoning—reasoning from (1) to (2)—would give you this justification. That is: Moorean reasoning would be a way one could *become* justified in believing (2).[20]

Let's explain this in a bit more detail. Suppose you start off not being justified in believing you're not a BIV. It's not that you merely lack a justified belief; you aren't justified *in* believing you aren't a BIV. That is, you lack propositional justification as well as doxastic justification. However, suppose you also lack good reason to believe you *are* a BIV. You don't have good reason to believe either you are or that you aren't a BIV, suppose. Now, according to dogmatism, when you look at your hands (or feel them), your experience of having hands is enough to make you prima facie justified in believing you have hands. You have no good reason, we can assume, to doubt your experience is accurate. (It was important to stipulate that you lack good reason to think you are a BIV; if you had such reason, it would defeat the prima facie justification you have from experience to believe you have hands.) Next, suppose you proceed to believe you have hands based on this experience. This gives you a justified belief that you have hands. Based on this justified belief, you then competently infer that you are not a BIV. This gives you a justified belief that you are not a BIV.

Or does it? In Chapter 4 (Section 4.2.1), we raised questions about whether forming a belief based on deduction from a proposition you know always provides further knowledge. Maybe when the deduction involved question-begging reasoning, you couldn't arrive at new knowledge this way. The same worry applies to justified belief. However, in Chapter 4, we proposed a closure principle that is neutral on these matters. The variant of that principle for justification is as follows:

Closure of Justified Belief

If your belief in P is justified and you know that P entails Q, then you are justified in believing Q.

The rationale here, as with the closure principle for knowledge, is that if you can't expand your justified beliefs by deduction that has to be because you already had a justified belief in the conclusion or at least had an independent ground for believing the conclusion. So, in any case, if you do have a justified belief in P and you know that P entails Q, you are in a position to obtain a justified belief in Q—either via deduction from P or independently. To be justified in believing Q just is to be in a position to have a justified belief in Q, and so this gives us the closure principle.

The interesting thing is that if both dogmatism and this closure principle are true, then you can become justified in believing you're not in a skeptical scenario, when you weren't beforehand, by having an experience as of P and believing P on its basis. For when you have the experience as of having hands, the dogmatist says this justifies you in believing you have hands. If you believed you have hands, based on the experience, you have a justified belief that you have hands.[21] But now, because of closure, you are justified in believing you aren't a BIV. What gives you the justification is your justified belief you have hands, together with the knowledge that this entails you aren't a BIV. You didn't have any independent source of justification that you aren't a BIV beforehand and you didn't acquire any simply by believing in accord with your experience. So, you continue not to have any independent justification for this. Nonetheless, by closure, you are justified in believing it. So, it must be that you *can* then expand your justified beliefs in this case through Moorean reasoning to arrive at a justified belief that you're not a BIV.

What's the problem with any of this? Yes, it does seem an awfully easy way to gain a justified belief that one isn't a BIV. But sometimes what's easily obtained is nonetheless the genuine article. We need an *argument* that one cannot gain a justified belief in this way. If we have such an argument, then we can conclude two things: First, the Moorean response to the skeptic fails; and second, more relevantly to this chapter, dogmatism is false.

Critics of dogmatism have given us precisely such an argument to fit the bill. The argument we will discuss is drawn from the work of Cohen (2002) and especially White (2006). It concerns probability. For our purposes in this chapter we can think of one's probabilities for various hypotheses as measuring how confident one *ought* to be in those hypotheses. So, to say that a piece of evidence E increases one's probability for a hypothesis H is to say that one's probability for H given E—one's conditional probability for H on E—is higher than one's (unconditional) probability for H. We can think of "increasing one's probability" for our purposes as boiling down to this: E raises one's probability for H if and only if, supposing the totality of what you learn is E, you ought to raise your confidence in H over what it ought to have been before learning E. (See Chapter 11 for more details.)

Here's the argument, in brief. Suppose that beforehand your probability for ~BIV (i.e., for the proposition that you are not a BIV) isn't high enough to make you justified in believing this. Going through the process of having the experience as of having hands and then performing Moorean reasoning doesn't increase your probability for ~BIV. So, if you weren't justified beforehand, you don't become justified afterward. But if you weren't justified in believing you aren't a BIV afterward, the belief you got through the Moorean reasoning wasn't justified. However, if dogmatism is true, the belief you get through Moorean reasoning in this case is justified. Thus, dogmatism is false.

Let's set this out in premise/conclusion form. To save words, let's call the process of having the experience and going through Moorean reasoning "the Moorean process."

The "Anti-Moorean" Argument

1. If before the Moorean process you aren't justified in believing ~*BIV* (but you lack good reason to think you are a BIV), then you don't become justified in believing ~*BIV* unless your probability for it is increased by going through the Moorean process.
2. Having the experience as of having hands doesn't increase your probability for ~*BIV*.
3. Going through the Moorean reasoning after having the experience doesn't increase your probability for ~*BIV* beyond what it was upon having the experience.
4. So, your probability for ~*BIV* doesn't increase through the Moorean process (from 2 and 3).
5. So, if before the Moorean process you aren't justified in believing ~*BIV* (but you lack good reason to think you are a BIV), then you do not *become* justified in believing this through the Moorean process (from 1 and 4).

If the anti-Moorean argument is sound, we can use its conclusion as a premise in an argument against dogmatism. We label this the "easy justification" argument against dogmatism because is a way of making more precise the worry that dogmatism makes it too easy to be justified in believing one isn't in a skeptical scenario.

The "Easy Justification" Argument Against Dogmatism

5. If before the Moorean process you aren't justified in believing ~*BIV* (but you lack good reason to think you are a BIV), then you do not *become* justified in believing this through the Moorean process.
6. If dogmatism is true, then in such a situation the Moorean process gives you a justified belief that you aren't a BIV.
7. If the Moorean process gives you a justified belief you aren't a BIV, then it had to be that you were justified in believing you aren't a BIV at the end of the Moorean process.
8. Therefore: Dogmatism is false.

As we have noted, (6) seems hard to resist given closure and the way we have defined dogmatism.[22] (7), too, is hard to deny, insofar as doxastic justification implies propositional justification.

Let's examine the premises of the anti-Moorean argument (i.e., steps (1)–(3)), starting with (1). Suppose going through the Moorean process doesn't raise your probability for ~*BIV*. Why would this show you don't become justified in believing ~*BIV*? The answer relies on an assumed connection between probability and justification. Suppose your probability for ~*BIV* doesn't increase after having the experience and going through the reasoning. It started, say, at .99 and didn't get any higher. But if the probability didn't increase, then how could you *become* justified in believing ~*BIV*? If a .99 probability isn't high enough for justification and you end up with a probability of .99 or lower, then your probability at the end of the Moorean process is not high enough for justification either.

This argument for (1) depends on the:

Threshold View of Justified Belief

There is some probability threshold such that, for any proposition P and at any time t, you are justified in believing P at t if and only if your probability for P reaches or exceeds that threshold at t.

We needn't try to specify an exact point value for the threshold; perhaps it's vague and/or mushy. The crucial points are two. First, there is some (possibly vague, mushy) boundary such that if you start out on the unjustified side of the boundary you can't cross over to the justified side of the boundary unless your probability for the proposition at issue goes up. Second, the same threshold applies to all propositions. If you are justified in believing P, then if Q is just as probable for you as P, you will be justified in believing Q as well. There are certainly ways to question the threshold view,[23] but it has substantial initial plausibility.

Turn, next, to (2)—that is, the premise that the experience as of having hands fails to increase your probability for ~*BIV*. Consider the hypothesis that you *are* a BIV. Let's make it part of this hypothesis that you have the very handish-experience you have at the beginning of the Moorean process. The hypothesis that you are a BIV then *predicts* you have these very hand-experiences (in a rather trivial way, but still it predicts them). When you learn that a prediction of a hypothesis is true, you are learning that something that you'd expect to find if the hypothesis is true is in fact true. Why should this lower your confidence in the hypothesis? It shouldn't, it seems. So, your hand-experiences don't lower your probability for the BIV hypothesis. It therefore must not raise your probability for its negation (i.e., for ~*BIV*).[24]

What about (3)? (3) asserts that merely going through the Moorean reasoning couldn't increase the probability of ~*BIV* beyond what it is after having the experience as of having hands. Why think this is true? Well, going through the reasoning increases your probability only if you acquire new evidence during this process that raises that probability. But how could merely going through Moorean reasoning give one the needed new evidence? You do learn new things as you reason (e.g., that you are reasoning, that you have such and such beliefs, etc.). But how does any of this raise your probability for ~*BIV*?

But wait, you might say: Don't you acquire a justified belief that you have hands when you base your belief on the experience of having hands? According to dogmatism, you do. But then wouldn't you have new evidence—that you have hands—which increases the probability that you are not a BIV? Note that the probability of not being a (handless) BIV given that you have hands is 100%! So couldn't the justified belief that you have hands be the new evidence that is acquired through the Moorean process and that increases your probability for ~*BIV* enough to make it justified?[25]

The only way you could acquire a justified belief that you have hands based on your experience is if the experience made you justified in believing you have hands. Did it? The dogmatist would insist: yes. But can the dogmatist really say this? Consider that your having hands obviously entails your not being a BIV. Because of this, your probability for *Hands* (i.e., the proposition that you have hands) cannot ever be higher than your probability for ~*BIV*.[26] But as we saw in discussing (2), after you had the experience and before you went through the Moorean reasoning, your probability for ~*BIV* did not increase from what it was before the experience. So, if you weren't justified in believing that ~*BIV* before having the experience, then you aren't justified in believing it after having the experience. Since at no time is your probability for *Hands* greater than your probability for ~*BIV*, it follows that after you had the experience and before you went through the Moorean reasoning, your probability for *Hands* wasn't high enough to make you justified in believing *Hands*, after all.

If these conclusions so far are correct, then you didn't acquire a *justified* belief that you have hands through the Moorean process, and so you didn't acquire the evidence that you have hands. The idea that you somehow bootstrapped your way to such strong evidence that you aren't a BIV from weak evidence by forming the justified belief that you have hands thus seems not to be a lifesaver for the dogmatist.

The threshold view of justified belief, together with the considerations about probability, places strict constraints on the relations between being justified in believing one has hands and being justified in believing one isn't a BIV, constraints that seem to make it impossible to have justification from experience for *Hands* without already and independently of any Moorean reasoning having justification for ~*BIV*. Thus, these constraints seem to take us back to the "first blush" intuitive thought that you can't be justified in believing you have hands without already being justified in believing you aren't a BIV—*contra* dogmatism.

It is an open question in contemporary epistemology how the dogmatist can resist the easy justification argument. Suppose at the end of the day that dogmatism stands refuted. How might we avoid retreating to either the indirect theory that we only have immediate justification from experience for beliefs about our experiences or to the Sellarsian view that experiences cannot justify any beliefs at all?

Crispin Wright (2004) argues for a view that is a middle ground between these extremes. On his view, experience by itself cannot justify beliefs about the world. Thus, perceptual beliefs about the world are not immediately justified.

However, experience is an essential component of what can justify such beliefs. Experience *plus* certain background beliefs or presumptions can do the trick. This position, of course, raises many questions: What are these background beliefs or presumptions? How do they get to be justified? If they're not justified, how can they together with experience justify anything? But if they are justified, are they justified by further evidence? If so, won't that evidence ultimately come from beliefs formed through past perception (beliefs like *this is a hand*), in which case we'd have to ask how *those* beliefs got to be justified. Or are such background beliefs somehow justified a priori? (See Chapter 4, Section 4.4.) Worries about the background beliefs and presumptions of Wright's account fuel the hope, and maybe the suspicion, that something is wrong with the anti-Moorean argument and so with the easy justification argument against dogmatism.[27]

6.7 CONCLUSION

This chapter explored a number of key questions about perceptual justification. Our primary question is how experiences can justify beliefs. (In an optional section, we considered the formidable Sellarsian Dilemma, an argument aimed to show that no experiences can justify any beliefs, not even beliefs about those very experiences.) We explored theories about how experiences might justify beliefs, including the indirect (according to which experiences directly justify beliefs about those experiences and only indirectly justify beliefs about the world external to us) and direct theories (according to which experiences directly justify beliefs about the external world). Most of our focus was on a popular version of the direct theory, dogmatism, according to which when you have an experience in which a thing is presented to you as F, this gives you immediate prima facie justification to believe it is F. We saw that there were grounds from the cognitive penetration problem and the speckled hen problem for restricting such a principle. Finally, we considered whether experience by itself is enough to justify beliefs about the external world, or whether justified background beliefs are necessary as well. The Easy Justification argument, we saw, is an important threat to dogmatism, even after it is restricted to cope with the problems of cognitive penetrability and the speckled hen.

We can see that the debate over how experiences justify beliefs is a lively one and that in tackling these matters epistemologists do well to help themselves to any useful resources from other parts of philosophy (e.g., philosophy of mind, philosophy of probability) as well as empirical psychology.

QUESTIONS

1. Under the heading of "any experience?" objections to dogmatism, we considered the cognitive penetration and speckled hen objections. Consider indirect theories, which take experience directly to justify only beliefs about experience. Do such theories avoid both, one, or neither of these two objections to dogmatism? Explain why or why not.

2. We considered cases in which a belief (e.g., an expectation) had an impact on experience. In the case we considered, the preformationist case, you might think the preformationist isn't justified in accepting his theory, and so his experience is penetrated by an *unjustified* belief. What would you say, though, about cases in which the experience is penetrated by a *justified* belief, or even by *knowledge*? Would this be a case of good cognitive penetration? Why or why not?

3. Suppose, following Wright (2004), you think experiences justify beliefs about the world but only with the help of background beliefs. Do you still have to worry about the cognitive penetration and speckled hen problems? Why or why not?

4. Susanna Siegel (2013b) distinguishes two ways cognitive states could affect which experiences you have. One is by *cognitive penetration,* in which the cognitive state affects processing by intervening in it, shaping it to some extent. The other is by *selection bias,* in which the cognitive state only affects which inputs are processed. So, for instance, studies on out-group hiring (e.g., a hiring committee of all males considering a female candidate) suggest that outgroup bias does not work by cognitive penetration so much as by selection bias (see Steinpreis et al. 1999). In-group employers might, for instance, not attend to a line on a résumé ("varsity tennis") for an out-group candidate but would for an in-group candidate. Question to consider: Suppose your experiences aren't cognitively penetrated but do result from selection bias; do they still provide justification for beliefs based on them? Why or why not?

5. Can you think of possible counterexamples to the threshold view of justified belief? You might consult Chapter 11 (Section 11.4.1) for ideas.

6. Consider the view that experience can justify beliefs about the external world but only with the help of background beliefs or presumptions. Is this view ultimately better off than classical foundationalism? Why or why not?

7. A relative of the "easy justification" problem for dogmatism is the "bootstrapping" problem (cf. Vogel 2000 and Fumerton 1995). This problem was originally raised for reliabilism, but it arguably affects dogmatism as well. Here is the problem (for dogmatism). Dogmatists claim you can be justified in having perceptual beliefs without independently knowing that believing based on perception is reliable. But consider the following bootstrapping reasoning. I open my eyes and believe what they tell me—this is a coffee cup; that is a scone, etc. I conclude that experience was accurate in all these cases. I keep doing this. So, through good inductive reasoning, can't I conclude that my experience is a reliable guide to how things are? But can I come to a justified belief that my experience is reliable *in that way*? This would be like determining that an oven thermometer was accurate simply by believing what it reads and trusting it, without any double-checking through other means. Two questions: (a) Is dogmatism committed to the claim that bootstrapping is a way to become justified in believing your experiences are a reliable guide to how things are? (b) If the answer to (a) is yes, is this a problem for dogmatism?

8. For readers of optional section 6.2.1: Consider the form of reliabilism developed in Chapter 2. Which horn of the Sellarsian Dilemma should someone who accepts this sort of reliabilism reject? Explain your answer.

FURTHER READING

BonJour, Laurence (1985). *The Structure of Empirical Knowledge*. Cambridge: Cambridge University Press, Chapter 4.

Brogaard, Berit (2013b). "Phenomenal Seemings and Sensible Dogmatism." In C. Tucker (ed.), *Seemings and Justification* (pp. 270–289). Oxford: Oxford University Press.

Goldman, Alvin I. (2008). "Immediate Justification and Process Reliabilism." In Q. Smith (ed.), *Epistemology: New Essays* (pp. 63–82). Oxford: Oxford University Press.

Pryor, James (2000). "The Skeptic and the Dogmatist." *Noûs* 34: 517–549.

Sellars, Wilfrid (1997). In Robert Brandom (ed.), *Empiricism and the Philosophy of Mind*. Cambridge, MA: Harvard University Press.

Siegel, Susanna (2012). "Cognitive Penetrability and Perceptual Justification." *Noûs* 46(2): 201–222.

Sosa, Ernest, and Laurence BonJour (2003). *Epistemic Justification*. Oxford: Blackwell, Chapter 7.

White, Roger (2006). "Problems for Dogmatism." *Philosophical Studies* 31: 525–557.

NOTES

1. Need perception involve experience? From experimental work in psychology, we know that people can show sensitivity to information to which they lack conscious access. For instance, in one study, subjects' impressions of an ambiguous story were affected by whether they had been exposed, subliminally, to negatively valenced or neutral words (see Bargh and Pietromonaco 1982). The reasoning is that this must be *unconscious* because the subject cannot report it but that it must be *perception* because the information processed influences *relevant* tasks by the subject. Within epistemology, Jack Lyons (2009) argues that experience is not essential to perceptual justification. Lyons's work is discussed in detail in Chapter 7.

2. The version of this argument given in the text is derived from Laurence BonJour's (1985) updated version of the argument. Thanks, also, to Jack Lyons for several useful suggestions.

3. Chapter 1 (Section 1.7) considered a number of arguments against immediate justification, including one due to Sellars. Any argument against immediate justification is an argument against justification by experience alone, at least assuming that experiences cannot be justified or unjustified. However, unlike the arguments considered in Chapter 1, the Sellarsian Dilemma does not depend on "higher-level" requirements (i.e., requirements that in order to be justified in believing that P you need to be justified in believing that you are justified in believing that P, or justified in believing that the source you are using is reliable). The Sellarsian Dilemma is also specifically about *experience* in a way that the arguments considered in Chapter 1 are not.

4. Note the parallels between our discussion here and the discussion of E = K in Section 3.7.2. There is an explanation for this. Plausibly, a reason for belief is evidence, and having a reason is having evidence.

5. We should note that BonJour (1985), Davidson (1986), Rorty (1981), and arguably Sellars himself, were sympathetic to coherentism.

6. Replying to the Sellarsian dilemma in this way releases one from the daunting task of explaining how having an experience could constitute having a reason. Even if we suppose experiences have assertive propositional content and even if we deny clause (iii) of PV, still it is doubtful that having an experience with content P entails having P as a reason. Consider a case in which you learn that an apple that looks green to you really isn't green at all: There's a hidden green light directed on what is really a pale yellow apple. In this situation, you don't have *this [the apple] is green* among your reasons. If you did, you would be justified in believing that the apple is green. After all, what better reason could you have to believe a thing is green than *it is green*? So, you don't have *this is green* as a reason in such a case, although you do experience it as green. Thus, experiencing the apple as green does not suffice for having *this is green* as a reason.

7. Epistemologists who claim that the only immediately justified beliefs are beliefs about one's own current mental states accept *Cartesian foundationalism,* to use the terminology of Chapter 1 (Section 1.7). Cartesian foundationalists accept an indirect theory of how experience justifies beliefs. In principle one might accept an indirect theory of how experience justifies beliefs but think that we do have immediately justified beliefs through other sources (e.g., rational intuition) about things other than our current mental states (e.g., that $2 + 2 = 4$).

8. As we saw in Chapter 2 (see the example of Chad in Section 2.3), doxastic justification requires more than basing one's belief on what provides one propositional justification. The "basing requirement" offers necessary but not sufficient conditions for doxastic justification. This is why we use "only if" here rather than "if and only if."

9. There is an interesting distinction, neglected in much epistemology, between how a thing looks to a person at a time and the looks of a thing. A willow oak leaf has a certain look, whether anyone is looking at it, and so whether it happens to look to a person at a time in any particular way. As J. L. Austin (1962) writes, "the fact that petrol looks like water is not a fact about me." If there are *looks* things have, which go beyond any particular set of experiences subjects have, how are they relevant to epistemology? In other work (McGrath forthcoming), I argue that these looks are objective features of objects and that normal human adults are justified in beliefs about how things are—their colors, shapes, and the kinds of things they are—because they are justified in beliefs about their looks. This is easier to argue in the case of classificatory beliefs, such as a belief that a certain thing seen *is a piano.* You are justified in a belief that a thing is a piano, in a simple perceptual case, by virtue of being justified in believing it looks like a piano. It is more challenging, I think, to mount the argument that our justification for the likes of *this is red* derives from a justification to believe that it looks red. In the body of the text, I will put aside these "objective looks," given that they have not (unfortunately, from my point of view) played an important role in perceptual epistemology. For the *locus classicus* of the view that looks are objective, see Austin (1962).

10. The term comes from James Pryor (2000). Many internalists accept the view, including Feldman (2003), Huemer (2000), Pollock (1975), Pryor (2000), and Tucker (2010). Many externalists, too, accept the view, sometimes with certain qualifications (considered below). Examples are Alston (1991), Goldman (1976), and Millar (2012).

11. Two things seem problematic here, as Siegel points out. It is problematic that the preformationist gains justification to believe the cell contains a tiny embryo. And it is also problematic that the preformationist gains justification for her theory. If we conclude the preformationist doesn't gain the first justification, then we can explain why she doesn't gain the second.

12. For more discussion of this reading of the cognitive penetration counterexamples to dogmatism, see McGrath (2013).

13. This division into lower- and higher-level features corresponds at least roughly to psychologists' division of visual processing into "early" and "late," the early processing often taken to process what we're calling lower-level features and the late higher-level ones. The talk of "early" and "late," however, shouldn't lead us to think there aren't back-projections from the brain regions associated with "late" processing (e.g., cells in the medial temporal area) to brain areas associated with "early" ones (e.g., V1). Such back-projections have been experimentally confirmed. See Gazzaniga et al. (2013).

14. Berkeley's *New Theory of Vision* itself is a landmark contribution to early vision science. But of course he did not have available to him the wealth of data we do today.

15. For information on associative agnosia, see Palmer (1999) or any textbook on perceptual psychology. See Berit Brogaard (2013a) for a response to the argument for the higher-level experience view from associative agnosia.

16. See Goldman (2008, 2009) and Lyons (2011a) for an account along these lines. See also Brogaard (2013b) for a form of dogmatism that employs reliabilist ideas.

17. The reader might consider the prospects for the two-stage reliabilism discussed in Chapter 2 (Section 2.5).

18. For further discussion, see McGrath (forthcoming).

19. Warning to the reader: The material in this section is challenging and in some places employs notions from probability theory. Time permitting, it might best be read in conjunction with Chapter 11. However, no familiarity with Chapter 11 is assumed.

20. What goes for justification here goes for knowledge as well (so long as what you are justified in believing is true nonaccidentally).

21. We would need to stipulate that the way you base your belief on your experience is appropriate. The character of the experience matters, for instance. It's not that you would believe you have hands based on any experience. It's the fact that it's an experience as of having hands that leads you to form the belief.

22. For an interesting account of how (6) might be false, see Silins (2008). For criticism of Silins's proposal, see Kotzen (2012). We ignore these complexities here.

23. See Chapter 5 (Section 5.2) and Chapter 11 (Sections 11.2.4 and 11.4) for resources for doing this.

24. For more on probability-raising, see Chapter 11 (Section 11.4). The ambitious reader might also wish to consider how these probabilistic matters bear on the prospects for the explanationist response to skepticism discussed in Chapter 4 (Section 4.4).

25. Admittedly, it's odd to think of acquiring a justified belief that you have hands by basing it on your experience (surely you had to already know you have hands!), but let's put this aside. We're asking about what is *possible* if dogmatism is true. If something that is impossible turns out to be possible if dogmatism is true, then we can conclude that dogmatism is false.

26. In the mathematical theory of probability, if A entails B, then the probability of A is less than or equal to the probability of B. Even if we conclude that probabilities as measuring rational credences do not obey the mathematical theory, it seems quite plausible that if it is obvious to you that A entails B, then your confidence in A shouldn't exceed your confidence in B. After all, every possibility in which A is true is one in which B is true—but not necessarily vice versa.

27. In the literature on dogmatism, you will find discussion of "warrant transmission failure" (cf. Wright 2004, Davies 2004, and Silins 2005). This topic is of a piece with the topic of easy justification. To say warrant fails to transmit across an entailment from P to Q is in effect to say that one cannot come to know—or gain warrant (justification)—for Q by inferring it from P (such warrant would be "too easy"). You will also see the terminology of "liberalism" for dogmatism and "conservatism" for Wright's (2004) view that experience justifies beliefs about the world only with the help of background beliefs. Confusingly, the position called "phenomenal conservatism" (see Section 6.5.2) is a form of liberalism, not conservatism (in this use of the term). We have avoided this confusing terminology here.

PART III
Naturalistic Epistemology

Epistemology, Cognitive Science, and Experimental Philosophy

Alvin I. Goldman

7.1 QUINE AND NATURALISTIC EPISTEMOLOGY

In the first six chapters of this book we have been *doing* epistemology. We have not reflected much on *how* epistemology is done, or should be done. In other words, we have not much discussed the *methodology* of epistemology. But epistemologists generally take a strong interest in methodology. Why shouldn't they discuss epistemology's methodology in particular? In this chapter and the one to follow, this is what will be undertaken. We will not be proposing utterly novel methodologies that nobody has in fact undertaken, but we will canvass some nontraditional methodologies that are currently being executed.

One feature of traditional philosophical method, which is certainly shared by epistemology, is the use of hypothetical examples to support or refute proposed analyses or theories. Epistemologists consult their intuitions about cases to decide whether, *intuitively*, they qualify as, or should be classified as, instances or noninstances of knowledge, justified belief, and so forth. This is often called an "armchair" method, because rendering an intuitive classification judgment requires no perceptual observation (once one has heard or read the example itself). One simply imagines or thinks about the case and an intuition about how it should be classified simply "wells up" in the mind. No doubt, some mental operations are taking place behind the scene. But these operations only touch base with other contents in the mind; no additional inspection of the external world is required. So these classification judgments themselves are not empirical judgments.

Stepping back a little, philosophers have historically divided beliefs or judgments into two categories: *a priori* and *a posteriori* (= empirical). A priori judgments are ones that do not rely for their epistemic credentials on perception. Judgments like 2 + 3 = 5, or everything is self-identical, are stock examples of a priori judgments, because they are (or can be) arrived at by pure *thought, intellection,* or *reason* alone. A posteriori, or empirical, judgments involve the use of the senses. According to the tradition, intuition is some sort of nonsensory, nonperceptual—hence a priori—faculty or process. Philosophers frequently pinpoint intuition as the source of our knowledge of mathematics, of logic, and of other conceptual relations. Science, by contrast, does not proceed in a thoroughly a priori fashion. Scientists generally dismiss the notion that one can find out things about the world by purely a priori means. At any rate, if questions are restricted to contingent facts about the world, empirical methods must be used.[1] So if philosophy's method is purely intuitional/a priori, its methodology must be (at least partly) distinct from that of science. But many philosophers regard science as the paradigm of respectable, reliable, or otherwise well-credentialed methodology. Walling philosophy off from science is a dubious idea, according to these folks. This is especially so because of the long-standing obscurity of a priori methods. There is much talk of intuition but little in the way of very satisfactory explanation of what it is supposed to be and why we are entitled to place any trust in it. This issue will be explored in Chapter 8. Meanwhile, science-oriented philosophers feel significant motivation to try to link philosophical method to scientific method if possible.

Willard van Orman Quine, the dominant figure of mid-twentieth-century philosophy, took this very much to heart. Like the logical empiricists whom he admired, he sought to reconcile philosophy with science, or perhaps more accurately, to blend philosophy into science. Logical empiricists held that the statements of philosophy are knowable a priori only because they are, if true, *analytic* (true by definition) rather than *synthetic*. But Quine himself rejected the analytic/synthetic distinction altogether. So where was he to turn? He viewed epistemology as the same thing as philosophy of science, and philosophy of science was always interested in the relation between evidence and theory. But the science of psychology is also interested in the relation between evidence and theory. As he wrote in "Epistemology Naturalized" (1969):

> [Psychology] studies a natural phenomenon, viz., a physical human subject. This human subject is accorded a certain experimentally controlled input—certain patterns of irradiation in assorted frequencies, for instance—and in the fullness of time the subject delivers as output a description of the three-dimensional external world and its history. The relation between the meager input and the torrential output is a relation we are prompted to study for somewhat the same reasons that always prompted epistemology; namely, in order to see how evidence relates to theory, and in what ways one's theory of nature transcends any available evidence. (82–83)

So Quine proposed that philosophy, or at least epistemology, should be considered *a chapter of psychology*. He despaired of any other ways to construe the project of epistemology. He was not interested in the "analysis" of knowledge, or justification, or rationality, and perhaps spurned these projects because he rejected analyticity. What, then, should be done with epistemology? With his characteristic scientific bent, he proposed a reconfiguration of epistemology as a subdiscipline of psychology. This was the take-home message of his essay "Epistemology Naturalized."

Few if any epistemologists have endorsed precisely this proposal, which seemed to advocate an abandonment of epistemology as we have known it. What happens, for example, to the *normative* or *evaluative* strands of epistemology under this conception, which seem so central to its mission?[2] Doesn't the project of explaining the nature of knowledge and epistemic norms evaporate under Quine's new portrayal of the field?

Other epistemologists, though disinclined to endorse Quine's very radical proposal, have thought there were sound reasons to connect epistemology with psychology, and with a larger family of empirical disciplines that study the mind, namely the cognitive sciences. Even if one believes that Quine's proposal to reduce epistemology to a branch of psychology should be resisted, perhaps the field would benefit by *getting help* from the cognitive sciences.[3] This notably weaker version of naturalistic epistemology is what we shall pursue in the remainder of this chapter (and the chapter that follows).

7.2 APPLYING COGNITIVE SCIENCE TO THE EPISTEMIC SUBJECT

We can distinguish two different ways of applying cognitive science to epistemology. One way is to apply it to questions about the epistemic *subject*. Epistemologists generally think and write about epistemic subjects either in terms of ordinary, commonsense concepts or in terms of selected formalisms that strike them as epistemically germane or indeed critical (logic, probability theory, statistics, etc.). In addition to these approaches, or in place of them, epistemologists might appeal to ways of understanding epistemic subjects by conceptualizing them as informational or computational processors, a ubiquitous depiction in cognitive science. Concepts imported from selected cognitivist fields might prove helpful in addressing traditional epistemological problems. Another way by which cognitive science can enter the picture is by applying its theories or findings to epistemic *judges,* or *attributors.* As we saw toward the end of Chapter 2, epistemologists have reason to seek greater understanding of what cognitive activities transpire when people (verbally and nonverbally) attribute epistemic achievements to themselves and others (knowledge, justification, etc.). Cognitive science may be well positioned to help with this task.

7.2.1 Applying Cognitive Science to the Epistemology of Perception

We start with the first kind of strategy, namely applying cognitive science to the study of the epistemic subject—that is, to individuals who might possess knowledge, justification, or what have you. As Chapters 1 and 6 indicated, basic beliefs represent an important strand of many epistemological theories. Not only pure foundationalism as such, but many other theories (including reliabilism) retain a substantial commitment to basic beliefs. How does perception enter the picture? Not all basic beliefs are perceptual beliefs, but an important subclass of (justified) basic beliefs are perceptual ones. They constitute, arguably, the most common variety of foundation-level justifica-tion. Now, most approaches to perceptual justification make central use of perceptual *experience* in their stories. As explained in Chapter 6, experience can play different roles in such a story, but there is substantial consensus that experience—conscious experience—is essential.

A very different account of perceptual belief and basicality is offered by Jack Lyons (2009), whose rationale for departing from the prevailing view is heavily predicated on inspiration from cognitive science. The first element in his rationale for dissent from orthodoxy is that it makes sense to regard experience as inessential for perception. Zombies are possible creatures extremely similar to humans—at least they occupy the same "functional" states as humans—but totally lack (conscious) experience. Yet they can still be described as "seeing" things, "hearing" things, and so forth. This kind of argument, of course, does not depend on an appeal to science. But we don't need science fiction to make the point: The actual world provides such ex-amples, as shown by psychological research.

James J. Gibson (1966) called attention to many instances of what he called "sensationless perception." One such example is the so-called obstacle sense of the blind. Blind people can detect obstacles such as walls, chairs, and the like without having any conscious sensation. This can also occur with sighted people wearing blindfolds, although they are less proficient than the blind. The blind tend to think they are picking up information through the skin of the face when in truth the information is coming in through the ears as a subtle form of echolocation (Lyons 2009, 52).

Another strand of Lyons's critique of traditional views involves combining a purely philosophical argument with a thesis that relies on the psychology of perception. Here is the general philosophical argument:

> The nondoxastic experiences that are alleged to justify the basic beliefs are either sensations or percepts . . . Sensations cannot justify the basic belief, in part because they cannot stand in the appropriate evidential relations to beliefs. Neither can percepts justify the basic beliefs, unless the percepts are construed as themselves beliefs, in which case they are not nondoxastic, and the beliefs they justify are not basic after all. (39–40)

Support for the two prongs of the argument appeals to what is known by vision scientists about "early" and "late" vision, respectively. The early part of the visual stream begins with retinal stimulation and the later part culminates in object or scene identification. The early part ("sensations") either lacks content altogether or lacks propositional/conceptual content that is needed to serve as evidential justifiers for beliefs. "Percepts" (alone) are also poor candidates to serve as justifiers for basic beliefs. This is because, without sensations, they are too much like hunches, or like Norman's clair-voyance sense (see BonJour 1985). From a subjective perspective they would seem to come out of nowhere, and therefore would not appeal to internalists as suitable justifiers.

Physical Events cause mental Events but does, Not Effect others
↳ Bi-product of Physical world — Similar to Behaviorism

Finally, consider Lyons's positive approach to justified basic belief. This is perhaps the most salient part of his theory that appeals to cognitive science. Lyons develops a variant of a modular approach to cognitive systems. According to Jerry Fodor's (1983) proposal, modules are information-processing mechanisms that are innately specified, domain-specific, informationally encapsulated (i.e., lack access to the beliefs and goals of the larger organism), and introspectively opaque. These are extremely stringent requirements. Lyons, rejecting the requirements of innateness and informational encapsulation, opts for a weaker notion of a module, which he calls a "cognitive system." A cognitive system in general is "an isolable virtual machine that performs some functionally cohesive task and is self-sufficient with respect to that task" (Lyons 2011b, 445). Perceptual systems are a species of cognitive systems. For one to have a perceptual belief is to have a belief that is an output of a perceptual system.

Elsewhere Lyons introduces a nonexperiential sense of "looks" that makes fruitful use of his notion of a perceptual system. He calls this the "perceptual output" sense of "looks." To introduce this special sense of "looks," he points out that learning frequently results in a change in how things look—in the desired sense—without necessarily changing how they look in an experiential sense (2005, 243–244). Here are some of his examples:

1. You and I have identical visual experiences, but the face looks like Joe to you but just looks like a face to me.
2. You and I come across a copperhead in a field. I am a professional herpetologist, and it looks like a copperhead to me, though it only looks like a snake to you.
3. I can now hear the difference between a melodic minor scale and a diminished scale; they sound quite different to me. Several years ago, they sounded the same as one another to me (i.e., I couldn't tell the difference), though neither sounds any different now than it ever did (i.e., the experiential state itself seems to be the same).

In each case, he says, the nonexperiential mode of looking can be identified as an output of a perceptual system.

Turn now to the more specifically epistemological application of these ideas, in particular their application to basic beliefs. Lyons suggests that belief outputs of perceptual systems are epistemologically basic. Thus, beliefs about ordinary physical objects, at an intermediate level of specificity ("table," for example, but not "Chippendale table"), are basic (for most people). In his terminology "basic" does not imply "justified." What, then, is required for a basic perceptual belief to be justified? Simplifying a bit, for a basic belief to be justified it must not only be the output of a perceptual system, but the system that outputs it must be reliable. So Lyons endorses a species of reliabilism. And in contrast with most traditional theories of basic perceptual justifiedness, there is no appeal to phenomenology or "experience" in the entire story.

The foregoing is just a sketch of a considerably more complicated theory. No attempt is made here to evaluate the theory; it is merely presented as an illustration of how findings and theoretical frameworks from cognitive science can bring an interestingly novel perspective to a traditional epistemological problem and possibly pave the way to an illuminating solution.

7.2.2 Psychological Research on Thought and Probabilistic Reasoning

At least two programs in epistemology have each proposed general perspectives on justification and knowledge that invite important contributions to the investigations from cognitive science. One of these programs takes an externalist, reliabilist perspective, the other an internalist perspective. The present author's book *Epistemology and Cognition* (1986) proposed that the job of identifying the right general standard, or criterion, of justifiedness falls to philosophy. If the chosen standard falls in a certain category, it becomes appropriate to call in cognitive scientists to supply many crucial details. One possible standard is a truth-conducive standard, the most common (but not the only) example of which is reliability (cf. Chapter 2). To apply this standard to human beings, the question immediately arises: What cognitive processes do human beings have available to them, and what are their respective reliabilities? This kind of methodological division of labor need not be confined, however, to reliabilism or externalism. John Pollock and Joseph Cruz (1999) have advanced a "naturalistic" approach of a broadly similar sort from an explicitly internalist perspective (though arguably an unorthodox one). They write:

> The promise of a substantial naturalistic epistemology was part of the attraction of externalism, as externalist views have seemed to be the only way to incorporate scientific information about biology and cognition into a theory of justification. We have, however, argued that this is a mistaken impression. Internalists can espouse a theory of justification that is just as naturalistic as externalist theories purport to be. (162)

They proceed to characterize naturalistic epistemology in a very similar ("weak") way that has been endorsed here: "A theory of justification is naturalistic if it maintains that epistemology should consist either partly or wholly in empirical disciplines, or should be informed by the results of empirical disciplines" (165).

The next question that arises is what specific contributions psychology or cognitive science can make or has made thus far. Obviously, these fields generate immense literatures, so we can only sample selectively from them. Let us therefore present some highlights of particularly influential perspectives on human cognition, to get a feel, or a "taste," for how they might contribute to the distinctively normative questions of epistemology.

One powerful current in the psychology of reasoning is a decidedly pessimistic one. It accuses human thought as "sinning" against rationality in virtue of using "heuristics" that often result in contraventions of proper principles of reasoning (e.g., principles of probability). This "biases and heuristics" strand of psychology, led by Amos Tversky and Daniel Kahneman, has been widely influential (Kahneman, Slovic, and Tversky, 1982; Gilovich, Griffin, and Kahneman, 2002). One of their earliest and most discussed examples is what they call the "representativeness" heuristic, which leads users (some of the time) to violate rules of probability.

A basic rule of probability theory is that a conjunctive event of the form A&B cannot be more probable than either of its conjuncts. The probability of its being cold and windy in Chicago tomorrow cannot be greater than the probability of its being cold. Anybody who rated the former probability higher than the latter would violate a formal rule of probability. Thinking in terms of a Venn diagram, it is obviously impossible for an A&B event to be more probable than either an A-event or a B-event. Do people avoid such violations? Sadly, they do not. Even highly trained people in relevant disciplines (e.g., statistics and decision theory) succumb to what Tversky and Kahneman call the "conjunction fallacy" (1983).

They gave the following description of somebody called "Linda" to participants in one study:

> Linda is thirty-one years old, single, outspoken, and very bright. She majored in philosophy. As a student, she was deeply concerned with issues of discrimination and social justice, and also participated in antinuclear demonstrations.

Subjects were then given a list of eight possible vocations or avocations Linda was pursuing and were asked to rank-order the vocations in terms of their probability. Here are the eight possibilities:

> Linda is a teacher in elementary school.
> Linda works in a bookstore and takes yoga classes.
> Linda is active in the feminist movement.
> Linda is a psychiatric social worker.
> Linda is a member of the League of Women Voters.
> Linda is a bank teller.
> Linda is an insurance sales person.
> Linda is a bank teller and active in the feminist movement.

Notice the logical relationship between being a bank teller (T) and being a bank teller and active in the feminist movement (T&F). This entailment implies that the probability of (T&F) cannot be greater than the probability of (T).

How did the participants perform? When using a within-subjects design (where each subject received all of the listed alternatives), almost all of the subjects ranked "feminist bank teller" (T&F) as more probable than "bank teller" (T). Eighty-nine percent of the undergraduates who completed the questionnaire violated a principle of probability. As Tversky and Kahneman put it, they committed the conjunction "fallacy." Even when the same questionnaire was administered to doctoral students in the decision-science program at the Stanford Graduate School of Business, all of whom had taken advanced courses in probability and statistics, 85 percent of these respondents also committed the conjunction fallacy.

How could this have happened? Tversky and Kahneman's explanation was rooted in the observation that the description participants were given of Linda portrays her as very dissimilar to the stereotype of a bank teller and hence more similar to, or more representative of, a bank teller who is active in the feminist movement. They further hypothesized that our cognitive repertoire includes a *representativeness heuristic,* an inferential pattern in which people assess the probability of something having property F by how much it is thought to *resemble,* or be *representative of,* things that have F. In many other examples used in experiments, they found confirmation for this idea.

Two other heuristics they pinpointed, which give rise to biases, were *base rate neglect,* a tendency to ignore frequencies of relevant events, and *availability,* a tendency to estimate a probability by the ease with which one can access an example of the category in question. To illustrate the availability heuristic, suppose that you are asked, "Are there more words of English that begin with the letter K or more words with K as their third letter?" People tend to answer such a question by assessing the ease with which instances of the two categories come to mind. This is an unreliable assessment method because it is easier to access words by their first letter than by their third letter. A typical text in English in fact has about twice as many words with K as their third letter than begin with K, although the availability heuristic leads people to make the opposite estimate.

Another influential group of cognitive scientists who study heuristics take a rather different stance toward them, regarding at least certain heuristics as outstanding exemplars of rationality rather than irrationality. This is the program of Gerd Gigerenzer and collaborators, who champion the virtues of so-called "fast-and-frugal" heuristics (Gigerenzer, Todd, and the ABC Research Group 1999). This group's standard of rationality is what they call *ecological rationality.* Ecological analysis takes an evolutionary perspective and tries to show how certain ways of reasoning are adaptive responses to people's environment. These simple and computationally "inexpensive" ways of reasoning, they argue, can be good at finding accurate (i.e., true) answers to questions, sometimes even better than more sophisticated and formally elegant procedures.[4] As indicated, their standard of rationality appears to be reliability, or truth-conduciveness (a feature that may be masked by a difference in terminology). It is appropriate, therefore, to view their standard as one of *epistemic* rationality. However, their conception of rationality also has a strong vein of the pragmatic, insofar as it emphasizes speed and resource conservation, each of which contributes to adaptiveness. However, with the current wave of interest in the pragmatic dimensions of the epistemic (see Chapter 5), many epistemologists might look favorably on the standards of epistemic evaluation that Gigerenzer and company highlight. Here the cognitive scientists might be ahead of the game, pointing not only, descriptively, toward what people *actually* do, but also toward what should earn them high epistemic grades.

What are the heuristics this group likes to tout? One of them is *take the best* (TTB, also called "one-reason decision making"). This provides a particularly clear instance of the "fast-and-frugal" idea. People often have (probabilistic) information about which cues concerning a pair of objects are correlated with a comparative property of interest about those objects. If people can rank-order cues in terms of their perceived reliability (or "validity," in the psychologist's sense), then they could decide which cues, and how many cues, to search for. A very frugal search-and-infer procedure would be one that directs an agent to search until he finds the single best cue he can—*and then stop*. In other words, instead of being thorough and trying to get information from as many cues as possible, he would engage in one-reason decision making. That's what TTB advises.

There is psychological evidence that people use this strategy, but could it really be as good as other, more thorough, procedures? Surprisingly, a study by the fast-and-frugal heuristics group suggests that it can. They first pitted TTB against other search-and-infer strategies. In a competition between TTB and five other fast-and-frugal heuristics, TTB outperformed all of them. In another competition, between TTB and several more powerful competitors like multiple regression, TTB again matched even the latter for accuracy. Another heuristic that Gigerenzer and colleagues tout is called the *recognition heuristic*. Although it is also very frugal, it enabled laypersons (in an experimental setting) to make very successful stock investments, outperforming even some expert traders.

The foregoing is just a sketch of the case made by Gigerenzer and company in support of selected heuristics, ones that people have psychological propensities to utilize. According to their approach, then, people have very considerable capacities for achieving high levels of epistemic attainment, even with the deployment of comparatively simple processes. The use of frugal heuristics is good to the extent that it is both reliable and leaves ample mental resources to devote to further epistemic tasks. This helps an agent do well on multiple tasks in a constrained timeframe. This is an important standard of epistemic prowess, perhaps as important as the kind of test mainstream epistemologists focus on (i.e., appraising individual doxastic "acts"). However, this is not to advocate the abandonment of epistemologists' longstanding concern with the justifiedness of belief in single propositions.

7.2.3 Epistemology and the Psychology of Deductive Reasoning

As a final example of psychological work that bears on epistemological questions, we turn to the psychology of *deductive reasoning*. Consider the problem epistemologists confront when they deal with necessary truths. If a person believes a necessary proposition, that belief is bound to be true; there's no way to come to believe that very same proposition without being accurate. But this should not imply that any such belief will be justified. Clearly, it is possible to have unjustified beliefs in necessary truths as much as in contingent truths. A similar problem arises if one classifies certain deductive relations between particular groups of propositions. If the premises jointly entail the conclusion, then anybody who classifies the argument as valid will believe a truth. Again, however, this does not mean that he or she is justified. To process reliabilists and their ilk, this shows that one must attend to the specific psychological processes a subject uses in arriving at his or her belief.

Apparently, this hasn't been an attractive row to hoe for epistemologists trained in philosophy of mathematics and logic. Many such philosophers adopt a rather antipsychologistic orientation, perhaps because of the huge influence of Gottlob Frege, who was strongly antipsychologistic vis-à-vis matters of logic. However, logic per se is not being discussed here; we are talking about the justifiedness of a person's *belief,* and that is not a matter of pure logic. In asking whether Jones is *justified* in believing tautology T or theorem θ, it is hard to avoid the question of the belief's provenance, or origin, which should be understood as its psychological origin. If S comes to believe T or θ by sheer guesswork, the belief will not qualify as justified or as knowledge no matter how necessary the proposition is. Can the justificational status be accounted for in terms of the method(s) used, where "method" is understood nonpsychologistically? Unlikely. This maneuver just pushes the problem back a step: Whatever formal techniques might be specified, they must ultimately be understood and executed by the agent in some psychologically appropriate fashion. Merely adopting and using a correct formal method by guesswork won't do the job (Goldman 1986, 52–53). One does not have to be a reliabilist to appreciate this point. Internalists like Pollock and Cruz should be on board with this point, as indicated by the passage from their work quoted above in Section 7.2.2.

Have psychologists made any significant headway on the topic of what processes we have for reasoning (appropriately) about logical relations? They have. The psychology of deductive reasoning is a well-developed field and deals with the right sorts of processes for purposes of assessing the epistemic credentials of logic-related belief. There is no firm consensus on the best framework for approaching the subject, but at least two sophisticated approaches have been developed and merit our attention. These are the "mental models" and the "mental logic" views, the leading developers of which are, respectively, Philip Johnson-Laird (1983; Johnson-Laird and Byrne 1991) and Lance Rips (1994). In addition there is considerable work on varieties of errors people make in deductive reasoning tasks (Wason 1966). This literature is also instructive, but it is harder to extract from it a unified family of processes on which to focus.

Rips's (1994) version of the mental logic approach is essentially a psychologized version of the natural deduction technique familiar to philosophers (e.g., from Quine 1950). It is intended to model actual human performance, warts and all. The theory proposes that humans naturally possess a logic-like system that enables them to construct legitimate proofs that enable them to move from many sets of premises to appropriate conclusions. That is, they utilize principles of proof that are truth-preserving. We do not naturally possess all the principles needed to construct all appropriate proofs. For example, a psychological implementation of *modus tollens* is not included in the system; this is because empirical research indicates that people do not "naturally" recognize *modus tollens* as a valid inference pattern (unlike *modus ponens,* which they recognize readily). Thus, Rips's mental logic approach does not credit people with an ideal or complete system for doing logic. Moreover, it is assumed that implementations of the deduction rules will employ working memory, a psychological subsystem with definite capacity limitations, which means that excess memory load can easily lead to errors.

The basic system Rips constructs consists of a set of deduction rules that construct mental proofs in the system's working memory. If the system is presented with an argument to evaluate, it will use those rules in an attempt to construct an internal proof of the conclusion from the premises. If the system is given a set of premises and asked for entailments of those premises, it will use the rules to generate proofs of possible conclusions. The model comes up with a proof by first storing the input premises (and conclusion, if any is supplied) in working memory. The rules then scan the memory contents to determine whether any inferences are possible. If so, it adds the newly deduced sentences to memory, scans the updated configuration, makes further deductions, and so forth until either a proof is found or no more rules apply. Thus, the inference routines carry out much of the work of the basic system.

Here is a sampling of a few routines in Rips's system, just to give the flavor of what they look like:

Forward IF Elimination

a. If a sentence of the form IF P THEN Q holds in some domain D,
b. and P holds in D,
c. and Q does not yet hold in D,
d. then add Q to D.

Forward Disjunctive Syllogism

a. If a sentence of the form P OR Q holds in some domain D,
b. then if NOT P holds in D and Q does not yet hold in D,
c. then add Q to D.
d. Else, if NOT Q does not yet hold in D,
e. then add P to D.

Rips calls his system PSYCHOP (short for Psychology of Proof). PSYCHOP's strategy in evaluating arguments is to work from the outside in, using "forward" rules to draw implications from the premises and "backward" rules (not presented here) to create subgoals based on a specified conclusion. It also contains "backward" rules that it can use. PSYCHOP has been constructed not to mimic an ideal deductive reasoner, but to mimic real human reasoners. But the jury is still out as to whether the "natural deduction" style of reasoning is empirically plausible as a model of human thought.

One reason for doubt is that other psychologists find evidence of a variety of error-prone features of actual performance, which raise doubts about how well people grasp the notion of validity. The validity of an inference, of course, has nothing to do with the actual truth of its premises or its conclusion (they all could be false). The fact that a conclusion is "unbelievable" in the sense that it conflicts with a participant's prior beliefs does not imply the argument's invalidity. Analogously, the fact that a conclusion is very believable does not show that an argument in which it occurs is valid. Nonetheless, studies reveal that people tend to let their prior belief or disbelief in a conclusion influence their answer to a validity question; this is what psychologists call "belief bias" (Evans, Barston, and Pollard 1983). And the question is whether people's having such a bias is compatible with their having a mental proof-based model of deductive reasoning.

The second general approach to deductive reasoning mentioned earlier uses a different template familiar from model-theoretic approaches to logic.[5] Mental models are internal representations of situations that can be derived from an argument with premises and conclusion—for example, a syllogistic argument. Deductive reasoning may then proceed in three stages. First, a mental model is constructed of the information in the premises. If you are told "All As are Bs" and "All Bs are Cs," you might construct a model in which three mental objects are labeled "C," two of these are also labeled "B," and one of the latter is also labeled "A." (Thus, the fact that both Bs in the model are also Cs and the one A is also a B is compatible with the two premises.) In the second stage, a tentative conclusion is generated and evaluated so it can be determined whether it is consistent with the model constructed in the first stage. In the example model, a tentative conclusion would be "All As are Cs." Third, and this is the most controversial aspect of the theory, the conclusion must be validated. This involves a refutation-oriented search, a search for alternative models consistent with the premises but not the conclusion. In the example, any alternative model will be consistent with the premises and conclusion. If such an alternative model is generated, however, the conclusion would be shown not to be a valid consequence of the premises, and an alternative conclusion would have to be generated and evaluated. A conclusion is a valid consequence only if there are no alternative models available to falsify it.

Empirical studies have shown that the extent to which people have difficulty in evaluating conditional and categorical syllogisms is directly related to the number of models required, so the mental model approach provides a good account of errors in deduction. The approach may also explain how believable but invalid conclusions are drawn, by positing a failure to generate and/or evaluate enough alternative models. A conclusion may be drawn without sufficient model-building and/or refutation. At the same time, the approach shows how accurate conclusions *can* be drawn for a certain subset of cases.

Each of these two theories depicts types of cognitive processes that are plausible candidates for how the mind undertakes to compute logical relationships. Each provides resources for picking out some sequences of belief-forming processes that are quite reliable and others that are definitely unreliable. Although it is hard to make empirical determinations of the overall superiority of these competing theories (and others), the epistemologist has reason to be optimistic that specifying the right *kinds* of processes is potentially attainable. This is progress of a relevant sort, progress that would surely elude us if we didn't attend carefully to the empirical research.

7.3 APPLYING COGNITIVE SCIENCE AND EXPERIMENTAL TECHNIQUES TO THE EPISTEMIC ATTRIBUTOR

Let us now turn to epistemological approaches that focus on *ascribers* or *attributors* of epistemic statuses rather than subjects of such statuses. This approach was discussed in Chapter 2 and briefly revisited in Chapter 5. Here we pursue it in greater breadth. In pursuing this approach, contemporary writers increasingly make appeal to specific psychological findings and theories, as well as experimental work of their own, to bolster or refute assorted epistemological theses. All in all, there is a burgeoning of empirically based work and citation of such work. Philosophers themselves have become proficient in doing experimental work very similar to experiments that psychologists perform, especially survey studies. This latter activity goes under the label of *experimental philosophy* (or X-phi). All in all, these activities represent a huge growth in "naturalistic epistemology."

7.3.1 "Solving" the Generality Problem with the Help of Psychology?

As we saw in Chapter 2, evidence that supports process reliabilism might be obtained by experimental work, in particular work on the verbal behavior of attributors. Before turning to this, however, let us step back a little and make further remarks about why we should turn the spotlight on the epistemic attributor. A focus on attributors seems to be an abandonment of the target we started out with. Why should attributors merit sustained attention?

A first response is to indicate that when we engage in our usual analytical activity, we have no "direct" evidence about epistemic properties inhering in the subject. Our evidence about this seems to lie in the attributions people (including ourselves) offer, or are disposed to offer, about cases on which they are queried. We ask whether subject S is justified or unjustified, but we use intuitions of attributors about S's E-statuses as our evidence. Furthermore, it is clear that, in a large number of simple and unproblematic cases, attributors *converge* on the same answer. They converge on saying that the protagonist in the scenario *is* justified or *isn't* justified (or has or lacks knowledge). If a good explanation can be provided of how this comes about, and if the explanation consists in part of noting that attributors judge a selected belief-forming process of the protagonist to be reliable or unreliable, that would be evidence in support of process reliabilism. This might be the closest thing to a "solution" to the generality problem as one might reasonably seek. If experimental work can provide such evidence, this would be a major "naturalistic" contribution to epistemological theory.

Erik Olsson (forthcoming) has made a novel proposal of this kind by calling attention to a well-supported psychological theory about conceptualization called *basic-level theory*. This theory goes back several decades and is one of the most robust findings in cognitive psychology.[6] It is the product of Eleanor Rosch and colleagues (Rosch et al. 1976), who investigated taxonomically related concepts (i.e., concepts linked together in a "tree" such that the extension of each concept is a subclass of its parent concept). A concept's "parent" concept is its superordinate; its "child" concept is its subordinate. In a zoological taxonomy containing "animal," "dog," and "Labrador," for example, the superordinate of "dog" is "animal" and a subordinate of "dog" is "Labrador."

It turns out that, across many conceptual taxonomies and semantic domains, intermediate-level concepts (illustrated by "dog" in the previous example) have a privileged status. This intermediate level within a taxonomy is called the *basic level*. Basic-level concepts are overwhelmingly preferred in free naming; they also have significantly more features associated with them than their superordinates, though not many fewer than their subordinates; they are the first concepts acquired by children; and they occur more frequently in text. Of special importance for present purposes is that it has been demonstrated that people tend to converge on reports at the same level of abstraction when asked to provide names or short descriptions for stimuli. Convergences have been found in several semantic domains, including physical objects, events, personality traits, and scenes.[7] Some of the convergences are very striking. Rosch and colleagues (1976) found that, out of 540 responses, 530 to 533 of them converged on the same word for naming a physical object.

As we discussed in Chapter 2, Olsson hypothesizes that people probably type token processes in a homogeneous way, as the basic-level research just reviewed would predict. In addition, he suggests that the reliability of these types will predict corresponding judgments of justification and knowledge. On his view, given that intuitive process-types exist, reliabilism can avoid the underspecification problem that goes by the name "generality problem." Of course, doubters about reliabilism have resisted the idea that there are broadly shared "intuitive" types. Feldman and Conee (2002) contend that, in the absence of linguistic cues, there is no single intuitive process-type to which a given process token corresponds. What can be said in the face of such skepticism?

Martin Jönsson (2013) has devised and conducted several experiments designed to address this issue. He reports their results and explains why he thinks they lend support to reliabilism. His first two experiments were free-naming experiments in which participants were asked how people in short film-clips form certain beliefs. His third experiment followed the pattern

Olsson had suggested (which was sketched in Chapter 2). One group of participants were asked to rate the reliability of the process-types under which they take certain belief-forming process tokens to fall, while the second and third groups were asked to judge the degree of justification or knowledge attainment of the protagonists in question.

To keep the discussion simple and brief, I here try to convey only Jönsson's summaries of his results. Convergence on belief-forming processes occurred for the majority of test items for most respondents. In describing the processes of belief-formation used by the characters in his film-clips, respondents converged on the same verbs, and for transitive verbs, most of them chose not to qualify the verbs with adverbial phrases. Since the clips did not have explicit linguistic cues for how to type the processes, Feldman and Conee's hypothesis that only such cues would make a particular type salient was disconfirmed. In a separate experiment, Jönsson reports, the claim was supported that reliability estimates assigned to belief-forming types can do a very good job of tracking justification and knowledge judgments. Finally, the reliability estimates assigned by the participants to each item were fairly similar across participants.

Jönsson then proceeds to offer a detailed and complex defense of the claim that these results support reliabilism; indeed, he offers six slightly different formulations of reliabilism, any one of which could find the experimental results very congenial. These formulations vary as a function, for example, of whether the types are associated with *thoughts* or with linguistic *verbalizations*. Jönsson concludes by saying that, although several subtly different versions of reliabilism might be advanced in light of the experiments, "the very striking correlations reported in [the last of his experiments] constitute a very strong fundament for reliabilist theories to build upon, and a major empirical confirmation of what reliabilists have been saying for a long time." These results and proposals by Olsson and Jönsson serve as a vivid illustration of how novel empirical work can in principle contribute to central epistemological projects.

7.3.2 The Gettier Problem Revisited (Experimentally)

As reported in Chapter 3, Gettier's claim that justified true belief is not sufficient for knowledge has been the orthodox view since his short article was published in 1963. However, in 2001, Weinberg, Nichols, and Stich reported an experiment that began to raise doubts about it. They gave Gettier-style scenarios to American students of Indian subcontinental descent and to students of European descent. The latter group gave mostly standard responses—that a protagonist in a Gettier-type situation "only believes" rather than "really knows." On the other hand, 61 percent of the South Asian group said that the protagonist "really knows." The result is not firmly established. Other investigators, such as Nagel, San Juan, and Mar (2013), have tried to replicate the finding and failed to do so. Some writers have criticized the methodology of this and other specimens of experimental philosophy

(Cullen 2010). On the other hand, a pair of psychologists, Starmans and Friedman (2012), did an analogous experiment with lay subjects and reported that 69 percent of them classified a Gettier-type protagonist as "really knowing." This raises doubts about the consensus view among professional epistemologists that protagonists in Gettier-type scenarios fail to know. Perhaps epistemologists have simply indoctrinated one another to accept a certain technical sense of "know." But shouldn't the use of the term by ordinary people (with no theoretical axes to grind of the sort epistemologists might have) be a better indicator of the ordinary sense of "know"? Is the overwhelming consensus among epistemologists really to be relied upon?

Responding to this challenge, some philosophers defend the traditional methodology on the grounds that professionals have greater *expertise* than laypeople do, so their intuitions should have greater evidential worth. But this answer might be dismissed as merely chest-beating, self-congratulatory propaganda. How can they self-confidently pursue their mission if they have no special expertise? Can any light be shed on this dispute by (further) empirical investigation?

John Turri argues as follows. If the expertise story is correct, philosophers may be better at noticing and appreciating the significance of subtle features of Gettier cases that untutored laypeople may miss. If this is correct, it should be possible to call attention to these crucial features by tweaking the presentation of the examples. This could give laypeople the same sensitivity to the relevant features of Gettier cases that trained philosophers, in virtue of their background, easily tune in on. If laypeople are assisted by such helpful cues, then they might agree both with Gettier himself and with the great preponderance of trained epistemologists that the Gettier characters do not know. This would lend support to what professional epistemologists have been saying about knowledge right along.

Turri conducted a series of such experiments with Gettier-like examples that were specifically designed to highlight what he calls a "conspicuous tripartite structure" (2013). Stories were presented in three stages. In the first stage the story's protagonist starts with a belief that clearly satisfies the justification condition. In the second stage an element of bad luck is introduced that would normally prevent the justified belief from being true. The third stage involves a conspicuously distinct element of good luck that makes the belief true anyway, although not in the normal way.

Participants were randomly assigned to one of two conditions: "Control" or "Authentic Gettier." All participants read a story in three stages. The first and third stages were the same in both conditions; the critical second stage differed. Here is a shortened version of the story, with different versions of the second stage for the two experimental conditions.

Stage One: Robert recently purchased a rare 1804 U.S. silver dollar, which he keeps over the fireplace in his library. Robert is throwing a dinner tonight for his neighbors and puts the coin over the fireplace. He shuts the library doors behind him and greets his neighbors, saying: "Guess what? There is an 1804 silver dollar in my library."

Stage Two: Authentic Gettier: When Robert shuts the library doors, a coin thief silently enters through the library window, steals his silver dollar, and quickly escapes. The coin is gone by the time he tells his neighbors, "There is an 1804 silver dollar in my library."

Stage Two: Control: When Robert shuts the library doors, the vibrations from the door cause the silver dollar to fall onto the rug; Robert doesn't hear anything. It has already fallen onto the rug when he says, "There is an 1804 silver dollar in my library."

Stage Three: Robert's house is an old mansion, built in the early 1800s. When it was originally built, a carpenter accidentally dropped an 1804 silver dollar into the mortar mix used to make the fireplace. No one has seen it for hundreds of years; it remains hidden in Robert's library.

Each stage of the experimental presentation appeared on a different screen. Participants in both conditions were asked one comprehension question at each stage—for example, "When Robert greets his guests, is there an 1804 silver dollar in his library? [Yes/No]" After the story was complete, participants were asked the *test question:* When Robert greets his guests, does he really know or does he only think he knows that there is an 1804 silver dollar in his library?

The idea was to dramatize the tripartite structure of Gettier cases, making conspicuous the difference across cases between a bad luck source and a good luck source. This was accomplished by dividing the story into three stages and asking participants to keep track of the truth of the key proposition. This had a dramatic effect on subjects' responses to the dichotomous test question. Eighty-four percent of participants in the Control condition said that Robert "really knows," whereas 89 percent of participants in the Authentic Gettier condition said that Robert "only thinks he knows." Turri concludes that "when suitably probed, laypeople across very different cultures, male and female, young and old, reveal that they overwhelmingly share the Gettier intuition" (34).

This is an intriguing example of how empirical experimentation can help illuminate important issues such as whether philosophers have any special expertise in responding to subtle features of scenarios like Gettier scenarios.[8]

7.3.3 Experiments About Pragmatic Encroachment

As we saw in Chapter 5, an intriguing development in recent epistemology is the "pragmatic encroachment" thesis. This thesis holds that knowledge is a function not just of purely "intellectual" factors like truth, evidence, and justification but also of "practical" factors having to do with interests and action. Perhaps the most prominent argument against pure intellectualism and in favor of pragmatic factors is the argument from "stakes." Within a ten-year period three different philosophers or pairs of philosophers claimed that people are less likely to ascribe knowledge to a subject in a "high-stakes" situation as compared with a similar "low-stakes" situation. Keith DeRose's

(1992) pair of bank cases, Stewart Cohen's (1999) pair of airport cases, and Jeremy Fantl and Matthew McGrath's (2002) pair of train cases made this point very salient. If the size of a believer's stakes affects the attributability of knowledge to him, it looks like this teaches us something very surprising, at least against the backdrop of traditional epistemological assumptions. Arguments for pragmatic encroachment coming from John Hawthorne (2004) and Jason Stanley (2005) added to this potentially volatile brew.

However, a recent group of experimental philosophers, not fully persuaded by these philosophers' armchair intuitions, set out to test these claims about what influences people's knowledge ascriptions. Would ordinary people, presented with pairs of high-stakes/low-stakes cases, attribute knowledge more readily to a subject with low stakes as compared to a subject with high stakes? First, let's formulate the issue more precisely. Following Buckwalter and Schaffer (forthcoming), consider the following thesis:

Folk Stakes Sensitivity

All else being equal, people are less likely to ascribe knowledge to a high-stakes subject than to a low-stakes subject.

What is meant by "all else being equal"? This means that all "traditional" epistemic factors like evidence and belief are held fixed across the two cases. When traditional factors are held fixed, will attributors still be sensitive to the stakes in the sense of having some probability of reacting differently in terms of knowledge ascription? A first wave of empirical studies on this question cast doubt on the claim. But soon a second wave of empirical studies were reported and said to vindicate folk stakes sensitivity. But even this was far from the end of the story. Buckwalter and Schaffer have delivered another negative judgment on pragmatic encroachment; they claim that the balance of evidence favors a very different view.

Folk Stakes Insensitivity

All else being equal, people are equally likely to ascribe knowledge to a high-stakes subject as to a low-stakes subject.

A more recent study by Buckwalter and Turri (under review) continues to reject the sensitivity of folk judgments to stakes. But in a new twist to the debate, they draw a distinction between two different kinds of pragmatic factors: the *stakes* factor and the *actionability* factor. "Actionability" here refers to how the agent should act. Hawthorne and Stanley, in their original treatments of the subject, focused pretty much exclusively on stakes. By contrast, Fantl and McGrath (2002; 2009) placed their main emphasis on defending pragmatic encroachment on actionability (as is true of McGrath's treatment here in Chapter 5 and Hawthorne and Stanley 2008). These two factors are not equivalent. And, lo and behold, the study by Buckwalter and Turri yields the result, as they explain it, that there is no deep and important direct connection between knowledge and stakes judgments, but there *is* a deep and important connection between knowledge judgments and actionability judgments.

The principal methodological innovation of the Buckwalter and Turri paper (relative to prior work by experimental philosophers) is their use of mediation analysis. Mediation analysis is a technique for clarifying how a predictor influences an outcome. Specifically, it helps estimate how much of the predictor's influence on an outcome is direct and how much is indirect. Indirect influence is mediated by other variables, whereas direct influence is not. We should be interested not only in *whether* practical factors influence knowledge ascriptions but also *how* they influence it, in particular the extent to which their influence is direct.

The results of their (two) experiments were that stakes judgments do predict knowledge judgments, but truth judgments mediate the relationship between stakes and knowledge judgments. Similarly, the stakes effect is mediated by evidence. Thus, there is no *direct* role for stakes in knowledge attribution once one controls for the effects of truth and evidence judgments. By contrast, in both experiments, judgments about how the agent should act were powerfully and *directly* related to knowledge judgments. They arrive, then, at the following summary statement:

> [W]e found that . . . practical factors [concerning stakes] have, at best, a modest indirect effect on knowledge attributions. However, . . . actionability . . . has a powerful direct connection to knowledge attributions. Indeed, if our results are any indication, actionability influences knowledge judgments as much as truth and evidence do. (Buckwalter and Turri, under review)

Without trying to evaluate the appropriate philosophical conclusions to be drawn from this work, it is obvious that these kinds of findings—especially in view of their greater statistical sophistication than others—cannot help but be very influential.

7.3.4 Contrastivism and Linguistics

In this final section of the chapter, we consider an approach to knowledge, *contrastivism*, that we did not manage to cover in Chapter 3 but certainly deserves close attention. Apart from its purely epistemological merits, it provides another illustration of the ways in which philosophy can profit from cognitive science. In this case, however, the input from cognitive science comes from linguistics rather than psychology. But linguistics is generally regarded as one of the core cognitive sciences, so it is appropriate to include such an example in this chapter.

According to the leading proponent of contrastivism, Jonathan Schaffer (2004; 2005), knowledge should not be conceptualized as a two-place relation (Ksp), as it is usually construed. It is should instead be conceptualized as a three-place relation (Kspq) between (i) a subject, (ii) a first proposition, and (iii) a second proposition, where the second proposition is a contrast to, or contrary of, the first proposition. (Alternatively, it might be optimal to conceptualize "knowledge" in *both* ways, linked in ways that will be exhibited below.) Under the three-place, or ternary, regimentation, knowledge attributions would be exemplified by constructions like "S knows that x is F rather than G." For example, "S knows that this drink is a Coke rather than a Pepsi." Contrastivism can be viewed as a close cousin of contextualism or, even better, a close cousin of the relevant alternatives approach (which was discussed in Chapter 3). In developing the connection with relevant alternatives, the idea is to define the standard two-place or binary relation of knowledge in terms of a ternary relation of knowledge as follows:

> S knows that P if and only if for every relevant alternative Q to P, S knows that P rather than Q.

However, in this section our focus is on the question of whether a ternary conception of knowledge is defensible in its own right, whether there is evidence of one sort or another (or of many kinds) that backs it up. We shall see how Schaffer uses the tools of linguistics to marshal evidence for contrastivism.[9]

A core part of Schaffer's contrastivist approach to knowledge is an account of what knowledge ascriptions are *for*. They are, he says, to certify that the subject is able to *answer a question* (2005, 236). When knowledge attributions are made, they aren't always tied to an explicitly posed question, but such a question is always recoverable from the conversational context. Such contexts provide speakers with the "live options" lying behind the question(s) tacitly in play.

Let me turn to the ways Schaffer exploits the resources of linguistics to argue for contrastivism. Schaffer advances the following principle of "encoding": "Knowledge ascriptions encode Kspq by encoding relations to questions" (2005, 244). He defends this by identifying three main surface forms of knowledge ascription and showing the mechanisms for question-relativity encoded in each. There are three syntactically different types of knowledge ascriptions. The first class is *interrogative* ascriptions, which employ a *wh*-headed complement phrase, such as "I know what time it is." The second class is *noun* (determiner) phrases, such as "I know the time." The third class is *declarative* ascriptions, which employ a *that*-headed complement phrase, such as "I know that it is midnight."

The mechanisms by which questions are encoded in knowledge ascriptions vary from type to type, and there are several ways of confirming them, but I shall explore only one of the modes of confirmation Schaffer discusses for each. Starting with interrogative knowledge ascriptions, they represent a syntactical type that straightforwardly embeds questions. Question-relativity is on the surface in the *wh*-clause cases. If one says, "I know who stole the bicycle," then the embedded question "who stole the bicycle" presents a set of alternatives such as [Mary stole the bicycle; Peter stole the bicycle; Paul stole the bicycle]. In the knowledge ascription, p is the selected answer and q is the rejected alternatives. If it was Mary who stole the bicycle, then to know who stole the bicycle is to know that p (= Mary stole the bicycle) rather than q (= either Peter stole the bicycle or Paul stole the bicycle). A confirmation of the fact that this is the way that interrogative knowledge ascriptions embed questions comes from existential generalization. If I know what time it is, then it follows that *there is a question* that I know the answer to, viz. "What time is it?" The question is what is being generalized on.

The existential generalization test also works for noun knowledge ascriptions, like "I know the time." If I know the time, then it follows that there is a question—namely, "What time is it?"—that I know the answer to. Similarly, if I know the murderer, it follows that there is a question—the question of who the murderer is—that I know the answer to.

Finally, the question-relative treatment of declarative ascriptions is also confirmed by the same test. If I know that the time is noon, then it follows that there is a question (namely, the question of what time it is) that I know the answer to.

Another paper (Schaffer 2004) draws on another set of tools borrowed from linguistics to defend contrastivism. For starters, it is clear that contrastivism would be going out on a limb if it posits a hidden contrast variable (q) that isn't on the surface of most everyday knowledge ascriptions. So, what might entitle a theorist to claim that such ascriptions contain a syntactically real contrast variable in their "logical forms"? Schaffer offers five arguments for q being syntactically real, all drawing on techniques from linguistics, most of which are too technical for present purposes. One is an argument from *overt counterparts.* A second is an argument from *binding* and a third is an argument from *ellipsis.* A fourth diagnostic is that of *focus,* and this one is more easily expounded.

The sentences "Ed prefers *drinking* tea" and "Ed prefers drinking *tea*" differ in truth-conditions. If Ed's overall preference ranking is drinking coffee, then drinking tea, and then bathing in tea, then the former is true but the latter is false. Knowledge ascriptions also have focus (or emphasis) sensitivity, as Dretske (1981) notes. In Dretske's example, to know that Clyde *sold* his typewriter to Alex is not necessarily the same as to know that Clyde sold his typewriter *to Alex.* To know that Clyde *sold* his typewriter to Alex is to know that Clyde sold the typewriter to Alex rather than that he gave it to him or loaned it to him. On the other hand, to know that Clyde sold his typewriter *to Alex* is to know that Clyde sold his typewriter to Alex *rather than Bonnie* (Schaffer 2004, 79).

Schaffer proceeds to argue that contrastivism has many virtues, including an attractive treatment of skeptical problems for knowledge. But the foregoing highlights of this work suffice to illustrate a way in which one of the subfields of cognitive science can provide great assistance to epistemological investigation.

QUESTIONS

1. Quine responded to the "absence of normativity" charge to his naturalized epistemology by saying that epistemology should become something like the "engineering" of thought. What might he have meant by this? Would this yield an appropriate conceptualization of epistemology within a psychological framework? Why or why not?

2. How might the two different psychological approaches to deductive reasoning sketched in Section 7.2.2 bear on the *epistemology* of deductive reasoning? Here is a possible scenario for your appraisal. The mental models method seems to invite more possibilities of mistakes than the mental logic method, at least when one does deductive reasoning "in the head." For example, it would be easy to overlook one or more models while trying to cover all possible ones. Hence, reliabilist epistemologists could conclude that the prospects of reliability under the mental models approach is worse than they would be under the mental logic approach. Does this seem like an appropriate application? Why or why not?

3. In recent years the "dual-process" approach to thought and reasoning has become very popular in psychology. (See the sources in the "Further Readings" list by Evans and by Kahneman.) The fundamental idea is that the human mind is, in effect, two different minds that attack the same problems but work very differently. System 1 is evolutionarily older, fast, cheap (in its use of resources), parallel, automatic, and largely unconscious. System 2 is more recent, slower, resource-reliant, serial, rule-based, deliberate, and subject to conscious control. System 1 is the locus of heuristics, while System 2 is the locus of more deliberate and reflective processes. Would it be right to conclude from this literature that all the epistemic traits valued by epistemologists are associated with System 2 rather than System 1? If so, should we conclude that people ought to use their System 2 more than they regularly do, or that epistemologists place an unreasonably high value on System 2-type activities (while undervaluing speed, conservation of cognitive resources, etc.)?

4. How might Feldman and Conee respond to Jönsson's experiments, which are said to provide support for the thesis that attributors converge on common descriptors of belief-forming processes and their reliability? Should skeptics of reliabilism try to find fault with his experimental results or deny that these results (plus the machinery behind "basic-level categories") support reliabilism? What is their best counter-thrust? Why?

5. What exactly does Turri's experiment show? That naïve subjects are potentially just as accurate in understanding a complex scenario as professional philosophers if the right features are specially highlighted? That they are therefore, when suitably guided, no less "experts" at making judgments about thought-experimental scenarios as are philosophers? That the worries raised by the Weinberg, Nichols, and Stich's (2001) study are entirely bogus? Any of the above?

FURTHER READING

Buckwalter, Wesley, and John Turri (forthcoming). "Descartes' Schism, Locke's Reunion: Completing the Pragmatic Turn in Epistemology."

Evans, Jonathan St. B. T. (2003). "In Two Minds: Dual-Process Accounts of Reasoning." *Trends in Cognitive Sciences* 7(10): 454–459.

Fantl, Jeremy, and Matthew McGrath (2002). "Evidence, Pragmatics, and Justification." *Philosophical Review* 111(1): 67–94.

Gigerenzer, Gerd, Peter M. Todd, and the ABC Research Group (1999). *Simple Heuristics That Make Us Smart*. New York: Oxford University Press.

Goldman, Alvin I. (1986). *Epistemology and Cognition*. Cambridge, MA: Harvard University Press.

Jönsson, Martin L. (2013). "A Reliabilism Built on Cognitive Convergence: An Empirically Grounded Solution to the Generality Problem." *Episteme* 10(3): 241–268.

Kahneman, Daniel (2011) *Thinking, Fast and Slow*. New York: Farrar, Straus, and Giroux.

Kornblith, Hilary (2002). *Knowledge and Its Place in Nature*. Oxford: Oxford University Press.

Olsson, Erik J. (forthcoming). "A Naturalistic Approach to the Generality Problem." In H. Kornblith and B. McLaughlin (eds.), *Alvin Goldman and His Critics*. Oxford: Blackwell.

Pinillos, Angel (2012). "Knowledge, Experiments, and Practical Interests." In J. Brown and M. Gerken (eds.), *Knowledge Ascriptions* (pp. 192–219). New York: Oxford University Press.

Quine, Willard van Orman (1969). "Epistemology Naturalized." In *Ontological Relativity and Other Essays* (pp. 69–90). New York: Columbia University Press.

Rysiew, Patrick (2008). "Rationality Wars—Psychology and Epistemology." *Philosophy Compass* 3(6): 1153–1176.

Turri, John (2013). "A Conspicuous Art: Putting Gettier to the Test." *Philosophers' Imprint* 13(10).

Weinberg, Jonathan M., Shaun Nichols, and Stephen Stich (2001). "Normativity and Epistemic Intuitions." *Philosophical Topics* 29(1–2): 429–460.

NOTES

1. This generalization has been challenged in recent times, but we need not concern ourselves with the exceptions in question for present purposes.

2. This point was advanced by Kim (1988). Quine himself, and several of his interpreters, denied that he abandons epistemic normativity.

3. This weaker, or softer, version of naturalistic epistemology was urged by Goldman (1986).

4. Patrick Rysiew (2008) provides a helpful overview of the contrasts between the "standard picture" of rationality offered by Tversky and Kahneman and the ecological picture offered by Gigerenzer and company.

5. The summary that follows is based on that of Smith and Kosslyn (2007, 445–446).

6. See Rosch et al. (1976).

7. For citations and summary of the relevant literature in which these discoveries were made, see Jönsson (2013).

8. This question will be probed in further depth in the next section and in Chapter 8.

9. For a more up-to-date, detailed, and revised approach, drawing even more heavily on linguistics, see Schaffer and Szabó (2013).

Philosophy's Intuitional
Methodology and
the Role of Science

Alvin I. Goldman

8.1 HOW TO DO PHILOSOPHY: IN THE ARMCHAIR
OR IN THE LABORATORY?

Every field of inquiry has a methodology, or should have one. What is philosophy's methodology? How does it go about the business of trying to establish the kinds of truths it seeks (whatever these truths may be)? If it is like empirical science, it would generate hypotheses about selected philosophical questions and then perform tests to decide which of these hypotheses is correct. Does philosophy proceed in anything like this fashion? It might seem that it does. As reported in Chapter 3, a once-popular theory in epistemology said that knowledge is justified true belief. Along came Gettier and sought to test this hypothesis. He presented two examples that he said falsified this theory. In each example a protagonist had justified true belief with respect to a certain proposition. The theory therefore predicted that the protagonist would be said to know that proposition. But, lo and behold, it didn't turn out way: The protagonist quite clearly did *not* know the proposition in question. Hence, down with the theory, said Gettier, and most epistemologists agreed with him. Wasn't this a test of the theory, and didn't the test outcomes falsify the theory? So it looks like philosophy, including epistemology, does conduct itself essentially like a science.

How much like science is this? Tests conducted in empirical science are tests in which the outcomes can be observed. Perhaps they can only be observed with the help of instrumentation (telescopes, electron microscopes, infrared spectroscopy, etc.), but that is still observation. What are the observed outcomes in philosophical tests? This is not straightforward. In Gettier's first example, the "outcome" might be the fact that Smith is justified in believing that the man who will get the job has ten coins in his pocket but does not know this. What kind of fact is this, however, given that the example is merely imaginary? And how is it observed?

Philosophical rationalists want to say that it isn't observed in the standard sense of the term. Perhaps there is a conceptual fact, which consists in a necessary relation between certain concepts. Such necessary relations are the sorts of things that might be detected by a capacity for a priori insight or intuition. Maybe this occurs when one considers a Gettier case and apprehends through such a faculty that the protagonist in the case fails to know. This is the kind of story that would-be rationalists want to tell about how philosophical "tests" are conducted. They are not cases of perceptual observation, as in science, but a different kind of detection of a test outcome. Thus, although there is some sort of similarity between philosophy and empirical science—both perform tests of theories in their respective domains—philosophical tests are very different from scientific ones. Philosophical tests are conducted in the armchair, whereas scientific tests are done in the laboratory (often literally, sometimes only loosely). So the methodology of philosophy is definitely unlike that of science in at least certain significant respects. Why is this so? And should it continue to be so? Rationalists think it is so and should be so. Naturalists are likely to disagree. The exact nature of the disagreement remains to be explored; naturalists may not all be of one mind.

8.2 THOUGHT EXPERIMENTS AND THE CONTENT OF GETTIERIZING JUDGMENTS

Most naturalists are suspicious of the role of intuitions or judgments arising from thought experiments (including Gettier-style thought experiments). How can philosophers use intuitive judgments about problem cases to arrive at some conclusion about a philosophical theory? How does this transpire, for example, in a Gettier case? What inference is made from somebody's intuition-based verdict about a single scenario to a conclusion concerning a concept, term, or relation that interests philosophical theorists?

Timothy Williamson seeks to demystify the philosophical practices that are often described in terms of "intuitions" (2005; 2007). He does not endorse the notion that we have a special capacity for a priori intuition; indeed, he regards the a priori/a posteriori distinction as too crude to be of use in epistemology. He argues that we should understand the use of thought experiments as a perfectly commonplace and unproblematic inference of a kind we regularly employ—namely, counterfactual reasoning.

Williamson first considers possible contents for Gettier-based conclusions that are presumed to be used in exploiting thought experiments to draw a theoretical conclusion. He wants an account of philosophical method that shows how one moves from something we learn about a particular Gettier case to something we conclude about knowledge in general. The account is intended to shed light on whether the investigation deploys empirical or a priori methods. Here is Williamson's preferred formulation of the initial conclusion:

COUNTERFACTUAL: If someone were to stand to a proposition in the way described by the Gettier text, then she would have justified true belief in that proposition but not knowledge.[1]

This is the first of two steps in the Gettierizing argument. This step by itself does not entail the falsity of the K = JTB thesis, which is the ultimate conclusion in view here, of course. However, the second step, says Williamson, is pretty straightforward. It is a step that says that the example described in the Gettier text is *possible*. When the truth of this POSSIBILITY proposition is conjoined with the truth of COUNTERFACTUAL, we have a conjunction from which the denial of K = JTB follows. (The example provides an instance of JTB being satisfied where K is not satisfied. If such a case is possible, the identity of K and JTB cannot obtain.)

Is COUNTERFACTUAL an apt rendering of a Gettier-type message? Williamson wants to persuade us of this because counterfactual reasoning, he feels, is a perfectly ordinary inferential operation that should not tempt anybody to invoke far-out ideas like "a priori reason," nor should it make anybody skeptical about the use of thought experiments in philosophy. If philosophical thought experiments can be understood as instances of counterfactual reasoning, the commonplaceness of the latter should defang any concerns about philosophy's purporting to use a "special" method that invites suspicion or skepticism. This is the attraction Williamson sees in it.

Is this interpretation correct, however? Ichikawa and Jarvis (2009) argue to the contrary. COUNTERFACTUAL renders the central premise of a Gettier-style argument as a contingently true counterfactual—only contingently true because the description of the case in the Gettier text does not entail justified true belief and does not entail nonknowledge. The story may be filled out in many different ways, only some of which involve justified true belief and nonknowledge. Instead of a relation of entailment, therefore, Williamson supplies a counterfactual relationship.

Here is an example Ichikawa (2009) uses to illustrate the point. First, there is an imagined Gettier-like text, describing a possible world of interest. Then, since counterfactuals are standardly interpreted in terms of what happens in the nearest possible world, a second such world is considered. Here is an imagined text:

> At 8:28 somebody looked at a clock to see what time it was. The clock was broken; it had stopped exactly 24 hours previously. The subject believed, on the basis of the clock's reading, that it was 8:28.

This text suggests, but does not actually entail, that the person who looks at the clock and believes that it was 8:28 does not know that it is 8:28. Now consider the nearest world in which this description is true but the clock observer knows *in advance* that the clock had stopped exactly 24 hours previously. In that world, even though the text is satisfied, the subject *does* know (on the basis of the clock's reading) that it is 8:28. So COUNTERFACTUAL is false. It is not true that if the person were to satisfy the Gettier text then he would not know; on the contrary, he would know. As Ichikawa and Jarvis further explain, Williamson's counterfactual interpretation makes the Gettierization of the JTB analysis depend on a particular structure of modal space, in particular on what holds in the nearest possible world. But the Get-tierization of knowledge does not so depend on the relevant configuration of modal space. Knowledge is Gettierized by the stopped clock example even if COUNTERFACTUAL is not satisfied in the specified world.

Anna-Sara Malmgren (2011) offers a similar counterexample to William-son's proposal and a more promising positive account of the form of the judgment implied by Gettier cases. Her positive account is as follows:

> POSSIBILITY: It is possible that someone stands to p as in the Gettier case (as described) and that she has a justified true belief that p but does not know that p.

Under this interpretation, the stopped clock example would be unprob-lematic. Even if that example itself would not be a Gettier case, a similar ex-ample in which the subject does lack knowledge would deliver the Gettier point. And it would deliver the point without any worry about the structure of modal space.

8.3 COGNITIVE OUTCOMES AS EVIDENCE

At the beginning of the chapter we pointed out that philosophy's methodol-ogy resembles that of empirical science to the extent that it uses "tests" to challenge and possibly reject one or more of the theories in play. The ques-tion next raised was what kinds of "outcomes" are involved in these tests. However, we haven't yet confronted the most common candidate for such outcomes. The prime candidate for such outcomes are *intuitions* or intuitional *states* understood as propositional attitudes of some sort that take as their contents answers to classification questions posed by thought experiments. In a Gettier case, the question would be: "Does the protagonist in the story know p?" The possible responses are "yes" and "no," or an affirmative or negative attitude. (In general, these states will be construed as nonlinguistic; or couched in the language of thought, not public language.) These intu-itional states can now be considered as *outcomes* of the thought-experimental test. The experimental subject could be anyone confronted with the hypo-thetical scenario: a professional philosopher, a student in a philosophy class, or a participant in an X-phi study who reads the scenario description and must check a box or click on a screen to indicate "yes" or "no."[2]

Perhaps the central question in the theory of philosophical methodology is this: "Are such intuitions, or intuitional states, *evidence*?" Can they legiti-mately be understood as conferring genuine evidential weight either in sup-port of or in opposition to some philosophical theory? Or, as some philosophical methodologists have claimed, are they really untrustworthy and unsuited to play the role of evidential items? After all, if we allow this class of mental states to serve as evidence, this will have definite epistemic consequences, for example, as to whether the respondent is justified in virtue of his or her intuition in drawing some conclusion, or revising his or her be-liefs, about an epistemological issue. Traditional philosophers who employ intuitional methodology generally assume that intuitions can and should serve as evidence, so that philosophers' theoretical conclusions based on intuitional methodology can be (in favorable cases) definitely justified. Skeptics of intuitional methodology doubt or deny that intuition-based methods can generate justified conclusions about philosophical matters. At a minimum, according to the skeptics, it is very unclear *how* they can legitimately provide such justification.[3]

In most philosophers' ears, talk of "intuitions" is talk of a specific class of mental states. This worries Williamson in his *Philosophy of Philosophy*. There he roundly rejects any attempt to "psychologize the evidence." He writes: "the current philosophical mainstream has failed to articulate an adequate philosophical methodology, in part because it has fallen into the classic epistemological error of psychologizing the data" (2007, 4–5). It is unclear, however, how this stance may be reconciled with his positive account of the respectable deployment of thought experiments. As we noted in Section 8.2, Williamson's account of the trustworthiness of thought experiments appeals to the reliability of counterfactual reasoning. But what is counterfactual reasoning if not a psychological process? Thus, Williamson himself seems to exemplify the tactic of "psychologizing the data" (or psychologizing the relevant "phenomena" anyway). How can he consistently present this as an "error" in the case of others but not an error in his own case?[4] In any event, epistemology has a wealth of approaches that appeal to psychological states and processes in making room for justification or knowledge. To claim that all attempts to exploit such states or processes in epistemology are destined for (unsalvageable) "error" is to make a sweeping claim that is insufficiently defended.

Returning to intuitions or intuitional states, the philosophical community is split when it comes to specifying what intuitions are supposed to be. There are two main candidates: (1) intuitions are belief states, and (2) intuitions are inclinations to believe or intellectual "seemings." By way of illustration, the first approach would say that a typical subject's intuition about the Gettier "ten coins" example is a *belief* that Smith does not know. The second approach would say that an intuition about that Gettier case is an *inclination* to believe or an *intellectual seeming* with the content "Smith does not know." An inclination to believe, or intellectual seeming, can be overridden by other factors so that it doesn't amount to a genuine belief, just as a perceptual seeming that one horizontal line in a Müller-Lyer illusion is longer than the other need not be a belief. We don't have to decide which of these two approaches (if either) to embrace. Either one, in principle, might serve the purpose of enabling a vindication of intuition-based methodology.

How could such a vindication arise? Whether an intuition is a belief or an intellectual seeming, it could be a kind of state that qualifies as *evidence*. Here is one familiar sense of evidence in which it might occupy this role. Something is often referred to as "evidence" if it is a *reliable indicator* of some other state of affairs. A falling barometer is evidence of impending rain, because when a barometer is falling, this is usually a reliable sign of imminent rain.

The number of rings on a tree trunk is evidence of a tree's age because if a tree trunk has X rings, this is a reliable indicator that the tree is X years old. In these cases, of course, the items of evidence are states of the external world, not mental states. But mental states can also be reliable indicators of other states of affairs (whether mental or nonmental) and thereby earn the status of evidence. Having a (seeming) memory of eating granola for breakfast this morning can be a reliable indicator that one did eat granola for breakfast. So the former can be (good) evidence of the latter. Undergoing a distinctive olfactory experience upon entering the house can be a reliable indicator that one's favorite dish is cooking in the kitchen. So it can be evidence for what is in the oven. Mentalist evidentialists like Feldman and Conee would certainly recognize and welcome the status of these mental states as specimens of evidence (see Chapter 2). True, they would resist the suggestion that their evidential status is grounded in reliable indicatorship. But they just suffer from a blind spot for reliability theories. Of course, not *all* types of mental states serve as evidence. Wishing that p, or imagining that p, may not be evidence of anything—or anything interesting.

To be more precise, when we ask whether a certain kind of mental state is evidence, we usually mean that it is evidence *for the truth of its content*. In the case of memory, your seeming to remember that you ate granola for breakfast would be taken to be evidence that you did eat granola for breakfast. When it comes to wishing, it is not impossible for a wish to be correlated with the truth of its content, but this will not normally obtain. As far as anything we have said thus far, then, intuitions might or might not be reliably correlated with, or have reliable indicator relations with, the truth(s) of their contents.

Arguments have been offered, however, to undercut intuitions' qualifications as evidence. Here is one such argument, adapted from Robert Cummins (1998, 116–118):

> The outputs of an instrument, procedure, or method constitute data we can properly treat as evidence only when that instrument, procedure, or method has been calibrated. Calibration requires corroboration by an independent procedure. Has intuition been calibrated? Has it been shown to be reliable by a method independent of intuition itself? There is no way to do this. Suppose we have a philosophical interest in fairness, and we ask people for their intuitions about the fairness of distributions described in certain hypothetical cases. We shouldn't trust their intuitions about these cases unless we have antecedently determined that their fairness intuitor is reliable, i.e., unless it has been calibrated. But how can we perform this calibration? We don't have a "key" by which to determine which outputs of their intuitor are correct, and there is no key to be found.

Defenders of the evidential status of intuitions might reply to this argument as follows. A requirement of independent corroboration, or calibration, is too stringent a condition to place on sources of evidence. There must be some sources of evidence that are "basic" in the sense that they cannot be corroborated by independent sources. Basic sources of evidence might include perception, memory, introspection, deductive reasoning, and inductive reasoning. These faculties are regarded as basic by many if not most epistemologists, and they are also regarded as bona fide sources of evidence. They are basic in precisely the sense that there is no independent faculty or method by which their reliability can be determined. Yet this does not undercut their evidence-conferring power. So we cannot accept Cummins's constraint on evidencehood on pain of general skepticism. His philosophical argument against the evidence-conferring power of intuitions is therefore unpersuasive.

8.4 CAN SCIENCE HELP US EVALUATE EVIDENTIAL STATUS?

Let us now turn to the prospect of investigating the evidential credentials of intuitions scientifically. Can this be done with the help of cognitive science specifically, or with the help of experimental philosophy? This would be highly continuous with the previous chapter's discussion of naturalistic epistemology. Is there precedent, however, for the scientific investigation of the evidential worthiness or soundness of procedures in other domains? It would help to have some guidance here.

Consider evidence presented in legal contexts. At least two types of standard evidentiary methods have been debunked by scientific investigation. The first was a study showing that eyewitness testimony is fraught with problems and errors (Loftus 1979). A more recent example concerns the most standard and established type of forensic evidence—that is, courtroom testimony by a forensic scientist to the effect that a pattern of fingerprints found at a crime scene constitutes a "match" with a defendant's fingerprints. Is this kind of testimony sufficiently reliable and hence worthy of being admitted into court? To ask this question is already to ask a second-order question about the evidence. It is to pose the question of whether there is good evidence that fingerprint methods provide good evidence (which is then conveyed via testimony).

Such second-order questions were recently raised in a very critical way in American courts of law. The so-called "ACE-V" method of fingerprint evidence has long been the gold standard of forensic evidence. But several high-profile cases occurred in which alleged "matches" generated by the FBI crime laboratory, long touted as one of the best forensic laboratories anywhere, turned out to be badly mistaken. This led academic specialists to dig deeper into the method. On closer inspection, what the community of fingerprint evidence specialists call "scientific" does not pass muster as very scientific (Mnookin 2008). Simply calling a method "scientific" does not make it so. The method's accuracy had never been subjected to proper statistical tests. So there was no scientific second-order evidence that this so-called evidence is good evidence. Commentators argued that that should change.

The example illustrates the point that being *taken* to be evidence does not make something *genuine* evidence, at least not *good* evidence. If a state of affairs does not reliably indicate the sorts of facts it purports to indicate, it should not be epistemically relied upon. The forensic science example also illustrates the point that empirical tests can often be designed to probe the reliability of a process or method, in order to decide whether its outputs are reliable indicators of that for which they purport to be indicators. These tests would be examples of second-order evidence. Finally, just as the legal system should surely demand good second-order evidence about the reliability of courtroom forensic testimony, it is reasonable for philosophers to seek analogous tests to obtain second-order evidence about the evidential quality of philosophical methods.

8.5 EXPERIMENTAL TESTS OF THE EVIDENTIAL QUALITY OF PHILOSOPHICAL INTUITIONS

Appealing to intuitions, as we have seen, is a species of evidential procedure. This is true whether we interpret intuitions to be beliefs or intellectual seemings. For present purposes, however, they may be viewed as *classification judgments* (i.e., judgments about how to categorize a given scenario or state of affairs). Not all uses of the term "intuition" are covered by this phraseology. In ordinary discourse "intuition" can refer to hunches or premonitions about the future, and in philosophical discourse it can refer to hypothesized faculties or senses employed in special domains of cognition, such as mathematics or ethics. But these other uses can be ignored for present purposes.

The central question on the table, then, is whether classification judgments, at least on philosophical topics, merit the status of high-quality evidence. Are they regularly reliable indicators of the truth of their contents? To express the point another way, are these states generally aligned with their truth-makers? Can this question be addressed with the help of experimental philosophy? Here is a possible approach. Suppose two people are presented with the same scenario and asked to classify some feature of it with respect to some property or relation of philosophical interest. Brown reports her intuition that the scenario is a case of F; Black reports his intuition that it is not a case of F.[5] On the surface, they cannot both be right. Indeed, exactly one must be right and the other wrong—a 50 percent hit rate. Should it turn out that survey participants regularly split down the middle in their classification judgments, this would be a terrible result for the evidential prospects of intuitions. They would be no better than chance at indicating the classificational "facts" being investigated—essentially, no evidential help whatever.

Experimental philosophers have run many surveys of roughly this kind (invariably with more than two participants). Presumably, they should therefore be in a position to report results either favorable or unfavorable to the evidential prospects of intuitions. For example, if for each of many philosophical categories that are tested, 60 percent of the participants intuit "F" and 40 percent intuit "not-F," at least 40 percent must be wrong. That is a very high error rate.

In the early years of experimental philosophy, "headline" studies produced data of roughly the foregoing kind. Jonathan Weinberg, Shaun Nichols, and Stephen Stich (2001) gave subjects a Gettier-like example featuring a
protagonist named Bob and asked them whether Bob "really knows" or
"only believes" a specified proposition. A majority (74 percent) of subjects
with Western ethnic origins responded that Bob only believes it, while a
majority (56 percent) of subjects with East Asian origins and a majority
(61 percent) of those with Indian origins responded that Bob knows. These
researchers were most interested in the discrepancies between answers
across participants of different ethnic origins, but the test could also be taken
as significant in terms of the proportion of errors that must have been made,
as inferable from the pattern of disagreement across ethnic groups.

On the topic of intuitions, experimental philosophers sometimes divide
themselves into two categories: *positive* and *negative* X-phi practitioners. Positive X-phi philosophers offer no challenge to the epistemological soundness
of intuitional-based methods; they just use the method to try to uncover
philosophically interesting results. Negative X-phi philosophers, by contrast,
deliberately aim to pose a challenge to the epistemic significance of intuitions. The announced goal of Alexander, Mallon, and Weinberg (2010) is to
"accentuate the negative"—that is, find evidence that raises doubts about the
quality of intuitional evidence. Their studies are intended to display *variation*
among subjects' responses. Variation is understood as intersubject disagreement, and when there is disagreement, as we have observed, one or more of
the parties must be mistaken. Too much disagreement would appear to
establish their negative, skeptical conclusion.

However, this oversimplifies the situation. When each of two people intu-
its, or judges, that x is F, where "x" is a referring term to a hypothetical scenario, are they assenting to the same proposition? Not necessarily. If one of
them understands, represents, or conceives of the scenario in one way and
the other in a different way, they may not be assenting to the same proposition. And if one of them affirms that "x if F" and the other denies that "x is
F," they may not be disagreeing with one another. Their verbal assent and
verbal denial may not constitute a pair of contradictory judgments; in fact,
they may both be right (Sosa 2007b). This possibility of explaining away apparent disagreement might protect intuition's evidential turf by averting excessive imputations of error. On the other hand, this may be excessively
charitable: If somebody has mentally misrepresented the scenario, and this
misrepresentation is the source of his misclassification, it is still *that* refer-
enced scenario that provides (part of) the content of his answer, and the basis
for judging it accurate or inaccurate. So when two intuitors differ in their
classification of the same scenario, it is arguably correct for the theorist to
conclude that one of them must be wrong, even if the source of the problem
is a misunderstanding of the scenario's description.

There are also other ways in which survey responses can lend support to
intuitional unreliability. Proponents of the "negative" form of X-phi argue
that if survey data reveal that intuitions are sensitive to factors "irrelevant"

to the contents of the thought-experiments themselves, this impugns their evidentiary status. This can again be understood in terms of how irrelevance is associated with unreliability. For example, if intuitions are to be trusted as accurate indicators of what obtains with respect to the scenario, the *order* in which cases are presented to subjects in the experiment should not influence their classification judgment. But one group of experimental philosophers found that order of presentation (being first vs. being second) did influence classification judgments (Swain, Alexander, and Weinberg 2008). This result was taken to show that intuitions are "unstable" and that when they are unstable, they will lack high reliability. Other factors that can produce "instability" include sensitivity to affective context, such as seeing disgusting stimuli like greasy pieces of old pizza while hearing the question posed (Nichols 2004).

These sorts of results show that scientific methods can potentially be informative about how intuitions arise, and this might indeed bear on their accuracy. In principle, we might learn that philosophers' naïve optimism about commonsense intuitions has been misplaced. Historically, science has overthrown many commonsense beliefs that had seemed so secure as to be immune from critical scrutiny. At the same time, one wants to be sure that only *high-quality* science should influence our on-balance assessments. Some critics of experimental philosophy argue that various specimens of X-phi are open to methodological objection or have simply not held up over time.

For example, debunkers of X-phi studies point out that in the first ten years since the founding X-phi study was conducted (Weinberg, Nichols, and Stich 2001), there have been no replications of these initial results (despite attempts to replicate them). In experimental science, of course, replication is essential. Others observe that the responses of the East Asians and South Asians in that initial study lie very close to the 50–50 split that experimenters often see when subjects are not interested in a problem but are merely answering randomly (Nagel 2012). The possibility of mere random answering in that study has not been excluded.

Another line of attack points out that X-phi survey studies often simply assume that survey responses can be equated with intuitions, yet this assumption is implausible. Intuitions should be distinguished from mere responses to questionnaires. The factors that influence survey responses include several things that may not influence (purely mental) intuitions. They include (1) the subject's background beliefs used when interpreting the vignette, (2) beliefs about what researchers are interested in, and hence "looking for" by way of responses, and (3) sensitivity to conversational norms. The second factor, sometimes referred to as "task demands," can skew a subject's responses. Such tailoring may not neatly correspond to actual intuitions. X-phi practitioners sometimes make dubious inferences from survey results to underlying intuitions, ignoring pragmatic and semantic factors known to play a role in guiding responses to surveys (Kauppinen 2007; Cullen 2010). In short, critics charge that X-phi philosophers have given insufficient attention to the required nuances of good survey methodology.

A third line of criticism is fueled by the hypothesis that student subjects, especially students who have not already studied the knowledge problem in an epistemology class, may lack the necessary *expertise* to comprehend the convoluted vignettes in which epistemology often traffics (especially in connection with the Gettier problem). This requires training and expertise that epistemologists (and philosophers in general) certainly have. By contrast, it cannot be assumed that routine participants in survey experiments have the needed tools to navigate the subtleties of the scenarios. Perhaps, then, there is no general flaw in their intuitional or classificational procedures; it is just the details of the target scenarios that they have difficulty tracking. This idea is given empirical support by Turri's studies reported in Chapter 7.

Even if some of these charges are correct, they do not cut against a main theme of the present chapter, namely that *properly conducted* science is potentially very helpful to the practice of philosophy in general and the effective deployment of intuitional methodology in particular. Whatever the reliability of intuitions happens to be, accurately determining this level of reliability may require, or at least benefit from, experimental methodology.

8.6 HOW INTUITIONAL JUDGMENTS CAN GO WRONG

Let us step back from the specific experimental work directed at classification intuitions. From a theoretical perspective, consider three ways in which a (classification) intuition might go wrong. First, it might go wrong if the subject has a mistaken concept, or conception, of the target category—knowledge, causation, reference, or whatever philosophical relation is in question. If one lacks a proper grasp of the category, one might easily be led to classify the target scenario inaccurately, thinking that Smith knows, for example, although he doesn't.

A second way it might go wrong is if the subject has an inadequate representation of the scenario. The main point of Turri's experiments (Section 7.3.2) was to show how an enhanced presentation of a scenario can call subjects' attention to critical features of a scenario, which can significantly affect a subject's full appreciation of the issue at hand. Without adequate attention or grasp of certain details, a classification can go astray. A third way to go wrong is by making a flawed implementation or execution of the classification process. Having formed a full and correct representation of the scenario, and having, much earlier, formed a correct representation of the category (e.g., knowledge), the attempt to classify the scenario with respect to the category might somehow go awry. The occurrence of any of these possibilities, or any combination of them, could lead to an erroneous classification judgment.

A vigorous defender of intuitional judgment might reply that neither of the first two types of error should be laid at the doorstep of intuition proper—that is, at the doorstep of the *process* or *operation* of intuition. Surely that process or operation cannot be blamed if other elements in the cognitive enterprise bungle the job of representing the scenario or the category. Those are flaws of another kind. When assessing the methodology of intuition, hadn't we better maintain a satisfactory grip on the role intuition per se plays in the methodology alongside other contributing factors? As we have just indicated, the accuracy of a particular classification judgment hinges on more than the classification step of the process. Responsibility should be shouldered by all the contributing factors, not by the intuitional (classification) process alone. If you discover that your watch is displaying the wrong time, the blame shouldn't necessarily fall on the watch mechanism itself; maybe the problem is your failure to reset the watch after moving to a new time zone. As this example illustrates, reliable indication can fail for any number of different reasons.

With these points in mind, the standard for evaluating classification intuition as a process can profitably be tweaked, in parallel with the way that process reliabilists tweak the theory of justified inferential processes (see Chapter 2). If an inferential process generates a set of output beliefs with a rather low truth-ratio, this might arise in several ways. It might be because the pattern of inference itself is defective. Alternatively, errors might arise because false premises are fed into the process on various occasions of its use. This could easily lead to numerous false conclusion beliefs. (Consider the adage "Garbage in, garbage out.") This prompts reliabilists to introduce into their framework the notion of *conditional reliability*—that is, having a high truth-ratio in those cases (only) where the input beliefs are true. This conditional reliability test is proposed as the proper standard of justificational quality for inferential processes (and other belief-dependent processes). Conditional reliability is a concept that can apply to the case of classification judgment as well:

> C-J RELIABILITY: A classification judgment process has high conditional reliability if and only if it outputs a high ratio of true classification judgments within that class of cases in which both the scenario representation and the category representation are accurate.

Just as the definition of conditional reliability for inference appeals to the truth-ratio of output beliefs *when all input beliefs are true*, so the notion of conditional reliability for classification judgments appeals to the truth-ratio of accurate classification judgments when all inputs to the process are accurate. The principal inputs here would include (i) the intuitor's mental representation of the scenario and (ii) her mental representation of the (target) category. This definition does not try to settle whether the process of classification intuition is or is not sufficiently reliable to merit our using it in philosophical practice. It just urges that the measure of reliability be set appropriately, where appropriateness would be conditional rather than unconditional reliability.

Once conditional reliability is included, however, a question arises whether it is even possible for classification intuition to make mistakes. If a subject has a concept of F that exactly matches (i.e., has the same content as) F itself, and if she also represents the scenario fully and accurately, how could the classification system deliver an erroneous answer to the question, "Does this scenario exemplify F?" How is a defective classification system even possible? It just would not be a system for classification as it is normally understood (Ludwig 2007).

Here again the resources of scientific psychology can be helpful. Classification is a topic heavily studied in cognitive psychology, usually under the heading of *categorization* (a term that will often be used here). Two illustrations of possible categorization errors will be presented, both drawing from psychology-based treatments of categorization.

First, consider a theory of concept possession, the so-called *exemplar theory*. This theory holds that concept possession consists of storing in memory a set of previously encountered exemplars of the target category (e.g., "dog"). Given that one has acquired such a concept, categorizing a visually sighted object as a dog or a non-dog begins by (a) retrieving from memory some subset of one's dog exemplars and (b) comparing for similarity the target object with the retrieved exemplars. If the similarity is close enough (at least to some of the retrieved exemplars), the target is categorized as a dog. If the object more closely resembles exemplars of a contrasting category (e.g., "cat"), then the target object is categorized as a non-dog.

Notice that the exemplar theory as presented above says that a *selection* is made during the retrieval process from the total set of exemplars of a category F. What guides this selection? Contextual factors might prime certain exemplars as contrasted with others. The "context model" of categorization, advanced by Medin and Schaffer (1978), offers this approach. If the retrieval process can be primed in this way, it would appear that the answers generated could be quite variable, and the question of their correctness becomes moot. If, however, the answer that would be generated by considering the total set of stored exemplars is different from the answer generated by some skewed subset of them, the latter would seem to be erroneous. So this is one way in which a classification mechanism might generate error.

Another example comes from the theory of heuristics (see Chapter 7). One heuristic proposed by Kahneman and Frederick (2005, see Sinnott-Armstrong, Young, and Cushman 2010) is a cognitive short-cut they call the *substitution heuristic*. Suppose a person wants to determine whether an object, X, has a target attribute, T. The presence or absence of this target attribute, however, is difficult to detect, perhaps due to the believer's lack of information or of time. Instead of directly investigating whether the object has the target attribute, the believer uses information about a different attribute, a "heuristic" attribute, H, which is easier to detect and hence convenient to substitute in place of T. In effect, the believer investigates a different question from the one she initially asks herself. Usually she is not consciously aware she is answering a different question; she simply forms a belief that the object has the target attribute if she detects the heuristic attribute, H. Whenever this substitution heuristic is at work, it is obviously capable of generating incorrect categorization judgments.

To sum up the previous few sections, there is ample reason to conclude that various kinds of empirically based findings, both from standard psychology and from experimental philosophy, can yield results that raise serious questions for the reliability, and hence evidential status, of intuitional methods. Thus, we have confirmed our earlier suggestion that empirical evidence is highly relevant to the question of whether intuitions are genuinely potent items of evidence, as orthodox philosophical practice assumes. This does not mean, however, that the current evidence about the evidential status of intuitions is entirely clear-cut. On the contrary, interpreting the higher-order evidence is a delicate matter, and new higher-order evidence will certainly be forthcoming. Meanwhile, as in all things, *caveat emptor*: Be careful what (intellectual products) you purchase.

In the next and final section of the chapter, we shall see that even if the intuitional prowess of individual intuitors is not only fallible but underwhelming, the community can still reasonably expect *some* applications of the intuitional method to generate very substantial evidential fruits.

8.7 INTUITIONAL METHODS AND SOCIAL EPISTEMOLOGY

We saw in the previous section that arriving at a correct classification judgment depends on at least three conditions: (1) the accuracy of the subject's scenario representation, (2) the accuracy of the subject's category representation, and (3) the conditional reliability of the subject's classification process. Each of these conditions, clearly, is a nontrivial condition to satisfy. So how can philosophers (many of them, anyway) be as confident as they seem to be about the correctness of intuition-based conclusions? Epistemologists seem very confident, for example, about several things pertaining to knowledge: for example, that knowledge requires truth, that knowledge requires belief (or something in that neighborhood), and that justified true belief isn't sufficient for knowledge. In light of the assorted worries that have surfaced here, how can philosophers *ever* be justifiedly confident of such beliefs based on intuitional methods?

This pessimistic stance, it will now be suggested, is premature. It might be warranted if a philosopher's only intuitional evidence were evidence from a single person on a single occasion. Suppose you are a philosopher thinking about knowledge, and you come up with a totally new example; or better, not just a new example, but a new angle, such as what happened when Gettier (or perhaps Bertrand Russell before him[6]) thought up the double-luck angle. You ask yourself for your own intuition about the new case, and it bubbles up with clarity: The character in the scenario *knows*! You have no doubt or hesitation about it. How confident *should* you be, however, based on your own intuition only? Given the clarity of the intuition, maybe you are entitled to be somewhat confident of it. But when you reflect on what you have read in the preceding pages of this chapter, maybe you feel that such confidence should be tempered. "Only degree-of-belief .65," you tell yourself, "no more."

Good, you are being cautious and conscientious. But thus far you haven't taken all steps that might be taken, and that many philosophers commonly do take. More evidence can be gathered. You can ask *other* people for *their* intuitions. You might ask your friends and acquaintances. You might submit a paper centered on the example to a conference and see what the audience members say in the Q&A. In Gettier's case, practically everybody agreed with him from the start. They agreed with his intuitions about the two cases. (They also agreed that the cases conflict with the JTB = K thesis, but that further step is irrelevant to the present discussion.) Only in such fairly rare cases are cautious philosophers fully persuaded by the results of the intuitional method, but maybe they are justified in being confident in *those* cases.

Traditionally philosophers have theorized about the evidential status of intuitional judgment by reflecting on the import of a *single* person's intuition. Sometimes discussion was restricted to a subject's *own* evidence based exclusively on his or her *own* intuition. Experimental philosophy has helpfully expanded our thinking about the subject by comparing and contrasting data from multiple participants. However, as we have seen, there has been a heavy emphasis on the negative evidential import of finding that participants disagree. Actually, an argument can be made on the opposite side of this issue: Conflicting responses among different survey participants is perfectly compatible (in principle) with the conclusion that a particular judgment has strong evidential support. In particular, this could be true if that judgment is the majority judgment of a large number of participants.

To see this, start with some examples. If a large number of people all observe a criminal act, and each testifies to what he or she saw in a trial, should jurors feel that their testimony, taken collectively, is only probative if their reports are identical in every detail? Or only if they all agree about the principal facts of what occurred? No. That is too stringent a requirement. If a solid majority agrees on what transpired, that should be evidence enough despite some dissenters. At least this is so if all opinions are independently arrived at. Similarly, a citizen is warranted in believing that human-caused climate change is a fact despite some level of dissent from some climatologists.

The general point here can be made more formally with the help of the Condorcet Jury Theorem, a mathematical theorem due to the eighteenth-century Frenchman Marquis de Condorcet (1785). The theorem also identifies important constraints that must be taken into account when "appealing to the numbers." Suppose that the following conditions are satisfied: (1) A yes/no question with an objectively correct answer is presented to a group of voters. (2) Each voter has a probability r of believing the correct answer, where r is greater than .50. (3) The voters' beliefs are mutually independent of one another. Then the theorem says that the answer judged true by a majority of voters has a greater-than-r chance of being correct, and this probability rapidly approaches 1.0 as the size of the group increases. In other words, if each member has a probability of being right only slightly better than 0.50 (and the other conditions are met), then the probability of a majority opinion being correct rapidly approaches 1.0 for large groups.[7]

If this theorem can be applied to classification judgment, it promises to have considerable significance. Suppose the probability of an isolated classification judgment being correct is quite modest, say .55, and that this probability is the same for everyone. Then, although a single isolated intuition provides pretty slim evidence in favor of the truth of the categorization claim, a large number of such intuitions could provide very weighty evidence. In fact, there doesn't have to be *consensus,* either unanimity or close to unanimity: A bare majority of any size in favor of one categorization can constitute weighty evidence if the total number of judgments is very large and they are made independently.

However, the requirement of independence is very questionable for the domain of classification judgment. Here it looks like there will be a very considerable amount of mutual influence, or *interdependence.* The problem isn't only the familiar one that many student participants in studies of intuitive judgments have studied epistemology and therefore have been directly influenced by their instructors and the authors they read. An even larger and more fundamental problem for independence is that in learning the meanings of words (including "know," one of the most common verbs in English), people have already encountered many sample classifications by others. These "models" of word use certainly influence them. What are the prospects, then, for the satisfaction of the independence condition in the domain of classification judgment? Of course, the reader should be reminded that the nonapplicability of a particular theorem such as the Condorcet Jury Theorem doesn't count against the reliability of a particular type of process; it just means that that particular tool is unavailable for the problem at hand. This initially promising way of making an "appeal to the numbers" runs into an important obstacle in the requirement of independence. There is much to be discussed here, but headway on these problems is difficult, so this seems like a reasonable place to pause, with acknowledgment that much remains unresolved.

Considering a social approach to what started out as a highly individualistic strand of traditional philosophy constitutes an instructive segue into the next two chapters of this text, grouped together under the heading of "Social Epistemology." That social epistemology can also bear on intuitional methodology seems like a noteworthy milestone in the growth of this branch of epistemology. The social part of epistemology is further explored in Chapters 9 and 10.

QUESTIONS

1. How might Cummins respond to the objection presented against his calibration argument? What kind of principled distinction could he make between intuitions and other sources of evidence that are widely held as basic, such as perception and memory? Could he somehow argue that intuition does have to be calibrated even if these other evidential sources do not? How would such an argument go?

2. Suppose that the chapter is right in arguing that philosophers should inquire into higher-order evidence for the evidential status of classification intuitions.

And suppose that the higher-order evidence must be (or must include) *empirical* evidence about the reliability of classification intuitions. How big a defeat would this be for a traditional rationalist position about philosophical methodology? After all, it might be compatible with the thesis that nonempirical processes are what occur at the first-order level of classification processes. So how big a deal is the nature of the higher-order evidence?

3. The chapter's formulation of *conditional reliability* (C-J Reliability) as the criterion of evidencehood for classification intuitions is a step in the direction of protecting evidential status for intuitions (see Section 8.6). Its acceptance means that any errors of classification that might be made can be imputed to something other than the classification process itself—for example, to flaws in scenario representations or concept representations. To avoid this clever defense of intuitional reliability, a would-be critic must find a flaw in the conditional reliability criterion of evidencehood. Can you help the critic find such a flaw?

4. Can you think of a way to rescue the "majority opinion" defense of intuitional methodology that avoids the problem of the lack of independence? Couldn't convergence of different people's intuitions speak to the indicator reliability of the concurring intuitions even if there is interdependence?

FURTHER READING

Alexander, Joshua, Ron Mallon, and Jonathan M. Weinberg (2010). "Accentuate the Negative." *Review of Philosophy and Psychology* 1(2): 297–314.

Casullo, Albert (2013). "Articulating the A Priori-A Posteriori Distinction." In A. Casullo and J. C. Thurow (eds.), *The A Priori in Philosophy* (pp. 249–273). Oxford: Oxford University Press.

Devitt, Michael (2005). "There Is No A Priori." In M. Steup and E. Sosa (eds.), *Contemporary Debates in Epistemology*. Oxford: Blackwell.

Goldman, Alvin I. (2010). "Philosophical Naturalism and Intuitional Methodology." *Proceedings and Addresses of the American Philosophical Association* 48(2): 115–150. Reprinted in A. I. Goldman (2012). *Reliabilism and Contemporary Epistemology*. New York: Oxford University Press and in A. Casullo and J. C. Thurow (eds.), *The A Priori in Philosophy* (pp. 11–44). Oxford: Oxford University Press.

Jenkins, C. S. I. (2013). "Naturalistic Challenges to the A Priori." In A. Casullo and J. C. Thurow (eds.), *The A Priori in Philosophy* (pp. 274–290). Oxford: Oxford University Press.

Malmgren, Anna-Sara (2011). "Rationalism and the Content of Intuitive Judgements." *Mind* 120(478): 263–327.

Nagel, Jennifer, Valerie San Juan, and Raymond A. Mar (2013). "Lay Denial of Knowledge for Justified True Beliefs." *Cognition* 129: 652–661.

Pust, Joel (2012) "Intuition." In Edward N. Zalta (ed.), *The Stanford Encyclopedia of Philosophy* (Winter 2012 Edition). Available at http://plato.stanford.edu/archive/win2012/entries/intuition/.

Williamson, Timothy (2007). *The Philosophy of Philosophy*. Malden, MA: Blackwell.

NOTES

1. This is the formulation given by Ichikawa (2009) and Ichikawa and Jarvis (2009). It is a translation into English of Williamson's logical notation.

2. It is assumed that a subject or participant gives an answer (either verbally or with a click) that expresses his or her genuine attitude. In other words, it's assumed that a subject responds sincerely rather than out of some strategic or other unusual motivation. This assumption can obviously be relaxed for certain experimental situations, but the working assumption here will be that of sincere report.

3. For a recent worthwhile attempt to say how intuition (or "awareness") might give us justification for beliefs about abstract objects in general, see Chudnoff (2013).

4. Moreover, Williamson provides more detail about the psychology of counterfactual inference. He endorses the idea that a number of others have suggested that counterfactual thinking is a species of "off-line simulation" (2007, 47–53). This move has its risks, however: There is ample evidence in the psychological literature that simulation, at least in its application to mindreading, is not terribly reliable. See Goldman (2006, 164–170) for an overview of empirical evidence that simulation-based mindreading is fraught with biases. The greater this threat, the greater the grounds for skepticism if the integrity of thought-experimental methodology hinges on the (high) reliability of offline simulation-based reasoning.

5. It is assumed that people are always correct in verbally reporting their intuitions. In the interest of simplicity, we grant subjects introspective infallibility, at least when it comes to classificational intuitions.

6. Russell (1912) introduced the stopped-clock example.

7. The original form of the jury theorem required all voters to have the same level (greater than chance) of competence. Modern formulations of the theorem loosen this demand by allowing heterogeneous competencies, where the average competence level is greater than a half and the distribution of competencies of the group members is symmetric. See Grofman, Owen, and Feld (1983).

PART IV

Social Epistemology

Testimony and Disagreement
Alvin I. Goldman

9.1 A GUIDE TO SOCIAL EPISTEMOLOGY

René Descartes created a roadmap for epistemology. The plan was to medi-
tate, reflect, and otherwise conduct one's intellectual affairs in a thoroughly
self-absorbed way. No consideration was to be given to other people's
thoughts or opinions, to how their knowledge might inform one's own. As
he reports in the following passage, Descartes rejected his teachers' precepts
and set out on a personal intellectual voyage to find the truth:

> That is why I gave up my studies entirely as soon as I reached the age when I
> was no longer under the control of my teachers. I resolved to seek no other
> knowledge than that which I might find within myself, or perhaps in the great
> book of nature. (Descartes [1637] 1960, 8)

The great bulk of epistemology has followed Descartes' image of an epistemic agent as a solitary investigator, seeking truth by his own devices. John
Locke endorsed a similar model in the following memorable passage:

> For, I think, we may as rationally hope to see with other Men's Eyes, as to know
> by other Men's Understanding. So much as we ourselves consider and compre-
> hend of Truth and Reason, so much we possess of real and true Knowledge. The
> floating of other Men's opinions in our brains makes us not a jot more knowing,
> though they happen to be true. (Locke [1689] 1975, I. iv. 23)

This is highly counterintuitive, however: Everyone seeks information from
others many times a day, if not from personal friends and professional colleagues then from Google and Wikipedia. We trust them (for the most part)
to tell us what they know, or what has been communally assembled as the
facts about a target subject. The social fabric of our epistemic lives is undeni-
able, and even if chunks of it are factually suspect (product commercials,

outlandish claims for and against political figures), a great deal of it seems both informative and beneficial. How could Locke have been so benighted?

As a general theory of knowledge, therefore, shouldn't epistemology make space for a social sector of the field? Some would argue for the priority of the social, on the grounds that society and culture influence the very epistemic standards we employ. At a minimum, social epistemology (SE) should explicate the epistemic standards communities use in cognitive interactions and propose improved and expanded ways to exploit the epistemic resources of our peers. Historically speaking, epistemology has been slow to find a capacious and focused niche for a social sector of the field.[1] But recent decades have witnessed an enormous growth in the development and clarification of a social branch (or branches). Work in SE now proceeds apace, as this chapter and the following one will indicate.

Contemporary SE may be divided into three branches (Goldman 2011):

1. Branch 1 of SE: Epistemic appraisal of doxastic decisions by individual agents using social sources
2. Branch 2 of SE: Epistemic appraisal of doxastic decisions by collective agents
3. Branch 3 of SE: Epistemic analysis of the informational features of social institutions, systems, and networks

The first branch of SE provides smooth continuity with the tradition, which always focused on individuals as the primary loci of doxastic states. What distinguishes this first branch of SE from the tradition is its preoccupation with what may be called "social evidence" (i.e., evidence arising from what others say or think). Consideration of social evidence is what makes this branch of epistemology "social."

Branch 2 introduces a quite novel element into epistemology: namely, collective or group agents. Group agents are another category of entities that are widely viewed, or treated, as subjects of doxastic attitudes (belief, disbelief, suspension of judgment, and levels of credence). Collective agents are distinctive in having members with doxastic attitudes of their own. A major question is how group attitudes arise from, or are aligned with, attitudes of their members. A second question is how to make epistemic evaluations of collective beliefs: by (roughly) the same criteria as we evaluate those of individuals, or by radically different criteria?

Branch 3 introduces yet another element quite foreign to traditional epistemology: institutions or social networks. Although institutions and networks, as such, are not doxastic decision makers, the contours of such social entities can dramatically influence epistemic consequences, either by promoting or retarding desirable epistemic ends. Science is a social institution that clearly aims at the generation of new knowledge. Education is a social institution that aims (or should aim) at the dissemination of previously discovered truths. Legal trials are social institutions aimed (among other things) at getting accurate verdicts. In each of these cases epistemologists can ask what institutional designs are best suited to achieve or advance the indicated epistemic aims.

The first branch of SE is explored in the present chapter, and the second and third branches in Chapter 10. Our main two topics here are (i) testimony-based belief and (ii) peer disagreement, with several related topics included in between.

9.2 THE EPISTEMOLOGY OF TESTIMONY: REDUCTIONISM VS. NONREDUCTIONISM

People start telling you things when you are just a toddler: "The stove is hot (so don't touch it)." Assuming you grasp the meaning of the statement, are you justified in believing it? As a grown-up in an unfamiliar city, you ask a passerby where the train station is located and he tells you how to get there. Are you entitled to believe what he tells you? What reason do you have to believe what this stranger says? You know nothing about his track record for lying or truth-telling.

Epistemologists often speak of epistemic "sources," usually referring to sources of knowledge. The most familiar candidates for such sources are perception, introspection, memory, deductive reasoning, inductive reasoning, and so forth. Each of these sources is thought to provide a method for acquiring knowledge. When we turn to social epistemology, we immediately encounter, at the very core of the subfield, an ostensibly new source: testimony. Knowledge can be acquired by reading or listening to the words of others. And this source does not appear on the traditional list of such sources simply because, until recently, epistemology was largely dedicated to "private," or purely "internal," sources.

What do we mean by "testimony"? Settling on a precise definition is a tricky matter. At a first approximation, testimony is any statement or other communication that purports to state a fact or provide information. ("Purport" is an important modifier. False statements intended to deceive are nonetheless acts of testimony because they imply an intention to state a fact.) In the context of epistemology the term "testimony" is not restricted to statements delivered by witnesses at trials, nor does it require a face-to-face encounter. If you read the Greek historian Thucydides' *History of the Peloponnesian War*, you encounter a sequence of communications directed to anybody who cares to read them, and philosophers would classify them as pieces of "testimony."

In the testimonial domain, however, social epistemology is less focused on acts of speakers than on acts of receivers. How the latter should respond to communications is what principally interests epistemologists. Does the receiver believe its content, disbelieve it, or suspend judgment? Is the receiver *justified* in believing its content, and does she acquire *knowledge* in the process? The chief aim is to elucidate principles of justification and/or knowledge for testimonial belief. The conditions in which a speaker is entitled to assert a proposition is also of interest, but will not be discussed here.

Two contrasting approaches to testimonial justification are *reductionism* and *nonreductionism*. David Hume was a prominent proponent of reductionism. To explain his position, assume as background that testimony is *somehow* a source of justification, in the sense that hearers often get to be justified in accepting someone's assertion in virtue of hearing or reading it. The reduction/nonreductionism dispute hinges on *how* such justification arises (when it does). Is the hearing of testimony a *basic* source of justification or is it *derivative* from other, more basic sources? A basic source provides justification on its own, without depending on other sources for its justificatory power. Introspection, perception, and memory are standard examples of basic epistemic sources.

The case of testimony may well be different from these. In his essay "On Miracles," Hume wondered whether we have warrant in accepting testimony from people claiming to have observed a miracle. He writes:

> [O]ur assurance in any argument of this kind [from testimony] is derived from no other principle than our observation of the veracity of human testimony, and the usual conformity of facts to the reports of witnesses. (Hume [1748] 1977, 74)

What Hume is saying is that we often observe people making reports (giving testimony) and often observe ourselves whether or not these reports are accurate. There isn't always an opportunity to verify other people's reports, but when there is such an opportunity, they are usually confirmed. Furthermore, memory enables us to justifiably believe that we previously observed pairings of report and fact. Next, induction justifies us in inferring from these past pairings the general principle that most testimonial reports are true. Finally, we can infer from this the general principle that where we encounter new items of testimony (the accuracy of which we cannot directly confirm), we are justified by the general principle in believing that they too are true. Thus, taken together, perception, memory, and inductive inference enable us to be justified in believing fresh items of testimony. So, testimony is not a basic source of justification, but it acquires justificatory power from the other three sources. This is therefore a *reductive* account of testimony's justificatory power, an account that *reduces* it to the power of the three other (basic) sources.

Hume seems to think that from our observations we can infer that testimony is generally reliable. But does each of us individually make enough observations to warrant this conclusion? Does each of us have a *diverse* enough range of individuals and subject-matters to justify us in accepting and applying such a principle to any topic that might be testified to, and to any person, even somebody we have never met? C. A. J. Coady argues to the contrary:

> [I]t seems absurd to suggest that, individually, we have done anything like the amount of field-work that [reductionism] requires. . . . [M]any of us have never seen a baby born, nor have most of us examined the circulation of the blood nor the actual geography of the world nor any fair sample of laws of the land, nor have we made the observations that lie behind our knowledge that the lights in the sky are heavenly bodies immensely distant nor a vast number of other observations that [reductionism] would seem to require. (Coady 1992, 82)

The Humean view, which is criticized in the previous passage, is often called *global reductionism*. In addition to having the problems just suggested, some people would say that general principles of testimonial trustworthiness aren't enough for a receiver to be justified in trusting particular acts of testimony. The receiver must have background evidence (based on observation and memory) about the specific speaker, in order to attain justifiedness. This approach is called *local reductionism*. Here it is expressed by Elizabeth Fricker:

> In claiming that a hearer is required to assess a speaker for trustworthiness, I [mean] ... that the hearer should be discriminating in her attitude to the speaker, in that she should be continually evaluating him for trustworthiness throughout their exchange, in the light of the evidence, or cues, available to her. This will be partly a matter of her being disposed to deploy background knowledge which is relevant, partly a matter of her monitoring the speaker for any tell-tale signs revealing likely untrustworthiness. (Fricker 1994, 149–150)

This high standard, however, seems too strict to many philosophers. It leads many to reject reductionism in favor of nonreductionism. Nonreductionism denies that testimony's justificatory power derives from other sources; rather, it is an *independent* source of justification. Quite apart from what we as individuals have observed in the past, merely hearing or otherwise encountering a new item of testimony gives us justification, at least prima facie justification, to believe it. This thesis is endorsed, for example, by Tyler Burge, who writes:

> [A] person is entitled to accept as true something that is presented as true and that is intelligible to him, unless there are stronger reasons not to do so. (Burge 1993, 457)

On this approach the mere hearing of testimony confers (or "transmits") prima facie justification on the receiver's accepting it, independent of the receiver's prior experience with testimony or background knowledge about the testifier. Prior experience can, of course, provide *defeaters* for this justification, so that on balance the receiver may not be justified. Absent such defeaters, however, justification arrives "for free"; the hearer does not need any relevant *positive* reason for believing the speaker's report.

The types of problems facing reductionism and nonreductionism, respectively, are familiar to philosophers. Reductionism sets a standard that seems too strong—that is, excessively demanding. Nonreductionism, on the other hand, seems too weak; it makes it too easy to be justified in believing random testimony. To illustrate the latter point, consider the following example from Jennifer Lackey (2008, 168–169). Suppose that Sam is taking a walk through the forest and sees someone that he can recognize as an alien from another planet drop a book. Sam recovers the dropped book and sees that it appears to be in English and that it seems to say (in a diary-like fashion) that tigers have eaten some of the inhabitants of the author's planet. But Sam, Lackey explains, has no epistemically relevant positive reasons to trust this source: He knows nothing about alien psychology and has no beliefs about the reliability of the book's author, no beliefs about the general reliability of aliens as testifiers, and no beliefs about how "diaries" function in alien culture. Is Sam justified in believing that tigers have eaten some of the inhabitants of the author's planet? Lackey says no. If this is right, it poses a serious problem for nonreductionism of the extreme kind that Burge defends.

9.3 THE INTERPERSONAL VIEW OF TESTIMONY

Testimony is widely treated as a type of evidence. Although this evidence involves another person, it is not fundamentally different from a wide variety of other events or states of affairs I can treat as "signs" or "indicators" of other states of the world. Just as thermometer and barometer readings are evidence about current or impending states of the local weather, so a person's asserting P is evidence that she believes P. And, if my background evidence is suitable, I can regard this as evidence that P is true. In other words, I can treat such evidence as a "truth gauge." Recently, however, some philosophers have proposed a rather different conception of testimony and its reception, a conception that rejects an understanding of testimony and testimonial belief on the analogy of the "truth gauge" model. One label for this approach is the *interpersonal view* of testimony (Moran 2006).

The first thesis of the interpersonal view (as the label suggests) is that a testimonial exchange is part of an interpersonal relationship, such as the speaker *offering her assurance* to the hearer that her testimony is true, or the speaker *inviting the hearer to trust her.* According to certain proponents of this view, such features can be partly responsible for conferring epistemic justification on the testimonial beliefs acquired. Second, the epistemic justification provided by these features of a testimonial exchange is *nonevidential.* At any rate, testimony is not *merely* "evidence" in the way that readings on gauges and instruments are. One of the proponents of this view, Hinchman, says: "[w]hen you have evidence of a speaker's reliability you don't need to trust her; you can treat her speech act as a mere assertion and believe what she says on the basis of the evidence you have of its truth. You can ignore the fact that she's addressing you, inviting you. You can *treat her as a truth-gauge*" (2005, 580). Similarly, Moran maintains that "if we are inclined to believe what the speaker says, but then learn that he is *not*, in fact, presenting his utterance as an assurance whose truth he stands behind, what *remains are just words*, not a reason to believe anything . . . the utterance as [a] phenomenon, loses the epistemic import we thought it had" (Moran 2006, 283). Like Hinchman, Moran holds that a significant aspect of true communication is missing when a speaker is treated as a mere truth gauge, offering nothing more than words. Moran claims that a speaker freely assumes responsibility for the truth of p when she asserts p, thereby providing the hearer with additional reason to believe that p, different in kind from anything given by evidence alone. Similarly, Hinchman's *trust* view holds that a speaker, in inviting a hearer to trust her, takes responsibility for the truth of p on her own shoulders. This gives the hearer a different, and additional, sort of entitlement to believe than mere evidence provides.

But is this genuinely *epistemic* entitlement that is so conferred? That is one central problem facing the interpersonal view. A speaker's offer of a guarantee has little epistemic worth unless previous such offers have served as reliable guides to the truth. Without evidence of any such reliable track record, or evidence of such track records by similarly placed informants, it is questionable whether hearers really have epistemic entitlement for trust. If they do have such entitlement, it may arise from this evidential background rather than the personal assurance offered by speaker to hearer.

Second, is such a personal assurance really essential? Is it really epistemically efficacious? Jennifer Lackey's "eavesdropper" case nicely shows otherwise:

> Ben and Kate, thinking they are alone in their office building, are having a discussion about the private lives of their co-workers. During the course of their conversation, Ben tells Kate that their boss is having an affair with the latest intern who has been hired by the company, Irene. Unbeknownst to them, however, Earl has been eavesdropping on this conversation and so he, like Kate, comes to believe solely on the basis of Ben's testimony—which is in fact both true and epistemically impeccable—that his boss is having an affair with Irene. Moreover, Kate and Earl not only have the same relevant background information about both Ben's reliability as a testifier and the proffered testimony, they also are properly functioning recipients of testimony who possess no relevant undefeated defeaters. (2008, 233)

The problem here for the interpersonal view is that Ben offered Kate his assurance that his testimony is true and invited Kate to trust him. But neither of these things characterizes Ben's relationship with eavesdropping Earl. Because of this, Earl ought to have an inferior level of epistemic entitlement than Kate does, according to the interpersonal view. But does he? If Kate and Earl each functions properly as a recipient of testimony, if each has the same background information, and so forth, then what could distinguish the epistemic statuses of their beliefs? There seems intuitively to be no such distinction, which sharply cuts against the interpersonal view.

9.4 BASING BELIEF ON THE ABSENCE OF TESTIMONY

Meanwhile, there have been some offshoots of the central problem of testimony. They are, if you like, "subproblems" of the core problem of testimonial belief. But some of them "stretch out" to the other branches of SE, including the third branch.

In the Sherlock Holmes story *Silver Blaze* there is a famous incident of a dog that didn't bark. Holmes takes the absence of a dog's bark to be a key piece of evidence that he uses to unravel the mystery. That the dog didn't bark is evidence that the person who committed the murder was no stranger to the dog. If barking is understood to be communication, here is a case in which the absence of communication has evidential value. Of course, barking isn't testimony—presumably because testimony must be linguistic and propositional. But *non*-barking certainly isn't testimony. Yet it may be telltale evidence nonetheless. In particular, it might qualify in special cases as "evidence to the best explanation." Some theorists of testimony offer an account of testimony-based belief in which the hearer makes an inference from another person's testimony-that-p to the conclusion that p is true, because the truth of p is part of the best explanation of the perceived testimony (Lipton 1998). Analogously, silence might serve as a piece of evidence for the truth of q in special circumstances in which q is part of the best explanation of the silence that is "heard."

This is precisely the idea that Sanford Goldberg (2010; 2011) sets forth. His formula consists in inferences of the form "P must not be true, because if it were true, I would have heard about it by now." If you are a regular consumer of online news, occurrences like catastrophes and media sensations will be broadcast widely and you will rapidly become apprised of them. If you haven't gotten wind of any plane crash, devastating typhoon, or other such event in the last twelve hours, it's a reasonable inference that no such events have occurred. Indeed, no matter the subject matter, if there is a rumor mill, a media system, or a dedicated blog that scrupulously reports on specified subjects, and you have received no posts or other kinds of messages from this system, then you might reasonably feel warranted in concluding that nothing newsworthy in this subject area has occurred. In these circumstances, silence can be almost as informative as a verbal message.

It is clear, however, as Goldberg argues, that the informational value of silence, or nontestimony, depends crucially on a social system. More fully, we might add, it depends on the existence of suitable technology (in our era, primarily Internet technology) and in the various forms of deployment of such technology (the World Wide Web, email, digital versions of newspapers and blogs, etc.). This socio-technological world, plus an individual's personalized connectivity to it, create a special environment in which the absence of a message, within that individual's unique connectivity pattern, may be quite informative.

Goldberg highlights five things that must hold of an agent's environment in order that silence, or nonreceipt of a message, would be informationally "propitious." First, some members of the agent's community (the "standard sources") regularly report about the topic in question. Second, the agent assumes that the standard sources are reliable in uncovering and publicizing truths about such matters. Third, she assumes that such sources have had sufficient time to discover the relevant facts and report on them. Fourth, she assumes that she herself would likely have come across such a report. Fifth, she has not in fact come across such a report. Goldberg calls a belief supported by this sort of reasoning a *coverage-supported* belief. An agent's reliance on such a source is called *coverage reliance*. Following Hilary Kornblith (1994), Goldberg shows how various social practices and institutions serve as a "social environment" in which coverage-supported beliefs can be reliably formed. We live in a world with a dizzying array of available information sources. We develop habits of selecting and utilizing a subset of these sources, and our resultant informational state depends heavily on the selections made and the extent and quality of what those sources cover. So our reliance on others is dramatic.

Goldberg proceeds to use this construction to defend a metaphysical thesis related to SE. Being a reliabilist, he agrees that the justifiedness of the beliefs based on negative testimony (i.e., nontestimony) depends on the reliability of the processes used. But since the reliabilities in question depend so heavily on the social environment, he argues, as against classical reliabilism, that the processes supervene on the social environment:

> The take-home point of the proposal is that a reliabilist assessment of coverage-supported belief can't just examine the belief-forming process that takes place within the mind/brain of the coverage-relying subject herself; such an assessment must also assess the various social institutions and practices that form the process(es) by which news is generated and disseminated in her community. Two different coverage-relying subjects, as alike skin-in as any two distinct individuals can be, might nevertheless differ in their [global]-reliability of their respective coverage-supported beliefs, as one subject lives in a community in which these institutions and practices provide her with highly reliable coverage on the issue at hand, whereas the other lives in a community where the coverage is less highly reliable. . . . Whatever difference there is in the [global]-reliability of their respective beliefs supervenes on more than what is going on in their respective heads; it also supervenes on the social practices and institutions that surround them. (Goldberg 2010, 179)

Here we set aside Goldberg's metaphysical "Extendedness" hypothesis. The social-*epistemological* morals, however, seem very important and should not be neglected. The subfield of testimony-based epistemology certainly expands when the communicational properties of the social world are accorded their full due.

9.5 CHOOSING AMONG EXPERTS

The standard format for the epistemology of testimony-based belief has three stages: (1) A speaker testifies that P. (2) A hearer (or receiver) of this testimony makes a doxastic decision vis-à-vis P, based on the speaker's testimony plus background beliefs. (3) A theorist or other evaluator makes an epistemic assessment of the hearer's doxastic behavior based on suitable epistemic principles (whatever they may be).

This is fine as far as it goes. But there are interesting epistemological stages and questions that are "prior," as it were, to this three-stage setup. As we already saw in the preceding section, epistemic agents are not always passive. They don't have to wait to be contacted by an eager communicator. They don't have to wait for the phone to ring, for a friend to begin the conversation, for the airport personnel to begin the boarding announcement. They can select a potential communicator and ask that person a question, thereby (often) prompting a piece of testimony on precisely the topic that interests them. They can select a particular column, book, or journal article to read based on their prior knowledge or belief about the author (or publication venue) and the topic that is conveyed by the title (or headline). In other words, epistemic agents can be pro-active and selective. They don't have to wait for the world (of communication) to come to them. They can consult selected sources of their own choosing. In short, epistemic agents can *gather evidence;* they don't have to confine themselves to evidence the world thrusts at them willy-nilly. This is particularly true and important vis-à-vis social evidence. Agents have choices to make in interacting with friends, acquaintances, and anonymous individuals, whether living or dead. Their ensuing epistemic successes or failures may depend heavily on how wisely, stupidly, or ignorantly they pursue social evidence.

One obvious corner in which to explore this theme (one of the oldest themes in SE, as it happens) concerns the choice of individuals to consult as *experts.* The world is full of people who claim to be an expert on this or that subject. What does it mean to really *be* an expert? Let us mean by an "expert" (a genuine expert) in domain D somebody who has more true beliefs and/or fewer false beliefs in D than most people do. Also they typically have skills or dispositions to generate more true answers to questions in D that they haven't previously thought about than most people would be able to generate. This is what it *means* to be an expert (Goldman 2001). But lots of people claim to be experts without satisfying the foregoing conditions. This problem worried Plato. In his dialogue *Charmides* (170d–e) Socrates wonders whether a man can distinguish someone who pretends to be a doctor from someone who really and truly is one.

The question about experts has been introduced by reference to how one might go about choosing an expert to consult. But many of the same problems emerge after you have chosen your experts and heard what they have to say in response to your question or problem. So let us focus on this stage. Suppose you are a total layperson with respect to (factual) question Q. You have little or nothing by way of beliefs vis-à-vis propositions in that domain, and no time to acquire training or expertise in D. You have selected two putative experts and asked each of them the same (true/false) question, Q. Each "expert" has responded, either briefly or at length. Their responses conflict. One says that the embedded proposition is true, the other that it is false. How can you decide, justifiedly, which one to trust? That is, which one should you believe; or how should you apportion your credences with respect to the proposition in question? According to nonreductionism about testimony, you initially have prima facie justifiedness in believing each of them. But this is of little help, because the testimony of each constitutes a *defeater* of the testimony of the other. Where should you turn? When experts disagree, can a layperson rationally determine which one should be believed (or assigned a higher credence)?

John Hardwig (1991) addresses the expert/layperson problem (or the expert/novice) problem by saying that a layperson's reliance on an expert must be *blind*. In effect, this says that laypeople can have no evidence for selecting between two experts; the social evidence is a "wash." Can we do better than this skeptical upshot? If not, this would be worrisome, because we all need expert advice in our incredibly complex world. There follow five ways that a layperson might proceed in order to make a justified choice between two opposing experts (Goldman 2001). Each way picks out a species of evidence one might seek to gather, either from the two putative experts alone or from others. Such evidence might or might not be forthcoming, depending on the situation.

1. Read or listen to arguments and counterarguments offered by the two experts. Appraise their relative strength and proceed accordingly.
2. Obtain the opinions of other (putative) experts on the same topic. If they mostly agree with expert A, identify A as your best guide and believe accordingly. If they mostly agree with B, align your belief with B.
3. Consult "meta-experts" about A and B. Try to find out which is the superior expert by asking people in a position to compare their relative expertise.
4. Obtain evidence about the experts' biases and interests, which might lead either (or both) to self-serving answers of dubious veracity.
5. Gather evidence of their respective past track records and apportion trust as a function of these track records.

Each of these proposed methods looks potentially helpful, but only a little probing reveals trouble. A characteristic feature of expertise is possession of *esoteric* knowledge. This implies that laypersons may lack the vocabulary used by the experts and lack some (or all) of their concepts. Thus, starting with Method 1, even if the layperson reads or hears answers and supporting arguments advanced by the experts, he may find them impenetrable or impossible to assess. He may be unable to assess the truth value of the asserted premises and unable to assess the strength of the premise/conclusion relationships. Trying to follow two competing, multistep arguments will probably leave a layperson little better off than when he started.

Next consider Method 2, which urges one to look to the numbers. This is a widely used method (at least implicitly), but it has a fundamental flaw: The fact that more (putative) experts agree with A tells you nothing at all about what these shared beliefs are based on, and, in particular, nothing about whether these concurring beliefs are independently or interdependently generated. Here is the kind of problem that arises from interdependence.

Suppose it turns out that A is joined in his or her belief by an overwhelming proportion of all people who have an opinion on the topic. They might all be the students of a single misguided but influential leader who, by dint of her prestigious position or flamboyant style, has persuaded vast numbers of

followers of the same thesis (and other theses). When the source of the concurring beliefs is identified, it is easy to recognize that little confidence
should be placed on numbers per se. The history of science as well as many
other subjects is littered with (what we now regard as) false hypotheses that
were the dominant position of the so-called experts at an earlier point in
time. Laypersons are not well positioned to make epistemically sound judgments about the significance of a given breakdown of the current distribution of the so-called experts.

Next consider Method 3, appeal to meta-experts. Implicit reliance on meta-
experts is common in society. When experts aim to impress others with their
expertise, they often point to their credentials or their prestigious appoint-
ments, presumably conferred by meta-experts. But a layperson is rarely in a
position actually to identify any of the meta-experts who were responsible for
an individual's credentials or appointment. And even if the layperson were
apprised of the meta-experts who played these roles, how can he be expected
to make sound epistemic appraisals of *them* if he cannot make sound epistemic appraisals of the initial putative experts, A and B? In short, no properly
informed application of Method 3 is available to most laypersons.

The fourth method, checking for possible interests and biases, is potentially useful when a layperson has access to such information. This may be
comparatively rare, however, unless one of the experts works for an entity
(e.g., a corporation) that has a financial stake in the question at issue. Where
this sort of information is available, it should definitely be used. But if both
experts have such interests and potential biases, this will be of limited help
to the layperson.

Finally, consider the fifth method, the track-record method. This looks like
a bust from the start: How can it even be seriously proposed? If the layperson
is just that, a layperson, how can he or she hope to determine whether past
beliefs of each expert (in domain D) were true or false, and hence whether
they have good or bad past track records? It's the inability of the layperson to
settle the truth-values of such propositions in the first place that launched
his turning to experts! How can the layperson now hope to assess the experts by turning to the sorts of facts of which he despaired from the beginning? It is the very esotericness of such facts that gets the problem rolling in
the first place.

These are natural thoughts, and they do seem to doom the fifth method to
uselessness. But in this case, the initial take on the method may be more discouraging than is warranted. Actually, laypersons sometimes are in a position to assess putative experts' track records because they *can* determine
relevant facts that bear on those track records. The key to this surprising
turn is that a given fact may be esoteric at one time, or from one epistemic
standpoint, but not at all times or from every epistemic standpoint. This is
easy to explain.

It may take an expert to predict when the next solar eclipse will be visible
in South America, say in Chile. So if a person in 2015 touts himself as an
expert in astronomy and predicts such an eclipse in Chile in 2025, a

layperson in 2015 cannot appeal to the (predicted) 2015 eclipse as evidence for or against the astronomer's track record. But once 2025 arrives and the same layperson is herself in Santiago, Chile, when such an eclipse occurs, she can easily verify the truth of the original prediction and chalk up one correct prediction to the astronomer's track record. The layperson's epistemic vantage point has changed, partly through the passage of time, and what was once esoteric for her no longer is so. However, this kind of case does not dissolve all problems of identifying experts, because as a practical matter this may not be a very exploitable fact across all situations. We must still face challenges of epistemic asymmetries between levels of expertise and nonexpertise that dot the social epistemological landscape.

9.6 THE PROBLEM OF PEER DISAGREEMENT

As indicated from the start, this chapter addresses individual doxastic decision making in response to social evidence (understood as evidence, mainly, about other *individuals*). The cases addressed thus far have featured substantial asymmetries between agents and their evidential sources. In trials, witnesses to pertinent events are asked to testify because they have superior event-relevant knowledge or information that jurors presumably lack, or because they have expert knowledge that exceeds that of the jurors. People seek to read what the *New York Times* reports about an event because its reporters have acquired knowledge about newsworthy events that ordinary citizens do not initially know. The purpose of these kinds of transactions, at least in the eyes of the receivers, is to reduce the epistemic asymmetry between them and their evidence providers. A somewhat different kind of social-epistemic situation has recently attracted considerable attention among philosophers, a situation in which there is more or less "perfect" epistemic symmetry between two agents, at least symmetry in evidence and in intellectual capacity. Despite this symmetry, however, the agents find themselves in disagreement, and the question here is what rationality then requires of them.

An example: You and I knew each other well when we were younger. We took many classes together and developed a high regard for one another's intellect, sophistication, and breadth of knowledge. Now we suddenly reencounter one another and have a lengthy conversation about a disputed event in the news. A political figure is charged with telling a big lie. You believe he really lied; I believe it's a phony charge. Despite this sharp disagreement, it emerges that we have read exactly the same evidence. We have each read everything in the media and on the Internet about the issue. So we are *epistemic peers* and regard one another as such. I believe you are just as smart, just as capable of forming well-reasoned beliefs, as I am, and that you are exactly as well informed (evidence-wise) on the present question as I am. You believe the same of me. Nonetheless, we disagree about the alleged lie. Once we learn all of this, should either or both of us change our view in light of our discovery of an epistemic peer who disagrees? Is it rational to stand one's ground, you believing L (= the politician lied) and I believing not-L (the politician didn't lie)? Or is the only reasonable thing for each of us is to sus-pend judgment rather than to continue to believe what we now believe? This is a *peer disagreement* problem.

Here is an argument for holding that it is unreasonable for either of us to stand our ground (i.e., maintain our initial position). The first premise is a high-level principle of epistemology called the *uniqueness thesis* (Feldman 2007). The uniqueness thesis holds that for any proposition P and body of evidence relevant to P, exactly one doxastic attitude is the reasonable attitude to take vis-à-vis P. (It might not be a belief in the truth, because the available evidence might be misleading.) Here it is assumed that, for any proposition, only three attitudes are available: belief, disbelief, and suspension of judg-ment. If the uniqueness thesis is correct, it cannot be reasonable for both of us to maintain our initial position, because (at least) one of us must be violat-ing what epistemic principles require given the specified evidence. If the principles require *belief* in L (given the evidence), then I am unreasonable in rejecting L. If the principles require *dis*belief in L (given the evidence), you are unreasonable in believing L. If the principles require suspension of judg-ment, both of us are being unreasonable in our respective doxastic attitudes. What *cannot* be the case, however, is that we are both reasonable in our (differing) attitudes.

All this holds of our initial doxastic attitudes; they cannot both be reason-able. The next question is what each of us should do *after* acquiring the new evidence concerning the other's doxastic position. Is it reasonable for either or both of us to remain *steadfast* in our initial position? Or should we revise our initial positions, and if so how much should we revise them? Although each of us would presumably recognize that (at least) one of us has been making an epistemic error, the fact that we acknowledge being peers keeps us from rationally concluding that the other person is (definitely) the one who is in error. If I cannot conclude that you are being unreasonable in light of our common evidence and you cannot conclude this about me, it looks like each of us ought to suspend judgment. No other attitude is reasonable to adopt (or retain) *now*.

An analogy can help solidify the foregoing argument. Suppose you and I are each interested in the current temperature, and we are next-door neigh-bors. You look at your thermometer, which reads 42 degrees, and form the belief that it is 42 degrees in our neighborhood. I look at my thermometer (at the same time) and see that it reads 38 degrees and form a belief to that effect. Next we compare notes and discover that we disagree. Since I have no reason to think that my thermometer is more likely to be accurate than yours, and you are in a symmetrical position, it would be quite irrational for either of us to persist in our initial beliefs. As concerns the precise temperature, each of us should suspend judgment (in light of our disagreement). Isn't the same reasoning plausible when we find ourselves in disagreement about the poli-tician charged with lying, where there is no instrument on which to pin the blame? Isn't a reasonable thing to do in this sort of case to "back off" and withhold (firm) belief? This position is called *conciliationism*.

9.7 CONCILIATIONISM AND ITS PROBLEMS

People in peer disagreement situations who abandon their initially firm beliefs and move in the direction of their peer (hence toward suspension) conform to conciliationism. The idea is that each should "conciliate" with his peer. This would apply even if we frame the problem of peer disagreement to include more fine-grained attitudes than belief, disbelief, and suspension of judgment. If *credences* are allowed as doxastic attitudes (see Chapter 11, Section 11.2), where credences can be any values or degrees of confidence in the unit interval, then a "disagreement" would be any two people's pair of credences vis-à-vis P that differ from one another, for instance .57 versus .63. We could then characterize conciliationism as the view that peers who differ in their initial credences should move at least somewhat closer to one another. A "hard" form of conciliationism (e.g., "split-the-difference" conciliationism) would require each peer to move halfway toward his opposite number, thereby "meeting" each other in the middle. Is conciliationism (of a soft or hard variety) the right prescription for all cases of peer disagreement?

One dissatisfaction with systematic conciliationism calls attention to a problem arising when the proposition on the table between the peers is itself a philosophical problem. Disagreement is rife in philosophy. People who study the very same body of philosophical work (and therefore share the same evidence) often disagree quite strongly, and since philosophers are almost all so smart, it is hard to deny that any pair of them are intellectual peers. If conciliationism were the correct position in general, then philosophers would regularly be required to suspend judgment. This looks like a recipe for radical skepticism about philosophy itself. If nobody is entitled to *believe* any philosophical thesis, as opposed to suspend judgment, this is just the state skeptics recommend, at least skeptics about philosophy itself (rather than ordinary external-world propositions). A very unsettling upshot!

A second objection to conciliationism is that it seems to sanction "throwing away evidence" (Kelly 2005). When two peers disagree about some proposition P, isn't it quite possible that one party to the disagreement, say Esther, has initially reasoned well while the other, Emile, reasoned poorly? Shouldn't Esther receive more epistemic credit for her initial assessment than Emile? This record of good vs. bad reasoning should not be erased from the epistemic ledger, as it were. It should not disappear from the two agents' lists of total epistemic credit in this particular epistemic task. In general they may deserve equal marks for reasoning well in the past (in virtue of which they are now peers). But on this particular occasion, since Esther reasoned much better than Emile did in the early phase of reflection, this fact should not be allowed to disappear from the record; it should not be "thrown away."

Conciliationism, however, seems to require just this sort of disappearance. Suppose Esther declines to conciliate. She is sure that she reasoned well at the start and should not be required to split the difference with Emile and converge on the same credence. If she is given less credit than Emile in virtue of her failure to conciliate, that seems to imply that the only evidence conciliationism counts as relevant are the two initial *attitudes* Esther and Emile took toward P. Those two *psychological* states are the only things inserted into their shared database from which Esther and Emile are expected to reason in the second phase of reasoning. What each did in the first stage is tossed out, and Esther earns no permanent credit for making a better initial credence assignment to P than Emile did. If we call the original reasoning that Esther and Emile did the "first-order evidence" and the psychological states they arrived at are called "higher-order evidence," it appears that only the higher-order evidence gets counted; the first-order evidence is ignored. This cannot be right (so says Kelly, for example).

A final objection to conciliationism, one developed by Adam Elga (2010a), is a *self-undermining* objection. If and when there is disagreement about disagreement, there will be many situations in which conciliatory views call for their own rejection. But it is incoherent for a view on disagreement to call for its own rejection; so conciliatory views are incoherent.

Let us walk through this more slowly. Why might conciliatory views sometimes call for their own rejection? Suppose your view on the problem of peer disagreement is conciliationism, but a respected philosopher friend disagrees. If your conciliatory view is correct, you should change it, moving at least partway in the direction of your friend. Repeated iterations of such an encounter would only move you still farther from conciliationism. In short, conciliatory views tend to undermine themselves.

Why is it incoherent for a view on disagreement to call for its own rejection? Notice that any view on disagreement is part of one's *inductive method*, one's *fundamental* method for taking evidence into account. An inductive method offers recommendations on what to believe given some evidence. Potentially, it could even offer a recommendation on which inductive method to use. In principle, it might even call for its own rejection. To show this, Elga offers the following example.

The magazine *Consumer Reports* rates appliances and gives recommendations on which ones to buy. Suppose it also rates consumer-ratings magazines. Then it cannot coherently recommend a competing magazine over itself. To illustrate, suppose that *Consumer Reports* says, "Buy only toaster X," while a competitor, *Smart Shopper*, says "Buy only toaster Y." And suppose that *Consumer Reports* also says, "*Smart Shopper* is the magazine to follow, not *Consumer Reports*." Then *Consumer Reports* either directly or indirectly gives inconsistent advice about toasters: On the one hand it says directly to buy toaster X, and on the other hand it says to trust *Smart Shopper*, which advises the purchase of only toaster Y. It is impossible to follow both pieces of advice. Just as a consumer-ratings magazine cannot consistently recommend a competing magazine, so an inductive method cannot consistently recommend a competing method. This applies to conciliationism because it is a species of inductive method. In order to be consistent, views on disagreement must be dogmatic with respect to their own correctness.

Elga concludes that a better conciliatory view is one that makes an exception when addressing possible self-application. It should not authorize conciliation about conciliationism. Would this be an arbitrary, or ad hoc, restriction? Elga argues to the contrary. Such an exception would not be peculiar to conciliationism but applies to any fundamental policy, rule, or method whatever. So it would not be ad hoc for a conciliatory view to have a special restriction against self-application.

9.8 DOES CONCILIATIONISM REQUIRE THROWING AWAY EVIDENCE?

Can conciliationism be defended, however, against the accusation of "throwing away evidence"? A defender of conciliationism might say that the view can be given a more favorable interpretation than this critique allows. When conciliationists say that peers should move toward one another or "split the difference," they should not be understood as saying that such revision of credences by peers guarantees *full* rationality. Instead, conciliationism should be seen as a view about the bearing of just one kind of evidence, viz. "psychological evidence," or what assorted people *think*. Psychological evidence should indeed be taken into account, but it isn't the whole story, and it isn't the only determinant of overall rational credence. It may be the last step in arriving at a certain (dated) credence, but previous steps should not be ignored. So, if Emile made a mistake at an earlier stage of attitude formation, that fact should play a role in a full evaluation of his rationality or reasonability. Similarly, if Esther performed well at the earlier stage, that should redound to her total credit. In other words, conciliationism should not be understood as holding that the original evidence was irrelevant or that Esther deserves no rationality credits for heeding it properly. She should get such credit; it's just not the entire story (Christensen 2009). Once the proper role of conciliatory moves is identified, conciliationism is absolved from the charge of "throwing away evidence."

9.9 CONCILIATIONISM, STEADFASTNESS, AND UNIQUENESS

As previously indicated, conciliationism acquires a large part of its pull (or push) from the principle of epistemic *uniqueness*. This principle says that exactly one doxastic response is (maximally) rational in any given evidential situation. If D is the uniquely correct doxastic attitude to take toward P in evidential situation E, then any agent in E who adopts a different doxastic attitude toward P is doing something epistemically *impermissible*. Now if two people have exactly the same evidence but take different attitudes toward P, at least one of them is being irrational (or not maximally rational). And if each regards the other agent as a peer, neither is in a position to hold that she is the one with the uniquely correct attitude while the other is "mistaken." Therefore, neither is permitted to remain steadfast and fixed in his or her credence. Therefore, each should conciliate. This is why conciliationism seems inevitable under the assumption of uniqueness. But is this correct? Does uniqueness require conciliationism?

The formulation of uniqueness is itself a bit squishy. When it says that exactly one doxastic attitude is rational, what does it mean by a "doxastic attitude"? Should attitudes be individuated *narrowly* (i.e., *sharply*) or *broadly*? If they are individuated broadly, a sample prescription might be: "If you are in evidential situation E, your credence must be within the interval from .75 to 1.0." Such an interval might be equivalent, in point-probability terms, to what epistemologists who like the "tripartite" division of attitudes simply call "belief." But if this is as precise a prescription as epistemic principles allow, then people in evidential situation E are permitted to adopt any of a fairly wide range of point-probability credences. One peer in situation E could rationally adopt .80 while another rationally adopts .90. If both peers are well informed about epistemic principles and their implications, each of them could say that she is being rational but that her opposite number is also being rational. From this it would be reasonable to conclude that each is entitled to remain steadfast (that is, not feel bound to conciliate). So, some interpretations of uniqueness are compatible with the denial of "global" conciliationism.

Another issue concerning the relationship between epistemic permissiveness and uniqueness is as follows. Even if the "correct" epistemic principles imply that D is the right doxastic attitude to have if one is in evidential situation E, what if a given agent does not know that this is what the correct principles imply? What if the agent believes—and even justifiedly believes—that the correct principles imply that D' (≠ D) is the right attitude to have? What determines what is permissible or impermissible—what the correct principles *actually* imply or what a given agent *justifiedly believes* the correct principles imply? These are difficult issues that complicate the picture concerning peer disagreement. But we shall leave them here, inviting the reader to pursue them independently.

QUESTIONS

1. Can you think of examples of how a generally reliable news or social network or lookout might fail to report something that occurred and is relevant? How might such failings be overcome?

2. Are there ways in which our social environment helps or hinders laypersons deciding between experts? In what ways could institutional structures be improved to further assist in this task?

3. How could proponents of going with majority expert opinion or meta-experts defend their view against the doubts or criticisms raised in this chapter?

4. What are some reasons why track records are sometimes difficult to ascertain by laypersons?

5. What do you make of the charge, advanced by Kelly, that conciliationism requires throwing away first-order evidence? And if the conciliationist makes the move that second-order evidence about what people believe only bears on one aspect of the problem, how should this second-order evidence be incorporated into an all-things-considered view of what peers should do?

6. Do you think that Elga's exception regarding self-application of inductive methods is ad hoc or not? Would his view have any negative implications in discussions concerning what inductive methods are best?

7. Can you think of other ways someone could object to the Uniqueness thesis, beyond the objection(s) raised in the chapter?

FURTHER READING

Burge, Tyler (1993). "Content Preservation." *Philosophical Review* 102: 457–488.

Christensen, David (2009). "Disagreement as Evidence: The Epistemology of Controversy." *Philosophy Compass* 4(5): 756–767.

Elga, Adam (2010). "How to Disagree About How to Disagree." In R. Feldman and T. A. Warfield (eds.), *Disagreement* (pp. 175–186). New York: Oxford University Press.

Feldman, Richard (2007). "Reasonable Religious Disagreements." In L. Antony (ed.), *Philosophers Without Gods* (pp. 194–214). New York: Oxford University Press. Reprinted in Alvin I. Goldman and Dennis Whitcomb, eds. (2011). *Social Epistemology: Essential Readings*. New York: Oxford University Press.

Goldberg, Sanford C. (2011). "If That Were True I Would Have Heard About It by Now." In Alvin I. Goldman and Dennis Whitcomb (eds.), *Social Epistemology: Essential Readings* (pp. 92–108). New York: Oxford University Press.

Goldman, Alvin I. (2001). "Experts: Which Ones Should You Trust?" *Philosophy and Phenomenological Research* 65(1): 85–110. Reprinted in Alvin I. Goldman and Dennis Whitcomb, eds. (2011). *Social Epistemology: Essential Readings*. New York: Oxford University Press.

Goldman, Alvin I., and Dennis Whitcomb, eds. (2011). *Social Epistemology: Essential Readings*. New York: Oxford University Press.

Kelly, Thomas (2011). "Peer Disagreement and Higher-Order Evidence." In Alvin I. Goldman and Dennis Whitcomb (eds.), *Social Epistemology: Essential Readings* (pp. 183–217). New York: Oxford University Press.

Lackey, Jennifer (2008). *Learning from Words: Testimony as a Source of Knowledge*. Oxford: Oxford University Press.

NOTE

1. A rare exception to this trend was the eighteenth-century Scottish philosopher Thomas Reid, who wrote: "The wise and beneficent Author of Nature, who intended that we should be social creatures, and that we should receive the greatest and most important part of our knowledge by the information of others, hath, for these purposes, implanted in our natures . . . a disposition to confide in the veracity of others, and to believe what they tell us" (Reid [1764] 1967, Chapter 6, Section 24, p. 196).

Collective and Institutional Epistemology

Alvin I. Goldman

10.1 COLLECTIVE EPISTEMOLOGY: GROUPS AS PLURAL SUBJECTS

This chapter continues to explore themes from social epistemology (SE) that we began in the previous chapter. We started with the proposed threefold taxonomy of SE. The first branch addresses individuals' beliefs formed on the basis of evidence about social sources—for example, what other people say and/or what they believe. In this chapter we shall explore the second and third branches of SE. The second branch, *collective SE*, considers groups or collectivities as epistemic agents and explores conditions under which the beliefs of such entities are justified or unjustified. The third branch of SE, *institutional* (or *system*-oriented SE), explores various kinds of social institutions that influence intellectual life and weighs the impact that those institutions may have on the (epistemic) successes or failure of the people using those institutions. This branch also studies certain patterns of influence or interaction among individuals and what the epistemic payoff is for those individuals.

We begin with the nature of group or collective agents, or the viability of the notion of a "plural subject" (an agent that is a "we" rather than an "I"). When doing collective epistemology, a philosopher assumes that there are such things as group agents. These are plural subjects in the sense that they are bearers of propositional attitudes and also composed or constituted by members who are themselves bearers of propositional attitudes.

In everyday discourse we often attribute beliefs and even degrees of belief to group-like entities. We might say, for example, that the Hoosiers are pretty confident they will win the championship. If we read in the newspaper that a certain commission, corporate board, or jury has rendered a certain factual judgment (regarding who did what when), we won't balk at the very idea that a group entity might make such a judgment; we will take it in stride. To ascribe beliefs or judgments to groups is to imply that they have a certain kind of *psychology*, namely a propositional-attitude psychology. This is a metaphysical commitment. Such a commitment turns epistemological only when the speaker (possibly a philosopher, though not necessarily) inquires into the *epistemic* properties of a group's beliefs. For example, under what conditions are group beliefs justified? Sometimes real-world events put pressure on us to make judgments of this kind. In 2003 the U.S. government claimed at the United Nations (through its Secretary of State Colin Powell) that Saddam Hussein, the ruler of Iraq, had weapons of mass destruction. Many governments had doubts. Was the U.S. government *justified* in making this claim, and in holding the belief that presumably lay behind the public claim? Before turning to the epistemological questions about groups, however, we must first confront some metaphysical issues. When can it be said of a group that it believes a particular proposition? How does a group's belief relate to its members' beliefs?

An early and widely discussed theory of group belief was advanced by Margaret Gilbert and may be called the *Joint Acceptance Account* (JAA):

> A group G *believes that p* if and only if the members of G jointly accept that p. The members of G *jointly accept that p* if and only if it is common knowledge in G that the members of G individually have intentionally and openly . . . expressed their willingness jointly to accept that p with the other members of G. (Gilbert 1989, 306; also see Schmitt 1994a, 265)

It emerges, however, that on JAA it isn't required that even a single individual member of G must believe p in order for G to believe it. This is implied, at any rate, by the following statement of Gilbert's: "It should be understood that . . . joint acceptance of a proposition p by a group whose members are X, Y, and Z, does not entail that there is some subset of the set comprising X, Y, and Z such that all of the members of that subset individually believes that p" (1989, 306–307).

Moreover, the following example, provided by Jennifer Lackey (forthcoming), shows how the general idea of "joint acceptance" does not entail belief by any individual group member. Suppose that a philosophy department is deliberating about the best candidate to recommend to the Graduate School for admission to their program. They agree to accept the proposition that Jane Doe is the most qualified candidate—that is, they agree (openly and willingly) to say this to their Graduate School. Actually, no individual member of the department believes this proposition; rather, they believe that Jane Doe is the candidate most likely to be approved by the Graduate School. (Alternatively, the story might be told that nobody thinks that Jane Doe is the best of the candidates, but there is no consensus on who is the best, and the members agree to present Jane Doe as the best.) According to JAA, the group thereby *believes* that Jane Doe is the best, despite the fact that no individual member believes this.

Joint acceptance, it seems, might be a good account of what it is for a group to *say*, or *assert*, that p, or at least to be *prepared* to say or assert that p. But it is not equivalent to *believing* that p.[1] Thus, belief that p cannot be explained in terms of what group members or representatives are licensed to *say*, but must be a function of, and suitably responsive to, at least some (if not many) of its members' beliefs. If the members of a group largely hold a belief in common, especially a belief that pertains to a joint activity of theirs, then the *group* may be said to hold that belief. It is not necessary that they have agreed to this proposition in any public or private deliberation. In our earlier example of an athletic team that is confident it will win the league championship, the members may not have given voice to this belief, or agreed publicly to defend it. Nonetheless, their sharing of the belief (i.e., holding it in common) may suffice to incline observers to ascribe this belief to the group. Moreover, one or two doubters would not suffice to cancel this ascription. This approach to conceptualizing group belief is sometimes called a *summative* approach.

In what follows we shall not firmly embrace a summative approach but we will explore the contours of group belief under this sort of conception. It has been facilitated by the work of Christian List and Philip Pettit (2011), who explore group agency under roughly the foregoing conception (although their preoccupation is more heavily tilted toward "corporate" groups with shared intentions).

10.2 COLLECTIVE BELIEF AND BELIEF AGGREGATION

At least for a certain range of groups, it is natural to think that a group's doxastic attitude toward a given proposition is grounded in (or supervenes on) the doxastic attitudes of its members. We can represent such a grounding or supervenience relation in terms of a function, or mapping, from beliefs of the members into a belief of the group. Such a mapping may be called a *belief aggregation function* (BAF). One example of a BAF is the majoritarian rule according to which a group believes P if and only if a majority of its members believe P. Another is a supermajoritarian rule, in which the group believes P just in case a qualified majority of its members do so (e.g., two thirds of them). Another example is dictatorship, in which the group belief is always the same as that of a single fixed member. We can initially think of a BAF as the product of an officially formulated and adopted rule, or set of rules. But not all groups have such official, formal rules. The same concept, however, can be applied to groups that lack such a formal rule but whose interpersonal practices and mechanisms of psychological influence give rise to patterns describable in similar terms.

Given such rules, practices, and/or mechanisms, there is an intimate connection between groups—at least some groups—and their members that List and Pettit describe as follows:

> The things a group agent does are clearly determined by the things its members do; they cannot emerge independently. In particular, no group agent can form propositional attitudes without these being determined, in one way or another, by certain contributions of its members, and no group agent can act without one or more of its members acting. (2011, 64)

Despite this "determination" relation, List and Pettit argue for a degree of autonomy for group agents from their members. Groups are neither identical to nor reducible to the set of their members. A group's propositional attitudes may be said to supervene on those of their members, but this is only a weak, holistic, supervenience relation, not a proposition-wise supervenience relation between the group's attitude toward P and its members' attitudes vis-à-vis P.[2] The upshot is that groups have "minds of their own." They are agents that are distinct from, and not reducible to, the minds of their members. This will be important in the considerations that follow.

It may be helpful to illustrate how a BAF might determine a group's doxastic attitude vis-à-vis some proposition based on its members' profile of attitudes toward the same proposition. This will also help us show how there are complications involved in collective (group) belief determination, especially when one also considers how the same group might reason from certain of its beliefs to further beliefs. Consider, then, a group consisting of all of the one hundred guards at the British Museum (Table 10.1).[3] Each of the first twenty guards (M_1–M_{20}) believes that Albert is planning an inside theft of a famous painting (= A). By deduction from A, each of them infers the (existential) proposition that there is a guard who is planning such a theft (= T). The remaining eighty guards do not believe A. Each of the second twenty guards (M_{21}–M_{40}) believes that Bernard is planning an inside theft (= B) and deductively infers T from B. The other eighty members do not believe B. Each member of a third group of twenty members (M_{41}–M_{60}) believes that guard Cecil is planning an inside theft (= C) and deductively infers T from C. The eighty others do not believe C. Thus, sixty members of G believe T by deduction from some premise that they believe.

TABLE 10.1

Individual-Level Beliefs	
About the Premises	**About the Conclusion**
20 members bel (A) (J'dly)	
20 members bel (B) (J'dly)	
20 members bel (C) (J'dly)	60 members bel (T) (J'dly)
80 members do not bel (A)	40 members do not bel (T)
80 members do not bel (B)	
80 members do not bel (C)	
Group-Level Beliefs	
About the Premises	**About the Conclusion**
G does not bel (A)	
G does not bel (B)	G believes T.
G does not bel (C)	

What does group G believe with respect to these matters? Here we must make some assumption about G's BAF. Let us assume that G's BAF is a supermajoritarian operation that proceeds in a proposition-wise fashion. Specifically, G believes a proposition Q if and only if at least 60 percent of its members believe Q. Applying this BAF to our example, it is clear that G will not believe either A, B, or C. That is because only twenty members believe each of those propositions and eighty members do not believe it. What about the group's attitude toward T? G does believe T because, as just recounted, sixty of the one hundred members believe T.

10.3 JUSTIFICATION AGGREGATION

So far, so good. Now we come to the principal *epistemological* question of interest here: the question of group, or collective, *justifiedness*. Is group G justified in believing T? Thus far, we have said nothing about the justificational statuses (J-statuses) of members' beliefs. We have been discussing only what beliefs the members have and what beliefs the group has, making certain assumptions about the group's "psychology" (which is part of its metaphysics). However, given what we have provisionally said about the dependence relation between a group and its members, it is perhaps to be expected that the *J-statuses* of the group's beliefs are determined by the *J-statuses* of its members' beliefs. This is, of course, an epistemological matter, not a purely psychological or metaphysical one. What we should look for, then, is a *justification aggregation function* (JAF), which maps the members' profile of J-statuses concerning a target proposition into a group, or collective, J-status vis-à-vis that proposition.

For illustrative purposes, consider an aggregation function for justifiedness that duplicates what was previously used for belief. Assume that if at least 60 percent of G's members justifiedly believe a proposition, then the group justifiedly believes it (or is propositionally justified to believe it). Further assume that all of the members' beliefs in the British Museum scenario are justified. What does this imply about G's justifiedness, in light of the preceding JAF? In particular, what does it imply about G's J-status with respect to T? As we saw, G does believe T, because 60 percent of its members believe P. And that same 60 percent of the members believe T *justifiedly*, so the group as a whole is justified in believing it. But this is not the only way to look at the problem. Although it's true that the group believes T, it does not believe A, B, or C. Hence, it does not believe any of those propositions justifiedly. The result is that the group has no other justified beliefs of its own from which it could infer the existential proposition T. So, from that point of view, it does not seem that G is justified in believing T. Which of these *conflicting* verdicts about the group's J-status is the correct one? This is one of the kinds of special problems, or puzzles, about justification that emerges in the field of collective epistemology.

We can think about the problem as follows. Distinguish two routes that a collective agent might take to earn positive J-status for a belief. One way is to *inherit* justification vis-à-vis a proposition Q from its members' justified beliefs vis-à-vis Q. This would be justification by *aggregation*. It can also be thought of as *vertical* justification, because the justificational juice "bubbles up" from "below." A second route for a collective agent to positive J-status for a belief is by inference from some of *its own prior (justified) beliefs* (used as premises). This might be called a *horizontal* route to justifiedness, because it all stays (during this route) at the group level. Which form of determination deserves to be the more important, or weighty, factor in collective J-status determination? This is a difficult problem, which we won't try to resolve here fully definitively. Instead, let us focus exclusively on *vertical* justification, which is the problem of *aggregating* the J-statuses of the members' doxastic attitudes into a group J-status, where aggregation takes place with respect to a single proposition and ignores antecedent beliefs of the group that might strengthen or defeat the J-status of the target proposition arising from aggregation.

10.4 THE (VERTICAL) DEPENDENCE OF GROUP JUSTIFICATION ON MEMBER JUSTIFICATION

At various points in our discussion we have suggested that group belief and group justifiedness have a special sort of *dependence* on members' belief and members' justifiedness, respectively. What kind of dependence, exactly, do we—or should we—have in mind? Two possibilities may be floated by considering two possible analogues: justificational dependence relations *across* individual agents and justificational dependence relations *within* a single individual agent.

Consider two agents, Robert and Sarah. Robert has acquired a lot of evidence in support of proposition P; accordingly, using appropriate reasoning skills, he has formed a belief in P. Robert's belief is justified. Sarah has thus far not encountered any evidence directly relevant to P. She suspends judgment on it. Can Sarah come to have a justified belief in P, just like Robert? Certainly. Robert can simply *tell* Sarah that P, by an act of testimony. If Sarah trusts Robert's testimony, this will give her justification for believing P. Right? Well, this partly depends on what is the correct theory of testimony-based justification, a topic explored in Section 9.2. Does a hearer need *positive* evidence for a speaker's trustworthiness in order to become justified in believing it? Or does it suffice *not* to have any *negative* evidence about the speaker's trustworthiness to become so justified? In either case, there are hurdles to clear for a hearer to become justified. Without jumping these hurdles, satisfying these conditions, the speaker's justifiedness in believing P is not *transmitted* to the hearer. And, of course, there is the fundamental requirement(s) that the speaker *communicate* his or her message that P to the hearer and that this communication be comprehensible to the hearer. In addition, the speaker might have to offer some evidence or reason for the truth of the proposition (which is credible to the hearer). In short, justification does not *automatically* jump across the gap between the two agents. There is no automatic, default dependence relation between hearer and speaker of the kind that obtains within a single epistemic agent.

What is the special justification dependence relation that holds within an agent? What contrast do we have in mind as compared with the inter-agent situation? In the intra-agent situation, justifiedness seems to be automatically transmitted across two kinds of gaps: inferential gaps and temporal gaps. If Sarah justifiedly believes both X and X→Y, and if she properly infers Y from these two premises, then her belief in Y is justified. If either of the two premises is unjustified, then even if she properly uses *modus ponens* to infer Y, the latter belief still isn't justified. The belief's J-status *depends* on the J-statuses of both of the premise beliefs. The important point is that the J-statuses of the premise beliefs are transmitted *automatically* to the conclusion belief. No separate act of *communication* analogous to testimony is required to facilitate or implement such transmission. Nor does Sarah have to engage in *epistemic ascent*, in which she must believe (and believe justifiedly?) that her premise beliefs are justified in order for their de facto justifiedness to be conveyed to the belief in Y. Similarly, consider the case of an agent's J-status with respect to a specified proposition at two different points in time, t_o and t_n. If Robert justifiedly believes L at t_o and holds L in memory between t_o and t_n, then his continued belief in L at t_o will still be justified (unless some defeaters have arisen in the interval that he neglects). If he unjustifiedly believes L at t_o and holds L in memory between t_o and $t_{n'}$ then his continued belief at t_o will also be unjustified. These examples of automatic (default) transmission of J-status *within* an individual agent illustrate a justification dependence relation of a different kind than any that seems to obtain *across* individuals.

Which kind of dependence relation holds between the J-statuses of member beliefs and the J-statuses of group beliefs (vis-à-vis the same proposition)? Assuming there is some such dependence relation between groups and their members, the vertical dimension, is it more like the *inter*personal case of individual agents (from one agent to a different agent) or more like the *intra*personal case, within a single agent? The present author embraces the latter answer. Although groups are distinct from their members, there is a special, automatic relation in which the J-statuses of member beliefs are automatically transmitted to group beliefs, although the member J-statuses might "compete" with one another to determine a J-status for the group. This "competition" constitutes the heart of the member/group J-aggregation process.

The next section sketches a theory of justifiedness for group belief that incorporates lessons from the foregoing discussion. The theory is a version of process reliabilism, an account of epistemic justification offered for individual justification in Chapter 2. To construct a suitable account for collective justification, some modifications must be made in the original. Nonetheless, the account preserves the distinctive themes of process reliabilism. As announced previously, the present focus continues to be the vertical dimension of group justification only, not the horizontal dimension (which concerns justifiedness relations among states of a single collective agent).

10.5 PROCESS RELIABILISM AND THE JUSTIFICATION OF COLLECTIVE BELIEF

As readers will recall, process reliabilism says (in abbreviated form) that a belief is justified if it is produced by a sequence of reliable belief-forming processes in the psychological history of the agent. Elsewhere this thesis has been advanced in connection with individual belief, but there are prospects, to be explored here, for extending the reliabilist approach to the domain of collective belief.[4] The first proposal to appeal to process reliabilism in accounting for group justification is due to Frederick Schmitt (1994a). However, Schmitt's account is based on a joint acceptance account of group belief, which was found wanting in earlier discussion here. Also, Schmitt pursues an approach that gives primacy to social justifiedness rather than individual justifiedness, which to many workers in social epistemology generates some mysteries. So the approach we shall explore tries to show how group justifiedness can emerge from individual-level justifiedness (at least to a substantial extent).[5]

According to process reliabilism, an important feature of justification is its *historicity*. The J-status of one of your current beliefs often depends on the J-statuses of beliefs you held at earlier times. For example, many years ago you may have observed several good deeds by a certain acquaintance, which led you to an overall impression of her as well-meaning and trustworthy. You continue to believe this about her overall character, although you would be hard put to pinpoint specific incidents on which your general belief is based. Nonetheless, your current belief about her good character is still justified, partly because you acquired them in reliable ways, retained them by (reliable) memory, and have never encountered any defeaters (or only the mildest of semi-defeaters) in the interim. In this fashion, the current J-status of your belief rests on this historical sequence of prior justified belief acquisitions (plus the absence of justified beliefs in conflicting evidence).

Under the current proposal, the historical character of J-statuses for individuals should be extended to groups. In the case of groups, this relevant history would extend backward not only to the group's earlier states (which would be on the horizontal dimension) but also to the group's current and earlier acquisition of beliefs from its members. Finally, since J-statuses of the members' beliefs would depend upon their respective histories, the total history relevant to a group belief would include many relevant cognitive events and processes in the members. Schematically, we may depict a prototypical sequence of the relevant kind as in Figure 10.1.

Figure 10.1 is a complex diagram, more complex than it looks. It describes activities and "upshots" at two different levels (although these levels are not visually depicted). First, there is the *psychological* level of description, in which doxastic states are generated within individual agents and a group agent by assorted psychological processes in their minds. (There may also be communicative interactions between members, but these member–member interactions do not especially concern us here.) Whether or not there are

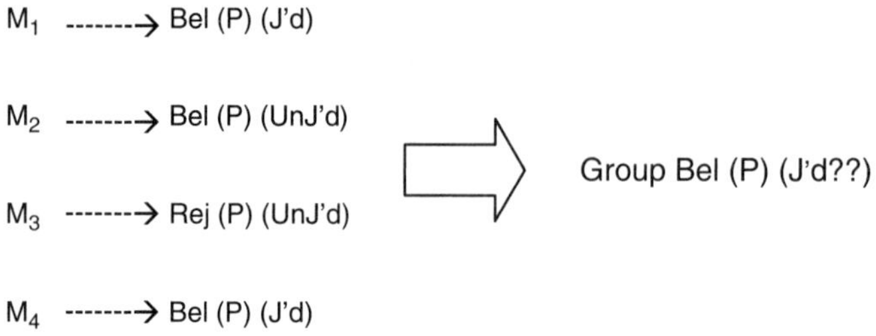

M_1 ------→ Bel (P) (J'd)

M_2 ------→ Bel (P) (UnJ'd)

M_3 ------→ Rej (P) (UnJ'd)   Group Bel (P) (J'd??)

M_4 ------→ Bel (P) (J'd)

FIGURE 10.1

member–member interactions, there definitely is an interaction between belief states of the members, on the one hand, and a belief state of the group. These arise from an aggregation process, in which a doxastic attitude is taken by the collective agent toward the same proposition about which member agents have attitudes of belief or rejection. All of these states and activities are at the psychological level as opposed to the epistemic, or justificational, level. The diagram, however, is also intended to depict certain matters of justifiedness. Just as the psychological states of the members *influence*, or *determine*, the psychological state of the group, so the J-statuses of the members' belief states *influence*, or *determine*, the J-status of the group's doxastic state. Of course, the two species of influence or determination are not at all the same; this is why we speak of two different levels. Broadly speaking, the determination at the first level may be termed "psychological," whereas the determination at the second level is "epistemic."

Even at the first level, however, there are complications. Within and among the members, influence is a combination of psychological and behavioral events. Members' beliefs are most directly caused by events in their own heads, but, as noted above, those events in turn can be caused by public acts of interpersonal communication. Finally (still staying at the first level), influence from member beliefs to the group belief is, arguably, more "metaphysical" than purely causal (where the metaphysical relation is one of supervenience or grounding). This is a particularly subtle relationship because aggregation always involves underlying mechanisms of a causal sort, ranging from methods of vote tabulation (in formal groups) to sociodynamical forces that may generate a state of consensus or semi-consensus that characterizes the group as a whole.

The second level (depicted very lightly by the diagram) is the *justificational* influence of members' beliefs on the J-status of the group belief. Thus, the large block does not just represent aggregation of beliefs or judgments; it also represents aggregation of J-statuses ("vertical" influence). The second aggregation relation is wholly nonpsychological and noncausal. Nonetheless, even the epistemic dependence relation may reflect, to some extent, the causal-psychological forces occurring at the first level. This can be explained as follows.

It should not be assumed that all members of a group have equal *weight* in influencing group belief. No "one-person, one vote" system should be presupposed as a general rule, or even as the default in matters of belief aggregation. In many organizations, a single person is the "head," "chairperson," "chief executive," and so forth, who in effect is either a dictator or an exceptionally weighty player in determining the organization's beliefs and intentions. Even with a less hierarchical organizational structure than this, some members' opinions may carry more clout than those of others, and some members' views may be ignored by the group entirely. Again, all this concerns member/group relations at the psychological as opposed to the epistemic level.

However, there may be some sort of correlation between the amount of impact a given individual's belief has on her group's belief and the degree to which the justifiedness of her belief has an impact on her group's justifiedness. Suppose that Marvin is a particularly weighty member in influencing the group's beliefs. Then it stands to reason that the J-status of Marvin's belief should also heavily influence the J-status of the group's belief, whether positively or negatively. Suppose, for example, that Marvin is an expert (or is reputed to be an expert) in detecting and assessing the threat-value of weapons of mass destruction. He was employed by the American government when it tried to determine whether Saddam Hussein had such weapons in 2003, and his opinion that Saddam *did* have WMD played an influential role in driving the American government's position toward that conclusion. If Marvin's belief was entirely unjustified—because he did a totally incompetent job in arriving at his conclusion—then (if we knew this) Marvin's own negative J-status would tilt strongly toward the conclusion that the U.S. government's judgment to that effect also had a negative J-status. (Of course, this verdict might be reversed if some other "weighty" contributor, Martha, also believed that Saddam had WMD and she had strong justification for her belief.)

In appealing to member J-statuses to determine group J-status, we follow the precept of traditional process reliabilism. There might have to be some tweakings of the approach, however, when we move from individual-level process reliabilism to group-level process reliabilism. In the original theory, for example, *all* input beliefs to a belief-dependent process must be justified if the output belief is to be justified on the basis of that process. This stringent requirement does not seem appropriate in the case of group-level justification, as the case of Martha suggests. But the necessity of such tweakings is to be expected whenever a theory originally formulated for one domain is subsequently applied to a different domain.[6]

10.6 PROBLEMS FOR SUMMATIVISM?

The foregoing presents one kind of approach to collective justifiedness. It may be classified as a species of *summativism*—at least partially so. Here is one possible way to characterize summativism:

Summativism
That a group G justifiedly believes that p is to be understood only in terms of some or all of G's members justifiedly believing that p.

The version of reliabilism sketched above for collective justifiedness is substantially summativist to the extent that a *vertical*, or *aggregative*, dimension of justifiedness is what underpins group justifiedness. Aggregation is not the only route to justifiedness, however, according to that approach. There is also the horizontal route, which has not been explored in detail. Still, it is appropriate here to consider problems that confront summativism, even if the approach sketched above is not purely summativist.

Schmitt lays the groundwork for his objection against summativism by introducing the notion of a *chartered group*. A chartered group is one founded to perform actions of a particular kind. When a group has a charter, it can normally perform actions only out of the office specified by its charter. Chartered groups have special standards for judging their own beliefs and "have no use for justification under an ordinary standard" (1994a, 273). For these groups, justification for the group and justification for members of the group "diverge" from each other. An example Schmitt gives concerns a court and the members of a jury trying a case in that court. The legal system excludes hearsay evidence, so a court could not be justified in believing that somebody is guilty if the evidence hinges on hearsay. But individual members of the jury, who have encountered hearsay evidence outside of court, may individually be justified in believing that the accused is guilty in virtue of the evidence they severally possess. But the court cannot admit, and hence cannot possess, that evidence. Thus, the court's J-status cannot be traced to the jurors' J-statuses. The group's J-status "diverges" from that of its members.

A rather analogous example is presented by Lackey (forthcoming), not to undercut a pure summativist view but to undercut an aggregative view of the type sketched in the preceding section. G is a group whose members consist of three nurses employed at a nursing home. The first nurse knows that she forgot to give O'Brien his first medication this morning, but she also justifiedly believes that this alone is insufficient to put him in danger of death. The second and third nurses are similarly situated with regard to the medication they forgot to give O'Brien on their shift. Thus, they all justifiedly believe that if O'Brien were to miss all three of his medications, he would be put at serious risk of dying. However, having not shared information with one another about their respective acts of negligence, each lacks crucial evidence that would have made them justified in believing that O'Brien is at serious risk of dying.

The putative dilemma Lackey poses for the aggregative approach is this. Given the evidence available to each nurse, each is justified in believing that O'Brien is not at risk of dying. Moreover, as individual epistemic agents, they are not neglecting any epistemic duties (although each did neglect a duty of information conveyance to others). As a group, however, matters are quite different. Given their obligations as nurses in this institution, they did have an epistemic duty (as Lackey describes it) to share relevant information. Had they done so, they would each have justifiedly believed that O'Brien is at risk of dying. Thus, while every member of the nursing unit justifiedly believes that O'Brien is not at risk of dying, the group is not so justified.

Neither of these examples strikes this author as terribly persuasive. Considered closely, the cases do not elicit very clear intuitions. A large part of the problem is that two kinds of normative systems get invoked, and it is difficult to keep them separate. In the first case, we are told about an institution with its own rules of evidence and justification, distinct from the ordinary ones (as Schmitt himself says). To express things a bit differently, the rules governing the court are what we might call rules of *shmustification*, not rules of justification. So let's not slide back and forth between these two different concepts. If we are going to compare the J-statuses of the individual jurors and the J-status of the court, it must be done consistently either by the (ordinary) standard of justification in both cases or by the shmustification standard in both cases. To apply one standard to the court and the other to the individual jurors is a recipe for confusion. A second problem is that the legal principles give instructions for what jurors should and shouldn't do while mentally addressing their judicial task. What they should do is ignore any evidence they have encountered except what they have heard in the courtroom. If they violate that instruction, what are they then justified in doing (doxastically speaking)? That is what the example invites us to consider. But the rules of shmustification, one suspects, are simply too indeterminate to make a clear-cut declaration. In general, when there have been violations of a normative system, the system may not have clear backup rules for what should transpire. (It is especially problematic in the present case, when epistemic verdicts are being invited for both individuals and an institutional system they are temporarily serving.)

The three nurses example suffers from similar indeterminacies. Why would we conclude that each individual nurse is justified in believing that O'Brien is not at risk of dying but that the group is not so justified? If the individuals' prior violations of a requirement to speak does not affect their subsequent epistemic situation, why should the very same set of violations by all three individuals affect the subsequent epistemic situation of the group that they compose? Is it because the group possesses a larger body of evidence than each individual possesses? That would require a highly suspect assumption about how to treat evidence possession in the case of groups—namely, the assumption that evidence possessed by any member is automatically possessed by the group per se. If we do not make this assumption, we do not seem committed to the clash of epistemic statuses that Lackey thinks she detects here.

10.7 THE SOCIAL EPISTEMOLOGY OF INSTITUTIONS AND SYSTEMS

We turn now from collective epistemology, the second branch of SE, to the third branch of SE: the SE of institutions and systems. Here we set aside issues about groups as plural epistemic agents and focus our attention on social institutions and systems in which individual agents operate. (There might be collective epistemic agents ensconced within such institutions, but that is neither here nor there for purposes of our next agenda.) The general idea is straightforward. Individual agents are involved in and are affected by many social institutions. They have an impact on many facets of their lives, including epistemic facets. To the extent that epistemic facets are affected, SE might want to get involved, at least in theoretical analysis and appraisal if not (ultimately) in offering policy advice.

Societies and cultures often have "choices" to make among alternative institutional forms or structures. If choices among these alternatives would have differential effects on epistemic successes or failures, SE should perk up and pay attention. It might have insights to offer as to which choice(s) would be epistemically better than others. Of course, there may not be many institutions that take epistemic matters to be their primary concern, but some of them do. Obvious examples here are (1) science, (2) educational systems, (3) journalism and media of all sorts, and (4) fact-finding bodies, such as legal adjudication systems (trial systems, in particular). Even an institution that is not concerned with epistemic issues at its foundation may still have an important stake in how epistemic problems are navigated within its dominion. So there is no shortage of topics in this branch of SE. We will focus on three illustrations of this branch of SE.

10.8 EPISTEMIC APPROACHES TO DEMOCRACY

In recent decades a substantial trend, or even movement, has been launched, in both political philosophy and theory, in support of epistemic approaches to democracy. What makes democracy such an attractive, and arguably even essential, mode of political organization? Why is it so enshrined in so much of the world, and does it deserve the unique position it occupies? What is the core rationale for its supposed superiority, and can it live up to all of the hype (even in the best of circumstances)?

Recent theorists have embraced two rather different kinds of epistemic approaches to the rationale for democracy. It is common to associate with democracy the procedure of *majority rule*. When elections and other decisions are made by a majority vote of the relevant electorate or legislative body, they are commonly accepted as legitimate or authoritative. What are the features of majority rule that give it this high—and probably unique— standing, and does it deserve its billing? Are there additional features that a full and acceptable form of democracy should have?

The first epistemic form of democracy says that the problems political bodies confront commonly have objectively right answers—that is, true or false answers. It is in the interest of the body politic to get right answers rather than wrong ones. That is a task of which good epistemic procedures should be chosen. Plausibly, in a public context, this should be a social procedure (in some sense). Finally, majoritarian decision making is the epistemically best social procedure to bring to bear on this problem. The most popular line of defense for majority rule is appeal to the Condorcet Jury Theorem (CJT), which we briefly utilized at the end of Chapter 8. We shall return to it again shortly.

A second kind of epistemic approach to democracy is the so-called deliberative democracy approach. This focuses more on the prevoting stage of political decision making. The idea here is that, whether or not there are "correct" answers to political questions, it is good for citizens to deliberate and debate with one another about the proposals on the table. This can be rationalized in a variety of ways. To take just one example, by deliberating together, people can justify their views on the subject to others, where justification is understood to be some sort of epistemic procedure. It might be a procedure that helps people recognize the "common good," or it might be helpful even if there is no such thing as the common good. If deliberation is a kind of argumentation, and argumentation is an epistemic tool, we again arrive at a rationale with an epistemic contour.

10.8.1 The Condorcet Jury Theorem: Its Promise and Problems

The revival of interest in the CJT has been a major impetus behind the first variant of the epistemic approach to democracy. This theorem says that among large electorates voting on some yes-or-no question, majoritarian outcomes have an exceedingly high probability of tracking the truth if a small number of conditions are satisfied. Since voting by majority rule is a cardinal feature of democratic procedure, this is seen as a vindication of the epistemic value of democracy. The crucial condition is that each voting member of the electorate has a probability of being right (a "competence") greater than chance. Even a small probability greater than .50 guarantees that the probability of the majority being right is greater than that of any such individual being right and approaches 1.0 as the group size increases. Isn't this a stunning and important finding?

Well, yes and no. It is stunning if the conditions set by the theorem are satisfied, or have a decent chance of being satisfied at least some of the time. Whether this is true or not is debatable. The three most important conditions are the following:

1. The yes/no question being voted upon must have an objectively correct answer, independent of the voting procedure used to arrive at the group's answer.[7]
2. In the original version of the theorem, all voters must have some one probability r of being right where r is greater than .50. (In an extension of the theorem, the condition specifies only that the median voter, not necessarily *all* voters, have a competence above .50 and the competent ones are symmetrically distributed.)
3. The voters' opinions are arrived at, or held, independently of one another.

Let us examine the prospects for satisfaction of these conditions in turn.

Starting with Condition 1, are political questions on which people vote typically ones with objectively correct answers? This in itself is a tough question to answer, but it's essential to the CJT variant of the epistemic approach. The main alternative view might be that typical questions on which people vote are (implicitly) questions about what policies or goals should be adopted or pursued by the body politic. In other words, the question is not "What is the best (or better) means to reach goal G?" but "What goal should we (the body politic) be aiming at?" Means-ends questions may well have objectively correct answers, but questions of what goals or ends *should* be pursued are normative/evaluative questions for which reasonable people may despair of there being objectively correct answers. If these questions have no objectively correct answers, this could well be a deathblow to the CJT variant of the epistemic approach, sometimes called the "aggregation" approach.

Let us assume, however, that the rightness approach somehow survives this challenge. The next set of problems concern the prospects for satisfying Condition 2, the voters' possessing a high enough level of competence with respect to the question(s) on which they will vote. Some theorists find it hard to imagine that citizens could *fail* to exceed a level of chance at being right. Surely people are fairly substantially competent—more likely to be right than wrong—on most ordinary questions; why should they be less likely to be right on political questions? But there are reasons for some pessimism.

The first obstacle is the kinds of evidence about political questions available to the ordinary voter. The trouble, this author would argue, is that a large sector of the evidence is "trash"—that is, is highly misleading evidence. Electoral questions, whatever exactly we take their content to be, are nothing like such simple factual questions as "Where is the nearest gas station?" or "Who won the gold medal in category X at the most recent Winter Olympics?" Such questions can be answered by making observations, consulting one's memory, or perhaps Googling them. The relevant evidence for political questions tends to occur in highly contested texts—for example, statements by biased actors on the political stage. Often they are hired to persuade an electorate of things that aren't true at all, or are at the margins of truth and falsity. Discriminating between the accurate and inaccurate statements can be extremely difficult. In short, the reliable evidence that voters need in order to be competent on political questions is difficult to identify as such. Political speech is continually shading the truth. So why should we expect voters to be uniformly competent, or even competent on average?

Moreover, even granted that there is some good-quality evidence to be discovered and discerned as such, why expect voters to expend the time and effort to seek it out and find it? Rational choice theorists argue that in large elections, it is not rational for people to vote because they are so unlikely to be swing voters. On an expected utility basis, they should not bother to vote, nor should they waste time gathering evidence about how best to vote. If they are even mildly rational, they will be *informational free riders* and unlikely to be competent on the issues in question (Landemore 2013, 193).

Finally, in addition to the CJT proper, there is also a mathematically correct "inverse" version of the CJT. Inverse CJT says that if the median voter is just slightly *in*competent (i.e., has a probability of being correct slightly *less* than .50), then as the size of the electorate increases, the probability of a majority making the correct choice rapidly approaches *zero* (not 1.0)!

On top of all of these challenges is the problem of satisfying Condition 3, the independence condition. Given that the evidence needed to be competent with respect to political questions almost inevitably requires dealing with "testimonial" evidence—including things said and/or written by one's contemporaries who are also voters—the combination of being competent and being independent is extremely difficult to fulfill.

10.8.2 Is There Help from Deliberation?

Given the serious problems facing the individual voter aspiring to competence on electoral issues, where is the voter to turn? Deliberation might be the required salvation. So it is easy to see why deliberative democrats highlight deliberation as a crucial phase of democracy prior to voting. Only if voters have engaged in deliberation with others, exchanging ideas and arguments about the political issues and candidates of the day, can they be expected to form beliefs to help the electorate make right decisions. So deliberation might be a suitable complement to the aggregative (or CJT) approach. This is what long-time advocates of the virtues of deliberation, like Bruce Ackerman and James Fishkin, have in mind.[8]

This sounds reasonable, but most deliberative democrats seem to offer rather different reasons for deliberation, and perhaps only a minority of them even assume there is objective rightness in the first place. A further difficulty with this proposal is that deliberation is clearly the epitome of *interdependence*, the antithesis of independence. If voters become competent by exchanging views with other voters, nobody will be voting independently of one another. This ruins all prospects for the electorate tracking the truth via the CJT, or any other *statistically* oriented strategy that requires independence.

Of course, nobody can say that truth tracking categorically requires the aegis of CJT or another probability-based theorem. The CJT only offers a *sufficient* condition for attaining a high probability of truth; it does not serve as a *necessary* condition. So forget the CJT, an epistemic democrat might say: Just focus on deliberation as the best path to truth all by itself.

Unfortunately, there is extensive empirical research on deliberation that casts a dark shadow on its prospects for paving the way to political truth. It is not only mathematical and philosophical theorizing that can weigh in on the prospects of potential epistemic tools. Empirical studies on what actually happens when people deliberate might give clues to the epistemic prospects of deliberation. Cass Sunstein (2006) has surveyed a wide range of such studies and delivers a report that may dim the hopes of deliberative democrats.

One finding Sunstein reports from a social scientific study is that when people of different political persuasions (e.g., liberals and conservatives) discussed some controversial issues of the day, they expressed more extreme views after discussion than beforehand. In other words, discussion increased "polarization." Can a form of interaction that polarizes people facilitate convergence on a single true answer? Another problem with deliberation is its tendency to generate "cascades." Cascades are patterns that occur when people are asked to explain their views to an assembled group, where this kind of occasion provides an opportunity for people to learn new things from others, to acquire fresh information that bears on the problem at hand. It is particularly important, Sunstein feels, for people to disclose what they know or believe, especially when it is a dissenting or minority opinion. How else can others benefit from this information? Cascades are sequences of statements by different individuals in which felt social pressure leads people to hide their real views and reiterate what preceding speakers said rather than sharing their fresh insights. A misleading amount of (ostensible) agreement is paraded, but people fail to acquire the heterodox information they need. This kind of social dynamic is something that philosophical and mathematical theorists tend to neglect, because thoughts like "This person won't approve of me if I disagree with him" appear to have significant real-world impact, but political philosophers and mathematicians don't build them into their models.

10.8.3 Alternative Voting Methods: Is Majority Rule the Best?

Traditionally, majoritarian voting is emblematic of democracy. In today's world as well, the test of a government's claim to being democratic hinges on its adoption and successful implementation of majoritarian elections. In democratic theory majority rule stays in the limelight in virtue of mathematical theorems like CJT. Of course, as we have seen, the CJT in itself offers no proof of its being a good method for getting the truth, given that *inverse CJT* makes the a priori likelihood of going *wrong* via majority rule exactly as great as going right.

It is time for alternative methods to receive a fair hearing, or at least *some* hearing. A number of such methods have been advanced as either superior to or the equal of majority voting from a purely epistemic point of view. By majority voting, I understand the institution of assigning to each voter one vote. Weighted voting is no longer majority voting. However, it is mathematically straightforward to see that when voters have nonidentical probabilities, or chances, of being right, the group no longer maximizes its probability of correctness when all voters are assigned one vote each. Consider a group of five individuals, three of whom have a .6 probability of being right and two of whom have a .9 probability of being right. Under majority voting, the group's probability of being right is .87. This chance of correctness is easily exceeded by instead choosing either of the two more expert individuals as dictator; this yields .90 for the group's probability of being right. And even this expected accuracy can be improved upon: If the two most competent individuals are assigned weights of .392 each and the other three voters are assigned weights of .072 each, then the group's expected judgmental accuracy is even better than under the dictatorship, namely .927. A maximally truth-conducive weighting scheme is one that assigns a weight w_i to each expert i that satisfies the following formula (Shapley and Grofman 1984):

$$W_i \propto log \, (p_i \, /(1 - p_i))$$

Yet another system touted as epistemically superior is different in other ways from (ordinary) majority rule. Richard Bradley and Christopher Thompson (2012) propose a system they call Multiple-Vote Majority Rule (MVMR). They preface their formulation and defense of it by commenting on the strengths and weaknesses of the standard majority rule system. The core of the standard epistemic defense of majority rule is that, by giving everyone an equal say, majority voting delivers group judgments that track the truth more reliably than those of dictatorial or oligarchical schemes. However, in cases in which voters are modest in number and the competence of individual voters varies from voter to voter and issue to issue, voting systems that give unequal weight to people who are more competent will produce better judgments, an epistemic advantage that is purchased at the cost of unequal participation. We saw how this worked above, in the Shapley–Grofman scheme that applies the log formula for assigning weights. The scheme Bradley and Thompson propound does not suffer similarly from inequality of participation. After laying it out, they argue that it produces a better balance of epistemic reliability and equality of participation than several other well-known rules including majority rule.

Suppose that a group must make decisions about a series of issues, say ten in all. Then everyone is allotted ten votes that they can place on any of the propositions. In other words, they can distribute the ten votes any way they like among the propositions. This includes using all ten votes on a single proposition, if they so desire. The collective decision is reached by adding up all of the votes for and against a given proposition and accepting it if and only if the votes for it exceed the votes against. If the individuals are interested only in the truth, they will try to place their votes where they will do the most good. Thus, if someone considers herself more competent on two of the propositions than on the others, she could concentrate more of her votes on those two propositions than on the others. Bradley and Thompson conjecture that when competence varies both between propositions and between voters, and when voters have second-order competence as to what they are competent on, then the MVMR rules can produce greater group competence than majority rule without sacrificing equality of participation (64–65).

10.9 SOCIAL DIMENSIONS OF SCIENTIFIC RESEARCH

Epistemology has long been closely linked to philosophy of science, which is warranted in light of the prevalent view that science is a paradigm of epistemic activity. Traditional philosophy of science, however, focused for a very long time on individual scientists rather than teams or communities of scientists. Or, to a large extent, it was (and is) focused on issues of scientific methodology that abstract from any particular choice of agents, whether they be individuals or groups. However, at least since Thomas Kuhn's influential *The Structure of Scientific Revolutions* (1962), the conduct of science has been studied from a more social point of view. Scientists, after all, are people; they are influenced by one another's ideas and can benefit (or get misdirected by) the theories that other scientists propound and the evidence they uncover. Scientists commonly work in teams and often compete with other teams to make important discoveries. All this provides a congenial environment for considering a social conception of the epistemology of science, one that makes room at a minimum for certain social *dimensions* of scientific epistemology.

Philip Kitcher (1990) made a break toward such an approach by talking about "divisions of labor" in scientific inquiry. Instead of scientists all pursuing one and the same research program within a given field of science, it might well benefit the research community to have distinct research groups deploying different methods in pursuit of a solution to the very same problem. He illustrated this by reference to what in fact transpired in biochemistry in the quest for the structure of the DNA molecule. He describes this in the following way:

> Once there was a very important molecule (VIM). Many people in the chemical community wanted to know the structure of VIM. Method I involved using X-ray crystallography, inspecting the resultant photographs and using them to eliminate possibilities about bonding patterns. Method II involved guesswork and the building of tinker-toy models. (11)

Kitcher points out that even if one of the two methods is the optimal method for a given individual seeking the solution to the structure-of-VIM question, it does not follow that the optimal distribution of community effort is to have all chemists use that one method. Assuming that no method is guaranteed from the start to generate a good outcome, the community may be well advised to diversify the methods used, however this diversification is implemented.

Different kinds of things might here be meant by "methods." On the one hand there are assorted techniques or procedures used by a given science at a particular point in its development. Certain types of experiments, perhaps, or certain kinds of mathematical analyses, or certain types of model-building strategies would be examples of "methods" under one interpretation of that term. But we can also speak of "methods" as *patterns of intellectual engagement* (including nonengagement) with other research groups. In different terminology, these might be called *intellectual styles* that characterize different individuals or groups in their interrelationships with others. An example of this kind of SE of science is presented by Michael Weisberg and Ryan Muldoon (2009).

Weisberg and Muldoon present a novel model of scientific research, one that is applicable in principle to all fields of science. In this model autonomous agents (embedded in a computational model) explore what the authors call an "epistemic landscape." The landscape consists of a flat plane plus two peaks (or Gaussian curves), and the aim of the scientists is to climb uphill in this landscape, where degree of elevation represents the significance of the results obtained in their field of research. Points that are topographically higher on either peak represent truths of greater scientific significance (importance to the field). Weisberg and Muldoon consider three research strategies, or patterns of intellectual interaction with other researchers (where one mode of interaction is *non*-interaction). The first kind of scientist is one who exemplifies the traditional lone-scientist model, working in his or her garage or basement. These scientists work wholly independently of others. They do not allow the discoveries of other scientists to influence their own actions. Their method of "foraging" through the landscape ignores the results of others. Scientists who exemplify this style are called *controls*, a term borrowed from experimental science where controls are subjects used for comparison purposes with other subjects.

The two other patterns of action represent some kind of response to what previous investigators have done. So-called *followers* (as the name suggests) follow the modes of research that their predecessors have undertaken. So-called *mavericks* take note of what predecessors have done but pursue something different, declining to imitate or build upon what others have done previously. The interesting question is how successful the various groups will be in terms of the heights they attain in climbing the peaks—that is, in obtaining highly significant truths. (It is assumed that scientists always obtain truths of one kind or another; the crucial question is how important the discovered truths are.)

As previously indicated, Weisberg and Muldoon use the notion of epistemic "significance" to represent levels of scientific attainment associated with their research. They deliberately do not try to specify what significance consists in, because this varies from field to field. But they assume that practitioners within any one field tend to agree on which findings are more significant than others. In the graphs of their model, significance is represented on the vertical axis, z. Accordingly, ascending a peak means making more and more significant findings. Their three-dimensional graphs feature two other axes, x and y, which jointly determine a particular "approach" to the topic. Each approach is described as occupying a "patch" in the landscape.

Being autonomous agents, their movements are all governed by algorithms, or rules, for traversing the terrain. Here is (part of) the rule for controls:

1. Move forward one patch.
2. Ask: Is the (new) patch I am investigating more significant than the previous patch I was investigating?
   If Yes, Move forward one patch.
   If No, Ask: Is it equally significant as the previous patch?
   If No, Move back to the previous patch. Select a new random heading. Begin again at step 1.

These controls move around the landscape relying only on what they can detect themselves about the significance of a path. They don't even notice if other investigators are currently working on the same patch. Agents using this type of algorithm are guaranteed to find at least a local maximum in finite time. In this case, a local maximum is one of the peaks.

Weisberg and Muldoon program their agents in such a fashion that they can then run *computer simulations* of the scientific activities in question. Thus, their work falls into an increasing popular method of doing SE, namely using computer simulations of social-intellectual activity. Such simulational exercises feature (1) designing models of patterns of activity and specifying algorithms for agents to follow starting from certain initial states; (2) performing a very large number of runs, varying the starting states from run to run; and (3) seeing what happens as upshots of the simulations. The hope is that the upshots will be instructive for SE purposes.

Here is one example among many of what Weisberg and Muldoon learn from their simulations about populations of controls. Large populations of controls can achieve high degrees of epistemic attainment (reach high levels on the vertical axis), but it takes a considerable length of time for this to happen. The main reason for this, it appears, is that controls don't learn from one another. In the next two strategies—followers and mavericks—scientists are strongly influenced by what their neighbors discover and attempt to learn from this. In one of these strategies, scientists are strongly biased in favor of doing what others have done—that is, employing the same research approaches. In the other strategy, they avoid the same approaches that others have used. How do these respective strategies fare in terms of epistemic success?

In important respects, followers do not do as well as controls. If a control finds her way to the edge of a hill, she will ultimately make her way to its top. But if followers bump into each other on the way up, they can get stuck following each other around on a suboptimal region of the hill. Finally, most followers who start out far from a hill end up following their own trail (and not making it to the peak).

Like followers, mavericks take into account the approaches that were previously explored and were successful. Unlike followers, however, mavericks *avoid* previously explored approaches; they prefer to do things their own way. How well do mavericks succeed? They are far more efficient at reaching both peaks than are controls. In addition, mavericks are far more efficient at finding peaks, in the sense that their mean time is much less than that of controls. Also, controls make far less progress in finding peaks per number of scientists than mavericks do.

Thus far, the reported results concern only pure populations of scientists—that is, pure groups of controls only, pure groups of followers, and pure groups of mavericks. The most interesting findings of the Weisberg–Muldoon simulations, however, concern mixed populations. Adding just ten mavericks to a population of one hundred followers resulted in a 214 percent increase in epistemic progress. This and similar statistics derived from the simulations indicate that even small additions of mavericks massively boost productivity by comparison with pure populations of followers. The increase in productivity is not only due to the direct actions of the mavericks themselves; it is also due to their effect on followers. Mavericks help many of the followers get unstuck and to explore the more fruitful areas of the epistemic landscape.

The moral of this, Weisberg and Muldoon suggest, is that if science wants to search a scientific landscape rapidly for the most significant truths, the best *system* to employ to attain this goal is a population of mavericks, at least as compared with populations of controls or followers. Even small populations of mavericks will be sufficient.

These results from computer simulations of group intellectual investigations fit neatly with a conclusion that other SE practitioners have been drawing recently, viz. the value of *diversity*. Assorted theorists of group problem solving have been arguing that it is epistemically desirable to include diverse members in a problem-solving group—that is, individuals with different life experiences from one another, different training, different specializations, different problem-solving styles, and so forth. This theme or moral has been defended at length, for example, by Lu Hong and Scott Page (2001; Page 2007), who contend that "diversity trumps ability" when it comes to group problem solving. Weisberg and Muldoon's demonstration that adding mavericks to form a mixed population greatly improves epistemic progress seems like an instructive confirmation of the epistemic value of diversity.

QUESTIONS

1. What are the most important cases in the social world in which it is imperative that groups or collective entities be credited with belief-like states? Courts of law? Governments? Corporations? If we do credit them with belief-like states, is it also imperative to credit them with *justified* (or unjustified) beliefs? How do you reply to critics who dismiss the notion of group beliefs entirely, contending that this is merely metaphorical talk? Groups don't *really* have beliefs or thoughts, do they?

2. What is the difference between a BAF (belief aggregation function) and a JAF (justification aggregation function)? Does a group's being *justified* in believing P require that the group *believe* that P? This seems to imply that the only kind of justification that applies to groups is *doxastic* justification. But what about *propositional* justification? Shouldn't that make sense for groups if doxastic justification makes sense for them? If no account can be given of propositional justification for groups, does this raise suspicions about the entire project of regarding groups as candidate agents with justificational status?

3. Does either Schmitt's example or Lackey's example (or both) show that the summativist, or aggregative, approach to collective justification is simply inadequate to the task? Explain your reasons.

4. Is it really possible that computer simulations of interacting agents, operating in hypothetical situations, and starting from randomly chosen positions, should shed genuine light on (social) epistemological questions? What exactly are the

(social) epistemic questions that this technique is designed to address? Exactly what questions does the computer-simulation methodology have prospects for illuminating? Would you consider it an empirical methodology or an armchair one?

5. Modern life and digital technology have generated multiple ideas and realizations thereof that might be called social epistemic *tools*—that is, devices to help us determine and/or disseminate certain truths more easily and more successfully than we might otherwise do. Three examples of these are "crowd-sourcing" in general, mass collaboration ventures like Wikipedia, and prediction or information markets, such as the Iowa Electronic Markets (see Landemore 2013 and Bragues 2009 for discussions of these tools). Do you agree in calling them "epistemic tools"? Are they contributions to epistemology? To applied epistemology?

FURTHER READING

Bragues, George (2009). "Prediction Markets: The Practical and Normative Possibilities for the Social Production of Knowledge." *Episteme: A Journal of Social Epistemology* 6(1): 91–106.

Goldman, Alvin I. (forthcoming). "Social Process Reliabilism: Solving Justification Problems in Collective Epistemology." In J. Lackey (ed.), *Essays in Collective Epistemology*. New York: Oxford University Press.

Kitcher, Philip (1990). "The Division of Cognitive Labor." *Journal of Philosophy* 87(1): 5–22.

Lackey, Jennifer (ed.) (forthcoming). *Essays in Collective Epistemology*. New York: Oxford University Press.

Lackey, Jennifer (in preparation). *The Epistemology of Groups*. Oxford University Press.

Landemore, Hélène (2013). *Democratic Reason: Politics, Collective Intelligence, and the Rule of the Many*. Princeton: Princeton University Press.

List, Philip, and Philip Pettit (2011). *Group Agency*. Oxford: Oxford University Press.

Pettit, Philip (2003). "Groups with Minds of Their Own." In F. Schmitt (ed.), *Socializing Metaphysics* (467–493). Lanham, MD: Rowman and Littlefield.

Strevens, Michael (2003). "The Role of the Priority Rule in Science." *Journal of Philosophy* 100(2): 55–79.

Sunstein, Cass R. (2006). *Infotopia: How Many Minds Produce Knowledge*. Oxford: Oxford University Press.

Weisberg, Michael, and Ryan Muldoon (2009). "Epistemic Landscapes and the Division of Cognitive Labor." *Philosophy of Science* 76(2): 225–252.

NOTES

1. Lackey (forthcoming) points out that unless one insists on this distinction, one won't be able to charge groups with *lying*, which would make hash of attempts to hold them appropriately responsible (e.g., in legal contexts). We have to be able to maintain that a specific group lied when it authorized its spokesperson to assert p on the group's behalf even when no member of the group really believed p. But JAA seems to imply that if all members of the group agreed to the authorization, then they *did* believe p. So how could the group be accused of lying?

2. In particular, List and Pettit say that there is no "proposition-wise" supervenience relation between a group's attitudes and its members' attitudes such that the group's attitude toward a given proposition is wholly determined by its members' attitudes *toward the very same proposition*. The group's attitude may also be a function of its members' attitudes toward other (related) propositions.

3. The example comes from Goldman (forthcoming).

4. For more details on this project, see Goldman (forthcoming).

5. Schmitt and others offer reasons for rejecting the primacy of individual justifiedness. We shall explore some of these reasons in Section 10.6 (and find them wanting).

6. For other examples of tweaking that might be needed, see Goldman (forthcoming).

7. In a modern extension of the original CJT, the result is extended to multiple-choice situations, in which the required level of competence can be lowered below .5. See Goodin and Estlund (2004).

8. See, for example, Ackerman and Fishkin (2004).

PART V

Probabilistic Epistemology

Probabilistic Epistemology

Matthew McGrath

Often epistemologists write as if only three sorts of cognitive states come up for epistemic assessment: belief, disbelief, and suspension of judgment. However, this three-way distinction isn't sufficiently fine-grained. Some of the things we believe, we believe with more confidence than others. A person might suspend judgment on two different propositions but be more confident of the truth of one of the propositions than the other. A psychology that ignored such differences in confidence would be inadequate. The same is true for an epistemology that ignored differences in how much confidence it is epistemically appropriate to have in various propositions. If you are like this author, it is epistemically appropriate for you to place great confidence in *Australia is in the Southern Hemisphere,* less in the proposition that you will catch the flu this winter, and even less (presumably) in the proposition that you will win a Grammy Award in the next twenty years. What does it take for such confidences (or "credences" in the lingo) to be epistemically appropriate? We could ask about different forms of epistemic appropriateness here. As we'll see, many philosophers think that to be *rational*, our credences as a whole must obey the axioms of probability.

Probability is important to epistemology, even apart from whether our credences rationally ought to obey the axioms of probability. As we have noted in previous chapters, it is plausible that evidence confirms an hypothesis just if it raises its probability. As we'll see at the end of the chapter, if we view evidential confirmation of a hypothesis as a matter of probability raising, we can better appreciate the power of skeptical arguments.

This chapter explores two broad sorts of issues in probabilistic epistemology: the epistemology of credences and the probability-raising theory of confirmation. Before we turn to these philosophical matters, though, we will review some basic facts from the mathematical theory of probability.[1]

11.1 BASICS OF PROBABILITY THEORY

Let's begin with the axioms of probability theory.

1. *Nonnegativity:*

$$Prob(P) \geq 0, \textit{for all propositions P.}$$

   Read this as: "the probability of any proposition is nonnegative."
2. *Normality:*

$$Prob(P) = 1 \textit{ if P is a logical truth.}$$

3. *Finite Additivity:* Suppose P1, . . . , Pn are pairwise incompatible—that is, each is incompatible with all the others. Then:

$$Prob(P1 \; v \ldots v \; Pn) = Prob(P1) + \ldots + Prob(Pn).$$

   The wedge "*v*" abbreviates "or." Finite Additivity tells us that where we have *n* propositions that are pairwise incompatible, the probability of the disjunction is the sum of the probabilities of the *n* disjuncts.[2]

To get an intuitive handle on these axioms, imagine drawing a card from a deck of normal playing cards. Let's pretend it is a logical truth that you will draw a card. So, *Prob (draw a card)* = 1. What is the probability that you draw either an ace or a jack? These are incompatible propositions. There are four aces and four jacks in a deck of fifty-two. Applying Finite Additivity, we can conclude:

$$Prob(\textit{Ace or a Jack}) = Prob(\textit{Ace}) + Prob(\textit{Jack}) = \frac{4}{52} + \frac{4}{52} = \frac{8}{52} = 2/13$$

What is the probability that you draw either a red jack or a spade? There are two red jacks in a deck and thirteen spades. Again, we use Finite Additivity to reach the answer: 15/52.

When we consider probabilities generally, outside of games of chance, a good way to visualize a probability function is as an inkjet that sprays ink over a page. Each part of the page represents some possibility and the whole page the totality of all possibilities. The inkjet takes a proposition as input and sprays a certain area of the page with ink as output. The ratio of the area of the ink sprayed to the whole page corresponds to that proposition's probability. When incompatible propositions are inputs, nonoverlapping areas of the page are sprayed with ink. When compatible ones are inputs, there is overlap in the sprayed areas.

Below are several useful consequences of the axioms of probability theory. Proofs of these can be found in the appendix to this chapter.

Negation Rule

$$Prob(\sim P) = 1 - Prob(P).$$

Contradictions

If P is a logical contradiction, $Prob(P) = 0$.

Logical Equivalents Rule

If P and Q are logically equivalent, then $Prob(P) = Prob(Q)$.

General Disjunction Rule

$$Prob(P \lor Q) = Prob(P) + Prob(Q) - Prob(P \& Q).$$

Entailment Rule

If P entails Q, $Prob(P) \leq Prob(Q)$.

In addition to asking about the probabilities of various propositions, we can ask about the probability of one proposition *conditional on* another proposition, or "given" another proposition. For instance, what is the probability that the card you draw will be a jack given that it will be a face card? You can see the answer is 1/3, because there are three sorts of face cards. In probability theory, the probability of P conditional on Q, written as $Prob(P/Q)$, is standardly defined as the ratio of $Prob(P\&Q)$ to $Prob(Q)$:

$$Prob(P/Q) = \frac{Prob(P \& Q)}{Prob(Q)}$$

It is defined only when $Prob(Q) > 0$. To visualize $Prob(P/Q)$, think first about the blob of ink representing the probability of P and an overlapping blob of ink representing the probability of Q (if there is no overlap, $Prob(P/Q) = 0$):

The ratio of the P part of the Q blob to the whole Q blob gives the conditional probability of P given Q. In Figure 11.1, this is the ratio between the darker region to the whole of the Q blob.

With conditional probability to work with, we can derive further useful consequences:

General Conjunction Rule

$$Prob(P\&Q) = Prob(P/Q) \times Prob(Q).$$

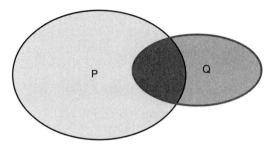

FIGURE 11.1 A representation of conditional probability. Here *Prob(P/Q)* is the ratio between the dark region of overlap and the whole of the Q oval. Similarly, *Prob(Q/P)* would be the ratio between the same dark region of overlap and the whole of the P oval.

This holds when *Prob(Q)* > 0. It is an easy consequence from the definition of conditional probability.

Special Conjunction Rule

$$Prob(P\&Q) = Prob(P) \times Prob(Q)$$

if *P* and *Q* are probabilistically independent.

The Law of Total Probability

$$Prob(P) = Prob(P/Q_1) \times Prob(Q_1) + \ldots + Prob(P/Q_n) \times Prob(Q_n),$$

if $Q_1 - Q_n$ is a partition of the entirety of logical space—that is, if the Q_i's are pairwise incompatible and their disjunction is a tautology.

Let's pause to see how we can use the various consequences we've derived so far.

- What is the probability you won't draw a heart?
  - Use the negation rule: *Prob(don't draw heart)* = 1 − *Prob(draw heart)* = 1 − .25 = .75.
- Assume you're playing a game in which the values of the cards go from 2 (which has the least value) through the number cards, through the face cards, to aces (the highest-value cards). What is the probability that you draw a face card or a card of higher value than a queen? Use *F* for "You draw a face value card" and *H* for "You draw a card of higher value than a queen."
  - Using the general disjunction rule:

$$Prob(F \lor H) = Prob(F) + Prob(H) - Prob(F\&H).$$

  If you compute these probabilities, you should get: 12/52 + 8/52 − 4/52 = 16/52 = 4/13.

- What is the probability you will draw a card that is neither a number card nor a face card?
  - You can see that this is equivalent to asking about the probability that you will draw an ace. Using the logical equivalents rule, the answer is 1/13.
- What is the probability, in two draws without replacement, of getting an ace on the first draw and an ace on the second?
  - Hint: Use the general conjunction rule.

We'll wrap up our brief primer of probability theory by examining Bayes' Rule and its applications. First, let's consider *Bayes' Theorem,* named after the eighteenth-century philosopher and cleric Thomas Bayes, who proved it:

Bayes' Theorem

$$Prob(H/E) = \frac{Prob(E/H) \times Prob(H)}{Prob(E)}$$

This holds provided E has a non-zero probability. The theorem is easily proved from the following two equations, which hold given the definition of conditional probability:

$$Prob(H/E) = \frac{Prob(H \& E)}{Prob(E)}$$

$$Prob(E/H) = \frac{Prob(E \& H)}{Prob(H)}$$

Because $H\&E$ is logically equivalent to $E\&H$, the numerators of ratios in these two equations are equal. Using this fact, we can rearrange the second equation to reach:

$$Prob(E/H) \times Prob(H) = Prob(H\&E)$$

We can then substitute the left-hand side in for the right-hand side in the first of the two equations for *Prob* (H/E) to arrive at Bayes' Theorem.

Some additional terminology will be helpful as we proceed: $Prob(H)$ is called the *prior probability* of H. $Prob(E/H)$ is called the *likelihood* of H on E. (The "of H on E" part is odd, but it is standard terminology.)

Bayes' Theorem is useful because we often know likelihoods and have some idea of the prior probability. We can use these together with Bayes' Theorem to get at something of more interest: how likely a hypothesis is given a certain piece of evidence. Of course, to get a value for $Prob(H/E)$

through Bayes' Theorem, we also need an estimate for *Prob(E)*. Sometimes we can estimate it using the Law of Total Probability. We have:

$$Prob(E) = Prob(E/H) \times Prob(H) + Prob(E/\sim H) \times Prob(\sim H).$$

If we know *Prob(E/H)* (the likelihood) and we know *Prob(H)* (the prior probability), all we need to compute this is *Prob(E/~H)*. When we have an estimate of this, we can plug in numbers in the formula below to estimate *Prob(H/E)*:

Variant of Bayes' Theorem

$$Prob(H/E) = \frac{Prob(E/H) \times Prob(H)}{Prob(E/H) \times Prob(H) + Prob(E/\sim H) \times Prob(\sim H)}$$

This is one of several useful variants of the theorem.[3]

Bayes' Theorem thus shows that the probability of an hypothesis given the evidence depends on the prior probability of the hypothesis and the likelihood. It is not a surprise to learn that how probable it is that you have tuberculosis conditional on your testing positive for it depends on how likely it is that you test positive for it conditional on your having it. Holding other things fixed, the more likely it is that you'll test positive for the disease given that you have it, the more likely it is that you have it given that you test positive for it. That's intuitive. But we often ignore the prior probabilities of hypotheses—here, the prior probability that you have tuberculosis. If a disease is very rare, then even if the probability that you test positive for it given that you have it is very high, it could still turn out that it isn't particularly likely that you have the disease given that you test positive.

Here's an example, called the *Harvard Medical School Test* (cf. Casscells, Schoenberger, and Grayboys 1978). Consider some dreadful disease; call it *D*. *D* is rare: It afflicts only, say, one in a thousand people on average. Suppose that if you have *D* it's 100 percent likely that you will test positive for it using the best and only test available. Suppose it's only 5 percent likely you will test positive if you don't have *D*. Now, suppose you test positive for *D*. Should you be a bit worried, rather worried, or terrified?

Well, let's see. Let *D* = You have disease *D*. Let *T* = You test positive for *D*. By Bayes' Theorem, we have:

$$Prob(D/T) = \frac{Prob(T/D) \times Prob(D)}{Prob(T/D) \times Prob(D) + Prob(T/\sim D) \times Prob(\sim D)}$$

Plugging in the numbers:

$$Prob(D/T) = \frac{1 \times (.001)}{1 \times (.001) + (.05) \times (.999)}$$

So, *Prob(D/T)* = .0196 or about 2 percent.

That is, the probability you'll have disease D given that you test positively for D is about 2 percent. Two percent rather than 95 percent! If you estimated it at 95 percent, or at least much higher than 2 percent, you're in good company: A majority of students and staff tested at Harvard Medical School gave the same answer.

But suppose, by contrast, that the prior probability of the disease is 1 in 10. Then *Prob(D/T)* is approximately .69, or 69 percent. What a difference the prior probability makes, even when the probability of testing positive given that you have the disease is 100 percent! In ordinary life, even when it matters, we unfortunately tend to neglect prior probability. Bayes' Theorem serves as a corrective to this. And it is not completely counterintuitive: Once you think about the background rate of the disease in the population, of course, it makes sense that it should matter to how likely it is that you have the disease given that you test positive for it.

The mathematical theory of probabilities has been usefully applied to a rich set of diverse phenomena in nature. We might naturally wonder how far it might be applied to understand the subject matter of epistemology.

11.2 THE EPISTEMOLOGY OF CREDENCES: WHAT ARE CREDENCES?

Before we ask if credences ought to conform to the probability axioms, we begin with a more fundamental question: Just what are credences?

11.2.1 The Classical Answer

The classical answer identifies credences with maximal prices one would pay to purchase a certain sort of bet (De Finetti 1974). Let's illustrate with an example. Suppose I'm 80 percent confident that it will rain tomorrow. Consider the following bet:

Bet on Rain: If rains tomorrow, you get $1 and if it doesn't, you get $0.

Suppose I'd like $1. Now what would seem to me to be a *fair* price to buy this bet from you (i.e., to pay for your guarantee to pay me $1 or $0 depending on whether it rains tomorrow)? If you gave the bet to me for free, that would be better than fair from my perspective—it would be favorable. That's because I'd have a bet that wouldn't lose me money and might give me $1. If you put the price at $1, that wouldn't be a fair price; I'd regard it as unfavorable. Certainly I wouldn't buy it, because I can see that I couldn't gain anything—my $1 for the bet at best would be matched by a $1 from winning the bet if it rains, and I'm 20 percent confident I'd lose my $1. Ninety cents is better, but still I wouldn't regard it as fair. The fair price is 80 cents, or $0.8. That's because, to use some jargon, the *expected value* of *Bet on Rain* is $0.8. The expected value (EV) of a bet is the sum of the values of each outcome weighted by the probabilities those outcomes obtain, using one's credence values as the probabilities. For *Bet on Rain*, we have:

$$EV(\text{Bet on Rain}) = .8 \times \$1 + .2 \times 0 = \$0.8$$

Examples like this one might tempt us to endorse the following account of *what it is* to have a credence:

Classical "Betting Price" Definition
To have a credence of d in a proposition P is to be willing to pay at most $\$d$ to have a bet that pays \$1 if P is true and \$0 otherwise.

Or, to eliminate reference to U.S. dollars in the account (not in the Italian De Finetti's original!), we could take values to come in units (call them utiles) and reformulate the analysis so that it claims that to have a credence d in P is a matter of being willing to sacrifice up to d utile for a bet that pays 1 utile if P and 0 utiles otherwise.

This is what is called an *operational* definition. It is a definition that gives a mechanical operation we could use to determine the application of a concept. It is mechanical in that it requires no judgment, no insight. A "dumb" computer could apply it. Prices for the bet are offered and it is recorded which prices the person is willing to pay. The person's credence is then identified with the highest price.

However, this is not a good definition of credence. A definition ought at the very least to be *extensionally adequate*. That is: If you are trying to define As in terms of Bs, each and every A must be a B, and vice versa. If some As aren't Bs or vice versa, we don't have a good definition. Of course, we want more than mere extensional adequacy in a definition: We want a noncircular explanation of the target phenomenon. But notice that the classical betting price account of credences is not even extensionally adequate. I might well have a .8 credence for rain tomorrow but not be willing to pay \$0.8 for the bet for any number of reasons: Perhaps I don't like betting; perhaps I miscalculate the expected winnings; perhaps I doubt that the \$1 will be forthcoming if I pay the \$0.8. There is simply no necessity that I be willing to pay \$0.8 for *Bet on Rain* if I have a credence of .8 for rain tomorrow. Nor is there any such necessity if we replace dollars with utiles.

Moreover, even if the betting prices I regard as fair line up with my credences, so that we have extensional adequacy, the definition gets the order of explanation wrong. It seems that the explanation of why I regard this betting price as fair must appeal to my credence in Rain. It is not some brute fact about me that I regard *Bet on Rain* as fair. I regard it as fair in part because of my credence in Rain; I don't have my credence in Rain because I regard *Bet on Rain* as fair.

The classical definition fails. Perhaps we do better to give up the hope of defining credences in terms of behavior. Behaviorist analyses of mental states like belief and desire, after all, haven't proved very successful. Perhaps a better bet, pardon the pun, might be to define credences in terms of other independently understood mental states. The natural candidate is *beliefs*. We investigate this possibility next.

11.2.2 Defining Credences in Terms of Beliefs

How might we define credences in terms of beliefs? The natural way to go is to turn to beliefs about probabilities. Credences, like probabilities, seem to come in degrees. There is such a thing as the minimal or zero credence. There is such a thing as maximal credence, which we can take as credence 1. Might we understand credences as beliefs that propositions have certain probabilities, where these probabilities satisfy the axioms of probability?

Here is the proposal we will examine:

Credences as Beliefs About Probabilities

To have a credence of d in a proposition P is to believe that the proposition P is d probable.

So, for example, for me to have a credence of .5 that the coin will land heads-up is for me to believe that it is .5 probable that it will land heads-up.

To evaluate this definition, we need to know more about what these probabilities are supposed to be. What we want is an *interpretation of probability*, one that goes beyond the axioms. The axioms tell us about the structure that probabilities must have. We want to know what probabilities *are*. (Of course, there could be more than one sort of thing that deserves to be called "probabilities.")

Traditional interpretations of probability broadly fall into two categories: *objectivist* and *subjectivist*. On the objectivist interpretation, probabilities are taken to be real mind-independent features of the world. The subjectivist, by contrast, takes probabilities to depend on our minds. If there were no human beings, there would be no probability, according to subjectivism but not according to objectivism.

The most common form of subjectivism takes probabilities to be relativized to particular subjects and times and in fact to just *be* the credences of those subjects at those times. This isn't very helpful to us if we're trying to define credences in terms of beliefs about probabilities. We can't define credences in terms of beliefs about credences.

There is a wide variety of objectivist interpretations of probability; the most popular one is the *frequentist interpretation*. On this interpretation, the probability of an event occurring is the proportion of events of that type occurring among events of a (possibly broader) reference class. So the probability of rolling a 4 using a normal die is 1/6, since 1/6 is the proportion of 4-results to results of rolling the die.

This interpretation faces a number of problems if it is to capture ordinary thinking about probability, even about dice. We'll just give one example.

Couldn't a die have a 1/6 probability of showing a 4, even though it is only rolled three times and never shows a 4? But wouldn't the proportion of 4-showings to all die-rolls be 0? We apparently need a broader reference class than the class of all actual die-rolls. Frequentists typically appeal to hypothetical further trials to cope with problems like this.

Could we define credences as beliefs about relative frequencies? The problem is that it's awfully hard to have beliefs about such frequencies when we go beyond the likes of dice and cards, but *easy* to have credences. Think about a proposition like *evolutionary theory is true*. What is the reference class for this proposition? Do ordinary people know it? But ordinary people could easily have a very high credence (even if it is hard to say what it is). It seems credences can't, therefore, in general, be beliefs about relative frequencies.

Other objectivist interpretations encounter the same problem. Take *propensity* accounts, which construe probabilities as tendencies, rooted in the physical properties of objects in certain situations to produce certain outcomes. (These fare better on the die cases than frequentist interpretations do.) As with frequentism, though, in many cases ordinary folk don't know things' propensities and so lack beliefs about their propensities, and yet they can have fairly precise credences.

What about an *epistemic* interpretation of probabilities? One epistemic interpretation takes the probability of *P* for a subject to amount to how much credence it would be epistemically rational/reasonable/justified for the subject to place in *P*. Clearly we cannot define credences in terms of beliefs about which credences it is rational to have. However, there is another epistemic interpretation: probabilities as credibilities. On this interpretation, a proposition's probability for a person is *how credible a proposition is* for the person. Credibility, it might be claimed, need not be explained in terms of credences it is rational to have. It seems the credibility interpretation avoids the problem of making credences too hard to come by. It isn't especially hard to have beliefs about how credible propositions are. In fact, such beliefs seem just as easy to come by as credences. This might lead you to think of credences as beliefs about credibilities.

One serious problem, though, is that it is quite unclear that credibilities satisfy the axioms of probability theory. Any interpretation of probability must take the probability of a logical truth to be 1. But surely there are logical truths that aren't 100 percent credible for us—if we don't know that they are logical truths. Open a logic textbook and turn to a problem in which you're asked to determine if the formula is a tautology. Just looking at the formula you might have no idea, and rightly so. It won't be 100 percent credible for you—until you do the truth-table.

One possibility is to drop the claim that credibilities satisfy the axioms of probability. We could still claim that to have a credence *d* in a proposition *P* is to believe it is probable—credible—to degree *d*. We would have to say that this account in terms of credibility aims to explicate an ordinary notion of probability, one that doesn't perfectly obey the axioms of probability.[4]

However we understand the relevant probabilities, we might have general misgivings about defining credences in terms of beliefs about probabilities. Having a credence seems only to require thinking about the content of proposition itself, but believing a proposition is probable seems to require thinking *about probability*. This is hardly a decisive reason to think credences can't be defined in terms of beliefs about probabilities, but it might give one pause.[5]

11.2.3 Defining Beliefs in Terms of Credences

Perhaps it is more promising to take credences as basic and try to define beliefs in terms of *them*. Not every credence in *P* is a belief in *P*, of course. I have a zero (or *extremely* low) credence for *I will win a Grammy*, but I don't believe it at all, not even a little bit. Nor do I believe, of a fair die, that a die will come up 5, but I have a credence that it will. Clearly, if belief is definable in terms of credence, it must be in terms of *high* credence. The two traditional proposed definitions are these:

> *The Certainty View*: to believe *P* is to have credence 1 in *P*.
>
> *The Threshold View*: to believe *P* is to have a credence above a particular threshold *d* for *P*. (Sturgeon 2008)

Is either of these tenable?

The certainty view is problematic. The main problem is that it seems we do believe pairs of propositions, even though we have a higher credence in one than in the other. Consider the pair: *I'll have dinner tonight, I had dinner last night*. I believe both, but I'm more confident in the latter. Under the certainty view, though, it is hard to see how this could be. To believe something is to be certain of it, fully confident of it—to have credence 1 for it. There is no greater credence than credence 1. So, I can't have more credence in some of the things I believe than in others.

The threshold view allows for different credences associated with different beliefs. So, that is an advantage over the certainty view. However, it seems not to capture certain putative facts about belief that serve as constraints as we look for a definition of belief:

Constraints on Belief

(Correctness) If you believe *P*, and *P* is false, you're incorrect (mistaken/wrong) about whether *P*.

(Commitment) If you believe *P*, and you believe that *P* implies *Q*, then you are committed to believing *Q*.

A word on each of these. According to *Correctness*, if you believe something that is false, you were wrong about it. So, if I believe Hilary Clinton will be the next president of the United States but she turns out not to be the next president, I was incorrect about this matter. This seems plausible enough.

According to *Commitment*, in the specific version here, believing a proposition that you believe implies another proposition commits you to believing that latter proposition. Think about an example. Suppose you and I are having a debate about some ethical issue, say same-sex marriage. Suppose I've asserted that *Democratic-leaning states allow same-sex marriage* and I've conceded *Hawaii is a Democratic-leaning state*. You, knowing that Hawaii doesn't allow same-sex marriage (as of 2013), will sense that you've nailed me: "Ah, so you believe that Hawaii allows same-sex marriage?" The interesting thing is that you seem perfectly in your rights to assume that I must believe this. It would be very odd for me to reply, "Well, yes, I believe Democratic-leaning states allow same-sex marriage, and I believe Hawaii is a Democratic-leaning state, but I don't believe Hawaii allows same-sex marriage." Belief seems to obey *Commitment*.[6]

Suppose the threshold view of belief is true. Are both these constraints on belief satisfied? We have to ask whether the following are true, where d is the threshold (and is a real number less than 1):

1. If you have a credence in P of d or higher, and P is false, you're incorrect about whether P.
2. If you have a credence in P of d or higher, and you have a credence in P *implies* Q of d or higher, then you are committed to having a credence in Q of d or higher.

These are what the constraints become when we replace "believes P" with "have a credence of d or higher in P," just as the threshold view would have us do.

Consider (1) first. Given all my evidence, it might be extremely unlikely that a die should come up 6 on three straight rolls. Suppose I give *it will come up 6 on three rolls* a credence of .0046. I might still think, "It might come up 6 three times in a row; I don't know it won't." Now you roll it. Oddly, it comes up 6 three times in a row. Were you incorrect about whether it would come up 6 three times in a row? You can say in your defense: "I didn't make any mistake—I just gave it a low credence."

Consider (2). Suppose $d = .9$. That is, suppose we're dealing with a threshold view on which belief amounts to having a credence of .9 or higher. If you have a credence of .9 in P and a credence of .9 in P *implies* Q, it looks like you *aren't* committed to having a credence of d or higher in Q. That's because you might well—and reasonably—have credences that fit the probability axioms, in which case, assuming P and P *implies* Q are independent, your credence for the conjunction P & P *implies* Q would be .81. If your own basis for confidence in Q comes from its being entailed by this conjunction, your credence for Q would be .81, below the threshold for belief. (We could make d any real number less than 1 and rerun the argument.)

So, if we take *Correctness* and *Commitment* to be true of belief, it seems we have to conclude that beliefs don't amount to having credences above a particular threshold. Thus, the threshold view would be false.

This argument is only as good as its main premise, which is that *Correctness* and *Commitment* are true of belief. *Commitment*, although admittedly plausible, might seem to require beliefs to have credence 1, which we've seen is too strong. Suppose I have the same credence for all these propositions: P, P implies Q, Q implies Q_1, ..., Q_{n-1} implies Q_n. My credence in all of them is some real number $d < 1$. Now suppose I believe them all. Then it follows from *Commitment* that I am committed to believing Q_n. But n could be huge—a million, say! If I follow the probability axioms, and if my credence for Q_n depends solely on this chain of reasoning, then my credence in Q_n must be pretty low. So, presumably if $n > 1,000,000$, it will be too low for belief. How could I be committed to believing Q_n? But if I'm not, then *Commitment* must not hold with full generality.

Yet even if we put aside *Commitment*, *Correctness* seems solid, and this alone might be sufficient reason to reject the threshold view.

11.2.4 Nondefinitional Views of the Relation Between Credences and Belief

There are other possible ways to think of the relation between beliefs and credences than attempting to define one in terms of the other. We will briefly discuss one (cf. Fantl and McGrath 2009, Ross and Schroeder 2014 for further discussion.) As you'll see, this view does not attempt to give a *definition*, since it makes full use of the concept of a belief in the account:

The Reason View

You believe P if and only if you have a credence in P high enough so that you are disposed to use P as a reason for further beliefs and actions.

You use a proposition as a reason if you base a belief or action on it. Thus, if you wave because you see your friend, you do something—wave—for a certain reason, namely that *he is your friend*. The reason is a proposition (or fact) that is your basis for waving at the person. Similarly, if you infer that he will wave back from the proposition that he is your friend and he saw you wave, you're using those propositions as reasons for belief. The idea behind the reason view, then, is that believing P amounts to having credence high enough to dispose you to take P as a reason in these ways.

The reason view allows for beliefs to come apart from credences in the following way, unlike either the certainty or threshold views: You can have the same credence for P and for Q but believe P and not believe Q. You might believe P and not believe Q because you are disposed to use P as a reason but not disposed to use Q as a reason. Suppose $P = I'll$ *have dinner tonight* and $Q = My$ *ticket will lose the lottery*. You might be equally confident of these— have the same credence for them—while being willing to use P as a reason, but not being willing to use Q (you won't throw away your ticket, say). The reason view needs further development: What counts as "disposed" to use P as a reason? If I'm in a high-stakes situation (e.g., whether to discontinue a certain medical treatment for my son), and I hold back from using *My son will be fine even if we discontinue the treatment* as a reason to discontinue the treatment, does this mean I don't believe that proposition? Couldn't I say, "Well, I believe he'll be fine if we discontinue the treatment, but I don't know he will, and so I'm going to play it safe"? These issues are tricky. Suppose the doctor tells me we can discontinue the treatment because my son will be fine if we do, but that it is up to me to make the decision. If I say, "Let's continue the treatment," he might say, "You don't believe he will be fine if we stop the treatment, do you?" We are pulled in different ways here: On the one hand, we are pulled toward the claim that I believe by the fact that I am very confident that *he'll be fine* is true; on the other hand, we are pulled away from that claim by the fact that I won't act on the supposed belief. We will not try to resolve these thorny issues here.

Whether the reason view proves correct or not, it is an example of the sort of view that is worth exploring, and that has not been thoroughly explored in the literature. It gives an informative account of the relation between credences and beliefs without attempting to define one in terms of the other.[7]

11.3 THE EPISTEMOLOGY OF CREDENCES: WHEN ARE CREDENCES RATIONAL?

On the supposition that credences can't be defined in terms of beliefs, our epistemology of belief will not apply automatically to credences. How then should we think about the epistemic status of credences? We will examine two common claims about the epistemology of credences: (1) that credences rationally ought to obey the probability axioms and (2) that credences rationally ought to change over time by a certain update rule, called *conditionalization*. The first is a claim about synchronic rationality, or rationality at a time, the second about diachronic rational, or rationality credences over time. We'll focus mainly on the first but touch briefly on the second as well in an optional section.[8]

11.3.1 Ought Credences Obey the Probability Axioms?

Let's introduce a label for the theory that credences rationally ought to obey the probability axioms:

Probabilism

It is irrational to have credences that taken together violate the axioms of probability.

You can see the appeal of probabilism in particular cases. Suppose I have a credence of .8 for *it will rain tomorrow* and have a credence of .8 for *it won't rain tomorrow*. Something seems very wrong with me. But probabilism is a very strong claim. Why think it is true more generally?

A common claim is that the laws of probability are to credences what the laws of logic are to beliefs. So, just as our beliefs ought to obey the laws of deductive logic (i.e., ought to be deductively consistent), so our credences ought to obey the laws of probability (i.e., ought to be probabilistically coherent). There are interesting questions to what extent rationality requires our beliefs to obey the laws of logic. If I believe, of each one of twenty friends, that he or she will come to my party, but I don't believe all twenty will, am I being irrational? What if we were talking about two hundred friends? It is not obvious there is irrationality here. So, arguing that credences ought to obey the axioms of probability based on an analogy with beliefs and the laws of logic is fraught with difficulties. It would be preferable not to rely on the analogy, but to argue directly for the conclusion about credences. We only have space to consider one sort of argument, *Dutch book arguments.*[9]

The basic strategy of a Dutch book argument is this: If your credences are probabilistically incoherent (i.e., if they fail to obey the laws of probability), you will be susceptible to "Dutch book"—that is, a clever bookie can sell you a series of bets that you will regard as fair or favorable but which collectively guarantee your loss as a matter of logic. This is claimed to be irrational.

To give a Dutch book argument, we show, for each of the axioms, that if your credences fail to satisfy that axiom, you are subject to a Dutch book. We'll consider how the argument goes only for the normalization axiom. Suppose your credence in some logical truth P is less than 1, say .7. Then a bookie can offer to sell you the following bet: If P is true, you get $0; if it is false, you get $1. How much will you be willing to pay? It seems the answer is $0.3. You'll regard that as fair. But now, observe: By paying *anything* for this bet, you guarantee your loss as a matter of logic. How so? Well, P is a logical truth. Thus, P is guaranteed to be true. Any bet on P that returns $0 if P is guaranteed logically to give you $0. You're paying $0.3 and guaranteed to get $0 from the bet, and so by paying the $0.3 you are guaranteed to lose a total of $0.3.

Let's grant that if your credences are probabilistically incoherent you will regard some bookie's selling prices for bets as fair, even though in doing so you would guarantee your monetary loss. Why is that irrational? It doesn't follow, unless we return to the problematic betting-price definition of credences, that you *will* accept the bookie's prices, and so it doesn't follow that you will lose money at all. You simply might not bet at all. Is it irrational to regard as fair or favorable prices for bets that, as a matter of logic, would guarantee your loss? If you *knew* that by paying the price for the bet you would end up losing as a matter of logic, then it would seem irrational to regard that asking price as fair. But it isn't part of the setup that you know you'd end up losing at all, let alone as a matter of logic. In fact, in this author's view, if you open up a logic textbook and look at a problem such as this (make it more complicated if you're a whiz at these things):

$$[(A \supset B)\&(\sim C \ v \sim B)] \supset \sim (C\&A)$$

you'd be perfectly rational to regard as fair or favorable a selling price of 1 cent for the following bet:

If P is true, you get $0; if P is false, you get $10,000.

Suppose the bookie says: "No time to do the truth-table; quick, right now—will you pay a cent?" What to do? This author would pay that cent! But, as it turns out, I'd be logically guaranteeing my loss. How could it be rational? Well, I don't know that it is guaranteeing my loss, and in fact my evidence suggests it might even be a contradiction (the proposition is in a textbook, with roughly 50 percent of the problems being nontautologies and 50 percent being tautologies).

It might be replied that I wouldn't be *blameworthy* in paying the cent for this bet, even though it is irrational. I'd have an excuse, namely that I didn't know better. However, wouldn't I be blameworthy for *not paying the cent*? This would be to disrespect my evidence. But if I am blameworthy for not paying the cent, it must be irrational not to pay the cent, and assuming this isn't some sort of dilemma case where all options are irrational, it would follow that it is rational to pay the cent.

It is hard to see, at least for this author, how Dutch book arguments can show that probabilism is true.

Despite these negative conclusions about this argument for probabilism, and indeed about probabilism, we shouldn't conclude that probabilistic coherence doesn't matter. We can all agree that there is something good about having a probabilistically coherent set of credences. Coherent credences, unlike incoherent ones, make us insusceptible to Dutch books. Moreover, if Joyce (1998) is right, then having coherent credences guarantees a certain sort of superior accuracy in our credences over incoherent credences. This seems to be an *epistemic* good.[10] However, it is one thing to acknowledge that coherent credences bring us epistemic goods we couldn't otherwise have (and help us avoid epistemic bads we otherwise would have); it is another to claim that it is irrational to have incoherent credences. The same holds for claims about having inconsistent beliefs. If you believe P and it turns out P is in fact a complicated logical contradiction, then you have an inconsistent set of beliefs. There is some consistent set of beliefs that is guaranteed to be at least as accurate in every possible world and more accurate in some possible worlds than your inconsistent set of beliefs. The corresponding claim wouldn't be true if your beliefs were consistent. But still, it might be rational for you to have your set of beliefs, because you don't know P is contradictory and in fact your evidence points toward P being true. Suppose your logic professor told you P is a tautology. The professor is almost always right and in fact has never led you astray on logic (you've checked out against your logic-pro software). However, in this one case the professor is wrong: P isn't a tautology. Wasn't it rational for you to believe P? This author thinks the answer is *yes*.[11]

11.3.2 Ought Credences Update by Conditionalization? (optional)

Conditionalization is a rule for updating credences. It is a rule for going from one *credence function* at one time to another at the next time. A credence function at a time is a mapping from propositions to real numbers meant to represent the person's credences at that time. To "conditionalize" on your total new evidence E is to make your new credences for propositions the same as your old credence for those propositions conditional on E—that is, to move from a credence function Cr to Cr($-/E$). Thus, if you have a .7 credence for *Rain tomorrow,* and then you see that the radar is clear to the west for five hundred miles, your new credence, according to the conditionalization rule, ought to be whatever your old credence was for *Rain tomorrow* given that the radar is clear to the west for five hundred miles. Suppose that this conditional credence is .2. Then your new credence for *Rain tomorrow* should be .2. In general, we have:

The Conditionalization Rule

Assume you begin with a probabilistically coherent credence function. Your new credence function upon receiving total evidence E ought to be $Cr_{new} = Cr_{old}(-/E)$. That is: Take your previous credence for any proposition P and replace it with your previous credence in P given E; this gives your new set of credences.

Just as we saw in the case of the basic axioms of probability, we can give a Dutch book argument for conditionalization. That Dutch book argument is vulnerable to all the same objections, and some in addition. Still, the conditionalization rule seems quite plausible on its face. Think about cases where you have clear conditional credences to begin with. Suppose you are going to draw a card from a deck. Your credence for *drawing a jack of diamonds* given *you draw a red card* is 1/26. Now you draw a red card but don't look at what card it is; you only see it is red. This is your total new evidence. How confident should you be that it is the jack of diamonds? Your old confidence that you'd draw a jack of diamonds was 1/52. Your new confidence should be—surely—1/26, exactly the same as your conditional credence. When we think about games of chance like this, the conditionalization rule seems exactly right.

However, there are problems for the rule. We'll discuss three.

- *Forgetting.* If the rule is correct, *forgetting* is irrational: Following the conditionalization rule, only new evidence can result in a change of credence for a proposition.
- *Rigid certainty.* If it is correct, then certainty is rigid: If you ever have credence 1 for a proposition, you must always continue to have credence 1 for that proposition. But couldn't you be rationally certain of something at one time but rationally less than certain of it at a later time?
- *Uncertain evidence.* If the rule is correct, all new evidence must have credence 1. Couldn't some evidence have credence less than 1?

Consider forgetting. Forgetting is a matter of losing information over time but not due to acquiring evidence that undermines that information. We all forget. Forgetting is perhaps epistemically unfortunate—we lose out on epistemic goods by forgetting—but it seems hardly irrational. Yet, if we can rationally update credences only by conditionalization on new evidence, since forgetting amounts to changes in credence not due to conditionalization on new evidence, forgetting is irrational.[12]

Next, the issue of rigid certainties. Suppose I rationally give credence 1 to P. Perhaps P is some proposition about logic or about mathematics. Later, I might get evidence against P; perhaps someone knowledgeable about these sorts of matters tells me P is false. It seems it might be rational to lower my credence in P. But this is ruled out by the conditionalization rule. Suppose $Cr_{old}(P) = 1$. Then $Cr_{new}(P) = Cr_{old}(P/E)$, where E is my new evidence. But if $Cr_{old}(P) = 1$, then $Cr_{old}(P/E) = 1$. (See proof in the appendix.)

Finally, uncertain evidence. Suppose a few days ago you told me you loved cooking with fenugreek. Today, suppose, I appeal to your telling me this as evidence that it's worth using more fenugreek in my Indian cooking. Must I have complete certainty that you told me this in order to have it as evidence? Couldn't I have some small credence, rationally, that perhaps you didn't tell me this, and that I am misremembering, while at the same time still having the proposition that you told me this as evidence? Here is another reason to think some evidence can be uncertain: Couldn't we have some evidence that was more certain than other evidence? If so, not all evidence must have maximal credence. Yet the Conditionalization Rule requires all evidence to have credence 1. Conditionalization requires that $Cr_{new}(-) = Cr_{old}(-/E)$, where E is your new evidence. Now put in E for "—" and we have:

$$Cr_{new}(E) = Cr_{old}(E/E).$$

Note that $Cr_{old}(E/E)$ is 1. So, $Cr_{new}(E)$ must be 1. Moreover, given rigid certainties, evidence always remains certain.

There is a well-developed answer to the worry about uncertain evidence. In place of the rule of conditionalization, we can substitute the rule of Jeffrey Conditionalization, named after the philosopher Richard Jeffrey. This rule assumes a person is simply saddled with a new credence for the evidence E and then takes the other new credences to come from the old conditional credences $Cr_{old}(-/E)$ weighted by the new credences for E and ~E. Thus, we have:

Jeffrey Conditionalization (Cf. Jeffrey 1983)

If your new evidence is E, then your new credence function $Cr_{new}(H)$, ought to be such that:

$$Cr_{new} = Cr_{old}(H/E) \times Cr_{new}(E) + Cr_{old}(H/{\sim}E) \times Cr_{new}({\sim}E).$$

Here's an example. Suppose that E, your new evidence after seeing the radar, arrives and that your credence for it—$Cr_{new}(E)$—is .8. Now what should your new credence be for *Rain tomorrow*? It is not simply $Cr_{old}(Rain/E)$. According to Jeffrey conditionalization, we have to consider the possibility that E is false and how likely *Rain tomorrow* is given that possibility.

Suppose $Cr_{old}(Rain/E) = .6$ and $Cr_{old}(Rain/{\sim}E) = .3$. Putting in the numbers, we have:

$$Cr_{new}(Rain) = Cr_{old}(Rain/E) \times Cr_{new}(E) + Cr_{old}(Rain/{\sim}E) \times Cr_{new}({\sim}E).$$

$$\text{So, } Cr_{new}(Rain) = (.6) \times (.8) + (.3) \times (.2) = .48 + .06 = .54.^{13}$$

We'll just mention one odd consequence of following Jeffrey conditionalization, which isn't a consequence of following the conditionalization rule: *order-dependence*. Under Jeffrey conditionalization, the order in which a person receives pieces of evidence has an effect on the rationality of her final credence. So, suppose you receive a piece of evidence E first and then later evidence F. Alternatively, suppose you receive F first and later E. We might think you should arrive at the very same credence function. Under conditionalization, you do. Under Jeffrey Conditionalization, you might not. Is this an acceptable result (cf. Field 1978)?

All in all, it looks as if the rule of conditionalization is too demanding. We have seen there are ways of relaxing it (e.g., Jeffrey conditionalization), just as there are ways of relaxing the requirement that one's credences obey the axioms of probability. Alternatively, it is often claimed that these requirements are requirements of *ideal rationality*. They represent an ideal to measure ourselves by. The difficult question, though, is about the normative force of this ideal. In some cases, we might *know* we're failing to be ideal and yet this is the rational thing *for us* to do. When I go from credence 1 to credence less than 1, I *know* I am not revising my credences in the way prescribed by conditionalization, and yet this might be the rational thing for me to do, given my evidence. One of the exciting challenges for those who deny probabilism and conditionalization but think that probabilistic coherence and conditionalization are ideals of rationality is to explain exactly how these ideals bear on real people normatively. The same challenge awaits those who think our beliefs ought, ideally at least, to be consistent. What is the normative force for us limited creatures of rules for an ideal mind?[14]

11.4 APPLICATIONS OF PROBABILITY IN EPISTEMOLOGY

Whether or not credences ought to obey the axioms of probability, or ought to be updated by conditionalization, the notion of probability has important uses in epistemology. We will discuss one primary use here as well as a specific application of it. The use is in giving an account of confirmation by the evidence.

11.4.1 Confirmation by Evidence

Let's start with some clear cases of confirmation. We'll be discussing confirmation in the sense of *providing some confirmation however small*, rather than confirmation in the sense of *establishing as true*.

- Drawing a heart confirms that you've drawn a red card.
- Drawing a red card confirms that you've drawn a heart.
- Today's being Sunday confirms the local churches will hold services today.
- A randomly sampled raven's being black confirms that ravens are black.

What do these cases have in common? One plausible candidate appeals to *probability raising*. In each of the above cases, the probability of the hypothesis conditional on the evidence seems greater than the unconditional probability of the hypothesis. Thus, consider the following theory of confirmation:

Probability-Raising Account of Confirmation

Evidence E confirms hypothesis H iff: $Prob(H/E) > Prob(H)$

We haven't said anything about what sort of probabilities are in question here. They presumably are *not* subjective. Just because you happen to distribute your credences in a certain way upon learning E, nothing about evidential confirmation follows. And just because E confirms H doesn't mean you are going to distribute your credences in any particular way. The subjective interpretation of probability is not appropriate here. What about other interpretations?

Objective interpretations are problematic for a different reason. Evidential confirmation should bear on rational credence. If you have confirming evidence for a hypothesis, this has an impact on what credences it is rational for you to have regarding the hypothesis. But the mere fact that, for instance, the relative frequency of H-type events within the class of E-type events is greater than the relative frequency of H-type events doesn't by itself bear on what credences it is rational for you to have in H if you have E as evidence. The same goes for propensities. If you have no idea, and rationally so, about the relation between litmus paper and acidity, observing that the paper turns pink needn't affect your credence at all in the proposition that the sample is acidic.

Epistemic interpretations are preferable. We have discussed two interpretations of probabilities as epistemic. On the first, facts about probabilities (for a subject) just are facts about which credences it is rational for a subject to have. On the second, facts about probabilities (for a subject) are facts about how credible propositions are for a subject, where such credibilities aren't definable in terms of rational credences but rather help to explain why certain credences are rational for the subject. Notice that if we employ either of these epistemic interpretations, we need to relativize claims about evidential confirmation. It is standard to relativize to background information. Thus, we arrive at:

Probability-Raising Account (with Epistemic Probabilities)

Evidence E confirms hypothesis H relative to background K iff:

$Prob(H/(E \& K)) > Prob(H/K)$, where *Prob* is an epistemic probability function.

This proposal secures the desired connection between evidential confirmation and rational credence. If I have evidence *E* and *E* is evidence for *H* relative to background information *K*, which is my background information, then if the above proposal is correct, learning *E* does bear on rational credence.[15]

Even supposing we can fix on the right sort of probability, we might worry that there are counterexamples to the probability-raising account. We will examine some well-known ones modeled after cases given by Peter Achinstein (1983). You'll want to judge for yourself if any of these undermines the account.

We'll start with proposed counterexamples to the sufficiency of probability raising for confirmation:

- Michael Phelps (the Olympic swimmer) swimming raises the probability that he will drown. But it is not confirmation he will drown.
- Buying a lottery ticket raises the probability that you will win the lottery. But it is not confirmation you will win the lottery.

Admittedly, we wouldn't normally say that Phelps swimming is evidence that he will drown. But isn't it just a tiny bit of evidence? After all, he can't drown if he isn't in water, so learning he is swimming and thus learning he's in water is some tiny evidence he will drown. The same response seems to apply to the lottery case.[16] The tiny evidence in each case confirms.

Next we turn to consider counterexamples to the necessity of probability raising for confirmation. (You can see that these counterexamples depend on an epistemic construal of probability.)

1. Suppose you see a totally new card game between two opponents. You have no information at all that would support your thinking that Player #1 will win, though you know that either Player #1 or Player #2 will win. You do see what Player #1's hand is. Consider the proposition (call it *E*) that you are given an exhaustive frequency analysis showing that 48 percent of the time if someone has Player #1's hand, that player wins. Now, as things stand *Prob(Player #1 wins)* is .5. You have no idea whether Player #1 will win or not. But *Prob(Player #1 wins/E)* = .48. So, this *E* lowers the probability of Player #1 winning. Still, it is evidence that Player #1 will win. (This example is found in Kung 2010.[17])

2. We already know for certain (suppose) about the anomalous advance of the perihelion of Mercury (call it *E*). Yet *E* is evidence for the General Theory of Relativity (which can explain it). But as the probability of *E* is 1, *Prob(GTR/E)* = *Prob(GTR)*, and so *E* doesn't raise the probability of the General Theory of Relativity. (This is the so-called problem of *old evidence*. For more, see Glymour 1980.)

We'll look at each in turn.

The idea behind the first counterexample is that you might begin with no evidence or reason at all to think a proposition *P* is true. In that case, the (epistemic) probability is .5. Consider the piece of frequency-based information that *P*-events happen about 48 percent of the time. Wouldn't that be evidence for *P*? But it lowers *P*'s probability.[18] Now, one might reply that although the frequency information is evidence for *P*, it doesn't confirm *P* for you. Confirmation is a matter of providing overall support, relative to the background information. Something could be evidence for *P* without providing overall support for *P*. (Another example of this is a case in which someone tells you that $1 + 1 = 2$. Yes, someone's telling you that is evidence it is true. But it doesn't confirm that it is true, because it doesn't provide support relative to your background information. Your probability stays put!) Such a response allows that *E* can be evidence for *H*, even though *E* lowers the probability of *H*. However, it claims that *E* can't confirm *H*—support *H* relative to your background information—unless *E* raises the probability of *H*.

The second counterexample presents the problem of "old evidence." If you already have evidence for *H*, and it has probability 1 for you, then it won't raise any probabilities of anything, including *H*, because nothing with probability 1 raises the probability of anything. Still, something could be evidence and could indeed be confirmation for *H* even if that evidence is known with certainty. The problem of old evidence is a lively topic of debate in confirmation theory. One strategy of coping with it is to back up to some earlier probability function at a time before the evidence had probability 1. But what if we're discussing a piece of evidence that's always been known? We might back up to an a priori probability function. But this brings problems of its own: Just what are the a priori probabilities of empirical events? And can we get the a priori probability of *GTR* given the anomalous advance of the perihelion of Mercury to be higher than the a priori probability of *GTR*? Or do we need to pack in further empirical information, making this probability not completely a priori?

The probability-raising account, then, may require some modifications, but it seems to do quite well in handling a great many cases of confirmation. This makes it a useful tool for epistemology. We will see a prime example of this in the next section.[19]

11.4.2 Skepticism and Confirmation

One style of skeptical argument, discussed at length in Chapter 1, is what we've called the *skeptical possibility argument*. The argument in outline goes like this: You don't know such-and-such skeptical possibility doesn't obtain; but if you don't know this, you don't know you have hands, or other ordinary things that you think you do know; and so, therefore, you don't know those ordinary things. To make it plausible that you don't know a skeptical possibility doesn't obtain, the skeptic should choose the skeptical possibility carefully. One way to do so is to choose a possibility that would seem to predict your having the very experiences and apparent memories and beliefs that you have. Thus, the skeptic might choose the hypothesis that you are a brain in a vat (BIV) with the very experiences, memories, and beliefs you actually have. *Why* does it seem you don't know you aren't such a BIV?

As we noted in Chapter 6 (Section 6.6), because the hypothesis that you are such a BIV predicts that you would have the very experiences, memories, and beliefs you have, it seems those experiences and so forth cannot be confirming evidence that you aren't such a BIV. With the probability-raising account of confirmation in mind, we can give an explanation of this intuition. To give the explanation, we need to run through a few crucial proofs of probability theory.

Recall Bayes' Theorem:

$$Prob(H/E) = \frac{Prob(E/H) \times Prob(H)}{Prob(E)}$$

Given the probability-raising account of confirmation, together with Bayes' Theorem, we can give a simple formula to test for confirmation. Often we know how likely a piece of evidence is on the assumption of a hypothesis, because we know what the hypothesis predicts. So, we are often—certainly not always, but often—in good shape to know $Prob(E/H)$, or at least how $Prob(E/H)$ compares to $Prob(E)$. We know whether such-and-such evidence is more or less likely assuming the hypothesis H is true. So, to determine if $Prob(H/E)$ is greater than $Prob(H)$—to determine if E confirms H—it would be useful to be able to answer the question in terms of $Prob(E/H)$ and $Prob(E)$ Given Bayes' Theorem, we can. We determine if the following ratio is greater than 1:

$$\frac{Prob(E/H)}{Prob(E)}$$

If it is, E confirms H. If not, not.[20]

Returning to skepticism, consider the following instance of Bayes' Theorem, where E is a statement of your total experiential, memorial, and introspective evidence:

$$Prob(BIV/E) = \frac{Prob(E/BIV) \times Prob(BIV)}{Prob(E)}$$

If *BIV* is chosen so as to entail E, then $Pro(E/BIV) = 1$. So, we know the ratio:

$$\frac{Prob(E/BIV)}{Prob(E)}$$

is greater than 1, since $Prob(E)$ was less than 1 and $Prob(E/BIV) = 1$. By the test above, and given the probability-raising account of confirmation, we can infer that E *confirms* the skeptical hypothesis that you are a BIV (with evidence E). The skeptic can then argue: Look, E is all the evidence you have;

but E confirms that you are a BIV with evidence E—perhaps only very weakly,[21] but confirms all the same. You can't *know* or be justified in believing you're not a BIV on the basis of evidence confirming that you are a BIV. But if you know or are justified in believing you're not a BIV, it must be on the basis of evidence. It follows that you don't know and aren't justified in believing you're not a BIV!

If the skeptic gets this far, the skeptic can continue the argument: Since you don't know you're not a BIV, you don't know you have hands; because if you knew you had hands, you'd know you're not a BIV; thus, you don't know you have hands. And the same would go for other ordinary propositions that you might have thought you knew through the senses.

This can look like—and this author thinks it *is*—a powerful argument for skepticism. There are ways we might try to resist it, as we in effect saw in Chapter 4. We could say that our evidence goes beyond experiences, apparent memories, and introspection. This raises worries about circularity, of course. Or we could insist that you needn't be in a position to know you're not a BIV in order to know you have hands. This is to deny the principle of closure for knowledge (see Section 4.2.1).

Recall how we chose the skeptical hypothesis. We chose it so that it entailed you had the experiential-cum-memory evidence you have. That's why $Prob(E/BIV) = 1$. If we scaled it back so that it is something like the hypothesis that you are a BIV stimulated to have realistic experiences of some sort or other, then this probability won't be 1 anymore. One might still claim $Prob(E/BIV)$ is still high, high enough to run the argument as before, but the details would be trickier.

Why *not* choose it so as to entail E? Well, there is a reason. The more the skeptic builds into a skeptical hypothesis, the lower its prior probability. So, if we explicitly build in E, that can only lower the prior probability. There is a danger—if there are infinitely many such skeptical possibilities—that $Prob(BIV)$ will go to 0! If it does so, the clever argument that $Prob(BIV/E) > Prob(BIV)$ will fail, and that's because $Prob(E/BIV)$ is undefined. So, the skeptic may have work to do to show that $Prob(BIV) > 0$ if she chooses BIV so as to imply that you have evidence E.[22]

You might have noticed that even if this probabilistically based argument for skepticism succeeds, it doesn't rule out our having a high credence—and rationally so—for both *I have hands* and *I am not a BIV*. Does this take its sting away? To some extent, yes. But it still leaves us with a startling conclusion: We don't know we have hands! Nor are we justified in believing this! The latter conclusion would strongly separate epistemic probability from justification. According to the sort of skeptic we are considering, you could have an epistemic probability of .9999 for *I have hands* but still not be justified in believing it. This very fact might make us want to think hard about whether our justification for ordinary propositions like *I have hands* comes merely from experiences-cum-memories. Perhaps we need a substantial role for a priori justification, after all![23]

Probability Problems

1. Suppose 80 percent of cabs in the city are blue, and the remaining 20 percent are green. Five percent of the time that eyewitnesses see a blue cab they will report they saw a green cab, and 90 percent of the time they see a green cab they report it is green. What is the probability that the cab the eyewitness saw is green given that an eyewitness reports that it was green? Use Bayes' Theorem. Is the answer 90 percent?

2. What is the probability, in four rolls of a normal die, of getting 6 each time? Assume the rolls are probabilistically independent.

3. Suppose a class has six students. We know that *either* it has four boys and two girls *or* it has one boy and five girls. All other possibilities are ruled out. We also know that it's 75 percent likely that there are four boys and two girls. Using the law of total probability, determine the probability that a student randomly selected is a boy.

4. What is the probability of drawing two aces back to back in a normal deck of cards (without replacement)?

5. The Monty Hall Problem (from Marilyn vos Savant's "Ask Marilyn" column [1990]): "Suppose you're on a game show, and you're given the choice of three doors: Behind one door is a car; behind the others, goats. You pick a door, say No. 1, and the host, who knows what's behind the doors, opens another door, say No. 3, which has a goat. He then says to you, 'Do you want to pick door No. 2?' Is it to your advantage to switch your choice?" Hint: Use Bayes' Theorem. Assume you've already chosen door No. 1. So, the probability that you did so is 1. Take the evidence E to be *the host chose to open Door No. 3*. Assume that the host will not open the door you pick nor the door with the car. Compute the probability that the car is behind Door No. 2 given E. If it is greater than .5, you ought to switch. Is it?

6. Suppose my credence for rain on Saturday is .7. Suppose my credence for *It won't rain on Saturday* is .4. Write out a series of bets that form a Dutch book for me.

7. (Challenging). It's a mathematical fact that if a function *Prob* obeys the probability axioms, then the function $Prob_E$ that comes from *Prob* by conditionalizing on E also obeys the probability axioms. (Assume here that $Prob(E) > 0$.) Can you prove this to be so? We will take you one third of the way. We'll show $Prob_E$ meets Normality. Suppose P is a tautology. Then $Prob(P) = 1$. We want to show that $Prob_E(P) = 1$ as well. By the definition of $Prob_E$, $Prob_E(P) = Prob(P/E)$. By the definition of conditional probability, $Prob(P/E) = Prob(P\&E)/Prob(E)$. Since P is a tautology, $P\&E$ is logically equivalent to E, and so has the same probability as E. Thus, $Prob_E(P) = 1$. Prove that $Prob_E$ satisfies Nonnegativity and Finite Additivity to complete the proof that if *Prob* obeys the axioms, so does $Prob_E$.

8. (Challenging). Suppose E raises the probability of H. Show that each of the following holds: (a) H raises the probability of E; (b) H lowers the probability of $\sim E$; (b) $\sim H$ raises the probability of $\sim E$; (c) $\sim E$ lowers the probability of H; and (d) $\sim E$ raises the probability of $\sim H$. Assume all of these propositions have non-zero probabilities. Hint: Use Bayes' Theorem.

Philosophical Questions

9. Consider the lottery paradox. For each ticket in a fair lottery, say of one thousand tickets, you have a very strong probability (both epistemic and subjective) that this ticket will lose, 999/1,000. This seems like enough for justified belief. It also seems that you are justified in believing a proposition when it is known to follow from one or more other propositions, each of which you are justified in believing. But these two assumptions lead to trouble. They assure us that you are justified in believing Ticket 1 will lose, Ticket 2 will lose, . . . , and Ticket 1,000 will lose, and that since these beliefs collectively entail Tickets 1 through 1,000 will lose, you are also justified in believing Tickets 1 through 1,000 will all lose. But you *aren't* justified in believing all these tickets will lose, since you know one of them will win. What gives? You might also think about how this lottery problem bears on the comparative plausibility of the certainty, threshold, or reason views of belief.

10. Does the reason view of belief satisfy the *Correctness* constraint? Why or why not? (The answer is not cut and dried; you'll have to make an argument one way or another.)

11. Suppose I know that Maria told Ian about her travel plans next summer. Maria tells me, "I think Ian and I will be in Vermont." This gives me good evidence she'll be in Vermont, though not decisive evidence. I increase my credence to, say, .7. Now Ian, Maria's husband, tells me, "I think we'll be in Vermont." Intuitively, I shouldn't increase my credence significantly more, if any more at all. Why? Didn't I receive evidence Maria will be in Vermont when Ian told me so? Explain.

12. A piece of evidence E could confirm H_1 and also confirm H_2 even if these are incompatible. Draw an ink blob diagram to show how this is possible. If you can, draw the blob diagram in such a way that E might seem to confirm H_1 *more* than it confirms H_2.

13. Call your memory-cum-experiential evidence E. Suppose the skeptic builds E into her BIV hypothesis, so that the hypothesis is that you are a BIV with evidence E. Suppose the skeptic says, "E confirms this BIV hypothesis. It also confirms the hypothesis that you have a body and perceive the real world through it. Since it confirms both hypotheses, you rationally should be neutral and give each a credence of .5." How would you reply?

14. To bolster Dutch book arguments, it is sometimes claimed that to value a bet differently depending on how it is (truly) described is irrational. So, for instance, consider two true descriptions of the same bet *B*:

    a. Description #1: Bet *B* pays $1 if a tautology is true and $0 otherwise.

    b. Description #2: Bet *B* pays $1 if the proposition below is true and $0 otherwise:

$$[(A \supset B)\&(\sim C \vee \sim B)] \supset \sim (C\&A)$$

    Consider Dahlia. If Dahlia was told that Description #1 applies to *B*, Dahlia would value *B* at $1. If Dahlia was told only that Description #2 applies to *B*, Dahlia would be more wary. She might say, "I'll pay only 50 cents for it." Is Dahlia irrational because of this pattern of her values? Why or why not?

15. The following problem is called the "Sleeping Beauty Problem":

    Some researchers are going to put you to sleep [on Sunday]. During the two days that your sleep will last, they will briefly wake you up either once or twice, depending on the toss of a fair coin (Heads: once [on Monday]; Tails: twice [both Monday and Tuesday]). After each waking, they will put you to back to sleep with a drug that makes you forget that waking. When you are first awakened, to what degree ought you believe that the outcome of the coin toss is Heads? (Elga 2000, 143)

    Here is an argument for having a credence (or degree of belief) of ½ (.5):

    The coin is fair, and so unless you obtain some information confirming or disconfirming the hypothesis that it came up Heads you ought to divide your credences equally between Heads and Tails and so give Heads a credence of ½.

    Here is an argument for having a credence of 1/3 that the coin came up Heads:

    There are three possibilities to take account of: it's Monday and the coin came up Heads; it's Monday and it came up Tails; and it's Tuesday and it came up Tails. (The probability that it's Tuesday and it came up Heads is 0, given the setup.) So, in only one of those three possibilities does the coin come up Heads. You have no reason to give more credence to one than the others. Thus, your credence in Heads ought to be 1/3.

    Which is the better argument and why? Are you a halfer or a thirder?

APPENDIX: PROOFS (OPTIONAL)

1. *Negation rule:*

$$Prob(\sim P) = 1 - Prob(P).$$

Proof: This is an immediate consequence of Finite Additivity. Take the incompatible disjuncts to be P and $\sim P$. We have $Prob(P) + Prob(\sim P) = 1$. Subtracting $Prob(P)$ from both sides gives us $Prob(\sim P) = 1 - Prob(P)$.

2. *Contradictions:*

$$\text{If } P \text{ is a logical contradiction, } Prob(P) = 0$$

Proof: This follows from the negation rule. If P is a contradiction, $\sim P$ is a tautology. So $Prob(\sim P) = 1$. Given that $Prob(P) + Prob(\sim P) = 1$, we can conclude $Prob(P) = 0$.

3. *Logical equivalents rule:*

$$\text{If } P \text{ and } Q \text{ are logically equivalent, then } Prob(P) = Prob(Q).$$

Proof: Suppose P and Q are logically equivalent. Then $P \vee \sim Q$ is a tautology, with incompatible disjuncts. Thus, $Prob(P \vee \sim Q) = Prob(P) + Prob(\sim Q) = 1$. So, $Prob(P) = 1 - Prob(\sim Q)$. But $Prob(Q) = 1 - Prob(\sim Q)$ Thus, $Prob(P) = Prob(Q)$.

4. *General disjunction rule:*

$$Prob(P \vee Q) = Prob(P) + Prob(Q) - Prob(P\&Q).$$

Proof: Because $P\&Q$ and $P\&\sim Q$ are incompatible and their disjunction is logically equivalent to P, we have by Finite Additivity: $Prob(P) = Pr(P\&Q) + Prob(P\&\sim Q)$. Similarly, $Prob(Q) = Prob(P\&Q) + Prob(\sim P\&Q)$. From Finite Addivity together with the logical equivalence of $P \vee Q$ and the disjunction $[(P\&Q) \vee (P\&\sim Q) \vee (\sim P\&Q)]$, we also have $Prob(P \vee Q) = Pr(P\&Q) + Prob(P\&\sim Q) + Prob(\sim Q\&P)$. Thus, $Prob(P) + Prob(Q)$ is greater than $Prob(P \vee Q)$ by the amount $Prob(P\&Q)$. Thus, it is the sum of those probabilities less $Prob(P\&Q)$, just as the general disjunction rule asserts.

5. *Entailment rule:*

$$\text{If } P \text{ entails } Q, Prob(P) \leq Prob(Q).$$

Proof: Suppose P entails Q. $Prob(Q) = Prob(P\&Q) + Prob(\sim P\&Q)$. But P is logically equivalent to $P\&Q$. So, $Prob(Q) = Prob(P) + Prob(\sim P\&Q)$. Since $Prob(\sim P\&Q) \geq 0$, it follows that $Prob(P) \leq Prob(Q)$.

6. *Special conjunction rule:*
   Where P and Q are *independent*,

$$Prob(P\&Q) = Prob(P) \times Prob(Q).$$

Proof: We define "independence" as follows: P and Q are independent just if neither raises the probability of the other—that is, where $Prob(P/Q) = Prob(Q)$ and $Prob(Q/P) = Prob(P)$. *I will draw an ace on the first draw* and *I will draw an ace on the second draw* are independent if we replace the card we draw on the first draw before making the second draw. They're not independent if we don't. We can prove the special conjunction rule in a few steps. From the definition of independence, if P and Q are independent, then $Prob(P/Q) = Prob(P)$. By the definition

of conditional probability, we have $Prob(P/Q) = \dfrac{Prob(P\&Q)}{Prob(Q)}$. So, putting

these together, we arrive at $Prob(P) = \dfrac{Prob(P\&Q)}{Prob(Q)}$. Rearranging, we

have the special rule: $Prob(P\&Q) = Prob(P) \times Prob(Q)$.

7. *The law of total probability.*
   This law states that: $Prob(P) = Prob(P/Q_1) \times Prob(Q_1) + \ldots + Prob(P/Q_n) \times Prob(Q_n)$, where Q_1-Q_n is a partition of the entirety of logical space—that is, the Q_i's are pairwise incompatible and their disjunction is a tautology.
   Proof: P is logically equivalent to $P\&Q_1 \, v \, P\&Q_2 \, v \ldots P\&Qn$. The disjuncts are pairwise incompatible and so we can conclude by Finite Additivity that $Prob(P) = Prob(P\&Q_1) + \ldots Pob(P\&Q_n)$. By the general conjunction rule, we can replace each of $Prob(P\&Qi)$ with $Prob(P/Q_i) \times Pr(Q_i)$. This gives us the Law of Total Probability.

8. *If your old rational credence for P is 1, then your old rational credence for P given E is also 1, if your old rational credence for E is greater than 0.*

   In symbols: If $Cr_{old}(P) = 1$, then $Cr_{old}(P/E) = 1$ if $Cr_{old}(E) > 0$.

Proof: We can drop the subscript 'old' and show that this holds for all credence functions obeying the probability axioms. Assume $Cr(P) = 1$ and that $Cr(E) > 0$. We show that $Cr(P/E) = 1$.
   E is logically equivalent to the disjunction $(P\&E) \, v \, (\sim P\&E)$. Logical equivalents have the same probability, and so the same credences. Moreover, $P\&E$ and $\sim P\&E$ are incompatible, and so by Finite Additivity we can compute the credence of their disjunction by adding their individual credences. So, we have:

$$Cr(P\&E) + Cr(\sim P\&E) = Cr(E)$$

Recall that $Cr(\sim P) = 0$. Because $\sim P\&E$ entails $\sim P$, as we've proved above, it cannot have a higher probability. Thus, we have $Cr(\sim P\&E) = 0$. But then it follows that $Cr(P\&E) = Cr(E)$.

Because $Cr(P\&E) = Cr(E)$, it follows that:

$$\frac{Cr(P\&E)}{Cr(E)} = \frac{Cr(E)}{Cr(E)} = 1.$$

So, applying the definition of conditional probability, we have:

$$Cr(P/E) = \frac{Cr(P\&E)}{Cr(E)} = 1.$$

FURTHER READING

Buchak, Lara (2013). *Risk and Rationality*. Oxford: Oxford University Press.

Christensen, David (2004). *Putting Logic in Its Place*. Oxford: Oxford University Press.

Eagle, Anthony (ed.) (2011). *Philosophy of Probability: Contemporary Readings*. London: Routledge.

Elga, Adam (2000). "Self-Locating Belief and the Sleeping Beauty Problem." *Analysis* 60(2): 143–147.

Hájek, Alan. (2008). "Arguments for—or Against—Probabilism?" *British Journal for the Philosophy of Science* 59(4): 793–819.

Howson, Colin, and Peter Urbach (2006). *Scientific Reasoning: The Bayesian Approach*. 3rd ed. Peru, IL: Open Court.

Moss, Sarah (2013). "Epistemology Formalized." *Philosophical Review* 122(1): 1–43.

Sober, Elliott (2008). *Evidence and Evolution*. Cambridge: Cambridge University Press.

NOTES

1. Although below we discuss some of the mathematics of probability theory, we only scratch the surface. For a much more thorough account of the mathematics, including its application to statistics, see Howson and Urbach (2006). Our focus throughout is on relatively foundational philosophical issues.

2. In the mathematical theory of probability, probability functions are defined over sets rather than sentences or propositions. In particular, probability functions are defined over *events* conceived as subsets of a background universe of possibilities (a further set). Events are closed under operations of union and complementation.

3. If we know how to partition $\sim H$ further (i.e., break it up into incompatible propositions whose disjunction is equivalent to $\sim H$), we can expand this formula further, by replacing the second summand in the denominator with a formula giving the sum of the probabilities of E given each proposition X_i in the partition of $\sim H$ multiplied by the probability of X_i. For instance, if we know that either John, Maria, or Claude committed the crime, we would partition the proposition *John didn't do it* into *Maria did it* and *Claude did it*.

4. For accounts of epistemic probabilities (that do not reduce them to subjective or objective probabilities), see Williamson (2000, Chapter 10) and Achinstein (2001, Chapter 5).

5. Rather than explaining credences in terms of beliefs about objective probability, we might try to explain the latter in terms of principles about credences. Thus, consider the *Principal Principle*, due to David Lewis (1980). Roughly, the principle tells us that if you know merely that the objective chance of H is d, where H is about the future, then your credence in H ought to be d.

6. This is a counterpart for belief of principles of closure for knowledge and justification (see Chapter 3 [Section 3.2]).

7. A number of other interesting questions arise about the relation between binary cognitive states, such as belief and knowledge and graded credal states. Sarah Moss (2013) argues for the thesis that credences, and not only high ones, can be knowledge. Thus, just as we can see credences as graded *beliefs*, so she claims we can see some credences, ones meeting Gettier-like constraints, as graded *knowledge*.

8. There is an interesting literature on the question of whether rational credences must be point-like or whether they can be "mushy," credences such as "Eh, somewhere between .6 and .8." To put it more precisely, could you rationally have an *interval* [.6, .8] as your credence for a proposition? For more discussion of these issues, see Joyce (2010) and Elga (2010b).

9. The reader interested in other arguments for probabilism (and willing to work through some relatively formal material) should consult Joyce (1998) for an "accuracy-based" argument for probabilism and Maher (1993) for an argument for probabilism based on so-called representation theorems. In consulting these papers, you should "follow the tautologies"—that is, see just how these authors argue that it is irrational to assign a tautology a credence less than 1, watching the assumptions they use (and asking about their plausibility). We will follow the tautologies below in our account of Dutch book arguments.

10. See also Goldman (1999) for an account of the epistemic goodness for credences.

11. For a different viewpoint, see David Christensen (2004, 153–157). Christensen distinguishes between factual and logical omniscience, arguing that failures of factual omniscience (not knowing all the empirical facts) are not a mark of rational defect, whereas failures of logical omniscience are.

12. Bovens and Hartmann (2003) develop update rules that allow for forgetting.

13. One slight inaccuracy in our account: Jeffrey does not consider the evidence itself uncertain (or certain). He wished not to identify evidence with propositions. Rather, what can be uncertain are directly evidenced propositions. See Jeffrey (1983).

14. See Weirich (2004) for attempts to devise a more realistic probabilistic epistemology and decision theory.

15. A number of hard questions arise here. For instance: Just what is it for K to be my background information—must I have rational credence 1 in K for it to be my background information? Also: Couldn't I rationally but falsely believe E doesn't confirm H; how should learning E bear on my rational credence for H in that case?

16. See Sherrilyn Roush (2004) for more on how to defend the probability-raising account in the light of such examples.

17. We should be clear: Kung's goal in the article from which this example is taken is *not* to refute the probability-raising account of confirmation but rather to show how that one can acquire a reason to believe something despite the fact that its probability isn't raised conditional on that reason. Nevertheless, it is instructive to see if the case does constitute a counterexample to the probability-raising account.

18. John Maynard Keynes' notion of the *weight* of evidence is relevant here:

> As the relevant evidence at our disposal increases, the magnitude of the probability of the argument may either decrease or increase, according as the new knowledge strengthens the unfavorable or favorable evidence; but something seems to have increased in either case—we have a more substantial basis upon which to rest our conclusion. I express this by saying that an accession of new evidence increases the weight of an argument. New evidence will sometimes decrease the probability of an argument, but it will always increase its "weight." (1921, 71)

19. We have only scratched the surface here. In addition to explaining confirmation—does *E* confirm *H* or not?—formal epistemologists have attempted to explain *degree* of confirmation—how *much* does *E* confirm *H*? (Cf. Sober 2008). We want to say that our total evidence provides a higher degree of confirmation for Evolutionary Theory than for Creationism. We also want to say that the success of surprising predictions—unexpected ones—in general provides more confirmation than unsurprising ones.

20. Here is why the ratio *Prob(E/H)/Prob (E)* is a test for confirmation. By Bayes' Theorem we have:

$$Prob(H/E) = \frac{Prob(E/H)\,Prob(H)}{Prob(E)}$$

Dividing both sides by *Prob(H)*, the left-hand side becomes *Prob(H/E)/Prob (H)*. This is greater than 1 if and only if *E* confirms *H*. The right-hand side becomes *Prob(E/H)/Prob (E)*. Thus, it follows that *E* confirms *H* if and only if *Prob(E/H)/Prob (E) > 1*.

21. On a good theory of degree of confirmation, *E* (including, say, the hand-ish experience) ought to provide more confirmation for *I have hands* than for *I am a BIV*. Still, it confirms both, at least on the probability-raising account.

22. There are difficult questions about how to understand probability for infinitely many pairwise incompatible events, questions that are beyond the scope of this chapter. To give the reader a taste: Suppose you have a ticket in a lottery with an infinite number of tickets. No ticket is more likely to win than any other. One ticket will win. What should your credence be for *ticket 255 will lose?* It cannot be any real number greater than 0. Could it be 0? But intuitively it seems you shouldn't be rationally certain ticket 255 will lose.

23. See Chapter 6 (Section 6.6) for a discussion of the role of probability in the "easy justification" argument against dogmatism about perceptual justification.

Works Cited

Achinstein, Peter (1983). "Concepts of Evidence." In *The Concept of Evidence*, ed. P. Achinstein, 145–174. Oxford: Oxford University Press.

Achinstein, Peter (2001). *The Book of Evidence*. Oxford: Oxford University Press.

Ackerman, Bruce A., and James S. Fishkin (2004). *Deliberation Day*. New Haven, CT: Yale University Press.

Adams, Fred, and Murray Clarke (2005). "Resurrecting the Tracking Theories." *Australasian Journal of Philosophy* 83(2): 207–221.

Alexander, Joshua, Ronald Mallon, and Jonathan M. Weinberg (2010). "Accentuate the Negative." *Review of Philosophy and Psychology* 1(2): 297–314.

Alston, William P. (1983). "What's Wrong with Immediate Knowledge?" *Synthese* 55: 73–95. Reprinted in *Epistemic Justification: Essays in the Theory of Knowledge*, 57–78 (1989). Ithaca, NY: Cornell University Press.

Alston, William P. (1985). "Thomas Reid on Epistemic Principles." *History of Philosophy Quarterly* 2(4): 435–452.

Alston, William P. (1991). *Perceiving God: The Epistemology of Religious Experience*. Ithaca, NY: Cornell University Press.

Alston, William P. (1995). "How to Think About Reliability." *Philosophical Topics* 23(1): 1–29.

Austin, J. L. (1962). *Sense and Sensibilia*. Reconstructed from the manuscript notes by G. J. Warnock. Oxford: Oxford University Press.

Bach, Kent (1984). "Default Reasoning: Jumping to Conclusions and Knowing When to Think Twice." *Pacific Philosophical Quarterly* 65: 37–58.

Bargh, John A., and Paula Pietromonaco (1982). "Automatic Information Processing and Social Perception: The Influence of Trait Information Presented Outside of Conscious Awareness on Impression Formation." *Journal of Personality and Social Psychology* 43(3): 437–449.

Beebe, James R. (2004). "The Generality Problem, Statistical Relevance and the Tri-Level Hypothesis." *Noûs* 38(1): 177–195.

Beebe, James R. (2009). "The Abductivist Reply to Skepticism." *Philosophy and Phenomenological Research* 79(3): 605–636.

Berkeley, George (1732). *An Essay Toward a New Theory of Vision*.

Berker, Selim (2013). "Epistemic Teleology and the Separateness of Propositions." *Philosophical Review* 122(3): 337–393.

Blumenfeld, David, and Jean Beer Blumenfeld (1978). "Can I Know I Am Not Dreaming?" In *Descartes: Critical and Interpretive Essays*, ed. M. Hooker, 234–255. Baltimore: Johns Hopkins University Press.

BonJour, Laurence (1985). *The Structure of Empirical Knowledge*. Cambridge, MA: Harvard University Press.

BonJour, Laurence, and Ernest Sosa (2003). *Epistemic Justification*. Oxford: Blackwell.

Bovens, Luc, and Stephen Hartmann (2003). *Bayesian Epistemology*. Oxford: Oxford University Press.

Bradley, Richard, and Christopher Thompson (2012). "A (Mainly Epistemic) Case for Multiple-Vote Majority Rule." *Episteme* 9(1): 63–79.

Bragues, George (2009). "Prediction Markets: The Practical and Normative Possibilities for the Social Production of Knowledge." *Episteme: A Journal of Social Epistemology* 6(1): 91–106.

Brogaard, Berit (2013a). "Do We Perceive Natural Kind Properties?" *Philosophical Studies* 162(1): 35–42.

Brogaard, Berit (2013b). "Phenomenal Seemings and Sensible Dogmatism." In *Seemings and Justification*, ed. C. Tucker, 270–289. Oxford: Oxford University Press.

Brown, Jessica (2006). "Contextualism and Warranted Assertibility Manoeuvres." *Philosophical Studies* 130(3): 407–435.

Brown, Jessica (2008). "Subject-Sensitive Invariantism and the Knowledge Norm for Practical Reasoning." *Noûs* 42(2): 167–189.

Brown, Jessica (2014). "Impurism, Practical Reasoning, and the Threshold Problem." *Noûs* 48(1): 179–192.

Brown, Jessica, and Mikkel Gerken, eds. (2012). *Knowledge Ascriptions*. Oxford: Oxford University Press.

Buchak, Lara (2013). *Risk and Rationality*. Oxford: Oxford University Press.

Buckwalter, Wesley (forthcoming). "The Mystery of Stakes and Error in Ascriber Intuitions." In *Advances in Experimental Epistemology*, ed. J. Beebe. New York: Continuum Press.

Buckwalter, Wesley, and Jonathan Schaffer (forthcoming). "Knowledge, Stakes, and Mistakes." *Noûs*.

Buckwalter, Wesley, and John Turri (manuscript). "Descartes' Schism, Locke's Reunion: Completing the Pragmatic Turn in Epistemology."

Burge, Tyler (1993). "Content Preservation." *Philosophical Review* 102: 457–488.

Casscells W., A. Schoenberger, and T. B. Grayboys (1978). "Interpretation by Physicians of Clinical Laboratory Results." *New England Journal of Medicine* 299(18): 999–1001.

Chisholm, Roderick M. (1957). *Perceiving*. Ithaca, NY: Cornell University Press.

Chisholm, Roderick M. (1966). *Theory of Knowledge*. Englewood Cliffs, NJ: Prentice Hall.

Chisholm, Roderick M. (1977). *Theory of Knowledge*. 2nd ed. Englewood Cliffs, NJ: Prentice-Hall.

Christensen, David (2004). *Putting Logic in Its Place*. Oxford: Oxford University Press.

Christensen, David (2009). "Disagreement as Evidence: The Epistemology of Controversy." *Philosophy Compass* 4(5): 756–767.

Chudnoff, Elijah (2013). "Awareness of Abstract Objects." *Noûs* 47(4): 706–726.

Coady, C. A. J. (1992). *Testimony: A Philosophical Study*. Oxford: Clarendon Press.

Cohen, Stewart (1998). "Contextualist Solutions to Epistemological Problems: Skepticism, Gettier, and the Lottery." *Australasian Journal of Philosophy* 76(2): 289–306.

Cohen, Stewart (1999). "Contextualism, Skepticism, and the Structure of Reasons." *Philosophical Perspectives* 33(13): 57–89.

Cohen, Stewart (2002). "Basic Knowledge and the Problem of Easy Knowledge." *Philosophy and Phenomenological Research* 65(2): 309–329.

Comesaña, Juan (2005). "Unsafe Knowledge." *Synthese* 146(3): 395–404.

Comesaña, Juan (2006). "A Well-Founded Solution to the Generality Problem." *Philosophical Studies* 129(1): 27–47.

Comesaña, Juan, and Matthew McGrath (2014). In *Epistemic Norms*, eds. C. Littlejohn and J. Turri, Chapter 3. Oxford: Oxford University Press.

Condorcet, Marquis de (1785). *Essai sur l'application de l'analyse a la probabilite des decisions rendues a la pluralite des voix.* Paris: De L'Imprimerie Royale.

Conee, Earl, and Richard Feldman (1998). "The Generality Problem for Reliabilism." *Philosophical Studies* 89(1): 1–29.

Conee, Earl, and Richard Feldman (2001). "Internalism Defended." In *Epistemology: Internalism and Externalism*, ed. H. Kornblith, 231–260. Malden, MA: Blackwell.

Conee, Earl, and Richard Feldman (2004). *Evidentialism: Essays in Epistemology.* Oxford: Clarendon Press.

Cooper, John M., and D. S. Hutchinson (1997). *Plato: Complete Works.* Cambridge, MA: Hackett Publishing.

Copenhaver, Rebecca (2010). "Thomas Reid on Acquired Perception." *Pacific Philosophical Quarterly* 91(3): 285–312.

Craig, Edward J. (1990). *Knowledge and the State of Nature.* Oxford: Oxford University Press.

Cullen, Simon (2010). "Survey-Driven Romanticism." *Review of Philosophy and Psychology* 1(2): 275–296.

Cummins, Robert C. (1998). "Reflection on Reflective Equilibrium." In *Rethinking Intuition: The Psychology of Intuition and Its Role in Philosophical Inquiry*, ed. M. R. DePaul and W. M. Ramsey, 113–128. Lanham, MD: Rowman & Littlefield.

Davidson, Donald (1986). "A Coherence Theory of Truth and Knowledge." In *Truth and Interpretation: Perspectives on the Philosophy of Donald Davidson*, ed. E. LePore, 307–19. Oxford: Basil Blackwell.

Davies, Martin (2004). "Epistemic Entitlement, Warrant Transmission and Easy Knowledge." *Aristotelian Society Supplementary Volume* 78(1): 213–245.

Davis, Wayne (2006). "Knowledge and Loose Use." *Philosophical Studies* 132(3): 395–438.

De Finetti, Bruno (1974). *Theory of Probability, Vol.I.* New York: Wiley.

DeRose, Keith (1992). "Contextualism and Knowledge Attributions." *Philosophy and Phenomenological Research* 52(4): 913–929.

DeRose, Keith (1995). "Solving the Skeptical Problem." *Phlosophical Review* 104(1): 1–52.

DeRose, Keith (2002). "Assertion, Knowledge and Context." *Philosophical Review* 111(2): 167–203.

DeRose, Keith (2009). *The Case for Contextualism: Knowledge, Skepticism, and Context, Vol. 1.* Oxford: Clarendon Press.

Descartes, René [1637] (1960). *Discourse on the Method of Rightly Conducting the Reason and Seeking Truth in the Sciences.* In *Discourse on Method* and *Meditations.* Indianapolis: Bobbs-Merrill.

Descartes, René (1641). *Meditations on First Philosophy.*

Dretske, Fred (1970). "Epistemic Operators." *Journal of Philosophy* 67(24): 1007–1023.

Dretske, Fred (1971). "Conclusive Reasons." *Australasian Journal of Philosophy* 49(1): 1–22.

Dretske, Fred (1981). "The Pragmatic Dimension of Knowledge." *Philosophical Studies* 40(3): 363–378.

Eagle, Anthony, ed. (2011). *Philosophy of Probability: Contemporary Readings*. New York: Routledge.

Elga, Adam (2000). "Self-Locating Belief and the Sleeping Beauty Problem." *Analysis* 60(2): 143–147.

Elga, Adam (2010a). "How to Disagree About How to Disagree." In *Disagreement*, eds. R. Feldman and T. A. Warfield, 175–186. Oxford: Oxford University Press.

Elga, Adam (2010b). "Subjective Probabilities Should Be Sharp." *Philosophers' Imprint* 10(5).

Eriksson, Lina, and Alan Hájek (2007). "What Are Degrees of Belief?" *Studia Logica: An International Journal for Symbolic Logic* 86(2): 183–213.

Evans, Jonathan S., Julie L. Barston, and Paul Pollard (1983). "On the Conflict between Logic and Belief in Syllogistic Reasoning." *Memory & Cognition* 11(3): 295–306.

Fantl, Jeremy, and Matthew McGrath (2002). "Evidence, Pragmatics, and Justification." *Philosophical Review* 111(1): 67–94.

Fantl, Jeremy, and Matthew McGrath (2009). *Knowledge in an Uncertain World*. Oxford: Oxford University Press.

Feldman, Richard (2003). *Epistemology*. Englewood Cliffs, NJ: Prentice-Hall.

Feldman, Richard (2007). "Reasonable Religious Disagreements." In *Philosophers without Gods: Meditations on Atheism and the Secular Life*, ed. L. M. Antony, 194–214. Oxford: Oxford University Press.

Feldman, Richard, and Earl Conee (2002). "Typing Problems." *Philosophy and Phenomenological Research* 65(1): 98–105.

Field, Hartry (1978). "A Note on Jeffrey Conditionalization." *Philosophy of Science* 45(3): 361–367.

Fodor, Jerry (1983). *The Modularity of Mind: An Essay on Faculty Psychology*. Cambridge, MA: MIT Press.

Fricker, Elizabeth (1994). "Against Gullibility." In *Knowing from Words: Western and Indian Philosophical Analysis of Understanding and Testimony*, eds. B. K. Matilal and A. Chakrabarti, 125–161. Dordrecht: Kluwer Academic Publishers.

Fricker, Elizabeth (forthcoming). "Unreliable Testimony." In *Alvin Goldman and His Critics*, eds. H. Kornblith and B. McLaughlin. Oxford: Blackwell.

Fumerton, Richard (1995). *Metaepistemology and Skepticism*. Lanham, MD: Rowman and Littlefield Press.

Gana, Kamel, Marcel Lourel, Raphaël Trouillet, Isabelle Fort, Djamila Mezred, Christophe Blaison, Valérian Boudjemadi, Pascaline K'Delant, and Julie Ledrich (2010). "Judgment of Riskiness: Impact of Personality, Naive Theories and Heuristic Thinking among Female Students." *Psychology & Health* 25(2): 131–147.

Gazzaniga, Michael, Richard B. Ivry, and George R. Mangun (2013). *Cognitive Neuroscience: The Biology of the Mind*. 4th ed. London: Norton.

Gendler, Tamar Szabó, and John Hawthorne (2005). "The Real Guide to Fake Barns. A Catalogue of Gifts for Your Epistemic Enemies." *Philosophical Studies* 124(3): 331–352.

Gibson, James J. (1966). *The Senses Considered as Perceptual Systems*. Boston: Houghton Mifflin.

Gigerenzer, Gerd, Peter M. Todd, and the ABC Research Group (1999). *Simple Heuristics That Make Us Smart*. New York: Oxford University Press.

Gilbert, Margaret (1989). *On Social Facts*. London: Routledge.

Gilovich, Thomas, Dale Griffin, and Daniel Kahneman, eds. (2002). *Heuristics and Biases: The Psychology of Intuitive Judgement*. Cambridge: Cambridge University Press.

Glymour, Clark (1980). *Theory and Evidence*. Princeton, NJ: Princeton University Press.

Goldberg, Sanford (2010). *Relying on Others: An Essay in Epistemology*. Oxford: Oxford University Press.

Goldberg, Sanford (2011). "If That Were True I Would Have Heard About It by Now." In *Social Epistemology: Essential Readings*, eds. A. Goldman and D. Whitcomb, 92–108. Oxford: Oxford University Press.

Goldman, Alvin I. (1967). "A Causal Theory of Knowing." *Journal of Philosophy* 64(12): 357–372.

Goldman, Alvin I. (1976). "Discrimination and Perceptual Knowledge." *Journal of Philosophy* 73: 771–791.

Goldman, Alvin I. (1979). "What Is Justified Belief?" In *Justification and Knowledge: New Studies in Epistemology*, ed. G. S. Pappas, 1–23. Dordrecht: D. Reidel. Reprinted in Goldman, Alvin I. (2012). *Reliabilism and Contemporary Epistemology*, 29–49. New York: Oxford University Press.

Goldman, Alvin I. (1986). *Epistemology and Cognition*. Cambridge, MA: Harvard University Press.

Goldman, Alvin I. (1992). "Epistemic Folkways and Scientific Epistemology." In *Liaisons: Philosophy Meets the Cognitive and Social Sciences*, 155–175. Cambridge, MA: MIT Press.

Goldman, Alvin I. (1999). *Knowledge in a Social World*. Oxford: Clarendon Press.

Goldman, Alvin I. (2001). "Experts: Which Ones Should You Trust?" *Philosophy and Phenomenological Research* 63(1): 85–110.

Goldman, Alvin I. (2006). *Simulating Minds: The Philosophy, Psychology, and Neuroscience of Mindreading*. Oxford: Oxford University Press.

Goldman, Alvin I. (2008). "Immediate Justification and Process Reliabilism." In *Epistemology: New Essays*, ed. Q. Smith, 63–82. Oxford: Oxford University Press.

Goldman, Alvin I. (2009). "Internalism, Externalism and the Architecture of Justification." *Journal of Philosophy* 106(6): 309–338.

Goldman, Alvin I. (2011). "A Guide to Social Epistemology." In *Social Epistemology: Essential Readings*, eds. A. I. Goldman and D. Whitcomb, 11–37. Oxford: Oxford University Press.

Goldman, Alvin I. (2012). *Reliabilism and Contemporary Epistemology*. New York: Oxford University Press.

Goldman, Alvin I. (2014). "Reliabilism, Veritism, and Epistemic Consequentialism." *Episteme* 11(4). (forthcoming).

Goldman, Alvin I. (forthcoming). "Social Process Reliabilism: Solving Justification Problems in Collective Epistemology." In *Essays in Collective Epistemology*, ed. J. Lackey.

Goodin, Robert E., and David Estlund (2004). "The Persuasiveness of Democratic Majorities." *Politics, Philosophy & Economics* 3(2): 131–142.

Grice, H. P. (1975). "Logic and Conversation." In *Syntax and Semantics, 3: Speech Acts*, eds. P. Cole and J. Morgan, 41–58. New York: Academic Press. Reprinted in *Studies in the Way of Words*, ed. H. P. Grice, 22–40. Cambridge, MA: Harvard University Press.

Grofman, Bernard, Guillermo Owen, and Scott L. Feld (1983). "Thirteen Theorems in Search of the Truth." *Theory and Decision* 15(3): 261–278.

Hájek, Alan (2008). "Arguments for—or Against—Probabilism?"*British Journal for the Philosophy of Science* 59(4): 793–819.

Hansen, Thorsten, Maria Olkkonen, Sebastian Walter, and Karl R. Gegenfurtner (2006). "Memory Modulates Color Appearance." *Nature Neuroscience* 9(11): 1367–1368.

Hardwig, John (1991). "The Role of Trust in Knowledge."*Journal of Philosophy* 88(12): 693–708.

Harman, Gilbert (1973). *Thought*. Princeton, NJ: Princeton University Press.

Hawthorne, John (2004). *Knowledge and Lotteries*. Oxford: Clarendon Press.

Hawthorne, John, and Jason Stanley (2008). "Knowledge and Action." *Journal of Philosophy* 105(10): 571–590.

Heller, Mark (1995). "The Simple Solution to the Problem of Generality." *Noûs* 29(4): 501–515.

Hinchman, Edward S. (2005). "Telling as Inviting to Trust." *Philosophy and Phenomenological Research* 70(3): 562–587.

Holton, Richard (1997). "Some Telling Examples: Reply to Tsohatzidis." *Journal of Pragmatics* 28: 625–628.

Hong, Lu, and Scott E. Page (2001). "Problem Solving by Heterogeneous Agents." *Journal of Economic Theory* 97(1): 123–163.

Howson, Colin, and Peter Urbach (2006). *Scientific Reasoning: The Bayesian Approach.* 3rd ed. Peru, IL: Open Court.

Huemer, Michael (2000). *Skepticism and the Veil of Perception*. Lanham, MD: Rowman and Littlefield.

Huemer, Michael (2013). "Epistemological Asymmetries Between Belief and Experience." *Philosophical Studies* 162: 741–748.

Hume, David [1748] (1977). *An Enquiry Concerning Human Understanding*, ed. E. Steinberg. Indianapolis: Hackett.

Ichikawa, Jonathan (2009). "Knowing the Intuition and Knowing the Counterfactual." *Philosophical Studies* 145(3): 435–443.

Ichikawa, Jonathan, and Benjamin Jarvis (2009). "Thought-Experiment Intuitions and Truth in Fiction." *Philosophical Studies* 142(2): 221–246.

James, William (1896). "The Will to Believe: An Address to the Philosophical Clubs of Yale and Brown Universities."

Jeffrey, Richard (1983). *The Logic of Decision*.2nd ed. Chicago: University of Chicago Press.

Johnson-Laird, P. N. (1983). *Mental Models: Towards a Cognitive Science of Language, Inference and Consciousness*. Cambridge: Cambridge University Press.

Johnson-Laird, P. N., and Ruth M. J. Byrne (1991). *Deduction*. Hove, UK: Lawrence Erlbaum Associates.

Jönsson, Martin L. (2013). "A Reliabilism Built on Cognitive Convergence: An Empirically Grounded Solution to the Generality Problem." *Episteme* 10(3): 241–268.

Joyce, James (1998). "A Non-Pragmatic Vindication of Probabilism." *Philosophy of Science* 65: 575–603.

Joyce, James (2010). "A Defense of Imprecise Credences in Inference and Decision-Making." *Philosophical Perspectives* 24(1): 281–323.

Kahneman, Daniel, and Shane Frederick (2005). "A Model of Heuristic Judgment." In *The Cambridge Handbook of Thinking and Reasoning*, eds. K. J. Holyoak and R. G. Morrison, 267–293. Cambridge: Cambridge University Press.

Kahneman, Daniel, Paul Slovic, and Amos Tversky, ed. (1982). *Judgment Under Uncertainty: Heuristics and Biases*. Cambridge: Cambridge University Press.

Kaplan, David (1989). "Demonstratives." In *Themes From Kaplan*, eds. J. Almog, J. Perry, & H. K. Wettstein, 481–565. New York: Oxford University Press.

Kauppinen, Antti (2007). "The Rise and Fall of Experimental Philosophy." *Philosophical Explorations* 10(2): 95–118.

Kelly, Thomas (2005). "The Epistemic Significance of Disagreement." *Oxford Studies in Epistemology* 1: 167–196.

Keynes, John Maynard (1921). *A Treatise on Probability.* London: MacMillan.

Kim, Jaegwon (1988). "What Is 'Naturalized Epistemology?'" *Philosophical Perspectives* 2: 381–405.

Kitcher, Philip (1990). "The Division of Cognitive Labor." *Journal of Philosophy* 87(1): 5–22.

Klein, Peter (1981). *Certainty.* Minneapolis: University of Minnesota Press.

Klein, Peter (2005). "Infinitism Is the Solution to the Regress Problem." In *Contemporary Debates in Epistemology,* ed. M. Steup and E. Sosa, 131–140. Oxford: Blackwell.

Kornblith, Hilary (1994). "A Conservative Approach to Social Epistemology." In *Socializing Epistemology,* ed. F. F. Schmitt, 93–110. Lanham, MD: Rowman and Littlefield.

Kotzen, Matthew (2012). "Silins' Liberalism." *Philosophical Studies* 159(1): 61–68.

Kripke, Saul (1980). *Naming and Necessity.* Cambridge, MA: Harvard University Press.

Kripke, Saul (2011). "Nozick on Knowledge." In *Philosophical Troubles: Collected Papers,* 162–224. New York: Oxford University Press.

Kruglanski, A. W., and D. M. Webster (1996). "Motivated Closing of the Mind: 'Seizing' and 'Freezing.'" *Psychological Review* 103(2): 263–283.

Kuhn, Thomas S. (1962). *The Structure of Scientific Revolutions.* Chicago: University of Chicago Press.

Kung, Peter (2010). "On Having No Reason: Dogmatism and Bayesian Confirmation." *Synthese* 177(1): 1–17.

Kvanvig, Jonathan (2003). *The Value of Knowledge and the Pursuit of Understanding.* Cambridge: Cambridge University Press.

Lackey, Jennifer (2008). *Learning from Words: Testimony as a Source of Knowledge.* Oxford: Oxford University Press.

Lackey, Jennifer (2010). "Assertion and Isolated Second-Hand Knowledge." In *Assertion: New Philosophical Essays,* eds. J. Brown and H. Cappelen, 251–276. Oxford: Oxford University Press.

Lackey, Jennifer (2011). "Testimony: Acquiring Knowledge from Others." In *Social Epistemology: Essential Readings,* eds. A. Goldman and D. Whitcomb, 71–91. Oxford: Oxford University Press.

Lackey, Jennifer (forthcoming). *The Epistemology of Groups.*

Landemore, Hélène (2013). *Democratic Reason: Politics, Collective Intelligence, and the Rule of the Many.* Princeton, NJ: Princeton University Press.

Lasonen-Aarnio (2010). "Unreasonable Knowledge." *Philosophical Perspectives,* 24(1): 1–21.

Lehrer, Keith (1965). "Knowledge, Truth and Evidence." *Analysis* 25: 168–175.

Lehrer, Keith (1974). *Knowledge.* Oxford: Oxford University Press.

Lehrer, Keith (1989). *Thomas Reid.* London: Routledge.

Lehrer, Keith, and Thomas D. Paxson (1969). "Knowledge: Undefeated Justified True Belief." *Journal of Philosophy* 66: 225–237.

Levin, Daniel T., and Mahzarin R. Banaji (2006). "Distortions in the Perceived Lightness of Faces: The Role of Race Categories." *Journal of Experimental Psychology* 135(4): 501–512.

Lewis, David (1996). "Elusive Knowledge." *Australasian Journal of Philosophy* 74(4): 549–567.

Lewis, David (1980). "A Subjectivist's Guide to Objective Chance." In *Studies in Inductive Logic and Probability, Vol.II,* 263–293. Berkeley: University of California Press.

Lipton, Peter (1998). "The Epistemology of Testimony." *Studies in History and Philosophy of Science* 29(1): 1–31.

Lipton, Peter (2004). *Inference to the Best Explanation*. 2nd ed. London: Routledge.

List, Christian, and Philip Pettit (2011). *Group Agency: The Possibility, Design, and Status of Corporate Agents*. Oxford: Oxford University Press.

Locke, John [1689] (1975). *An Essay Concerning Human Understanding*, ed. P. H. Nidditch. Oxford: Clarendon Press.

Loftus, Elizabeth F. (1979). *Eyewitness Testimony*. Cambridge, MA: Harvard University Press.

Logue, Heather (2011). "The Skeptic and the Naïve Realist." *Philosophical Issues* 21(1): 268–288.

Logue, Heather (2013). "Visual Experience of Natural Kind Properties: Is There Any Fact of the Matter?" *Philosophical Studies* 162(1): 1–12.

Ludwig, Kirk (2007). "The Epistemology of Thought Experiments: First Person Versus Third Person Approaches." *Midwest Studies in Philosophy* 31: 128–159.

Lyons, Jack C. (2005). "Perceptual Belief and Nonexperiential Looks." *Philosophical Perspectives* 19(1): 237–256.

Lyons, Jack C. (2009). *Perception and Basic Beliefs: Zombies, Modules, and the Problem of the External World*. Oxford: Oxford University Press.

Lyons, Jack C. (2011a). "Circularity, Reliability and the Cognitive Penetrability of Perception." *Philosophical Issues* 21(1): 289–311.

Lyons, Jack C. (2011b). "Precis of *Perception and Basic Beliefs*." *Philosophical Studies* 153(3): 443–446.

MacFarlane, John (2005). "The Assessment Sensitivity of Knowledge Attributions." *Oxford Studies in Epistemology* 1: 197–233.

Maher, Patrick (1993). *Betting on Theories*. Cambridge: Cambridge University Press.

Malmgren, Anna-Sara (2011). "Rationalism and the Content of Intuitive Judgements." *Mind* 120(478): 263–327.

Markie, Peter (2006). "Epistemically Appropriate Perceptual Belief." *Noûs* 40: 118–142.

McGrath, Matthew (2013). "Phenomenal Conservatism and Cognitive Penetration: The 'Bad Basis' Counterexamples." In *Seemings and Justification*, ed. C. Tucker, 225–247. Oxford: Oxford University Press.

McGrath, Matthew (forthcoming). "Looks and Perceptual Justification." *Philosophy and Phenomenological Research*.

Medin, Douglas L., and Marguerite M. Schaffer (1978). "Context Theory of Classification Learning." *Psychological Review* 85(3): 207–238.

Millar, Alan (2012). "Skepticism, Perceptual Knowledge, and Doxastic Responsibility." *Synthese* 189(2): 353–372.

Mnookin, Jennifer L. (2008). "Of Black Boxes, Instruments, and Experts: Testing the Validity of Forensic Science." *Episteme, A Journal of Social Epistemology* 5(3): 343–358.

Moore, G. E. (1959). *Philosophical Papers*. London: George Allen and Unwin.

Moran, Richard (2006). "Getting Told and Being Believed." In *The Epistemology of Testimony*, eds. J. Lackey and E. Sosa, 272–306. Oxford: Oxford University Press.

Moss, Sarah (2013). "Epistemology Formalized." *Philosophical Review* 122(1): 1–43.

Nagel, Jennifer (2008). "Knowledge Ascriptions and the Psychological Consequences of Changing Stakes." *Australasian Journal of Philosophy* 86(2): 279–294.

Nagel, Jennifer (2010a). "Epistemic Anxiety and Adaptive Invariantism." *Philosophical Perspectives* 24: 407–435.

Nagel, Jennifer (2010b). "Knowledge Ascriptions and the Psychological Consequences of Thinking About Error." *Philosophical Quarterly* 60(239): 286–306.

Nagel, Jennifer (2012). "Intuitions and Experiments: A Defense of the Case Method in Epistemology." *Philosophy and Phenomenological Research* 85(3): 495–527.

Nagel, Jennifer, Valerie San Juan, and Raymond A. Mar (2013). "Lay Denial of Knowledge for Justified True Beliefs." *Cognition* 129: 652–661.

Neta, Ram, and Guy Rohrbaugh (2004). "Luminosity and the Safety of Knowledge." *Pacific Philosophical Quarterly* 85(4): 396–406.

Nichols, Shaun (2004). "After Objectivity: An Empirical Study of Moral Judgment." *Philosophical Psychology* 17(1): 3–26.

Nozick, Robert. (1981). *Philosophical Explanations*. Cambridge, MA: Harvard University Press.

Olsson, Erik J. (forthcoming). "A Naturalistic Approach to the Generality Problem." In *Alvin Goldman and His Critics*, eds. H. Kornblith and B. McLaughlin. Oxford: Blackwell.

Pace, Michael (2010). "Foundationally Justified Perceptual Beliefs and the Problem of the Speckled Hen." *Pacific Philosophical Quarterly* 91(3): 401–441.

Page, Scott E. (2007). *The Difference: How the Power of Diversity Creates Better Groups, Firms, Schools, and Societies*. Princeton, NJ: Princeton University Press.

Plato. *Meno*. In *Plato: Complete Works*, eds. John M. Cooper and D. S. Hutchinson (1997).

Pollock, John (1975). *Knowledge and Justification*. Princeton, NJ: Princeton University Press.

Pollock, John L., and Joseph Cruz (1999). *Contemporary Theories of Knowledge*. 2nd ed. Lanham, MD: Rowman & Littlefield Publishers.

Pritchard, Duncan (2005). *Epistemic Luck*. Oxford: Oxford University Press.

Pritchard, Duncan (2010). "Knowledge and Understanding." In *The Nature and Value of Knowledge: Three Investigations*, eds. D. H. Pritchard, A. Millar, and A. Haddock, Chapters 1–4. Oxford: Oxford University Press.

Pryor, James (2000). "The Skeptic and the Dogmatist." *Noûs* 34: 517–549.

Pryor, James (2004). "What's Wrong with Moore's Argument." *Philosophical Issues*. 14(1): 349–378.

Pryor, James (2005). "There Is Immediate Justification." In *Contemporary Debates in Epistemology*, eds. M. Steup and E. Sosa, 181–202. Oxford: Blackwell.

Pylyshyn, Zenon (1999). "Is Vision Continuous with Cognition? The Case for Cognitive Impenetrability of Visual Perception."*Behavioral and Brain Sciences* 22: 343–391.

Quine, Willard Van Orman (1950). *Methods of Logic*. New York: Holt, Rinehart, and Winston.

Quine, Willard van Orman (1969). "Epistemology Naturalized." In *Ontological Relativity and Other Essays*, 69–90. New York: Columbia University Press.

Palmer, Stephen (1999). *Vision Science: From Photons to Phenomenology*. Cambridge, MA: MIT Press.

Radford, Colin (1966). "Knowledge—By Examples." *Analysis* 27: 1–11.

Reichenbach, Hans (1938). *Experience and Prediction: An Analysis of the Foundations and the Structure of Knowledge*. Chicago: University of Chicago Press.

Reid, Thomas [1764] (1967). *Inquiry into the Human Mind*. In *Philosophical Works*, ed. W. Hamilton. Hildesheim, Germany: Georg Olms.

Reid, Thomas (1785). *Essays on the Intellectual Powers of Man*.

Riddle, Karen (2010). "Always on My Mind: Exploring How Frequent, Recent, and Vivid Television Portrayals Are Used in the Formation of Social Reality Judgments." *Media Psychology* 13: 155–179.

Rips, Lance J. (1994). *The Psychology of Proof: Deductive Reasoning in Human Thinking*. Cambridge, MA: MIT Press.

Rorty, Richard (1981). *Philosophy and the Mirror of Nature.* Princeton, NJ: Princeton University Press.

Rosch, Eleanor, Carolyn B. Mervis, Wayne D. Gray, David M. Johnson, and Penny Boyes-Braem (1976). "Basic Objects in Natural Categories." *Cognitive Psychology* 8(3): 382–439.

Ross, Jacob, and Mark Schroeder (2014). "Belief, Credence and Pragmatic Encroachment." *Philosophy and Phenomenological Research* 88(2): 259–288.

Roush, Sherrilyn (2004). "Positive Relevance Defended." *Philosophy of Science* 71(1): 110–116.

Roush, Sherrilyn (2005). *Tracking Truth.* Oxford: Oxford University Press.

Russell, Bertrand (1912). *The Problems of Philosophy.* London: Oxford University Press.

Russell, Bruce (2013). "A Priori Justification and Knowledge." *The Stanford Encyclopedia of Philosophy,* Summer 2013 ed., ed. E. Zalta.

Rysiew, Patrick (2001). "The Context-Sensitivity of Knowledge Attributions." *Noûs* 35(4): 477–514

Rysiew, Patrick (2008). "Rationality Wars—Psychology and Epistemology." *Philosophy Compass* 3(6): 1153–1176.

Schaffer, Jonathan (2004). "From Contextualism to Contrastivism." *Philosophical Studies* 119(1/2): 73–103.

Schaffer, Jonathan (2005). "Contrastive Knowledge." In *Oxford Studies in Epistemology* 1: 235–271.

Schaffer, Jonathan, and Zoltán Gendler Szabó (2013). "Epistemic Comparativism: A Contextualist Semantics for Knowledge Ascriptions." *Philosophical Studies.* http://link.springer.com/10.1007/s11098-013-0141-7.

Schellenberg, Susanna (forthcoming). "The Epistemic Force of Experience." *Philosophical Studies.*

Schmitt, Frederick F. (1994a). "The Justification of Group Beliefs." In *Socializing Epistemology,* ed. F. F. Schmitt, 257–287. Lanham, MD: Rowman and Littlefield.

Schmitt, Frederick F., ed. (1994b). *Socializing Epistemology.* Lanham, MD: Rowman and Littlefield.

Schroeder, Mark (2008). "Having Reasons." *Philosophical Studies* 39(1): 57–71.

Sellars, Wilfrid (1956). "Empiricism and the Philosophy of Mind." In *Science, Perception, and Reality.* New York: Humanities Press.

Sellars, Wilfrid (1997). *Empiricism and the Philosophy of Mind,* ed. R. Brandom. Cambridge, MA: Harvard University Press.

Shapley, Lloyd, and Bernard Grofman (1984). "Optimizing Group Judgmental Accuracy in the Presence of Interdependencies." *Public Choice* 43(3): 329–343.

Siegel, Susanna (2010). *The Contents of Visual Experience.* Oxford: Oxford University Press.

Siegel, Susanna (2012). "Cognitive Penetrability and Perceptual Justification." *Noûs* 46(2). 201–222.

Siegel, Susanna (2013a). "The Epistemic Impact of the Etiology of Experience." *Philosophical Studies* 162(3): 697–722.

Siegel, Susanna (2013b). "Can Selection Effects on Experience Influence Its Rational Role?" *Oxford Studies in Epistemology* 4: 240–270.

Silins, Nicholas (2005). "Transmission Failure Failure." *Philosophical Studies* 126(1): 71–102.

Silins, Nicholas (2008). "Basic Justification and the Moorean Response to the Skeptic." *Oxford Studies in Epistemology* 2: 108–142.

Sinnott-Armstrong, Walter, Liane Young, and Fiery Cushman (2010). "Moral Intuitions." In *The Moral Psychology Handbook*, ed. John M. Doris, 246–272. Oxford:
Oxford University Press.

Smith, Edward E., and Stephen M. Kosslyn (2007). *Cognitive Psychology: Mind and
Brain*. Upper Saddle River, NJ: Pearson/Prentice Hall.

Sober, Elliott (2008). *Evidence and Evolution*. Cambridge: Cambridge University Press.

Sosa, Ernest (1999). "How to Defeat Opposition to Moore." *Philosophical Perspectives:
A Supplement to Noûs* 33: 141–153.

Sosa, Ernest (2007a). *A Virtue Epistemology: Apt Belief and Reflective Knowledge*, Vol. I.
New York: Oxford University Press.

Sosa, Ernest (2007b). "Experimental Philosophy and Philosophical Intuition."
Philosophical Studies 132(1): 99–107.

Stanley, Jason (2005). *Knowledge and Practical Interests*. Oxford: Clarendon Press.

Stanley, Jason (2011). *Knowing How*. Oxford: Oxford University Press.

Starmans, Christina, and Ori Friedman (2012). "The Folk Conception of Knowledge."
Cognition 124(3): 272–283.

Steinpreis, Reah, Katie Anders, and Dawn Ritzke (1999). "The Impact of Gender on
the Review of the Curricula Vitae of Job Applicants and Tenure Candidates:
A National Empirical Study." *Sex Roles* 41(7–8): 509–528.

Stine, Gail (1976). "Skepticism, Relevant Alternatives and Deductive Closure." *Philosophical Studies* 29: 249–261.

Stroud, Barry (1984). *The Significance of Philosophical Skepticism*. Oxford: Oxford University
Press.

Sturgeon, Scott (2008). "Reason and the Grain of Belief." *Noûs* 42(1): 139–165.

Sunstein, Cass R. (2006). *Infotopia: How Many Minds Produce Knowledge*. Oxford:
Oxford University Press.

Swain, Stacey, Joshua Alexander, and Jonathan M. Weinberg (2008). "The Instability
of Philosophical Intuitions: Running Hot and Cold on Truetemp." *Philosophy and
Phenomenological Research* 76(1): 138–155.

Tucker, Christopher (2010). "Why Open-Minded People Should Endorse Dogmatism." *Philosophical Perspectives* 24: 529–545.

Tucker, Christopher, ed. (2013). *Seemings and Justification*. Oxford: Oxford University
Press.

Turri, John (2011). "Manifest Failure: The Gettier Problem Solved." *Philosophers' Imprint*
11(8).

Turri, John (2013). "A Conspicuous Art: Putting Gettier to the Test." *Philosophers' Imprint*
13(10).

Tversky, Amos, and Daniel Kahneman (1983). "Extensional Versus Intuitive Reasoning: The Conjunction Fallacy in Probability Judgment." *Psychological Review* 90(4):
293–315.

Unger, Peter (1975). *Ignorance: A Case for Scepticism*. Oxford: Clarendon Press.

Van Cleve, James (1999). "Reid on the First Principles of Contingent Truths." *Reid
Studies* 3: 3–30.

Van Cleve, James (2003). "Is Knowledge Easy—Or Impossible? Externalism as the
Only Alternative to Skepticism." In *The Skeptics: Contemporary Essays*, ed. S. Luper,
45–59. Aldershot, UK: Ashgate.

van Fraassen, Bas (1989). *Laws and Symmetries*. Oxford: Clarendon Press.

Vogel, Jonathan (1987). "Tracking, Closure and Inductive Knowledge." In *The Possibility of Knowledge*, 197–215. Towota, NJ: Rowman and Littlefield.

Vogel, Jonathan (2000). "Reliabilism Leveled." *Journal of Philosophy* 97(11): 602–623.

Vogel, Jonathan (2005). "The Refutation of Skepticism." In *Contemporary Debates in Epistemology*, eds. M. Steup and E. Sosa, 72–84. Oxford: Blackwell.

Vogel, Jonathan (2007). "Subjunctivitis." *Philosophical Studies* 134(1): 73–88.

vos Savant, Marilyn (9 September 1990). "Ask Marilyn." *Parade Magazine*: 16.

Wason, P. C. (1966). "Reasoning." In *New Horizons in Psychology*, ed. B. M. Foss. Baltimore: Penguin Books.

Weinberg, Jonathan M., Shaun Nichols, and Stephen Stich (2001). "Normativity and Epistemic Intuitions." *Philosophical Topics* 29(1–2): 429–460.

Weirich, Paul (2004). *Realistic Decision Theory*. New York: Oxford University Press.

Weisberg, Michael, and Ryan Muldoon (2009). "Epistemic Landscapes and the Division of Cognitive Labor." *Philosophy of Science* 76(2): 225–252.

White, Roger (2006). "Problems for Dogmatism." *Philosophical Studies* 31: 525–557.

Williamson, Timothy (2000). *Knowledge and Its Limits*. Oxford: Oxford University Press.

Williamson, Timothy (2005). "Armchair Philosophy, Metaphysical Modality and Counterfactual Thinking." *Proceedings of the Aristotelian Society* 105(1): 1–23.

Williamson, Timothy (2007). *The Philosophy of Philosophy*. Malden, MA: Blackwell.

Williamson, Timothy (2013). "How Deep Is the Distinction Between A Priori and A Posteriori Knowledge?" In *The A Priori in Philosophy*, eds. A. Casullo and J. Thurow, 291–312. Oxford: Oxford University Press.

Wright, Crispin (2002). "Anti-Sceptics Simple and Subtle: G. E. Moore and John McDowell." *Philosophy and Phenomenological Research* 62(2): 330–348.

Wright, Crispin (2004). "Warrant for Nothing (and Foundations for Free)?" *Aristotelian Society Supplementary Volume* 78(1): 167–212.

Wright, Crispin (2007). "The Perils of Dogmatism." In *Themes from G.E. Moore: New Essays in Epistemology and Ethics*, eds. S. Nuccetelli and G. Seay, 25–48. Oxford: Oxford University Press.

Wunderlich, Mark E. (2003). "Vector Reliability: A New Approach to Epistemic Justification." *Synthese* 136(2): 237–262.

Zagzebski, Linda (1994). "The Inescapability of Gettier Problems." *Philosophical Quarterly* 44(174): 65–73.

Index